MUSSOLINI'S ROMAN EMPIRE

Also by Denis Mack Smith

VICTOR EMANUEL, CAVOUR AND THE RISORGIMENTO
MEDIEVAL SICILY: 800–1713
MODERN SICILY: AFTER 1713
ITALY: A MODERN HISTORY
GARIBALDI
CAVOUR AND GARIBALDI 1860: A STUDY IN POLITICAL CONFLICT

Editor

THE MAKING OF ITALY: 1796–1870

MUSSOLINI'S ROMAN EMPIRE

DENIS MACK SMITH

THE VIKING PRESS · NEW YORK

Copyright © Denis Mack Smith, 1976

All rights reserved

First published in 1976 by The Viking Press
625 Madison Avenue, New York, N.Y. 10022

LIBRARY OF CONGRESS CATALOGING IN PUBLICATION DATA
Mack Smith, Denis, 1920–
Mussolini's Roman Empire. New York, Viking Press
Bibliography: p. [1976]
Includes index.
1. Italy—Politics and government, 1922–1945.
2. Mussolini, Benito, 1883–1945. I. Title.
DG571.M22   945.091'092'4   75-46618
ISBN 0-670-49652-9

Printed in the United States of America
Maps by Paul J. Pugliese

PREFACE

If a politician has to be assessed by whether his speeches are in any way profound or prophetic, or even just sensible, then Benito Mussolini was no better than third-rate. If instead the test is how far he changed his country and the rest of the world, the rating would be far more in his favour, although, if the criterion also includes whether he left the world a better place, the inventor of fascism would in nearly everyone's estimation score no marks at all. Mussolini would himself have preferred to be judged by whether he succeeded in frightening Europe and making his country of greater account in the world, on which reckoning even his enemies would probably have to admit that he was a very considerable personality indeed.

Such hypothetical assessments must always depend on personal and subjective considerations, but a preface is a place where assumptions and prejudices can be stated without apology. The theme of this book is how Mussolini deliberately and even carefully steered his fascist movement into imperialism and into a succession of wars which eventually left Italy prostrate. The defeat was as total as it was unexpected, and those fascist leaders who survived were thereby persuaded in retrospect not only to admit that much must have been wrong with fascism, but also to put most of the blame on Mussolini personally. Although their motives are suspect, it is hard to disagree with this conclusion. Nevertheless the apportionment of blame is not a particularly interesting or important matter. Many grave offences were committed by the Fascists in their twenty years of rule and they would have had much to answer for in a court of criminal law, but no Italian was ever brought before the Nuremberg tribunal, and local Italian courts preferred wherever possible to ignore or exonerate in an understandable attempt to reduce animosities and black out what was painful in the past. History, however, has as its purpose not

v

exoneration, nor condemnation, and certainly not the blacking out of what may be painful and embarrassing, but rather the attempt to comprehend and make intelligible. Among other tasks it must examine what the Fascists wanted to do and how far they succeeded in doing it.

When Mussolini himself recalled what he liked to think of as his greatest successes in foreign policy, he singled out first his conquest of Abyssinia (1935–1936); next, his blocking of communism by sending troops to help General Franco in the Spanish civil war; thirdly, his mediation at the Munich conference of 1938, which seemed to save Europe from a major war; and then his intuitive choice of June 1940 as the best moment for making war on Britain and France. Subsequently he also boasted about his decision to invade the Balkans in October 1940, though when he declared war on Russia and the United States in 1941 he himself seems to have realised that these were the actions of a gambler whose luck was beginning to run out.

How far any one of these decisions justified his self-satisfaction will be discussed later, but by his own standards he was certainly successful in much of what he tried or pretended to do. In so far as he aimed to make Italy feared and hated in the world, he achieved his purpose, even though he also provoked the additional and unexpected reaction of scorn and contempt. He used to say that he wanted to test the mettle of Italy in war, and here too he succeeded. He meant to assert Italy's "rights" to territorial expansion even if, in his own words, this would involve setting fire to Europe and bringing civilised life to a halt. He was as good as his word and many hundreds of thousands of Italians died in consequence, though he accepted such losses philosophically because he prided himself on being a realist who saw life as struggle and perpetual combat. He therefore accepted blood-letting as not only normal but desirable. The fact that he incidentally brought economic ruin and civil war to Italy, and also advanced the cause of communism in Europe, was unintended and obviously unwelcome, but he nonchalantly ascribed such disasters wholly to the malevolence of his opponents.

In the last period of his life, as he mused on his own triumph and defeat, Mussolini could not accept that he had any major responsibility for what had gone wrong. He thought that if only others, and in particular Hitler and Churchill, had listened to him and yielded to his better judgement, Europe could have been saved from disaster. He was proud to think that historians would see him in a better light than contemporaries might. He believed that future generations would above all admire the way he had created fascism, a set of ideas which in his opinion was destined to survive defeat and remain the central theme of the twentieth century. They would admire the way he had made such a rebellious and changeable people as the Italians obey him for twenty years—something no one else had ever succeeded in doing. This success in dealing with Italians he once called his political masterpiece, even though he was ready to admit that his fellow-countrymen proved unworthy of him and of what he tried to do in their name. Such arrogance and insensitivity were characteristic of the man. Nevertheless one should remember that, despite appearances, Mussolini possessed considerable intelligence and an unusual political skill. Even though he spoke more rubbish than most other contemporary politicians, he generally did so deliberately and after carefully gauging his audience, and was quite able to talk good sense when he wanted or needed to.

Where he seldom went wrong was as a propagandist communicating with the masses. Even though he said he cared little for public opinion, and perhaps thought that he meant what he said, Mussolini spent a great deal of time trying to mould popular beliefs, because he discovered that he had the capacity for making his listeners believe almost anything he liked. He was by training and profession a journalist, and through editorship of several newspapers had first—as he himself put it—felt the pulse of the Italian people. No sooner had he succeeded in identifying an audience through his leading articles, than he proceeded to use them as a lever for attaining political power. As he freely admitted, lies might sometimes be more useful than truths, and for the purposes of propaganda he deliberately manufactured a false image of himself, a carefully tended and increasingly distorted personification which became the kernel or central structure round which the fascist movement was built. Aided by an army of petty intellectuals and journalists, he fashioned a make-believe effigy of the Duce, who was depicted as a leader of vast intelligence, personal magnetism, and profound humanity: a man of immense power who was admired and feared by the whole civilised world. These journalists sometimes spoke of him as a real God to whom all personal liberties must be sacrificed; in return for such a sacrifice, he would transform the nature of Italians and make them mighty and irresistible.

In this sense it can be claimed that journalism and public relations were the most essential of all professional activities under fascism. If one examines the ruling elite in the Grand Council of fascism, at times almost half the members of this body held union cards of the journalists' trade union; as Mussolini was ready to acknowledge, it was these journalists in the inner councils of the party who were the best Fascists and the most useful of all his collaborators. In return for high salaries and prestige, they helped him to give Italy, if not the reality of strength, at least the appearance of it, which he thought might come to almost the same thing so long as ordinary people could be made to believe it. For this reason any history of Mussolini's foreign policy has to be also, or even mainly, a history of propaganda. By persuading foreign governments that he was the strong leader of a strong country, he made it possible to pursue a belligerent foreign policy without having to waste scarce money on providing the material sinews of war. By convincing Italians that he and he alone could lead them to greatness and riches at negligible cost to themselves, he won the plenitude of power for himself without much opposition.

Mussolini's greatest skill was in the manufacture and communication of such myths, and in his hands they became as important a part of the substance of history as were the external "facts" of fascism. But in retrospect it is important to distinguish facts from propaganda, to see what was reality and what was illusion. Failure to make this distinction was one important reason why so many of the older generation of Italian liberals misunderstood fascism, and gratuitously helped Mussolini into power by taking his propaganda at face value. A similar failure then led the next generation to disaster just because he convinced them of his own genius and of their invincibility. Today, however, it is easier to discern what was counterfeit and see how the trick was carried out.

In recent years a great deal of historical writing has built up a clear picture of how fascism succeeded in establishing its authority during the early and middle 1920s, but much has still to be done to investigate what Mussolini came to stand for in later years. Inevitably, the archives of government departments for the 1930s are still very largely inaccessible. Nor in Italy were there official enquiries about the Second World War like those carried out, admittedly in an often partisan spirit, about the First. And some of the official and semi-official histories, for instance of the army, navy, and air force, have been excessively purged of controversy before publication. The mere fact that, thirty years after Mussolini's death, fascism or the memory of fascism is still a political issue in contemporary Italy, means that the subject is not yet open for completely dispassionate investigation.

The present volume is an essay on one very important aspect of Italian fascism. Its prior assumption is that the nature of Mussolini's political career is better revealed by what fascism became than by how it began: *ex fructibus eorum cognoscetis eos*. It is a study of political and military defeat and the reasons for that defeat. It is incidentally a study of the effectiveness and the dangers of propaganda. Fascism largely succeeded in isolating Italy from the rest of Europe. It employed not only the press and radio, but Italy's whole educational system, to build up a series of convenient myths. These myths were intended to make Italy a dominant power in the world, but instead, because Mussolini silenced criticism, led to bankruptcy and destruction.

Denis Mack Smith

Oxford, 1975

CONTENTS

xi

CONTENTS

MUSSOLINI'S ROMAN EMPIRE

I

FASCISM TAKES OVER

Benito Mussolini became prime minister of Italy in October 1922, at a time when fascism was a party not of ideas and doctrine but of action. His followers were a gang of truculent and ambitious men who wanted power, and who were backed by some intelligent and influential members of society who saw the usefulness of just such rowdies in helping to suppress socialism, curtail parliamentary liberties, and if possible make the name of Italy feared abroad. Violence and the desire to be feared were strong components of Mussolini's character and, as soon as he had tamed parliament, were bound to spill over into his conduct of foreign policy. He wanted to command not only in Italy but outside it, and to get such power he would take risks—even, in the last resort, the risk of a world-wide conflagration.

Though from early boyhood a violent person, Mussolini had not always been a militarist or a patriot. Efforts were later made to conceal the fact that he had been on occasion a dogmatic pacifist.[1] He had gone to prison for opposing Italy's invasion of Libya in 1911 and 1912, and in 1914 he tried to organise a proletarian revolution to stop his country's involvement in the First World War. Many of his earlier pronouncements—notwithstanding later attempts by Fascists to deny it—were strongly anti-patriotic, for he was more interested in class war than the greatness of Italy, and in this period he shared the Socialist attitude that patriotism was just one more mask of capitalism.[2]

No doubt Mussolini was sincere—or at least genuinely confused—in some of the contradictory intellectual postures which he assumed throughout his life, but usually he judged ideas by whether they could be employed as ideological levers to obtain and keep authority. His lack of attachment to principle was an important ingredient in his success. When he edited a socialist newspaper in the years before 1919, he readily accepted subsidies from capitalist arms manufacturers, and negotiated for secret financial backing from the far-from-socialist governments of France, Britain, the United States, and even Tsarist Russia.[3] Yet this same man had been an enthusiastic follower of Marx,[4] and Lenin was one of the contemporaries whom he most admired—although he claimed to dislike in Leninism the violent and intolerant methods which in fact characterised fascism.[5] Mussolini moved easily from one opinion to another whenever his instinct for publicity suggested to him a winning formula, and though he based his later career on anti-communism, it is hard to be sure that this represented an entirely genuine conviction rather than a tactical move with one eye on the main chance.

Eventually Mussolini's regime came to stand for patriotism, militarism, and anti-bolshevism, and references to earlier apparently discordant phases in his thought were, where possible, expunged from the record. An early sign of this change came in 1923 when the new prime minister brought about a fusion between his Black Shirts and the Blue Shirts of the Nationalist Party, thus adding to his group a number of intellectuals and practical politicians of ability. The Nationalists had a real foreign policy. During the period from 1910 to 1912 they had come into existence as an elite party advocating an exaggerated patriotism. They shared common ground with Mussolini in a hostility to democracy and parliament, and he particularly liked the anti-humanitarian, anti-internationalist views which had already been elaborated by Enrico Corradini, Luigi Federzoni, Alfredo Rocco, and Francesco Coppola, the leading figures in the nationalist revival. Indeed, much in the essential nucleus of fascist beliefs derived directly from the writings of Corradini and Rocco.[6] These Nationalists maintained, anticipating fascism, that foreign affairs had priority, that the greatness of the nation was the first objective of policy, and that Italy must break the existing equilibrium in Europe with the deliberate intention of becoming an undisputed great power possessed of an overseas empire.[7] According to the Nationalists, it was they who laid down at least some of the conditions for a fusion with fascism, for example recognition of the monarchy and of Catholicism, also the defence of social order against the extreme left,[8] and above all the need for a strong army and a sometimes aggressive attitude to the rest of the world.[9] Federzoni, after he joined Mussolini's cabinet as minister of colonies and then of the interior, put into one phrase what was to be the essence of fascist foreign policy: "we Italians like to be loved, but prefer to be envied and feared".[10]

When Mussolini came to power he had still not completed his move into this phase of nationalism, nor did he possess a coherent attitude to foreign affairs, but rather looked at foreign policy as a useful weapon in strengthening his position at home. While he was ready to admit in theory that foreign affairs were more important than domestic,[11] he was still trying to attract support from almost the whole spectrum of Italian politics, and hence he emphasised that fascism would not strive after originality,[12] but would respect treaties and try to be an element of equilibrium and peace in Europe.[13] As he looked back at the world war, he was prepared to accept that the settlement of 1919 had won for Italy most of what she wanted; only gradually did he see change towards asserting that "a mutilated peace" was forced on Italy by the Treaty of Versailles.[14] He was ready to condemn all imperialism, including Italian imperialism,[15] ready to say that he wanted not to be adventurous even while protecting his country's interests. Though occasionally he spoke of intending to annex Dalmatia and establish a protectorate over Albania, he did not immediately side with the have-not nations who wanted a revision of the Versailles settlement. He professed to be above all a pragmatist, against the bringing of morals into international politics, unenthusiastic about a League of Nations which gave disproportionate representation to the rich and conservative nations, yet anxious also for Italy to join the League and exploit it to suit her own needs.[16]

Mussolini's career between 1914, when he was expelled from the Socialist Party, and 1922, had been that of a newspaper proprietor and editor, in which profession he had shown a quite exceptional ability. But if in the course of writing editorials he had picked up a lot of casual information about foreign affairs, it was only when he became prime minister and foreign minister in 1922 that he faced real international situations which required more than the easy answers of journalism. As he did not lack common sense or intelligence, he was ready in his first months of power to accept advice from foreign-office officials and to leave as many options open as possible. He announced that he did not want an ideological foreign policy. Though opposed to liberalism and democracy, he would not let this opposition dictate Italian conduct abroad, since fascism was not for export, and "we will not act as missionaries who have a revealed truth to impart." [17] This at least was what he said, whether or not it reflected his inner thoughts. Perhaps he was deliberately playing down his nationalism and bluffing the international community into thinking he was a man who could be trusted.

Mussolini had political intuition as well as intelligence, but he knew very little from personal experience about foreign countries. As a young man he had spent two years in Switzerland in several low-paid jobs and in prison. As prime minister he made half a dozen quick visits to other European states, for two or three days each, but abroad as at home he was interested more in the impression he was creating than in trying to understand the ways and ideas of others. At a small conference at Lausanne in November 1922 he somehow persuaded himself that he had personally scored a great diplomatic success, though there was nothing to show for it. [18] In December he made his only visit to England, and again wrote over-dramatically to his ministers that he was helping to decide the fate of Europe; but he was then jolted into taking offence at the frank questions of journalists and into an indecorous quarrel about who should have the best suite in Claridges Hotel. After three days during whigh he committed one *gaffe* after another and aroused general indignation he left London with a sense of some personal humiliation, and he determined henceforward to meet foreign statesmen on home ground where his own dignity could be properly stage-managed. Perhaps he sensed the disappointment of his staff over his evident weakness as a negotiator. [19]

Italy asserted a right to special responsibilities in the Balkans, because she had a common frontier with the newly created state of Yugoslavia and had ambitions over Albania. Strategically and economically this area was full of promise to anyone who thought imperially, and it was here that Mussolini first began to show his hand. As became customary, his instinct was to speak in several senses, then wait to see whether he might gain more by a policy of forceful insistence or, alternatively and more cheaply, by good neighbourliness. Much depended on whom he was speaking to. At one point he agreed to renounce any ideas of expansion on the far shore of the Adriatic, but more privately he confessed that his long-term aim was to win political primacy in the Balkans.[20] In speeches destined for wide circulation he continued to deny the accusation that he nurtured imperialist ambitions, whereas to a more exclusively fascist audience he called the whole Adriatic by rights Italian. In this latter mood he used to disparage the Slavs as an inferior and barbarous people. He could talk even in these early years of Italy dominating the Mediterranean, and the word "dominate" was one that came easily to him.[21] He knew on the one hand that the prosperity of the Italian frontier port of Trieste might depend on preserving peace and friendship in the Balkans, and on the other hand that renouncing Italy's "rights" would upset members of the Fascist Party; indeed, there were moments when this last possibility produced threats of a revolt against his leadership.[22] With considerable skill he threaded his way through a number of contradictory attitudes and eventually agreed with Yugoslavia to renounce some of his more extreme demands in return for its recognition that the border port of Fiume was Italian. This cut off Fiume from its economic hinterland and condemned the town to poverty, but fascist dogma put prestige above mere economics and most patriots were delighted, while the rest of the world took note that Mussolini could show realism and a sense of discretion in foreign affairs.

A more menacing form of nationalism led Mussolini in August 1923 to make an armed landing on the Greek island of Corfu. The pretext, which was the murder of an Italian general in Greece, seemed a ridiculous reason for such aggressive behaviour, and subsequently it emerged that the Italian navy had been told to prepare their attack a month before the murder took place,[23] so without doubt he had been seeking an excuse to control the mouth of the Adriatic by annexing this strategically placed island. No one ever discovered whether Greeks were responsible for the murder, and it has even been suggested that the assassin may have been in Italian pay.[24] It was a dangerous sign that Mussolini had not first bothered to consult the permanent officials in the foreign office. It was equally ominous that, because his orders were unclear, the occupying forces bungled their part, with the result that, though no resistance was offered, an Italian bombardment caused unnecessary casualties and made the expedition seem both brutal and inefficient. But most frightening of all was Mussolini's assumption that Italy, by virtue of being a great power, could resort to force whenever prestige was even minimally involved.[25]

Although Mussolini had wanted the Italian forces to stay in Corfu, he was obliged to submit to world opinion and withdraw them. This rankled with him, and he said he would not forgive the British for making him back down; [26] but among Italians, liberals as well as conservatives, the first example of violence on an international scale won him a useful reputation for courage and patriotic zeal.[27] Mussolini knew from his years in journalism how to manipulate public opinion, and was able without provoking ridicule to call his attack on Greece Italy's most important action since 1860.[28] He preferred to remember it as the occasion when the British submitted to his iron will,[29] and the fascist press dutifully praised what they called a magnificent display of strength against Greek aggressiveness and a first step in conquering for Italy a place in the sun.[30] Dino Grandi, a younger Fascist who soon became an authoritative spokesman on foreign policy, called it a "real contribution to European peace." [31] Such was the chorus of applause, that Mussolini never realised what damage he had done nor how dangerous for Italy as well as other countries this one-sided idea of national prestige might be. On the contrary, he took positive pleasure in having made people afraid of Italian power; he had learned that the other states of Europe would not stand together against a treaty-breaker, and that by control of the newspapers he could at any time rally opinion in Italy in favour of bullying a smaller and weaker state.

Except for a short interval with Grandi from 1929 to 1932, Mussolini was his own foreign minister until 1936, but he was responsible for so many different departments that he could occupy himself with foreign-office business only irregularly, and foreign ambassadors found this a constant hindrance.[32] He nevertheless resented any suggestion that the permanent officials of the ministry might be in charge of foreign affairs,[33] and the decision over Corfu was obviously his own, as also was the strange decision in 1923 to support French military action against Germany in the Ruhr. This last action Mussolini never properly explained: if he was trying to create a continental bloc with France in order to isolate Great Britain, he did not succeed. So far as one can tell, his senior officials were nevertheless reasonably content with his first steps in diplomacy; almost no one resigned after fascism came to power, and there is little sign that they were anything but happy with Mussolini's talk of pursuing a forceful nationalist policy. Not all of them were so pleased with the removal of the foreign office from the Consulta palace to the much smaller Palazzo Chigi, because it led to disorganisation of the archives and hence a confusing fracture with the past.[34] Yet this was a comparatively minor matter, and the fact that they remained in their jobs smoothed the transition from liberalism to fascism.

Officials of the foreign office did quite a lot to educate Mussolini during these early years of the regime. They improved his habits of dress and also, up to a point, his social behaviour and his table manners. Perhaps they helped to modify his violent language and control his pleasure in wounding the *amour propre* of foreign statesmen and governments. But these were restraints which he could find tiresome. In course of time he antagonised some of the older diplomats and encouraged their resignation. One useful reform was that he opened the foreign service to those without private means—an important break with tradition. In particular he did not like feeling dependent on the permanent secretary, Salvatore Contarini, and the latter hinted to foreign diplomats that he was beginning to resent Mussolini's disregard of his colleagues.[35] The extreme Fascists were pleased when Contarini resigned in 1926, because his moderate, old-fashioned, and conciliatory ways of procedure did not fit the bluster and bludgeoning that was one inescapable facet of the new regime.

One success for moderation was Mussolini's signature of the Treaty of Locarno in October 1925, when along with Germany, France, England, and Belgium he guaranteed the Franco-German frontier which had been laid down by the Treaty of Versailles. Mussolini later claimed, in a way which became familiar, that the original idea was his own, and he used this as an example of how he was changing the direction of European history;[36] the suggestion was even advanced that he qualified for a Nobel peace

ITALY AND THE
MEDITERRANEAN BASIN
IN THE 1930s

prize.[37] Nevertheless, although he continued to stress that the Locarno Treaty was a fundamental fact of European politics,[38] it was one of those many pieces of paper which he signed for little other reason than to avoid being left out on his own. As his colleagues have since explained, Mussolini was glad to sign almost any treaty because treaties always made news and so gave him a sense of importance: few other countries signed so many pacts as fascist Italy, and yet treaties meant little to him.[39] One incident which made Locarno an unhappy experience was that Mussolini was ostentatiously boycotted there by foreign journalists in protest against news censorship in Italy,[40] and though he later invented a more flattering version of the episode,[41] at the time he was very angry indeed, and never again did he visit any country where journalists were free to treat him as an ordinary mortal.

In the discussions at Locarno, when the French offered to guarantee Italy's northern frontier, Mussolini surprisingly refused this helpful suggestion. Since fascist foreign policy was more often a matter of attitudes and prestige than of hard realities, he thought he had more to gain by a refusal and preferred to despise the French for their reliance on "pieces of paper". Thinking of propaganda more than of reality, he wanted to be able to tell his own people that fascism was quite capable of guaranteeing the Brenner frontier on its own; in other words France needed his guarantee but he did not need hers.[42]

Mussolini occasionally found it useful to say that fascism was a purely domestic matter, because he knew that this would reassure foreigners; hence he was at pains to emphasise that he had no interest in carrying out propaganda abroad.[43] In reality, however, a special press office was set up with a sizeable budget and the task of working on foreign journalists, politicians, and industrialists; its director was charged "to exploit everything that might be used to further the cause of Italian fascism abroad".[44] By 1925 there were hopeful signs of fascist movements at work in Japan, Germany, Portugal—even, it was thought, in Russia—and one hopeful agent guessed that there might be 150,000 active Fascists in England.[45] On occasion the Duce could not deny himself the pleasure of saying not only that fascism was a movement vastly more revolutionary than bolshevism, but that before long it would engulf the greater part of Europe.[46] No doubt Mussolini was here just trying to impress his entourage, but it is possible that he was also deceiving himself. His instincts told him that foreigners and Italians alike should be kept guessing, in a constant state of anxiety and in expectation of some astonishing *coup de maître*. Propaganda was steered into creating the illusion that the whole of Europe looked to Rome with envy and apprehension.[47]

One useful element abroad was those Italians who had temporarily or permanently emigrated. With what one may take to be the usual fascist hyperbole, there were said to be 10 million of them: nearly a million in France, 1.7 million in the Argentine, 1.9 million in Brazil, and 3.7 million in the United States. A strange illusion was kept alive that in case of war many of these exiles might return home and be mobilised into the Italian forces; hence embassies abroad were required to carry out the wholly impossible task of providing a secret biennial census answering twenty-nine questions about this huge number of people, so as to be ready for such an emergency. Much money was also spent, not very successfully, in trying to prevent the assimilation of Italian emigrants into other national communities,[48] and when Rudolf Valentino renounced Italian citizenship there was an attempt to boycott his films in displeasure at such manifest treason. Official denials could not hide the fact that government money was being used to give these exiles political instruction and even semi-military training, and the knowledge caused much offence in other countries. Nevertheless, only a small proportion of Italians abroad seem to have come into the net of this fascist propaganda machine, and much scarce foreign currency must have been wasted or corruptly diverted.[49]

Foreigners could not immediately make much sense of the various and sometimes contradictory aspects of Italian fascism. Mussolini used the technique of what he called the "Scotch douche", blowing hot and cold, being friendly and provocative by turns, and continually changing his ground so that he could appear both democrat and authoritarian, radical and reactionary, socialist and anti-socialist. It was therefore quite a long time before foreign governments felt that they knew where they were with him,[50] for he could speak at one moment of demolishing the British empire,[51] and a few days later be all sweet reasonableness. British and French politicians did not take him too seriously at first, but though most of them were not much impressed with his personality, they were no more impressed by any possible alternatives to him. Italy's successive liberal administrations between 1919 and 1922 had failed to produce an effective government or an effective politician. Then in November 1922 a predominantly liberal parliament voted overwhelmingly for Mussolini, and foreigners observed that most of the Italian liberal leaders were among his supporters on that occasion. Newspapers in Paris and London did not conceal that fascism used brutal and illegal means in coming to power, but official Italy was manifestly in favour of fascism, and one could hope that the experience of power would soften its more violent attitudes. In their reports from Rome, foreign diplomats sometimes suggested the possibility of using outside pressure to overturn Mussolini, but added that the likely alternatives were anarchy, bolshevism, or military dictatorship, all of which could be worse;[52] also that he was extremely touchy and quite equal to bringing war to Europe if he were not treated with care and some indulgence. Probably his tenure of office would be short, and he would only rally more support if foreigners tried to criticise after such a large parliamentary vote.

Ronald Graham, the British ambassador in Rome, went further than most in thinking Mussolini to be basically sane and reasonable. Dangerous and often unpleasant as fascism in his view might be, the good might yet outweigh the evil.[53] It was common among conservatives in London to think that Mussolini might save his country from a bolshevik revolution. Winston Churchill, who was in Italy during some of the worst outrages of fascist violence, continued to think of fascism as standing for law and order, and went out of his way to praise it, and was in turn praised by the fascist press.[54] Lord Rothermere's newspapers were generally favourable; Lord Rosebery gave Mussolini his splendid villa at Posillipo; Lord Inchcape wrote to *The Times* to suggest that England and France needed Mussolinis to introduce economies into government; and Sir Walter Runciman publicly hailed him as a second Napoleon, a genius whose salutary use of bludgeon and castor oil had put his country to rights.[55]

Public opinion in Great Britain and France was of course divided about fascism. If any general feeling existed it was that here was a desperate and violent remedy for an almost impossible situation, and while people were understandably ignorant about what fascism meant, they had to accept it at least until greater clarity existed about any possible alternatives. Among the conservatives some differed from the general view and thought of Mussolini as some kind of socialist and for this reason continued to oppose him,[56] while others among French conservatives feared him as representative of extreme Italian nationalism.[57] The financiers of the City of London, despite what many have thought, were not generous enthusiasts for lending money to fascist Italy, and there was plenty of horrified opposition on the right as well as the left to the continued political violence in Italy.[58] Mussolini expressed annoyance about such hostility. Anti-Fascists, on the other hand, were equally annoyed that the British and French governing classes were not helping to remove Mussolini from power, and without doubt the friendliness of many foreigners must have assisted him in convincing moderate Italians that he was a reliable and responsible person. The British police of Scotland Yard, in what one may hope was not their usual practice, even helped him to locate anti-Fascists in England and Italy.[59]

Mussolini kept in close touch with foreign newspaper editors and proprietors, notably with William Randolph Hearst and Lord Rothermere. Lord Rothermere wrote to thank him "for his great services to civilisation and humanity", and Hearst praised the "astounding ability" of this "marvelous man".[60] The Duce had a personal letter printed in *The Times* on 26 June 1925, insisting that fascism in Italy had no intention of curtailing elementary liberties, and possibly his words were believed by some readers. The Italian ambassador in London paid special attention to *The Times*, because of its influence and its reputation for detachment and unbribability; though not always successful, he begged it to underplay the views of the anti-fascist exiles, and said that otherwise there would be a risk of losing Italian friendship.[61] Camillo Pellizzi, the founder of the London *fascio*, obtained money from Rome to set up a company for coal and iron imports, but which in fact was for bribing English journalists and writers.[62] What Pellizzi wanted to put across was that fascism was not reactionary, not chauvinistic, and not anti-Jewish.[63] In an article which Mussolini first approved, British readers were told that fascism was neither a dictatorship nor a danger for Europe, but stood for a revival of religion and the family.[64] Luigi Villari was another indefatigable propagandist of these themes in London and New York

13

and managed to persuade several publishers and the editors of the *Encyclopaedia Britannica* that his views were authoritative and trustworthy.

A good deal of success was obviously obtained by such means, and Mussolini's destruction of the liberal press in Italy made it hard for outsiders to learn the other side of the picture. Most of their knowledge inevitably came from the official Stefani agency in Rome. The permanent correspondents of foreign newspapers in Rome told the truth at their peril, and could not easily explain, for example, about the murder of the socialist leader Giacomo Matteotti by the Fascists in 1924, nor could any editor who wanted to keep a correspondent in Italy avoid conniving at this kind of censorship.[65] Any criticisms of fascist policy were confined rather to editorial comment, and few people in Italy would ever hear of such criticism except on the occasions when Mussolini saw fit to reproduce it as a means of arousing popular xenophobia.

More important than press comments was the fact that the British foreign office, in particular under Austen Chamberlain (1924–1929), decided to pin its faith on the hope that Mussolini would ultimately become respectable and a pillar of law and order. Chamberlain claimed to disapprove of fascism, but pretended that he had no right to quarrel with the Italians' choice of their own system of government. On four occasions he went to meet the Italian dictator, though these meetings produced few practical results and indeed eventually taught him that his confidence in Mussolini had been misplaced.[66] Yet there is no doubt that such solicitous attention helped to give fascism a gratuitous title of respectability which was easily exploited, especially when, in a highly undiplomatic gesture, Lady Chamberlain asked for Mussolini's fascist badge and pinned it ostentatiously on her dress for the photographers to see.

2

GROWING SELF-CONFIDENCE

For anyone prepared to read or listen, Mussolini made it obvious
that he was becoming a nationalist with great ambitions for his
country. He liked to boast that Italians were a race which had
three times given civilisation to a barbarian world, and in an
excess of rhetorical self-indulgence he called them the most solid
and homogeneous people in Europe, who were destined to raise
the flag of imperialism throughout the Mediterranean and make
Rome once again the centre of western civilisation.[1] He could be
strangely irritated when foreigners spoke to him of the glories of
Italian art and climate, because he imagined, and resented, that
Italians had the reputation of being disinclined to fight and eager
for pleasure. He determined to change their reputation and make
them less nice, more hateful, and more violent.[2]

An easy acceptance of brutality and violence had been characteristic of Mussolini even as a schoolboy. As a young man he had
lived for combat and pointedly rejected the view that war did not
pay, since "only blood could turn the bloodstained wheels of history".[3] As prime minister he told Italians to consider themselves
in a permanent state of war, and remarked that his first priority
was to increase military readiness to the very maximum. Carried
away again by his own words, he said that he could quickly
mobilise an army of five million men,[4] and though he privately
reassured foreign diplomats that he was not serious, he could not
back down easily from words spoken in public; indeed he repeated
the assertion and informed parliament in 1927 that he would
create an air force so large as to blot out the sun. After discoursing
on the beauty of machine guns and artillery, he declared that war
alone could make a people truly noble, and set himself ten years to
militarise the country so as to be able to force a war upon Europe
and obtain for Italy what he called her due.[5]

A lot of this can have been only half serious, but it is not always easy to know where fascism drew the line between truth and exhortatory fiction, and some Fascists were not content with liking such views but improved on them, and sometimes carried their leader along in a flood of wordy rhetoric. Newspapers argued not only that war was the one solution to Europe's problems, but that it should be desired for its own sake. A positive desire for war was even said by the extremists to be the main belief distinguishing fascism from democracy,[6] and some of the doubters were evidently attracted to fascism by the very belief that it was making Italy an object of respect but also of fear abroad.[7] Rejecting his early anti-imperialism, Mussolini began to demand that the Mediterranean should again become *mare nostrum* and that Italy should enlarge her overseas empire.[8] Already in the mid-1920s, contingency plans were prepared for a possible occupation of Ethiopia, and by 1928 the revival of imperialism and militarism was stated with pride to be virtually an accomplished fact.[9]

Mussolini did not come to power in 1922 by a military pronunciamento, but it helped him that many in the higher army commands were sympathisers. His first two ministers of war, Marshal Armando Diaz and General Antonino Di Giorgio, were not members of the Fascist Party, and both resigned when Mussolini would not accept the basic structural reforms which they thought necessary. This enabled him to appoint himself minister for army, navy, and air force for the next four years, though his lack of competence in military matters prevented him seeing how only radical reforms in organisation and armament could produce a really modern fighting service. As minister responsible for seven different departments he had insufficient time to think out long-term policy in any of them, and by abolishing freedom of the press he prevented anyone drawing attention to this crucial deficiency or trying to repair it.[10] The dead hand of fascism soon lay heavily on the army as party membership became necessary for promotion to higher rank.

By constitutional law it was the king who commanded the armed services, and Mussolini aimed to circumvent this awkward fact. In June 1925 he created a new official, the chief of general staff, who was directly responsible to the minister and not to the king. The first incumbent was Marshal Pietro Badoglio, a man who some knowledgeable people thought bore the main responsibility for the disastrous defeat of the Italian army at Caporetto in 1917, and who lacked the character and brains to compensate for Mussolini's failings. The duties of this post were left so vague that one of the older generals, Giuseppe Ferrari, was brave enough to say that the result of its creation might be to paralyse the whole higher command. As this prophecy came true, it is worth adding that Ferrari was an early champion of far more mechanisation of the army; he also advised the careful use of government purchases to build up an armaments industry, and urged more serious planning for various hypothetical war situations.[11] Unfortunately, serious study and discussion were not part of the "fascist style". Mussolini could sometimes listen to critical views, but was psychologically incapable of real discussion, for he hated having his authority or prescience called in question. So the supreme commission of defence wasted much of its time on such matters as the cut of military uniforms, and whether beans or cabbage should predominate in military rations; like the office of chief of staff, this commission was used by Mussolini to create the illusion among the public that serious thought and preparations were taking place.[12] As for General Ferrari, he had reached the end of his career, and the younger fascist generals were made of different stuff.

In 1927 Mussolini declared, without any justification except the desire to impress, that the technical preparation of the armed forces was well enough advanced for war to be something of which Italy should not be afraid.[13] Flattered and deceived by his subordinates, he possibly already thought that his judgement on such matters was reliable, and grandiosely announced not only that military problems were the most fundamental problems of all, but that he dedicated the greater part of his time to them. Relying on his own intuition, he liked to convey the impression that he did not need expert advice, and so it happened that on the same day he could sign contradictory decisions in his different ministries without even reading them.[14] Some of the generals found it expedient to flatter him and encourage his delusions, while others were upset by his complete ignorance about military affairs, but said nothing.[15] And yet this was the man who concentrated all military authority in his own hands by appointing himself head of the militia as well as minister for each of the three services, and who ultimately, as first marshal of the empire, supplanted the king in command of all armed forces in the field.

One dangerous military illusion propagated by government order, and even compulsorily included in school textbooks, was that Italy alone of all the countries involved in the First World War had been victorious. Her army had repeatedly saved England and France from defeat, and by rights Italy should therefore have dictated the peace settlement, though out of generosity and foolishness she let herself be robbed of her deserts. Fascism was not above tinkering with the documents in order to substantiate this assertion. As explained by the foremost fascist historian, Gioacchino Volpe, the textbooks in France which told a different story were scandalously biased, whereas Italians in his view were by nature incapable of narrow nationalism and were, alone of all peoples, skilled in judging such historical questions with impartiality.[16]

Admittedly the peace settlement of 1919 gave Italy none of the ex-German colonies she would have liked, but, as Mussolini himself once admitted, it had won her in Europe itself greater gains than any other participant country. Before long it suited him to develop the quite different theme that the peace had been a disaster, and the official historians of the regime therefore substituted the idea of an Italy wrongfully cheated of her imperial ambitions.[17] By the late 1920s revision of the Versailles treaty became the central theme of fascist foreign policy, and this meant drifting into opposition against Britain and France, whose interest, on the contrary, was to defend the peace settlement and keep Europe stable. An early sign was the attack on the Greek island of Corfu in 1923. Another was the treaty with Hungary in 1927, which stressed the common interests of these two powers against the Slavs and the democracies. Italy, like Hungary, was now said to be an "unsatisfied" power, and hence tended to take up a position against Czechoslovakia and Yugoslavia, which had both gained from the 1919 settlement: it was thought that perhaps Italy could undermine these two countries to the point where they would split up and give way to the spread of Italian influence along and south of the Danube.[18] According to Dino Grandi, speaking as second in charge at the foreign office, there were possibilities of imperial expansion farther away in Asia Minor, and also against the French in Corsica.[19] Germany was approached to associate herself with Italy over joint action to obtain colonies in Africa,[20] and Grandi also instructed Italian diplomats to keep in touch with separatist movements inside Russia and various Balkan states. Mussolini's idea was to be ready to exploit any occasion, and at one point he even toyed with the idea of using Afghanistan as a means of entry into the politics of central Asia.[21]

Grandi had earned his spurs as a brutal squad leader during the fascist conquest of power. He entered the foreign office just before Contarini resigned, one of his first tasks in 1926 being to put the senior diplomats under pressure to join the party; then in 1927 the first batch of fascist militiamen were given posts in the foreign office, and Mussolini explained that he wanted the whole service to become thoroughly fascist within a year.[22] Some of the new men possessed no qualifications except loyal service in the squads and the party; many of them had little education, little knowledge of other countries or languages, and their boastful, uncouth behaviour in foreign capitals threw considerable discredit on the fascist revolution.[23]

Two small details in 1928 reveal further aspects of the development of foreign policy as the diplomatic service became more fascist in its composition and in its objectives. One was that, after signing the Kellogg Pact for renouncing war, Mussolini almost at once made sarcastic remarks about it in parliament. He explained that if any similar treaty was put up to him he would again hurry to sign as he had signed at Locarno, yet his policy would continue to be based on a strong army and on the fact that it was war and not peace which would bring the necessary changes in Europe.[24]

The other concerned the international control of Tangier. By a treaty of 1923, Spain, France, and Britain—but not Italy— shared in the administration of this town, and Mussolini made a major issue out of Italy's joining the others on terms of parity. He described the situation as full of potential conflict, and it was in the interest of fascism to keep such irritants alive as long and as acutely as possible until they were solved in his favour. In October 1927 he dramatically despatched to Tangier a squadron of ships commanded by the Prince of Udine, and the crews were welcomed ashore by local Fascists with an ostentatious display of blackshirt bravado. Eventually, in the summer of 1928, he won his point and Italy was invited to join the international administration.[25]

Nearer home, Albania received a good deal of his attention; indeed, this tiny country became for a time the main hinge of fascist foreign policy. Italian troops had occupied Albania during the First World War, but had left after a patriotic rebellion against the invaders in 1920. It was Mussolini's intention to recover this lost situation because possession of Albania, which ran along the far side of the Straits of Otranto, would supposedly give Italy control of entry to the Adriatic.[26] He began by backing a local chieftain, Ahmed Zog, in his successful struggle for power at Tirana, then encouraged Italian investment there and persuaded the British to surrender some of their oil concessions. Next, after obtaining a strong hold over the economy of the country, he made it into an Italian satellite by a treaty in November 1926. This treaty was held up proudly by Mussolini as typical of the "fascist style" in politics. One of its aims was to create a threat on the frontier of Yugoslavia; another, to counter French influence in the Balkans; and yet another, to extend Italian economic and political influence in southeastern Europe before Germany was strong enough to compete.[27] Although Mussolini continued to protest that he had no designs against Albanian independence, his actions told in a different sense; he used clear threats of force in establishing his Albanian protectorate and said he would not allow any interference by the League of Nations.[28] When the French reacted by drawing closer to Yugoslavia, this only increased his determination to force the issue, while other countries, though they would have liked to avoid any Balkan confrontation, were not ready to use force against him and so could be held to have tacitly acquiesced.

This was another example of revisionism and of his intention to break free of international agreements wherever these stood in the way. By 1927 Italian officers were training the Albanian army in expectation of war against Yugoslavia, which could hardly have been in the interests of the local population. Some Italian administrators did a good job in Albania, but many others were notoriously corrupt, and to curtail criticism they succeeded in suppressing the opposition newspapers which had drawn attention to this fact. Yet friendship was not so easily purchased. Some wouldbe friends of fascism among the British conservatives at last learned from this clumsy imperialism in the Adriatic that Mussolini was a dangerous force in Europe.[29] The antagonising of Yugoslavia may have flattered Italy's self-esteem, but it lost old friends and created new and gratuitous enmities. Moreover, by increasing tension in the Balkans, Mussolini was only helping the very advance of German influence that he was hoping to prevent. In addition, his policy of bolstering the Albanian economy cost money which Italy could hardly afford, and several million dollars a year had to be given to Zog in the not very confident hope that this would prevent him turning instead to the Yugoslavs.[30] Sometimes expensive military action had to be taken to keep him in line. Alternative methods of control were less effective, and though Mussolini once tried to find an Italian wife for the king of Albania, Zog insisted on nothing less than a daughter of the king of Italy, and the offer was withdrawn in some confusion.[31]

Albania was not to be annexed by Mussolini until 1939, but already in 1928 the Italian foreign office thought of it as virtually national territory. Vague plans were being drawn up to settle large numbers of Italian peasants there after forcibly removing Albanian citizens from the more fertile areas—a policy that was defended as being no worse than Americans killing off redskins with drink. Albania was thus to become "the first stage in our imperial journey"; it was "the proof by fire for fascist Italy"; once established there, once having subjugated "the decadent Albanian race", Italy could move forward to more distant objects of expansion in Africa and the Levant.[32]

Not often did Mussolini have a well-thought-out and coordinated foreign policy. What he preferred, and what was more consonant with the relative weakness of Italy, was the much less exacting objective of small individual successes, making a nuisance of himself by small-scale provocations in the hope that a situation might emerge which he could exploit. He had little sympathy with the idea that diplomacy might be a matter of slow negotiation based on compromise.[33] As well as providing weapons for insurgent groups in Hungary and Austria, he sent arms to Greece and Spain, and secret military training in Italy was offered to soldiers from Spain and Germany.[34] In the Balkans, fascist policy was to encourage any irredentist movements that might help to multiply tension.[35] With the Yugoslavs, however, he was more ambivalent: one idea was that they should be persuaded to accept Italy rather than France as a patron; another was that, Yugoslavia being an "artificial creation" of Versailles, it might disintegrate under pressure, in which case Italy was ready with her claim to Croatia and the whole Dalmatian coast of the Adriatic. Mussolini had plans ready for a possible invasion of the country as a means towards asserting his position as the chief power in the Balkans and the Danube basin, the area which he called "Italy's hinterland".[36]

A first step was to encourage separatist movements inside Yugoslavia. By the early 1930s two secret camps had been set up in Italy where Croat exiles were instructed in terrorist activity.[37] In Macedonia, Grandi was in touch with two rival dissident factions, one of which, the Macedonian Revolutionary Organisation, used Italian money to finance a campaign of apparently quite casual murders and other outrages. Its objectives were not particularly clear, but apart from politics it seems to have been a financial racket which usually sold its services to more sides than one, and was probably also obtaining money from the Soviet Union. How much the Fascists spent on such an unreliable body cannot be known, but it was money squandered.[38] Public opinion in Italy of course knew nothing about this aspect of foreign policy; official propaganda confined itself to maintaining that the Croats and the other insurgent movements were the defenders of western values against barbarism, whereas the Serbs, who were the dominant element in Yugoslavia, were "savage aggressors drunk with the spirit of conquest and dangerous for the peace of the world".[39]

At the time of the march on Rome, Adolf Hitler, then a little-known party leader in Germany, tried to get in touch with Mussolini because he had been greatly impressed by the success of the fascist movement. He made it clear to the Italians that he intended to restore German power and hoped for their support in doing so. He admitted that he wanted a union or *Anschluss* between Germany and Austria, and if Italy would agree to this he in return would guarantee her frontier with Austria at the Brenner Pass, and discountenance the German-speaking population south of that pass which Italy had incorporated in 1919.[40] Mussolini realised that a German alliance might one day be useful to him, and already in September 1923 was wondering if Germany was strong enough to check the French army should he ever decide to attack Yugoslavia on his other frontier.[41] Whether or not he helped Hitler in the attempted Nazi *Putsch* of November 1923 is in doubt, but shortly afterwards he was secretly sending money and arms to help the German nationalists to undermine the Weimar Republic.[42] Though he continued to speak of the Nazis with some contempt,[43] he gave hospitality to Göring when he came to Italy to convalesce from a wound in 1924. Hitler wrote to ask—though in vain until 1931—for a signed photograph of Mussolini, and a bronze bust of the Duce was prominently on display whenever Fascists visited the Nazi headquarters at Munich.[44]

Fascism continued throughout the 1920s to maintain a number of contacts with right-wing movements north of the Alps. Hints came from militarist elements in Germany that they would like Italian help one day in defeating France, after which Italy would be allowed to annex much of North Africa.[45] There were talks in 1926 between General Capello and General von Seeckt, who then personally visited Mussolini, and Italian industrialists were interested in secretly setting up plants to help Germany make poison gas.[46] Italian diplomats, and especially the president of the Italian chamber of commerce in Berlin, Major Giuseppe Renzetti, saw Hitler from time to time, and in 1928 Mussolini said he was ready to meet the Nazi leader, though officials continued to deny that the two movements were in contact.[47] Hitler was anxious to minimise any possible differences between the two countries, so as to make a joint programme possible: what he proposed was a long-term aim to arrange separate spheres of interest, Italy taking the Mediterranean, Germany having a predominant influence over northern and eastern Europe. His main wish was to prise Italy loose from the coalition which she had enjoyed with France and Britain from 1915 to 1918.[48]

If Mussolini occasionally seemed lukewarm in his response, the chief reason was his recognition that an *Anschluss*, by bringing a major European power down to the Brenner Pass, would annul the one major success of Italy in the First World War, namely the defeat and dismemberment of the great Austro-Hungarian empire. He made up his mind that he could not possibly allow such a damaging blow to fascist prestige.[49] For the moment, however, this particular danger looked remote and he could not see he had much to lose in the short term from a German comeback in Europe. He had on the contrary something to gain from it, because Italy was strongest when she could oscillate between rival power groups,[50] and for this reason he needed a counterpoise to Britain and France in the European equilibrium. At the same time he was anxious to reinforce right-wing groups in Austria, because his own fascist movement would gather strength and reputation if it spread into other countries before the Nazis could do so.[51] Italian diplomats and generals therefore arranged in 1929 to assemble caches of arms near the Austrian frontier for use in a projected rising by the para-military *Heimwehren* to take over power in Austria.[52] Such a policy was not entirely consistent, for help was simultaneously given to the Nazi movement in Austria which was opposed to the *Heimwehren*, and vast sums were still being given, at heavy cost to the Italian exchequer, to the Austrian government itself in an attempt to maintain Italian influence at Vienna and create a more substantial barrier against any aggressive move by Germany. Presumably it was hoped that one or another of these policies would help Italian interests.[53]

Mussolini was simultaneously sending weapons, again in breach of treaty, into Hungary. The extent of this arms traffic from Italy is not known. When one consignment was discovered in January 1928, documents were fabricated by the Italian foreign office to cover it up, and the possibility was discussed of finding someone patriotic enough to make a false confession and go to prison so as to exculpate the government. Although an investigation by the League of Nations was hushed up at Italian request, foreign journalists established that Italy since 1922 had been smuggling arms to various fascist parties in Europe. In 1929, a few days after becoming foreign minister Dino Grandi authorised the continuance of secret subsidies for subversion in Hungary and Austria,[54] and it was planned to give Hungarian soldiers secret military training in Italy.[55]

On Mussolini's personal instructions, a similar arrangement was made with other countries whose revisionist ambitions might be useful to him. Long before Hitler came to power, Germans were surreptitiously coming to Italy for military instruction, and the German government investigated the possibility of setting up munitions deposits there so as to evade the terms of the 1919 treaty.[56] A number of training units were established, and successive groups of German pilots wearing Italian uniforms came to Italy for practice in bombing and air combat. Mussolini said he was delighted to give any help he could in thus secretly reconstructing the German air force in defiance of the terms of the Treaty of Versailles.[57]

Fascist foreign policy was sometimes governed quite excessively by ideological considerations, but at other times went to the opposite extreme and boasted of the realism with which Mussolini, though anti-communist, befriended the Soviet Union. Though the Fascists never lost sight of the value of posing as the great opponents of bolshevism, the Duce took pride in calling himself the first statesman in Europe to make an agreement with the Soviets, and the assiduity with which this legend was repeated suggests that the claim was important to him, though it was not quite accurate; indeed, Mussolini's anti-bolshevism may even have delayed a diplomatic recognition of the Soviet regime which Italian liberal governments had prepared before 1922.[58] Some fascist newspapers showed a remarkable sympathy with Russia, at least until 1936; some continued to wonder whether both regimes by different paths were not moving so close together as to be almost identical. It at least crossed Mussolini's mind that Russia might prove a safer ally than Germany.[59] He himself in 1934 seems to have been momentarily deluded by his own press into thinking that Russia had abandoned Marx and might be persuaded to look instead to the founder of fascism.[60] Though the Russian leaders would have found such presumptuousness bizarre, they too were equally determined not to let ideology prevent a much closer relationship with fascism than other communist parties in Europe can have liked.[61]

By the time Dino Grandi took over the foreign ministry from Mussolini in September 1929, he was already beginning to acquire the reputation of being a moderate, as experience of office made him more liberal, less belligerent, and less ideological. But he prudently continued like the other ministers to advertise his determination to let policy be dictated by Mussolini himself,[62] and few people in the fascist hierarchy were more grovelling than Grandi in their flattery of the leader. Though he set more value than his colleagues on good relations with other countries, and though he did not always like Mussolini's tendency towards grand gestures and intransigent phraseology, he claimed that his own intentions were essentially the same, namely to break free from "the so-called friendship" with Britain and France.[63]

Fascist policy at this period was still one of collaboration with the League of Nations. Mussolini's attitude to the League had from the first been ambiguous because, although he might have preferred it not to exist, he could not afford to be left out. What especially annoyed him was the parliamentary tradition of open discussion which was still maintained in Geneva long after fascism had proclaimed the inevitable victory of the alternative virtues of authority and discipline. He once tried to have the secretariat of the League moved to Vienna, where Italian influence counted for more. He then had the idea that non-European nations should be excluded. Both these suggestions failed, but he did succeed in having some of his own nominees appointed to senior positions in the League bureaucracy and gave them precise instructions on how to use their office for furthering Italian interests.[64] He nevertheless announced that Italy would eventually leave Geneva if the League were not radically reformed by giving greater weight to the vote of the larger powers.[65]

When the French foreign minister, Aristide Briand, began to talk about the possibility of setting up a loose federal union in Europe, this looked like a bid to increase French influence and hence had to be resisted. To counter any advance of democratic ideology, an "independent" international fascist institute had already been set up with Italian money in Switzerland,[66] and against Briand's idea a new journal called *Antieuropa* was started in Italy with government subsidies to put forward the alternative of fascist expansion in the world. Mussolini charged its editor, Asvero Gravelli, to investigate the possibility of creating a fascist international society which would make Rome an alternative centre to both Geneva and Moscow.[67] *Antieuropa* proclaimed without false modesty that fascism was the greatest revolution of modern times; that Mussolini alone had the intellect and the will to impose proper discipline on Europe and to challenge the values of democracy, communism, and Americanism; and moreover that Italy alone, of all countries, had a position of spiritual primacy which everyone would acknowledge.[68] The Europe of tomorrow, wrote *Antieuropa*, would be fascist and unashamedly aggressive because there was no room left in the world for the weak and the fearful. England would have to be dethroned from supremacy in the Mediterranean, and Italy would then be restored to her dominion over *mare nostrum*.[69]

Gravelli was not being entirely original when he developed these themes. Many fascist intellectuals and politicians had other journals which they used for building up their own power groups inside the regime, and in which they advocated monotonously whatever ideas were currently acceptable. As well as Coppola's *Politica*, Franco Ciarlantini's *Augustea* and Edmondo Rossoni's *La Stirpe* were already arguing for *latinità* against Americanism, and for establishing a new Roman empire in the Mediterranean.[70] Giuseppe Bottai's *Critica Fascista* was another magazine which, though it had a reputation for moderation and better than average sense, was prophesying a new order for Europe in which Italy would be the leading constituent. It maintained that only Italy could provide the necessary element of vitality and constructive power; Italy was already the "axis of Europe" and would in time become the "axis of the whole world".[71] The wisdom of Rome could not be compared with the mere egoism of Washington and London. Fascism was now for export, and indeed was the only export article which Italy had in abundance. The nice, gentle Italy of yesterday was changing into something hard, intransigent, and masculine, which had learned that national greatness was determined by the degree of alarm aroused elsewhere.[72]

Parallel to this was the demand for a new "spiritual imperialism" in Italy, a positive belief that Italian culture was best and alone would be capable of educating the rest of the world: not untypical of such an attitude was the proud assertion that foreigners such as Byron and Shakespeare owed their success to what they had learned from Italy.[73] Equally strong was the demand to put up barriers against foreign art and literature, because it was thought wrong that, despite fascism, many Italians still were in love with things foreign and with what Leo Longanesi called "the French disease, liberty". According to one prominent intellectual, Carlo Costamagna, an internationalism of ideas was as dangerous as an internationalism of finance or politics: if you went to an Italian art gallery, he said, most likely you would see not virile Italian and fascist art, but decadent derivatives of French impressionism; if you opened a treatise on medicine or economics, eight names out of ten quoted were foreigners, and this was wrong.[74] Fortunately, it was observed, the minister of education had issued an order that half of every public music programme should be of Italian music, though it was thought scandalous that concert managers needed a law to compel them to introduce such an obvious reform.[75]

Even worse was the more subtle invasion of Italy by the American way of life. Mussolini disliked the United States for its new laws restricting immigrants from Italy, at the same time as he inconsistently disliked the fact that so many Italian emigrants had already crossed the Atlantic in the past fifty years and been "lost" to the fatherland. He envied Americans their wealth and reputation, resented their claim for repayment of debts incurred during the First World War, and despised what he called their abject materialism. In April 1929 he told the British that Europe should unite speedily against the Americans or else "they will eat us all up".[76] He was frightened as he saw the films, the fashions, the various canons of taste and behaviour, and even the speech of America invading Italy, especially as Italian youth was showing great enthusiasm for these novelties; this was a dangerous sign that fascist culture might be proving unacceptable to the new generation which he had tried so hard to educate. Hence in 1929 there was an organised campaign of propaganda directed against Americanism, that "grease-stain which is spreading through the whole of European life". From the example of American writers— the name of James Joyce was cited—it could be seen that "the average intelligence of an adult male in the United States was about that of a European fourteen-year-old boy"; theirs was a society modelled on ants and termites; Europe should unite behind the beneficent leadership of fascism and resist such a baleful influence.[77]

Critica Fascista meanwhile advanced the argument that too many foreign books were being translated in Italy by publishers exploiting the ignorance and poor taste of the reading public, so much so that French and Russian novels were "contaminating" youth and threatening to undo all the hard work of devoted fascist educators. One worrying example was H. G. Wells, whose *Outline of History* had been condemned as worthless in England but was bringing contraband ideas into Italy.[78] Three-quarters of the books being published in Italy were from abroad, wrote *Antieuropa*, and fascist writers had good reason to regard this as unfair competition. One certainly could not accept the principle of tolerance advocated by the international P.E.N. club of authors; on the contrary, the finest works of art had always emerged from an atmosphere of intolerance, and fascist Italy must encourage them to go on doing so.[79]

The extremes of cultural and political nationalism appealed to the rhetorician in Mussolini, and from 1930 onwards his speeches seem to have become less careful and more extravagant: fascism was not something merely for Italy but was of universal application, because he could now foresee a fascist Europe and an Italy which had broken out of its "imprisonment" in the Mediterranean. He spoke of the rise of the Italian people towards greatness as something inevitable, something divine, but which could probably be obtained only by armed might or the threat of it. "Words are beautiful things, but muskets and machine guns are even more beautiful." The whole Italian people "would eventually constitute a single human mass and, more than a mass, would become a shooting star that could be hurled against anyone anywhere".[80]

With such official benediction of extremism, the organs and spokesmen of the propaganda machine took up the chorus and told Italians to renounce the hedonism of yesterday, so as to make national power the only goal, to rejoice in the new sense of being admired and also disliked. Italians were a superior people with a need for empire. Official statements by the Fascist Party accentuated the theme that Italy was the envy of the whole world and was ten years ahead of other nations on the road which all must travel: she was being led to her imperial destiny by a superman who was already "coordinating and directing the politics of Europe".[81]

The minister Grandi, at the same time as he fulfilled his public task of reassuring foreign diplomats of Italy's peaceful intentions, privately encouraged Mussolini in this trend towards belligerent declamation, advising him to be more fierce, more Machiavellian, less interested in disarmament and the League, but "to arm and isolate Italy more and more" until everyone acknowledged his rightful place as the arbiter of Europe.[82] Sometimes the fascist technique was to deliver speeches praising the glories of war and dominion, and then half make amends by explaining to foreigners that such speeches were for domestic consumption only.[83] Not everyone thought it inconsistent that Mussolini liked to strike the quite different attitude of the peacemaker, indeed of being the only world statesman really bent on maintaining peace.[84] He had learned that consistency was not important in public utterances, less important at least than being excessive, brazen, and audacious.

During the early 1930s, when there was much discussion about reducing the arms race between nations, Mussolini and Grandi played a helpful part, not least because the drive for armaments threatened to prove very expensive for a poor nation and because any move towards disarmament was likely to increase the relative strength of Italy. In particular they would have liked to limit the building of the more costly items such as battleships, tanks, and heavy artillery. This attitude was probably quite sincere, but equally sincere was Mussolini's contradictory determination to obtain naval parity with France, since to be outdistanced by France would diminish Italy's stature in the world.[85]

As the time came for deeds rather than words, in July 1932 Mussolini took over the foreign office again, dismissing Grandi, who left unwillingly to become ambassador in London. There was a disappointing sense that, after all the Duce's grandiloquent promises, Italian foreign policy had been achieving very little; though the newspapers said that Italy was dominating the world, those who could read foreign papers knew that in fact this was far from the truth.[86] Grandi could be conveniently held responsible for this fact, the implication being that he had pursued a policy too much in favour of the League and the western democracies.[87] But Grandi would not have acted without precise instructions, nor would he have been sent to London if he and Mussolini had seriously disagreed. His orders had been to champion the traditional, realistic Italian policy of seeking a balance of power in

Europe where Italy might act as the makeweight. Now Mussolini wanted a more aggressive stance.[88] By the early 1930s the gradual return of Germany to a position of strength was already leading to an awareness in France that Italian colonial claims could not be resisted forever, and this gave Mussolini a greater interest in personally taking over the conduct of foreign affairs: it was indeed his intention to accentuate the warlike mood in Germany so as to make France give way over the issue of colonies.[89] In part, Grandi's dismissal was a criticism for his not having played a more prominent role in the disarmament conference at Geneva, and for the fact that, after the failure of that conference, fascism would have to confront a burdensome armaments race.[90] Without doubt the dismissal also reflected disappointment that the ever more grandiose pretensions of fascism were receiving so little recognition outside the country; Mussolini intended to claim for himself any credit for the more dynamic moves now being prepared for the future.

3
ITALY AND HER COLONIES,
1922–1932

Until fairly late in life, Mussolini's thoughts about the colonial question were few and superficial, and he was far from dogmatic imperialism. On the contrary, as a good Socialist he had criticised the Italian liberals for their atrocities against colonial peoples and for spending money on prestige imperialism rather than on the solution of difficult domestic problems.[1] But once in office, fascism very soon proclaimed the need for empire, and with much the same arguments as the liberals in 1911; an imperialist policy would increase Italian prestige, satisfy the extreme nationalists, divert attention from pressing problems at home, and quite simply enrich the nation by finding markets to exploit and raw materials to supplement deficiencies at home. According to Giuseppe Bottai, one of the more measured and temperate figures in the fascist leadership, already in 1926 it was clear that materialistic reasons were less important than the Italian people's patriotic duty to start on the road of conquest which other nations had taken; Italians had to make Italy more grand, must seek out empire for its own sake, not for any supposed economic advantages.[2] Fascism was before long said to be imperialist by definition, and Italy to be far more fitted than France or Britain to become a major colonial power.[3]

Though many Italians believed in them to the bitter end, the economic reasons for empire proved a delusion; if only free debate had been allowed by fascism, those reasons could at least have been challenged. The argument of colonies as wealth had been greatly exaggerated by the imperialists and by some industrialists, whether out of honest ignorance or by deliberate deceit; until the Italian empire collapsed in 1941, between half and three-quarters of the budget of each colony continued to depend on generous subsidies from the mother country. Nor in practice was there any truth in the argument that colonies would absorb the "surplus"

Italian population which hitherto had emigrated in its millions to France and the Americas. Party leaders and even some respectable industrialists continued to perpetuate the illusion that Libya and East Africa would become areas of settlement for Italians on a big scale,[4] but no one in the colonial administration dared to give this sensitive but vital matter a thorough investigation. By 1930, in the existing Italian colonial empire which included the Dodecanese Islands, Libya, Somalia, and Eritrea, there were about 50,000 Italian residents,[5] but Mussolini talked glibly of exporting ten million souls to the colonies, and one colonial governor thought there would be room for at least fifteen million white settlers in East Africa alone. Other fascist propagandists multiplied this figure still further as they tried to outdo each other in a zealous glossing of the fascist gospel.[6]

In the First World War Italy's allies had promised her "equitable compensation" in the field of colonies, and Mussolini here found himself with an uncashed cheque to negotiate. Many possible areas for Italian expansion were suggested during the 1920s. Parts of Anatolia and the Euphrates valley were considered. Syria was often mentioned until it began to be suspected that national feeling might be too troublesome there. One possibility was Kenya; another was to purchase the Portuguese colony of Angola.[7] All that happened, however, was that in 1924 the British agreed to give up a portion of the Juba valley between Kenya and Italian Somalia, and the next year compelled Egypt to cede the oasis of Jarabub on the Libyan frontier; these were minor concessions and were greeted with anything but enthusiasm.

Mussolini backed his colonial claims by a forward policy in the Middle East. He tried to persuade King Fuad to copy fascism and suspend the Egyptian constitution;[8] he made use of Italian Jewish settlements in the eastern Mediterranean for the penetration of the Levant by Italian propaganda;[9] and young Catholic missionaries were exempted from military service as part of an attempt to replace French and Spanish influence by Italian in the Holy Land. An Italian right of patronage over the holy places of Jerusalem was claimed by mediaeval tradition, though this was rejected by the British, who held an international mandate for Palestine.[10] A little more successful was Italian infiltration of the Yemen, where from 1923 onwards munitions were being sent, along with a good deal of money, to sustain a chronic conflict against the British which was thought to be in Italian interests; but ultimately there was nothing to show for the money thus spent.[11] Some Italians even wondered if it would not be more rewarding to give up colonial pretensions and side with local nationalist movements against the declining colonial powers. For a brief period in 1930, even the Duce's monthly magazine *Gerarchia* was suggesting that the age of colonies might be over, so that white and native peoples should be treated as absolute equals.[12] Mussolini here came close to tapping one of the big revolutionary forces of the century, before falling back on the easier and less imaginative doctrines of imperialism and racial supremacy.

In the early 1920s colonialism was certainly no harsher in Italian territories than elsewhere, though fascism, being a doctrine based on hierarchy and force, eventually showed its true principles, which were those of subjugation and the inherent superiority of Italians to both the native populations and other colonialist powers. Yet these principles were costly and ineffective in practical application. Great sums of money were continuously spent in the colonies without much return, and the balance of trade, whatever people may have hoped, at no stage favoured Italy. Her colonial administrators often did a good job, sometimes very good; they built a large network of roads; and by the legal abolition of slavery, the control of pestilence and famine, and the administration of justice, they sometimes gave the local population more active help than their neighbours in nearby British colonies. The reduction of inter-tribal warfare in Somalia was a considerable achievement, though the cost of this in lives is impossible to count.[13]

When the fascist leader Cesare De Vecchi arrived as governor of Somalia in 1923, only the southern third of this colony was directly ruled from Rome; the northern sultanates were under a vague protectorship which in practice had not been exercised at all. No true Fascist could allow such a typical product of liberal mentality, so a series of expensive campaigns from 1925 to 1927 reduced the north to obedience. It was greatly appreciated in Italy that De Vecchi thus made Italy's name feared and respected, giving the natives a full sense of the force and authority of fascist rule. The history of these campaigns is known only in small part and almost exclusively from fascist sources, so it is right to stress that Mussolini himself admitted and deplored that De Vecchi's authoritarian methods had been accompanied by cruel and gratuitous acts of slaughter.[14]

In 1929 it was agreed to introduce into East Africa a practice already formulated in Libya, whereby, if land was not being actively cultivated, the government could allocate it to Italian settlers. This did not go entirely without question in the Italian parliament, but the rule was said to be essential for any colony of settlement, and the few native landowners in Eritrea and Somalia who protested were bought off with small sums.[15] It is said that only a restricted area was confiscated in this way, though it was a large proportion of the more easily and more profitably cultivated land, and a few Italian farmers were encouraged by it to take their savings and start a new career in Africa. The operation was not a great success and they found life much more difficult than expected.[16] In 1935 the government came to their rescue by setting up a banana monopoly so that only the inferior and overpriced bananas of Somalia could be sold in Italy; although there were strong objections to this by Italian consumer interests,[17] the banana plantations survived and became an important part of the local economy.

The government did not hesitate to introduce conscript labour into these plantations. Italians had taken a leading part in having forced labour banned by international law, and attempts were made to deny that it was being used in East Africa,[18] but the authorities were adamant that the local economy could not do without it, and some Fascists acknowledged that in practice this perpetuated the slavery which they claimed to have abolished. Official accounts confirm that conscripted workers were regularly given short rations to make them work harder, and beaten or imprisoned if they failed to do the tasks imposed on them.[19]

Until the middle 1930s only a little was done for education in either Eritrea or Somalia. Eventually a government textbook was introduced in 1936, but until then the education in these colonies was based on the old Koranic schools and the missions, and there was room for only a few thousand pupils.[20] As time went on, however, the colonial civil servants realised the urgent need for a more positive policy, and hoped that by teaching Italian language and history they would succeed in arousing more enthusiasm for fascism.[21] There was a real danger that the local nationalism which was developing in Kenya and Uganda might spread to the Italian colonies. There was also a problem that the evangelical mission schools might be producing a new generation of citizens who would be less easy to govern,[22] and the call went out to expel these missions so as to make education more "purely Italian" and fascist in its content.

Italy had conquered Libya from the Turks in 1912, but the first experience of colonial government there had not been happy. In retrospect it is clear that one mistake of these early years was to have introduced practices of government from mainland Italy without sufficient study of existing local traditions or of the French experience in Morocco and Algeria. Italian rule was not welcomed, and the caliph ordered that resistance should continue. The result was a rising in 1914–1917 which was little known in Italy because of contemporary events in the European war, but which has been called one of the great colonial tragedies. By 1918 Libya and the Fezzan had virtually won their independence, and Italian rule was confined to little more than four towns on the coast.[23] After the war, in 1919, an agreement was reached with Muhammad Idris, the leader of the Senussi confraternity in Cyrenaica, who by now considered himself a secular as well as a religious ruler. In return for recognition of Italian suzerainty, the Rome government granted a large degree of autonomy, paid subsidies, and acknowledged that the local population was no longer "subject" but had a special Italian citizenship. Freedom of speech, of meeting, of teaching, and of property were granted to an extent not often found in colonial empires of the time, and two parliaments were set up at Tripoli and in Cyrenaica. This was said to work splendidly.[24]

Many Italians, however, accepted this only as a temporary arrangement, since it was thought to be incompatible with the prestige of a colonial power.[25] The governor of Libya, Giuseppe Volpi, who had already shown skill and ruthlessness in building up a huge financial empire in the Balkans, decided to overturn the agreement and launch a reconquest by force of arms. It was said that he kept his intention secret from the liberal government at Rome, though this is improbable, and it should be remembered

that many of the liberals were strongly in favour of colonial conquest.[26] Employing for the most part black levies from Eritrea and
independent Ethiopia, during the period from 1922 to 1925 Volpi
brought most of the tribes of Tripolitania back into subjection.[27]
The operation was carried out efficiently, though arguably with
excessive harshness,[28] and the result, according to the Fascists
who were by then in power, was that the natives were taught to
love Italy and "to take pride in subjection to our country." [29]

Further along the coast, in Cyrenaica, an added difficulty was
that the various tribal units made common front in support of
Idris, but here too military action continued, and by 1929 the
boastful and not entirely accurate claim was made that almost the
whole of both these Libyan provinces was back under Italian sov-
ereignty. Mussolini did not make the task of his local governors
easier when he gave them contradictory instructions; for example,
to continue their offensive far into the south so as to achieve a notable victory at any cost, but also to use fewer troops and reduce
an expenditure which was becoming excessive. As he said, a
handful of blackshirts ought to be enough to inculcate respect
into a sparse Berber population, and the fact of reducing the
number of troops would have the incidental advantage of showing
these "rebels" that he was not afraid of them.[30] Meanwhile the
minister of colonies, the former nationalist Luigi Federzoni, ended
what he called the unseemly farce of the two parliaments, on the
assumption that neither self-government nor reliance on the advice
of tribal sheikhs was consonant with fascist authoritarianism.[31]

Mussolini underestimated his enemy out of ignorance and
pride. He wanted to think that theirs was a simple political rebellion without social or religious content, so he and his generals did
not sufficiently investigate the small world of the bedouin who
were struggling for survival, fighting for their lands and their ancient way of life. Professor Evans-Pritchard, who spent several
years among the Senussi, could discover very little in all the Italian literature on Cyrenaica to show that anyone tried to understand nomadism: he found that the nomad was assumed to be a
barbarian and treated accordingly, wherever possible forced to
settle on the land or become a wage-labourer for the occupying
power.[32] According to Evans-Pritchard there were rarely more
than a thousand rebels active at any one time against Italian rule,
but these thousand men, by guerrilla tactics which Giuseppe

Garibaldi would have understood, received open or tacit help from almost the whole of the population and exploited a deep-seated resentment of boastful foreigners and infidels. By dividing into small bands, they were able to live off the land and keep fighting for almost ten years against a substantial Italian army. Only reluctantly did Mussolini come to admit that, far from being able to withdraw troops, he was involved in a serious war.

Such reports as existed on economic conditions in North Africa did not suggest that large-scale settlement by European farmers would be feasible,[33] but the Fascists could not afford to accept such a negative verdict. Count Volpi, as soon as any area of Tripolitania had been recaptured, tried to fix the tribes in restricted areas,[34] and since existing laws did not allow confiscation of private property, he changed the law just as others were to do in East Africa, and declared that the government could confiscate all uncultivated land: a right of appeal was allowed, but no more than as a basis of possible compensation.[35]

The argument was advanced that nationalisation of landed property would be a positive help to the native population and no interference with their rights,[36] but of course it was only the best land that was worth nationalising, and safeguards for local interests were progressively abandoned as the fascist policy of white settlement developed. Similarly, when the Italians reoccupied Cyrenaica in 1928–1932 the bedouin were cleared off the fertile plateau and confined to the steppe.[37]

Federzoni in 1927 was planning to settle 300,000 Italians in Libya, and others hoped for up to half a million, the basis of calculation being that Italy must try to do as well as the French, who had a one-to-five ratio in Algeria;[38] hence intensive propaganda was carried out to find this number of settlers, and concessions were given to almost all Italians who asked for them.[39] The government understandably found it easier to grant very large areas at a time, and hence favoured capitalists rather than genuine settlers. Volpi himself was rewarded with a very large estate, as was Mussolini's private secretary, and also at least one Fascist whose crimes made it advisable to keep him away from Italy: this was Amerigo Dumini, one of Mussolini's professional murderers and hatchet men, who became wealthy in Libya on police subsidies and strong-arm intimidation.[40] But the allocations were made without due calculation, so the prime objective was nowhere near achieved, and by 1933 only 1500 families had been settled on the half million acres which had been arbitrarily commandeered.[41]

Mussolini could not tolerate that the Italian army should be engaged in almost continuous fighting for year after year against poorly armed tribesmen and have so little to show for it. In 1929 he therefore gave the governorship of both North African provinces to the chief of staff, General Badoglio, so as to use the full resources of the Italian state in bringing these rebels to heel. Badoglio's initial reports were depressing, and he pointed out that fascist colonisation was associated with scandalous profits made by contractors and even by army officers. He reported that the colonial police and judiciary were being infiltrated by the mafia, while corruption was affecting his own officers, who were presenting him with a flood of claims for medals and promotion even after quite insignificant military episodes; he even hinted that the war was too financially advantageous for the army to want to finish it.[42] As sporadic fighting continued, it became clear that the search for prestige was very costly: prestige demanded that a force be sent south to occupy the Fezzan, where, although some rebel leaders were prepared to negotiate, the Italian generals refused to parley on the grounds that negotiation would have been humiliating.[43]

Perhaps Mussolini realised that he was demanding too much. At all events, for a few months in 1929 he decided to try a change of policy and began discussions with Idris, the Senussi leader who was now in Egypt.[44] A truce was also arranged with the sheikh Umar al-Mukhtar, a remarkable man of over seventy who led the rebels in Cyrenaica, and this truce was stipulated for five months during which Idris would negotiate a stable peace. It was not a helpful sign that Badoglio could not restrain himself from calling the truce a submission by the rebels.[45] Negotiations did not in fact take place, so in October 1929 Umar announced that he would resume fighting. Badoglio from now onwards was under orders to give no quarter at all; any leaders taken were to be hanged, and any Italian generals who wanted conciliation were dismissed. A proclamation was issued to say that if the enemy did not submit they would be exterminated, everything would be destroyed, property would be forfeit, and even families of offenders would be punished.[46]

In June 1930 Badoglio and General Rodolfo Graziani agreed on the bold but disturbing policy of removing the whole population of Cyrenaica into five concentration camps along with all their flocks and possessions, since in no other way could Umar and his men be deprived of food. A few months later the local shrines of the Senussi confraternity were closed, all their large religious endowments confiscated, and their property of some half a million acres seized; a mobile military court handed out summary justice to any who resisted. Graziani denied that his men used any excessive zeal in this period of repression,[47] but other evidence suggests that there may have been a real reign of terror, with hundreds or thousands executed, villages sacked or starved into submission, and savage reprisals taken against bedouin communities whose members joined the enemy.[48] Early in 1931 Graziani rounded off this policy by building a high barbed-wire fence four metres thick along the 275 kilometres from the port of Bardia to the oasis of Jarabub, and so cut off supplies reaching Umar from Egypt.

This severe policy was generally accepted as right even by the surviving Italian liberals able to speak in parliament, who pointed out that the concentration camps were "truly worthy of Italian civilisation", and that the standard of life inside them was far higher than the population had hitherto enjoyed outside.[49] Cut off from their normal caravan routes, the population became partially dependent on purchases from overseas, which was much appreciated by Italian men of commerce.[50] But the crowding of eighty thousand people and nearly a million animals into these small crowded camps resulted in what the Fascists admitted were "excessive deaths";[51] the herds, on which the population depended entirely, were almost wiped out, and something like twenty thousand people may have died.[52]

In September 1931 the wounded Umar was at last captured after being pinned down by his horse in a running engagement. Badoglio and General De Bono, the new minister for colonies, decided that he should be publicly executed, and twenty thousand bedouin were brought from confinement to witness an event designed to show them that the old days of compromise and Italian weakness were over.[53] The Italian officer appointed to defend Umar at his short and summary trial was punished when he weakened the desired effect by pleading that the accused had never submitted and so could not be a rebel, but should be treated as a prisoner of war.[54] There was outrage in the Moslem world over this execution, and even Fascists recognised it as a gross error when they saw from French experience that generosity to insurgent leaders was more rewarding and a far more obvious sign of strength. Instead they were creating a nationalist feeling that had hardly existed before.[55]

By January 1932 resistance was virtually at an end. The campaign had cost a good deal, but the great majority of Italian casualties were among black troops from East Africa: for this very reason, as well as for Mussolini's obvious need to play down a somewhat unfascist non-success, the war was not keenly felt at home. The bedouin of Cyrenaica, on the other hand, were reduced in number by at least half, in other words to a hundred thousand or not many more.[56] Italy, according to Mussolini, gained in prestige by the victory. According to others she lost greatly in prestige because of the time taken to win and the cruel means employed.

Cyrenaica suffered a great deal and continued to suffer. When Graziani offered pardon to those who surrendered, Badoglio reproved him and insisted that severity was the only fascist policy,[57] while Mussolini himself wanted to go even further in rigour.[58] From now onwards nomadism had to be limited and strictly controlled. For the bulk of the native population there was no going back from the camps to their old lands and way of life, because memories of ancient Rome gave Mussolini the idea that North Africa must become a source of wheat for Italy: nomadism would not only endanger settled agriculture but would make colonies of settlement impossible, and he was determined to have white settlers in special white villages all along the fertile coast of Libya. As Graziani said, Italians had to be compensated for the cost of the rebellion, and government money therefore went rather into giving them farms than into restoring the flocks of the bedouin. The sequestered Senussi estates were thus not kept as public property but allocated where possible to Italians. Those of the subject population who were left became largely a sub-proletariat for the road works and building operations of the fascist empire.[59]

One or two voices were heard in Italy protesting that this might be inexpedient as well as morally offensive, but official policy would allow no second thoughts.[60]

What was promised in return, and quite genuinely, was higher living standards, improved medical care, and in general "civilised values". Expenditure allocated to popular education was thus relatively high.[61] Before fascism, in 1912–1914, educational policy had been to have schools in common for Italians and Arabs, the intention being to assimilate and Italianise the child population; then in 1919 almost the opposite principle was adopted, under which education for native children was to be in Arabic with Italian just an optional language. The Fascists had a yet different answer. Education should be "in the interests of the colonial power"; it ought not to encourage the natives beyond a certain point but should ensure white domination.[62] Italian became the main language of instruction, and Arabic secondary schools were closed down altogether so as not to develop higher studies among non-Europeans. At the same time a good deal was spent on elementary schools and on training colleges to provide teachers for them.[63] A main consideration was to teach pupils the fascist principles of discipline, obedience, and militarism, especially as Mussolini already had in mind to create a large black army.

From the semi-official press in Italy during the early 1930s one can see that there was a concerted attempt to drum up enthusiasm for colonialism. Colonies were said to be essential for the economic welfare of Europe, and should be administered in the interests of the whites, since white domination was necessary for the future of Europe civilisation; comparison would show that the French and the British were quite wrong to favour the local populations in nearby Algeria and Kenya. Italians were told that they could claim a right of priority in Africa; they both needed and deserved colonies more than any other European power; they had a moral and intellectual primacy over all other nations in Africa, and were the acknowledged leaders there in the work of civilisation and redemption. Other nations would have to come round to the fascist principle that there must be "an absolute predominance of whites over blacks and an indestructible separation between dominators and dominated." Of course white rulers would govern

in the interest of the natives, but there must be no false senti-
mentalism and no challenge to the basic doctrine of white
supremacy.[64]

This propaganda campaign was intended to convey to ordinary
Italians the sensation that they were a colonial power. The very
fact that such a campaign was needed suggests that most Italians
had little feeling and no enthusiasm for the colonies, and this
apathy or antipathy was often admitted.[65] Some Italians who
talked freely about the colonies would have been hard put to say
where they were on the map.[66] Despite many appeals, despite the
fact that Mussolini had publicly announced that Africa was to be a
predominant continent in the twentieth century, people with
money did not like investing in the colonies; moreover intellectuals had little interest in them, and whereas there were over
150,000 members of the German colonial association, fascist Italy
in 1930 had only 6,000 members in hers.[67]

The government had stumbled into a colonial policy for economic and prestige reasons which were highly dubious, yet without popular support, without the indispensable preliminary studies which were patently necessary, and without the trained
colonial administrators and technicians necessary for success.[68]
Most politically minded Italians, on the other hand, were far less
preoccupied by the possibilities of African expansion than by the
immediate and pressing problems confronting them in Europe.

4

THE SHADOW OF HITLER

As early as 1923 Mussolini had been sure that "the axis of European history passes through Berlin".[1] By 1930 he was actually hoping that Germany might go fascist. He was in touch there with the right-wing *Stahlhelm* and perhaps to a lesser extent with the Nazis,[2] ready to associate with any group which was effectively opposed to liberalism and democracy. As he got to know more about Hitler he wondered sometimes if the nazi leader were not possibly a little mad,[3] but this apprehension was more than offset by the prospect that German revisionism might be exploited to help Italy.[4] The chief intermediary between the two men was Renzetti, who was a familiar guest at Hitler's house and possibly had considerable influence with the nazi leader. Messages of admiration were sent through him to the Duce, and in return Renzetti communicated Mussolini's advice—for example that the Nazis should not tie their hands by coming to power too meekly as part of a parliamentary coalition. No doubt it was on Mussolini's instructions that Renzetti tried to bring Hitler closer to other German right-wing movements.[5] On several occasions in 1931 and 1932 Hitler asked if he could come to talk with Mussolini, but evidently the latter was no longer so keen to see him,[6] and probably he was not altogether sure that the Nazis were the best candidate in Germany for Italian support. The Duce tried to read *Mein Kampf*, but found it too boring to finish.[7] Only in 1938 was there sufficient interest for the full text to be published in an Italian translation.

Many Fascists did not much like Hitler and were allowed to express their hostility in public. Some disliked his brutality, others his evident lack of principle or else what Mussolini called his commonplace ideas.[8] Opposition came from Catholics worried by nazi neo-paganism, also from exaggerated patriots such as Roberto Forges Davanzati and Italo Balbo, who could not easily forget that Germany in 1918 had been the national enemy.[9] Ezio Garibaldi represented the patriotic tradition of friendliness for the French republic, which his grandfather had fought for during the Risorgimento, and Garibaldi's magazine *Camicia Rossa* was more consistent than most in stressing the differences between fascism and nazism. In Garibaldi's opinion, German behaviour in burning books, persecuting Jews, and despising Italians was intolerable,[10] and he shared the belief which Mussolini had once expressed that German traditions of imperialism might easily conflict with Italian interests. Apart from the indications in *Mein Kampf* about the annexation of Austria to Germany, there were memories of economic and political rivalry in the Balkans. Hitler privately said in 1930 that Trieste would one day have to be taken back from Italy to become a German port, and this remark was known and noted in Italy.[11]

Doubts about nazism could be found among extremist as well as moderate Fascists. Roberto Farinacci, one of the more strident and extravagant, claimed to despise the Nazis for not killing more of their opponents, as he despised them for not being more openly revolutionary in discarding parliamentary methods. More than anything else he resented Alfred Rosenberg's ideas about German racial superiority, because he foresaw that these could be used against southerners like himself as well as against Jews.[12] The racial question was crucial, and strong offence was taken south of the Alps at talk about the superiority of tall, blue-eyed, fair-haired peoples. Some Italians spoke with contempt and dismay of this "spiritual Wotanism". When the anti-Slav, anti-Jewish Rosenberg lectured in Italy about purity of blood, Professor Francesco Orestano, who was a leading Italian philosopher and a member of the prestigious royal academy, intervened to say that the lecturer's remarks were nonsense since every nation was a hybrid, and he took care to speak in German so that Rosenberg would understand; more pointedly, Orestano added that there was a large element of Slav blood among the Germans.[13] Mussolini himself, while he admitted that there might be good political or psychological reasons in Germany for such racial propaganda, thought at this stage in his life that Hitler was ill-advised to provoke so strong an enemy as the Jews,[14] but he was not entirely against racialism and before long confessed to an admiration for Rosenberg's writings. In pri-

vate he could already encourage the Germans in their anti-semitism, perhaps hoping that they would embroil themselves too
far.[15]

In 1932 the fascist royal academy summoned an international
congress for academics and politicians to consider the future of
Europe. The leading spirit behind this congress was Francesco
Coppola, the former nationalist leader, who stage-managed the occasion as an essay in public relations. He limited Italian representation to the more mild and respectable elements of fascism in case
foreign visitors should receive the wrong impression, and at the
same time foreign delegates were asked not to talk politics "lest we
should have to listen to some objectionable or even intolerable
opinions",[16] though any praise of fascism, needless to say, was
more than welcome. France and Britain were somewhat under-
represented: Valéry, Maurras, Bainville, Gaxotte, and Weygand
were among those who refused an invitation, as were Churchill,
Keynes, Kipling, Lloyd George, and Trevelyan; but enough foreigners came for the organisers to claim it as proof that the leadership of fascist Italy was becoming recognised. There was Stefan
Zweig from Austria and Count Alberto Apponyi from Hungary.
From France came Daniel Halévy, Louis Bertrand, and the historian Jérôme Carcopino. England provided Christopher Dawson
and Paul Einzig. And from Germany, apart from Göring and
Rosenberg, came Alfred Weber, Werner Sombart, and Hjalmar
Schacht.

The gist of the Italian speakers' remarks at this conference was
to call on Europe to unite against bolshevism and the black races,
but equally against what Coppola called the doctrinaire, pacifist,
and individualistic civilisation of America. Professor Bodrero
capped this by stressing the virtues of war as a generator of moral
values. Though a few tactful protests were made by some foreign
delegates, in each case an Italian broke in to defend imperialism
and authoritarianism, and to condemn the League of Nations for
its outmoded belief in democracy and national equality. A former
British ambassador to Italy presided over the main session addressed by Coppola and Rosenberg, and Göring was in the audience when Sir Charles Petrie lent his support to the opinion that
the parliamentary system was now defunct: to the annoyance of

French delegates, Petrie flattered his hosts by agreeing with their view that Napoleon should be thought of as an Italian.[17]

Mussolini's preoccupation with war became more outspoken in the early 1930s until it began to seem almost an obsession. He spoke more insistently of how "war alone can carry to the maximum tension all human energies and imprint with the seal of nobility those people who have the courage to confront it; every other test is a mere substitute." He indicated the fascist tendency towards imperial expansion as a clear sign of national vitality, and claimed fascism was "the one powerful and truly original force in our century." Within ten years the whole of Europe would be fascist, so he announced in a public speech, and the army was told to get ready for a surprise attack on France or Yugoslavia. The new watchword was "better one day as a lion than a hundred years as a sheep", and this mindless slogan was soon stencilled on thousands of walls and houses up and down the country.[18]

Such remarks, made in this case while an international disarmament conference was sitting, were expounded and annotated by an obedient press. The Italian people, it was stated again and again, were proving themselves to be the greatest people in the world; they should and would become one of the strongest. Since the Duce had said that the national character must be changed, all Italians would support him in this purpose and in making Italy for the third or fourth time the chief propulsive force in western civilisation. The inscrutable laws of history demanded that such a people should assert themselves in the wider world, and article after article therefore praised imperialism as the only doctrine fit for the Italy of Mussolini.[19]

In the early months of 1933 the press was instructed to accentuate this kind of message after the Grand Council, the supreme directorate of the fascist movement, prescribed that "the expansion of fascism in the world" was official policy. Mussolini spoke of revising the Treaty of Versailles, and foretold a speedy end to the League of Nations if it did not accept such revision: one example which he brought up again was that France should one day be forced to cede Corsica to Italy. In a book he was reading he underlined a phrase referring to the primacy of the Italian people and their being "a new Israel in Europe".[20] This "primacy" of

Italians became a necessary theme for all political journalists who wanted to improve their fortunes. They had to reiterate continuously that fascism had the only answer for Europe's problems, and that where she led, all other nations were bound to follow.[21]

Another and by now familiar theme of Italian journalism was that fascist Italy was the envy of the whole world. Such mild self-flattery was to prove dangerous in the long run, but it was consoling to be assured that Italians were now the teachers and that dictatorship was coming back into fashion.[22] Some people in Germany saw good reasons for contributing to such flattery and expressed the conviction that all Europe must soon follow the Italian example;[23] they also worked on Mussolini's personal susceptibility, and when a play which he had helped to write was given at Weimar, Hitler and Hess unexpectedly arrived to see it.[24] One of Mussolini's magazines described how American intellectuals were flocking to Italy to study and admire fascist legislation, and how they were agreeably impressed by the virile foreign policy exemplified by his attack on Corfu.[25] A new magazine, *Universalità Fascista*, made its chief theme the praise which Italian fascism was said to receive elsewhere, and such praise was taken as proof that liberalism was dead and democracy no more than a sick joke: "The workers of North America exclaim in chorus 'if only we had a Mussolini'. . . . Fascism is conquering the world by its example. . . . You cannot open a foreign newspaper without finding articles in its praise. . . . In a logical, inevitable process it converts thousands of new believers every day, and no longer can anyone be found to criticise our regime."[26] Nor was anyone in Italy free to say that this was abject nonsense.

Within a few hours of achieving power in January 1933, Hitler sent a personal message to Mussolini with his "admiration and homage", expressing his urgent need for closer relations, and hoping that they could soon meet personally. Though he admitted that their two movements were not identical, on all essential points he was ready to accept Mussolini's *Weltanschauung* and tactfully acknowledged that he would not have been successful without the latter's example. He did not conceal that it was his long-term intention to restore German power in Europe and probably incorporate Austria, but once again he hinted that Italy, in return

for allowing this, would have his support in asserting her authority over the rest of the Danube basin.[27] At all events, he still
maintained the thesis of *Mein Kampf* that an alliance with Italy was
a fundamental necessity of German policy.[28]

On hearing of Hitler's success, Mussolini confirmed that it was
a victory also for Italian fascism. He was pleased to think that he
had helped the Nazis with arms and money, though he had no intention of giving way to them over Austria. Along with warm
congratualtions he sent his hopes for the continuance of a very
close relationship, which would be all the easier after the acceptance by Germany of Italian predominance throughout southeast
Europe.[29] In the next few weeks he conveyed further advice to
Hitler on how best to consolidate his power, how anti-semitism
could be a danger, and how Germany had no alternative but to
copy the fascist corporative system of organising the labour un-
ions.[30] To the British ambassador he confided his opinion that
Hitler was the best element in the new German regime, though
he admitted that other Nazis—he instanced Göring, who had
been in Italy several times again in 1931 and 1932—might be
dangerous.[31]

The Italian press of course welcomed the Nazi coup and emphasised that Germany was copying an Italian example. Here was
one more sign that Europe would soon be fascist, and Italy alongside Germany would create a political bloc in Europe which could
alter the course of history. Newspapers sometimes added the conventional expression of belief that Hitler in power would be a new
force for peace in Europe, bringing greater justice and a more balanced equilibrium in international relations, though some journalists already foresaw with unconcealed pleasure that Hitler in actu-
ality would represent not an element of order in Europe, but one
of disorder and discord.[32]

In June 1933 a pact of collaboration was signed in Rome between Italy, Germany, England, and France. Mussolini intended
it to signify that the League of Nations was being superseded by
an international system where a few stronger states predominated,
because this would exemplify the fascist principles of authoritarianism and of *gerarchia* or hierarchy. He envisaged Rome as the
main centre of Europe, from which he was now ready to direct

policy for the whole continent.[33] Hitler, on the other hand, agreed to this Pact of Rome with reluctance; France and Britain did so after insisting that it should in no sense diminish the League, and only after a hint from Mussolini that secretly he meant it as a curb on German ambitions.[34]

The agreement never came into operation. Nevertheless, Mussolini was radiant with a new sense of power: he had been able to demonstrate that the leading statesmen in Europe were in Rome to sign a pact which, so it was said with some exaggeration, was just his personal idea and had been maturing for years in his mind.[35] Newspapers were instructed to explain that it made Italy the arbiter of the destinies of Europe; it guaranteed peace for the next ten years, and, according to the propagandists, was being hailed in Europe with unanimous applause such as had never greeted any previous treaty. The world was said to have recognised in this pact "the unchallenged authority of the Duce", and it would thus enable Italy to demand the colonial possessions denied to her in 1919. Grandi commented that only a genius could have scored such a "colossal diplomatic success . . . and inflicted such a mortal blow on France", while the philosopher Giovanni Gentile lent his authority to the statement that the date on which it was signed would become one of the major dates in world history.[36]

In 1933 Mussolini again took over the three ministries of the army, navy, and air force—he had relinquished them in 1929 —and official propaganda revealed a new element of assertiveness as he laid down the objective of Italian primacy "on land, at sea, and in the sky".[37] Being the greatest revolution the world had known, fascism alone could provide the spiritual values needed to save white civilisation from the non-white races. A new order was being founded which would be based on a proper hierarchy of nations, and Italy was showing and leading the way, while the Pact of Rome accorded Mussolini the right to preside over the future destinies not only of Europe but of the whole world.[38] It could now be recognised that this was "the century of Mussolini", because he had suddenly indicated how problems could be solved for which liberalism had no answer at all. "It is no exaggeration to say that the whole of world policy is now polarised on this one man", and from his wisdom all other nations would now learn that authoritarian regimes must inherently be better than democracies.[39]

Among surviving Italian diplomats of the old school there was strong sympathy with Mussolini's view that Italy had a right to expand outside Europe and to find colonies in Africa. A widely accepted belief was that one day, after a war against France, they would annex Corsica, Nice, Savoy, Dalmatia, and Tunisia. On such an expectation there were good arguments for Italy backing a resurgent Nazi Germany which had a parallel interest in revisionism, and Mussolini himself had little doubt about this as a long-term policy,[40] though there were difficulties in the short term and the more timid of his foreign-policy staff thought it would be wise to move cautiously.[41] Possibly mere threats would be enough to make the French give up some of their colonies and agree to let Italy have a free hand in Ethiopia[42] in which case France and Italy would continue to block German imperialism. Hitler, too, was becoming a little less friendly as he learned more about Italy. Perhaps he did not relish Mussolini's condescension. Whatever he said to Italians, Hitler's private opinion was that Roman fascism, though it might possibly be useful to him, had mistaken "the real meaning of our era,"[43] and in the German foreign service there were many who continued to think of Italy as the nation which had deserted Germany in 1915 and might do so again.

Where the interests of the two countries most obviously collided was Austria, and Mussolini repeated to Austrian leaders that they could rely on him to fight to defend their country's independence. He was paying a lot of money to bolster the Austrian economy. Against nazi terrorism in Austria he was prepared to use terroristic methods, and continued to support with money and arms the rival and pro-fascist *Heimwehren*.[44] At the end of December 1932, forty railway wagons of small arms crossed from Italy into Austria with the connivance of frontier officials, and probably this was not the first or last such occasion. These weapons were possibly for use by the *Heimwehren*, or possibly some of them were going to Macedonian and Croat insurgents, since they were listed in the name of Paolo Cortese, the foreign-office official responsible for organising terrorism in the Balkans. On this occasion socialist railway workmen in Austria exposed what was happening, so alerting Europe to the fact that Italy was smuggling arms in defiance of treaties which she had signed. Yet the attempt also suggests that Mussolini was alarmed by the increasing success of the nazi movement in Austria: dealing with Nazis, he said, was worse than dealing with an elephant in a china shop: "they are like thousands of elephants." [45]

In October 1933 Hitler suddenly leap-frogged Mussolini and withdrew from the League of Nations. The latter was outspokenly annoyed,[46] partly because this was in open disregard of the four-power Pact of Rome which was his great pride, partly because the German ambassador had seen Mussolini a few hours earlier without consulting him or informing him.[47] It looked almost as though the Germans might not be taking fascism with sufficient seriousness. Some of them were known to think that they had invented a better version of fascism; they were daring to be almost deliberately offensive, as for example when they suggested that Vikings and not Italians had discovered America.[48] One of Mussolini's aides was therefore sent to Germany to give a lecture about fascist achievements, with instructions not to speak in German lest the Nazis should see it as an admission of inferiority: he should speak in Italian even if no one understood, and the central theme of his lecture should be "to convince these Germans that there is nothing left for them to invent." [49] Seen from Rome, national socialism was showing signs of being not the daughter of fascism, nor even its sister, but something possibly quite different, something mysteriously Teutonic, and Mussolini occasionally hinted that there might be no more than superficial resemblances between the two regimes.[50]

His self-confidence nevertheless did not desert him, and even though he could have little doubt that the Germans wished to annex Austria one day, he was confident that he could stop them without outside help.[51] To make doubly sure, in September 1933 he sent a virtual ultimatum to the Austrian chancellor, Engelbert Dollfuss, intimating that further support from Italy would be conditional on introducing a fascist regime on the Roman model and eliminating other parties, if necessary, by force. Dollfuss had little option but to take this advice, though it cost him an armed battle with many dead among the urban workers of Vienna. Mussolini failed to see that by crushing the Austrian Socialists he was removing one of the last barriers to an eventual German *Anschluss*.

He was warned of such a possible result, but did not let it deter him from his immediate aim, which was to demonstrate that fascism was gaining ground against nazism in central Europe.[52] To confirm this he again publicly guaranteed fascist support for the independence of Austria.[53]

Unfortunately, in the same speech he could not resist the temptation to announce publicly that Italy had ambitions for expansion in Africa and Asia. Here he was moving into dangerous waters because he was simultaneously challenging France as well as Germany, something far beyond his means. Hitler took his chance and proposed again that he and Mussolini should meet, pointing out that fascist colonial ambitions in Africa could hardly be satisfied by the French, but only by a victorious war in alliance with Germany.[54] Mussolini's more successful moments in foreign policy occurred when he could press both France and Germany simultaneously to see which had more to offer, but of course there was always the risk that, without due care, he might antagonise both of them and so be left helpless. Another risk was that he might make different or even incompatible assurances to both sides—something he had learned to do in domestic politics—trusting "that in the ensuing complications he could find a path of escape from contradictory engagements." [55]

By June 1934 Mussolini judged that the time had come at last to meet Hitler, though he balanced this by also inviting the French foreign minister to Rome, and tried by the threat of an agreement with Germany to persuade France to give up "a few palm trees and some sand" in North Africa.[56] The French put off an answer, but Hitler accepted and their meeting took place near Venice. For some four hours the two men spoke alone without an interpreter. Though it is difficult to know from various second-hand accounts precisely what happened, one can assume that Mussolini did not understand some, possibly a lot, of what was said.[57] According to one Italian version, Hitler repudiated the idea of an *Anschluss* but asked Mussolini to withdraw his protection from Dollfuss. If true, it was a transparent ruse. Another account says that Hitler tried hard to persuade the Italians to be firmer in controlling the Church.[58] One Italian version tells of Hitler's being greatly impressed at finding himself treated on level terms by so great a man as Mussolini. It was reported that Hitler spoke for almost all the time and with great excitement, tears coming frequently to his eyes, and at one point he was said to have proposed that they should take Europe by surprise and jointly attack France.[59] Mussolini subsequently recounted that Hitler was like a gramophone which had only seven tunes to play and kept on starting all over again; he concluded that the nazi leader was an ideologue, not a realist, but something of a buffoon, and certainly not the man of great physical presence and martial attitude whom he had been expecting. They had each stated their views, but had not agreed with each other.[60]

It is likely that Mussolini at this meeting was hoping to reinforce his own sense of superiority. Unsure of himself in personal conversation, he relied more on the subtler arts of stage management,[61] and arrived in uniform to meet a Hitler who was caught off guard in an unimpressive raincoat and civilian clothes. Hitler was not invited to preside at the military review in the central square of Venice, and perhaps this was as well since the parade was embarrassingly unmartial; there were some disorderly scenes, and at a concert given for Hitler in the Palazzo Ducale the audience, evidently on orders, went on applauding Mussolini throughout the evening.[62] Though the Germans were excited by the splendours of Venice and made flattering remarks about Mussolini personally, they were not enthusiastic about what they saw of fascism and were far from convinced of the worthiness of Italy as an ally.[63]

Throughout 1934 Mussolini continued to declare that this year would mark a decisive step in the spread of fascism throughout the civilised world. Democracy and liberalism, he contended, were no longer dying but dead. So was any question of disarmament. In May 1934 he emphasised in another of his more publicised and less intelligible statements that "war is to man as maternity to women," and it was this same speech which was said to have launched the process of Italian rearmament.[64] The newspapers meanwhile rammed home that Mussolini was "the helmsman of the European ship." He had taught Italy to be a military nation and to accept that war was the supreme test of a people's worth. Not only were warlike ideals said to pervade all of civilian life, but

Mussolini had completely solved Italy's military problems. Under his personal supervision the three services had a unity of direction they had never possessed before, and he was said to have motorised the army "up to the limit of what is possible." [65] Such a belligerent pose appealed to many who were outside the hard core of fascism, for example to King Victor Emanuel, who forgot his earlier liberalism as he welcomed the emphasis on military tradition, and who frankly confessed that his own ideal life was based on war and the hunt. [66] It equally excited some younger radicals who, disillusioned by the more conservative aspects of fascism, spoke enthusiastically of "the sanctity of war" and the need for every country to prove its greatness by military victory. [67]

Judging by the tone of newspaper headlines, an excellent index under fascism, Italo-German relations became more friendly with Hitler's visit, but almost at once became tense again when in June the Nazis murdered Röhm and his associates. This was an act more calculatedly brutal than anything in fascist history, and yet must have reminded Mussolini of the violent, murderous aspects of fascism which, in his new guise of semi-respectability, he may have preferred to forget. The news was softened slightly for the Italian public, but Mussolini himself claimed to be appalled, and he easily forgot his own partial responsibility for the recent killing of many Viennese Social Democrats by Dollfuss a few months earlier. Possibly he was offended most of all when the Germans started a rumour that he had advised Hitler to carry out just such a cold-blooded purge. [68]

A month later, in July 1934, worse happened when Dollfuss was assassinated in a *Putsch* organised by the Nazis. Coming so soon after Mussolini's guarantee of Austrian independence, it was a great blow to the international reputation of fascism; particularly insulting was the fact that the wife of Dollfuss was at the time a guest of Mussolini and had to be informed of the murder by her host. The Germans were immediately pilloried in the Italian press as assassins and paederasts, accused of bare-faced imperialism, and told that the whole of Europe was ready to unite against them. [69] It was announced that four Italian divisions were poised to occupy the Austrian Tyrol, and although the German intelligence services were fairly sure that this was bluff since the divisions were well under strength,[70] for the next twelve months military plans were adjusted to fit the hypothesis of a war against Germany.[71] Mussolini, in a statement which he later denied having made, pledged once again that he would fight for Austrian independence,[72] and his magazine *Gerarchia*, which had earlier depicted Hitler as a Catholic and a leader of an essentially Catholic movement, now veered to the different and equally dubious extreme of arguing that Austrians were in no sense Germans by culture or sentiment, but belonged rather to a Roman, Mediterranean, and Catholic civilisation.[73]

Moving troops to his northern frontier gave Mussolini a sense of power and excitement, in which he was abetted by Achille Starace, the secretary of the Fascist Party, who unctuously declared that the Duce far exceeded the generals in his knowledge of even the technical minutiae of military affairs. Starace confirmed that the army was now entirely fascist in spirit and that the senior generals had all become members of the party.[74] This encouraged Mussolini to boast that Italians were not only a military but a militaristic nation; they were an altered people who now possessed the virtues of absolute obedience, sacrifice, and dedication to the fatherland; the whole life of the nation, even its spiritual life, would therefore be bent towards military necessity, since war was "the court of appeal among the nations".[75]

Mussolini's own newspaper referred to him as a genius whose word in such matters was gospel, and he himself found that he could raise easy applause by talking of the corpse of disarmament buried beneath mountains of tanks and cannon. His statements became ever more oracular as Starace learned how to organise the mass meetings which lent themselves to rhetoric and bombast. "Only God can bend the will of fascism, men and things never," announced the leader. "It is the plough that traces the furrow, but it is the sword which defends it, and both plough and sword are made of tempered steel like the faith in our hearts".[76] In private Mussolini sought to explain that in such statements he was merely trying out the mettle of his audience,[77] but in fact he was swamping his own judgement in a fantasy of words. Perhaps he even believed his own statements about mountains of tanks, or about five million soldiers and an aircraft industry which had reached a peak of perfection.[78]

This slenderly based belligerence was associated with a temporary but violent about-turn against the Germans which was a direct result of Dollfuss's murder. In a speech of September 1934 Mussolini pitied the uncivilised northerners who presumed to preach to Italy, yet who had been primitive illiterates when ancient Rome knew Caesar and Virgil.[79] In private he spoke of Hitler with indulgent sarcasm, irritated by him, claiming to despise him, also jealous and afraid that the other fascist groups in Europe might prefer Berlin to Rome. To assert his own autonomy he now pretended that Italian fascism recognised the rights of individuals, whereas Hitlerism was merely barbaric autocracy,[80] though at the same time Hitler was accused of having come to power not by honest force, like Mussolini, but by disreputable parliamentary compromises. *Gerarchia* also argued that national socialism was just a continuation of the Kaiser's imperialist Germany, while the sheer originality of Italian fascism was "the admiration of the whole world"; the former was purely Teutonic, whereas fascism was Roman and universal.[81] Publicists who knew how to trim their sails—notably Farinacci and Preziosi, who before long found it expedient to be strongly pro-German once again—wrote of nazism as offensive to the conscience of mankind and something that would inevitably push Europe into the ultimate indignity of communism. This tone of shocked antagonism characterised the whole of the Italian press for several months, until the German ambassador protested that no nation with a sense of honour could tolerate it.[82]

The arguments against national socialism ran a wide gamut. Some said it was too socialist, and this at a time when many Fascists oddly thought of themselves as champions of individualism.[83] More often it was accused of being anti-Catholic if not anti-Christian or atheistic,[84] and Mussolini, though himself temperamentally anti-clerical, was proud of Rome being the centre of Catholicism, and needed the extra influence given to him by his alliance with the Vatican. Criticism continued unabated of the nazi doctrine that the Germans were a chosen race with a divine mission to rule over lesser breeds. Italian writers ascribed such arrogant views to an inferiority complex, since the Germans were parvenus who felt despised by other peoples and needed to compensate for their lack of culture; hence they had taken up the purely linguistic discoveries of Max Müller about aryanism and twisted them into the belief that the Germans and English belonged to a separate Nordic, Aryan race, a belief which Italians knew to be nonsense, and which might be used to demote Italy from her rightful position in the forefront of the hierarchy of nations.[85] German books about the inferiority of the non-Nordic peoples were by now beginning to reach Italy, and it was especially resented that some of these writings were directed against fascism, even naming Jews who were highly placed inside the Fascist Party.[86]

Mussolini took offence at German racial exclusiveness. He seems to have raised the matter with Hitler in June 1934 and in reply was read a lecture about how Mediterranean peoples were tainted with Negro blood.[87] On later reconsideration, Mussolini insisted that German racialism was in itself of Semitic origin and he denied that any German race could possibly exist at all. There were at least six different peoples in Germany, he said, and among them symptoms of degeneration were innumerable; in some villages of Bavaria seven per cent of the inhabitants were weak-minded.[88] After such outspoken words, any Fascists tempted by racialism were taken sharply to task. Racial doctrines, wrote *Critica Fascista*, were not fascist but a major threat to the new fascist civilisation, and any idea that Germans had superiority in technology or organisation likewise had to be nailed for the lie it was. Fascist Italy had nothing at all to learn from the Germans or anyone else. The magazine *Antieuropa* published a whole issue dedicated to a criticism of nazi racialism. The strongly anti-Jewish Giovanni Preziosi had no doubt, at all events for the next few months, that German talk of an Aryan race had absolutely no scientific basis, and indeed the truth was that men of genius were usually of mixed blood. Even the theorist of racialism, Rosenberg, showed by his name that he might be a Jew, and Hitler himself was fairly obviously of tainted ancestry.[89]

5

THE ETHIOPIAN WAR

Mussolini's first major war began in October 1935 when he invaded Ethiopia. This vast empire, temptingly placed alongside Italian Eritrea and Italian Somalia, was the one place in Africa where other European countries had no special concern and where Italy's predominant interest was widely recognised by them. In the 1920s Mussolini's main objective had been peaceful economic penetration, although from the very beginning of fascism there had been hypothetical talk of war to obtain political control.[1] Either way Ethiopia, like Albania, was looked upon by Rome as an Italian reserve, so much so that throughout the 1920s it was already providing most of the soldiers for the Italian army fighting in Libya.[2] A treaty of friendship between the two countries had been signed in 1928, but Mussolini intended this as one stage towards establishing an economic protectorate over Haile Selassie's empire, and was genuinely offended when the latter avoided the trap by simultaneously seeking friends elsewhere.[3] Fascism therefore prepared to use more forcible measures.[4]

One view held in the foreign office was that Africa and not Europe should be the main concern of Italian foreign policy. Possibly Ethiopia should be annexed outright, perhaps in the fairly near future; among incidental reasons adduced were fascism's need of the prestige of a military victory, and also its need to control a larger catchment area for the recruitment of a big colonial army. When the foreign office favoured a rapprochement with Germany, one reason was so as to bring pressure on France and thus win French approval for what Grandi in 1930 called Italy's "mission to civilise the black continent."[5] Mussolini at first had doubts about annexing Ethiopia and was suspicious that the French might be luring him into a difficult African adventure.[6] Ethiopia did not look especially attractive to him as a possible colony, yet he was more than ready to accept the need for a prestige victory. Officials held out an even more ambitious prospect of advancing right across the African continent, with the possibility of persuading the French or the British to cede an outlet on the Atlantic ocean.[7]

This was a long-term plan. More immediately, taking advantage of the uncertain frontier demarcation, Italian troops from at least 1929 onwards surreptitiously occupied places inside Ethiopia. When Haile Selassie asked for talks to determine the line of the frontier, Mussolini told his officials to delay matters and agree to nothing.[8] In the next few years the army staff, the colonial office, and the supreme commission of defence all discussed plans for the possible conquest of Ethiopia,[9] but this was just another distant possibility, and for the moment Italy continued to sell arms to her future enemy.[10] On the other hand it was argued that the longer they waited, the more Haile Selassie would be able to strengthen and centralise his ramshackle empire, and the more a foreign-educated intellectual elite at Addis Ababa would have time to organise resistance against Italian infiltration.[11]

A determining factor may have been Hitler's coming to power in Germany, because this on the one hand created the tension in Europe which would give Mussolini greater freedom to act, and on the other hand suggested that Italy had better conquer Ethiopia soon, if she wanted her troops back on the northern frontier before the Germans were strong enough to attack Austria. The Duce carefully calculated that the German army would be too weak until 1937. A war plan was therefore devised in the summer of 1934,[12] and in December he began active preparations to conquer Ethiopia in the autumn of 1935. The army was told to act on the supposition that poison gas could be used. They could also assume that other European nations would not protest so long as the conquest was quick enough, especially as it was intended to arrange matters so that Ethiopia would appear the aggressor.[13]

Another event took place at the end of 1934 which contributed to the growing tension in Europe. This was the assassination at Marseille of King Alexander of Yugoslavia, and the murderers were Croat refugees who had been living in Italy and had arms and money provided by the Italian government.[14] Just possibly

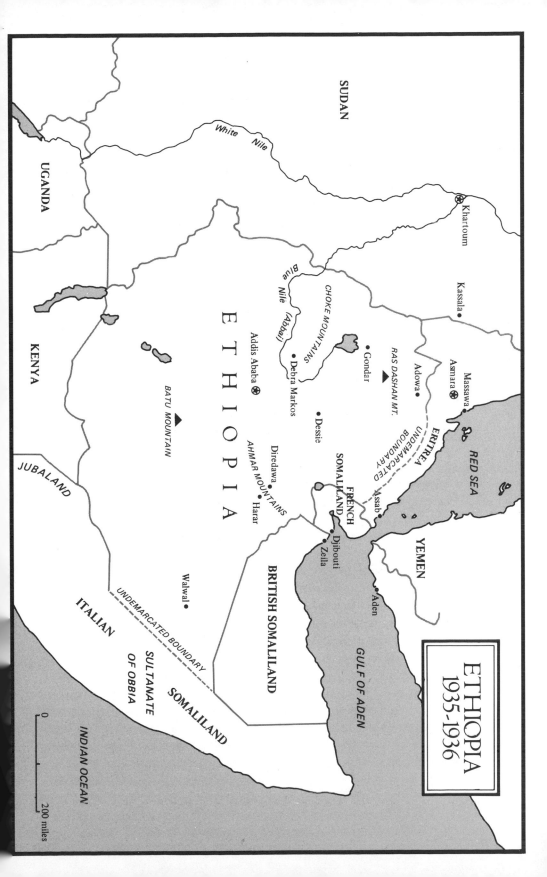

the Fascists knew about this murder in advance—we know that on other occasions they planned to murder the king of Albania and the king of Greece—and were hoping that it would lead to a civil war in Yugoslavia which would give them a chance to push farther into the Balkans before Germany became too strong.[15] If so, they miscalculated, because the murder was an embarrassment to them,[16] but it would not have been their first or last miscalculation. More likely, however, the Croat leader, Ante Pavelic, was exploiting Mussolini's help for his own purposes, knowing that indications of Italian collusion would let him blackmail the fascist government into keeping silent.

In December 1934 Mussolini organised an international congress of fascist parties at Montreux, to which the Nazis, the one other major fascist party in Europe, either were not invited or at least did not come. He may have thought of this "fascist international" as a possible way of replacing the League of Nations with something more vital and authoritative, and there was certainly an intention of asserting the superiority of Italian fascism over national socialism.[17] The note of anti-Germanism was constantly sounded in the Italian press, perhaps because of Italy's temporary fear that the Germans were close to an agreement with France which would leave her powerless.[18] There were references in the newspapers to Hitler's megalomania, to German barbarism, and to a German danger to European peace. Hitler was named "anti-Christ", and crude jokes were made against the vanity of Göring and Goebbels which would not be allowed by the censors a year later. The German and Roman systems of law were declared to be antithetical, and *Gerarchia* in July 1935 remarked that the differences between fascism and nazism, underneath a superficial similarity, were now "profound and unambiguous".[19] According to the German ambassador, the fascist regime showed every sign of moving over into the conservative camp of the defenders of the Treaty of Versailles, and he thought that, if only the western powers would agree to Italy's expansion in Africa, Mussolini was bound to think their friendship more useful than that of Germany.[20] Some of the fascist leaders obviously shared such a view.[21]

If he wanted Ethiopia, Mussolini's best hope was to paralyse any European opposition by first trying to set France against Germany, and in the meantime to galvanise Italians into a more warlike stance. In his capacity as minister of war, in December 1934 he hurriedly enacted a law which said that every Italian citizen was a soldier and should be educated militarily from the age of eight onwards; the claim was made that this law not only put Italy ahead of every other nation in readiness for war, but would rank as a decisive fact in Italian history. His view was that "a nation, to remain healthy, should make war every twenty-five years," and the inculcation of a military spirit should start in elementary school.[22] In this way he intended to make others take Italy more seriously as a military nation,[23] and his law was thus greeted with delight by the fascist leaders: indeed it was declared to have the unanimous support of everyone, since it would by itself ensure success in war, and since it was the universal wish no longer to waste time in talk but to act and carry the flag to some glorious victory.[24]

Meanwhile the progress of Italian rearmament was discussed in February 1935 by the supreme commission of defence. If, as some suppose, Mussolini's main reason for wanting war was to give a boost to the lagging national economy, this planning body should now have taken some major decision: for instance, the replacement of the army's antiquated artillery. But from what Mussolini said it seems that the chief object of its discussion was an essay in public relations, to assure the general public that the really serious problems of war and peace had been thoroughly considered. It is hard to see that any genuine stimulus was given to either army reorganisation or war production. Further conclusions were reached about what was called the decisive importance of a totalitarian military education for youth.[25] An equally irrelevant and purely theoretical decision was taken to begin repatriating Italian emigrants abroad who might be of use in the army or in armament industries.[26] Civil defence was also discussed and it was agreed to buy gas masks for civil servants.[27]

But the most important conclusion after five days of discussion was that the Italian people should, for propaganda reasons, be told a series of major untruths intended to convince them that war was

feasible as well as desirable. Mussolini thus announced that domestic cereal production was enough for Italy's wartime needs,
and although meat production was insufficient this would soon be
remedied, so that people could be told that Italy now had all the
food she needed. They could also be reassured that the government aimed at doing without oil imports, and indeed that within
Italy itself there was already sufficient fuel for the needs of the
military machine. Likewise in textiles there would be self-sufficiency. Foreign imports of coal would be necessary in peacetime,
but Mussolini explained, and just possibly believed, that in wartime he could quickly bring domestic supplies of low-grade lignite
into production. All this signified that, because of fascism, their
long economic slavery was at an end and Italians were no longer
poor in raw materials. As he commented finally, the news should
have a tonic effect on the nation,[28] which could now be given an
assurance that Italy had a war capacity never before even con-
ceived, and which would positively guarantee victory.[29]

Early in 1935, when troops began leaving for Africa, the
country was left in no doubt that a major colonial war was being
prepared which would be vital for the solution of Italy's economic
problems. Among the economic arguments advanced there was
the pledge, by now familiar, that millions of Italians would be
able to live and work in East Africa. There were exaggerated
reports about gold, platinum, oil, coal, and untold agricultural
riches in Ethiopia, and Italians were said to have a duty to make
this wealth available to the civilised world.[30] Some fascist leaders
must have known or suspected that such dreams were make-
believe, but official propaganda preferred to depict the country as
a kind of El Dorado.[31] It would be a point of honour to look after
the welfare of the natives, but no one would expect Italy to show
"an excess of attention for the African population",[32] and hence
imperialism might be highly profitable.

One reason for haste was the fear that other countries, taking
advantage of the inexperience and lack of interest among Italian
exporters, might be forestalling Italy in this bonanza. Japan, for
instance, was capturing Ethiopian markets by what was held to be
unfair competition; there was some astonishment that such "an
uncivilised people" could undersell Italians so easily, and the
suggestion was even made that other countries should join Italy in
economic sanctions against them.[33] As well as Japan, Germany

was selling arms to Ethiopia; [34] the French were investing in mines where Italian finance was not forthcoming; [35] and an entirely false rumour had it that the British were buying up oil concessions all over the country, and so depriving Italy of what might be the solution to her energy problems. [36]

The economic motives for imperialism, though effective as propaganda, would not have borne close and serious investigation. More substantial was the matter of prestige, because Mussolini urgently needed to reinforce in Italians the belief that fascism stood for something big, important, and successful. [37] Where necessary, such selfish motives could be covered with a varnish of idealism by claiming to defend Christianity and the white races against the barbarian Ethiopians and coloured Japanese. [38] The very same Fascists who had lately been appealing to Gandhi to rise against the British in the name of Indian nationalism, now appealed to the British to show solidarity with another white nation. [39] The propaganda machine made this a major theme, summoning other civilised peoples to stand together with Italy against cannibals and slave-owners who were a threat to European superiority. [40]

The diplomatic preparations for war were less easy than the preparation of Italian public opinion, and in some important respects were left to take their chance. The British had already agreed that Italy possessed a predominant economic interest in Ethiopia. They clearly could not be told about an invasion, but it was to be hoped that they would not oppose it when it happened. France was easier, especially as the French foreign minister, Pierre Laval, had privately hinted that Mussolini might one day move into Ethiopia. [41] In January 1935, when the two men met in Rome, they agreed on the terms of a treaty, and also on military staff talks in view of a possible war against Germany; at the same time Laval made an uncertain verbal agreement to leave Italy some kind of free hand in Africa. In all probability he did not explicitly agree to an Italian invasion, [42] but perhaps there was a tacit understanding, and some historians think that Laval may have given an unambiguous approval. [43] After this meeting Mussolini certainly acted as though he had the backing of one major power and could safely begin an aggressive war. [44]

The French and British governments recognised that Hitler was the main danger for the western world and were prepared to pay for Italy's help against him. When their representatives met Mussolini at Stresa in April 1935 to discuss forming a common front, they avoided the question of Ethiopia, hoping that, since Mussolini did not himself raise it, he agreed with them in wanting to concentrate on the German danger. He was informally warned that an Italian invasion would arouse strong opposition, but no more than that, and while some British diplomats thought this smudging of the issue a cowardly mistake,[45] others felt it to be a justifiable risk, and some presumably went to the point of thinking Ethiopia expendable if it was a question of saving Europe from Hitler.

Even though not formally cautioned, Mussolini was left in little doubt that world opinion would oppose him if he started an African war: the British said so privately at Stresa, and spelt it out unequivocally and in public at Geneva on 15 April, then again in both Rome and London,[46] while speeches in the British parliament were outspoken enough for one Fascist to challenge the Labour leader, Clement Attlee, to a duel.[47] But Italian propaganda preferred to anaesthetise such awakward thoughts by giving two dangerous and almost contradictory reasons for continuing with war preparations; first, that Britain had secretly encouraged Italy to fight, and might even like a piece of Ethiopia as the price of her support;[48] second, that the British were frightened of Italy and frightened that war would destroy their own foreign investments. As Mussolini told his colleagues, the British would not dare oppose him over Ethiopia, since they knew he was strong enough to take Egypt and the Sudan.[49] This was one of a number of elementary miscalculations. He simply assumed that other governments would act as unscrupulously as his own and have no regard for Ethiopia; he assumed that they would act with equal disregard of their own public opinion; and he also felt sure that Britain and France would keep quiet as they needed his help against Germany.

Mussolini gave responsibility for preparing the war not to the chief of general staff, nor even to the army, but to a special planning committee in the colonial office. He was ready to listen to the army's advice, but insisted that it was to be a fascist war under his own direction, and as field commander he appointed Emilio De Bono, a leading Fascist who was a veteran of the African campaign of 1887 and had retired from the army many years earlier. It was hoped that many or most of the soldiers would come not from the regular army but from the blackshirt brigades of the fascist militia. As can be seen from De Bono's diary, a main consideration was to obtain military glory for the regime, so Badoglio and the army staff would have to take second place. The first place would go to Mussolini himself, who, as well as being commander-in-chief of the militia, would be in personal charge of operations, and who would be in East Africa for the moment of victory.[50]

De Bono at first thought he would need just three divisions, but Mussolini decided to send ten as he preferred to be on the safe side,[51] and in the end sent twenty-five: this haphazard, extempore over-provision typified the whole campaign. The boast was made that every request was met in triplicate and that expense was no object. Eventually 650,000 men, along with two million tons of materials, travelled the thousands of miles to East Africa. This was a remarkable feat, but some observers thought that ten times as much material was sent as could be used, and stores perished on quaysides because there was no transport to move them. Another sign of amateurishness, as De Bono had to complain, was that thousands of his blackshirt militiamen had received no military training whatsoever and arrived with a single shirt, no underwear, and rifles that were jammed with rust.[52]

As the huge build-up of troops proceeded through 1935, outsiders could not doubt what was afoot. Some thought that Mussolini was becoming dangerously unbalanced and that his statements could certainly no longer be trusted.[53] Even if he still hoped to stop short of war,[54] the time had probably come when he could no longer back down without losing the prestige which mattered so much to him. The British foreign minister, Anthony Eden, hurried to Rome in June with a plan to avoid war by persuading Ethiopia to surrender some areas to Italy and to receive in return British colonial territory which would give this inland country an outlet to the sea. The Italian foreign office hoped for more substantial concessions than this, and agreed with Mussolini that the offer was unacceptable, especially as an Ethiopia with an independent seaport would be less subject to Italy's economic influence.[55] With true fascist perversity Mussolini excused himself from an official lunch in Eden's honour, only to appear ostentatiously in his motorboat within a few yards of the beach restaurant where his guest was being entertained:[56] one may wonder what he hoped to gain by this odd piece of discourtesy. Eden came away from Rome with the impression that Mussolini was not someone to whom one could make concessions, since he would take them as only a sign of weakness; nor could he be relied on to keep promises.[57] Mussolini, on the other hand, assumed from the offer that Britain could be pushed even further into appeasement, and hence increased his warlike preparations.[58]

Unfortunately Mussolini was deceived by his colleagues, who played on his own hopes by suggesting that public opinion in France and Britain would be on his side.[59] Unfortunately, too, he managed to get a copy of a secret British report which led him to imagine, wrongly, that Britain would not oppose him if he resorted to war. The thought of leading his country to military victory was a great temptation. He could now envisage an Italian empire stretching right across central Africa; the four corners of the earth would have to bow before the might of fascism, and if the Ethiopians dared resist him, their country would be put to pillage and fire.[60] As he now said—and it does not sound like another pose—he wanted war for war's sake; he needed revenge for the Ethiopian victory over Italy at Adowa in 1896; and he wanted this even "if it meant that the whole of Europe went up in smoke", even if it meant war against Britain and France.[61] *Gerarchia* meanwhile reassured its readers that Italy was stronger than the western democracies,[62] and other journals and periodicals took up once again the early fascist and futurist motifs about "the poetry of hatred and the beneficent hygiene of war".[63]

Meanwhile at Geneva fascist representatives were doing their best, by bluster and procrastination, to ensure that the League of Nations did not interfere. Their orders were to say that Ethiopia was threatening aggression against Eritrea, and the vast Italian armada carrying war materiel through the Suez Canal was only for defence.[64] The truth was that Mussolini had carefully decided months earlier on "the total conquest of Ethiopia" so as to create an Italian empire before the Germans became too strong in Europe. He had timed his attack for the end of the rainy season in the autumn of 1935, and was ready with a frontier incident to serve as pretext, after which he would attack on two different fronts in Eritrea and Somalia, with Egypt and the Sudan as later objectives and possibly Kenya as well.[65] Already he had prepared a plan of attack, using gas and bombing planes against whatever centres of population could be found, and the army had orders to use terroristic methods in the knowledge that the Ethiopians had no air force for retaliation.[66]

In September 1935, when the British reinforced their fleet in the Mediterranean so as to be ready for whatever might happen, the fascist press retorted that the British navy and air force were no match for those of Italy,[67] and fascist leaders assured Mussolini that in a single night he could sink the whole British fleet and change the course of history.[68] The British on the other hand were aware, as Mussolini apparently was not, that Italians had no armour-piercing bombs, and felt sure that, if it came to war, Italy's sea-borne trade could easily be cut off and reinforcements be prevented from reaching Ethiopia.[69] The Italian general staff knew this too and thought that the British could attack almost anywhere they wanted to and win. The suggestion has been made that the Duce's over-confidence might be explained by the fact that he was being deceived, perhaps by people who needed to cover up various errors of omission; [70] or possibly he was still just trying to impress public opinion. At all events he privately reassured the British that, for all his warlike talk, he meant no harm.[71]

Unlike Hitler, Mussolini had an uncontrollable passion for secret information, especially for telephone taps and anonymous police reports, and spent a large part of his time personally studying this kind of unreliable material. From the early 1930s, a number of foreign embassies in Rome had their telephones bugged or their private documents photographed.[72] No doubt this was fairly common practice among major powers, but Mussolini was unusual in that he did not always try to check such information, and also in that he could not help using it in a way which made clear where it came from.[73] He knew from intercepts that the British were determined to concentrate on the two chief dangers in the world, Germany and Japan, and had no actual plans to fight over Ethiopia. He also learned that their Mediterranean fleet was short of ammunition,[74] and decided to risk basing policy on this fact, not realising that the report might be misleading nor that

Italian shortages were even greater.[75] Mussolini's ministers knew that one of the quickest ways of getting information to him was by working it into private telephone calls which they knew the police were monitoring, and it is not beyond the bounds of belief that ambassadors sometimes did likewise. Certainly it seems that Mussolini's indiscretions gave the game away to the British that their ambassador's private safe was being opened, and the fact that in later years he continued to receive information from this source must indicate either remarkable inefficiency by the British foreign office or else that they were planting information on him. Neither possibility can be excluded.

Mussolini began the invasion of Ethiopia on 3 October 1935, not stopping to declare war and of course unconcerned that he was violating a number of treaties. The Grand Council was not consulted, because he intended the victory to be very much his own personal success. Public opinion was not enthusiastic: without being against imperialism as such, some Italians feared a possible defeat and were worried by cutting loose from the League and the western democracies. According to police reports the bureaucracy, the aristocracy, and the leaders of the armed services were against the war, and in cinemas there was sometimes a dead silence as news reels were shown, or whistles of derision.[76] Even some leading Fascists were for peace, and Mussolini himself admitted that the war was generally unpopular.[77] Yet there could be no suggestion of backing down. Moreover, whereas his diplomatic preparations for the war had been poor, in propaganda he had a sure touch, and he goaded the party into recapitulating the message that the conquest of Ethiopia would be the supreme moment in modern history, the test of Italy's greatness and of her mission to teach other nations. Bottai described it as a war of civilisation and liberation. A proud Italy full of energy was determined to emerge from its poverty and sense of inferiority, while the whole civilised world was said to be watching with admiration.[78]

So confident was Mussolini that he did not bother about the prearranged pretext which had been intended to disguise his aggression, and this left even Laval unable to defend his action.[79] A few days after war began, the League, including France, therefore condemned Italy as an aggressor nation and imposed economic sanctions on her. Possibly, if sanctions had then been rigidly imposed, Mussolini might have been stopped and notice would have been served on the dictators that warmongering was unprofitable. But the world was not ready to face a major war over Ethiopia. The League's action, since it was not firm enough and did not include oil in its embargo on sales to Italy, just gave Mussolini a splendid opportunity to rally national sentiment against this "aggression" by fifty-two other nations. As he later admitted, it was the imposition of sanctions which "broke the last resistance to fascism in Italy" and permitted what would otherwise have been impossible, the conquest of an empire.[80] The propaganda industry had a popular and easy target when it labelled the western democracies as decadent, bloodless, cowardly, and unable to stand up to the vigour and idealism of fascist Italy.[81] Mussolini was determined to show the British and French how unhealthy it was to despise him, and when he spoke on this subject he spoke without control.[82] Britain would have to be destroyed like Carthage.[83] The chief intellectuals of the regime were mobilised to support this theme and to express their sense of outrage that other European governments could prefer "a horde of barbarian negroes", when they should know that fascist Italy was "the most intelligent among the nations", "the mother of civilisations", "the creator and custodian of the European spirit".[84]

The threat of sanctions against Italy was decisive in swinging public opinion behind the war, and hundreds of journalists were drafted to Ethiopia to help increase the sense of excitement. A few of the anti-fascist exiles returned to Italy to show their solidarity with the regime over this particular issue, and elder liberal statesmen such as Benedetto Croce, Luigi Albertini, and Vittorio Emanuele Orlando seemed to share the belief that this was a patriotic and a just war. When Mussolini called on citizens to give their wedding rings and other precious objects to the common cause, there was a remarkable response: no doubt much of the proceeds of this collection was misappropriated,[85] but the public act of faith, shared by ordinary citizens along with the royal family and cardinals of the Church, was fine propaganda for fascism.

De Bono's initial advance was another great tonic for the nation, particularly his easy occupation of Adowa, for this wiped out the terrible memory of defeat forty years earlier, which had become a positive obsession with Italian patriots. But after a week the advance came to a halt for lack of petrol and other supplies. Mussolini assumed that international intervention might before long bring the war to an end and wanted De Bono to occupy as much territory as possible before that happened.[86] The latter, however, was proving to be a bad choice of commander. The appointment of this man of sixty-nine, only an amateur soldier, timid and unimaginative, convinced some in the fascist leadership that the Duce was losing touch with reality and was surrounding himself only by nonentities and flatterers who would confirm his own sense of superiority.[87] The idea of using the fascist militiamen had been another example of thoughtlessness. Many of the blackshirt officers were by now comfortable middle-aged placemen who stayed on just for the uniform and the privileges; some had so far lost touch with fascist ideals that they begged not to be sent out to Africa, while others were given higher commands with almost no training whatsoever. Though many patriotic Italians, fascist and non-fascist, volunteered to fight, other recruits had to be rounded up by party officials from among the unemployed.[88]

Within a few hours of the campaign's beginning, Mussolini realised his mistake and began to think of replacing De Bono.[89] At a time when public opinion wanted more spectacular successes, Mussolini's repeated orders to attack went unregarded, so De Bono was promoted to the rank of marshal and replaced by Badoglio. Still the Italian front remained stationary for another two months and further reinforcements were sent out to this already enormous army. As the wall maps in Rome showed no advance, the press was told to play down what was happening,[90] and foreign correspondents were expelled if they ventured to report any engagement where the Ethiopians were victorious.[91] But alarm began to spread inside the party, along with rumours that Mussolini might fall from power.[92]

Early in December there was further talk in fascist circles of peace, possibly with Italy's granting Ethiopia a corridor to the Red Sea in return for admitting that the Italians had "won." A curious episode which shows up the naiveté and even the possible corruption in Italian army circles concerns a Palestinian, Chukry Jacir Bey, a plausible and charming adventurer who, after apparently being in trouble in various European countries, talked the Italian general staff into paying him to bribe Haile Selassie to agree to terms. If the emperor should refuse, Jacir Bey would then arrange with both sides for a fictitious battle to be fought in any way the Italian generals required, from which they would of course emerge victorious. A formal agreement was drawn up which army representatives signed, and a lot of money changed hands, but Jacir Bey then decamped, and subsequently black-mailed the fascist government by the threat that he would reveal the whole comic story.[93]

Yet another suggestion for peace was put forward in December by the foreign ministers Laval and Samuel Hoare, who thought they might persuade Mussolini to accept a compromise giving him about half of Ethiopia. He seems to have been on the point of ac-cepting this attempt at appeasement,[94] but Haile Selassie was not, nor was British public opinion.

When military operations resumed in December, Badoglio used much sterner tactics than De Bono had done. This was by Musso-lini's express order, namely that, although they should try to keep such things secret, the army could use any means: the bombing of hospitals, the use of poison gas "on a large scale" if this were needed, and even bacterial warfare.[95] In a convention ratified in 1928, Italy had repudiated chemical warfare as "uncivilised", but Mussolini had transported quantities of gas to Ethiopia and in-tended to use it after pretending that the Ethiopians had done so first.[96] Official statements were made then and later that Italy used only humane methods of warfare, and that the stories about Italy using mustard gas were a pure invention by foreigners to dis-credit fascism.[97] Newspapers were censored to help this denial, and photographs of casualties which reached London were cle-verly discounted by the Italian embassy there as being cases of leprosy.[98] Mussolini meanwhile told the *Daily Mail* that the bar-barities of Haile Selassie were an outrage, and a yet more imagina-tive stroke of fancy was the story that the British were furnishing the Ethiopians with gas for use against Italy.[99]

Italian planes had for some time been experimenting with spe-cial sprayers so as to vaporise a fine rain of mustard gas over large areas. Though rarely fatal, the results could be appalling, and Major-General Fuller, a British Fascist who was in Ethiopia reporting for the *Daily Mail*, suggested that it proved a decisive tactical factor in the war.[100] The Ethiopians were thereby presented with the gratuitous argument that, without the use of gas, Italy might even have lost.[101] A more serious objection was that this weapon antagonised some pro-Fascists abroad and possibly also some Catholic soldiers in the Italian army.[102] The Vatican claimed that it was not in a strong enough position to condemn the use of gas, but the Archbishop of Canterbury, in a freer situation, was able to do so.[103] A good deal of scepticism was aroused about the fascist claim to be fighting for Christian civilisation against barbarism.

Badoglio had such a superabundance of force that in any case he can hardly have needed such questionable means. When finally he launched an offensive it was entirely successful. Mussolini tried, as with De Bono, to direct operations personally from his office in Rome, but Badoglio resisted these efforts,[104] and the Duce fell back on encouraging rivalries among the field commanders as the best way of increasing his own influence over the course of events.[105] So as to raise the prestige of fascism, the party secretary, Achille Starace, was given an active command and despatched on what was built up into a legandary "march on Gondar", said to be among the great epics of colonial history,[106] though the army leaders knew that it was nothing of the sort.[107] Other fascist leaders were given commands in Ethiopia and their ambition for medals was legendary;[108] indeed the plethora of medals and the notorious falsity of many fascist exploits brought the regime into some ridicule.[109] Roberto Farinacci, a former party secretary, was another garlanded hero whose loss of a hand in action earned him the special acclamation of parliament,[110] even though it was common knowledge that the "action" had been the inexpert using of grenades to catch fish in a lake near Dessié.[111]

Just as Farinacci had bypassed the normal training program and was quickly given a commission in the air force to enable him to take part in the Ethiopian expedition, so Mussolini's two older sons were given commissions, Bruno illegally before he reached the age of seventeen, and it was a legitimate piece of propaganda to say that these two young boys were typical of fascist heroism.[112] The elder, Vittorio, wrote a book on his experiences to tell Italian youth about the beauties of fighting and how every Italian boy should one day try war, because it was an exciting sport, indeed "the most beautiful and complete of all sports". Vittorio's favourite adjective to describe events in which he took part was "diverting". It was sad but diverting to watch groups of Galla tribesmen "bursting out like a rose after I had landed a bomb in the middle of them".[113] He did not mention that the enemy had no fighting planes at all and almost no defence except rifle fire. Both children were given silver medals for their courage in the face of "fearful odds", as also were Farinacci and other fascist *gerarchi* who had seen even less active service.

As late as March or April 1936, Mussolini was ready to make a compromise peace with the Ethiopian emperor, annexing perhaps only half his territory,[114] because the rainy season was coming near and Italy's army could not be kept in the field for another campaign season without grave danger and intolerable financial loss. But in the fortunes of battle were favourable and made a more totalitarian solution possible. In May, after an advance group of Badoglio's army occupied Addis Ababa, it was announced that they had won "the greatest colonial war known to history", and the population of Ethiopia was said to have turned against their government and joyfully welcomed Italian rule.[115]

Mussolini claimed the glory for himself personally, and took steps to see that Badoglio and Graziani were given something less than the full hero's welcome in Rome which both thought they deserved: it was his firm principle, while being lavish with financial rewards, to ensure that no other Fascist shone except by reflected light.[116] If this was slightly ungenerous, it was good politics, and it is undeniable that his own determination and energy had made a fundamental contribution to the victory. After officially proclaiming the existence of an Italian empire, he left other countries to accept the fact with as good a grace as possible. When Haile Selassie came to Geneva for one last protest at the League of Nations, a dozen Italian journalists earned a small place in history by booing and whistling for fifteen minutes so that his speech could not be heard. This was said to be a spontaneous act on their part, but in fact it was on orders from Rome, and a much-respected Italian diplomat handed out the whistles for them to use; they later received a prize for the most distinguished service to journalism of the year, and one of them remembered that no other act of his career earned him so much enthusiastic support in Italy.[117]

Mussolini, with his natural talent for propaganda, squeezed every possible advantage out of victory, and managed to convince many people that it would bring jobs for everyone and admiration from the whole world. Official accounts of the campaign were suitably doctored to make the fascist version more plausible,[118] and it was described as one of the great campaigns in world history, a masterpiece of strategy against an enemy which the military experts of Europe had guaranteed would be absolutely unbeatable.[119] Badoglio put out a slightly different story that all the staff officers in Europe, "and particularly the British", had expected that Italy would need three years to win, whereas he had confounded them by winning in seven months.[120] No one in Italy was likely to know that at least one foreign expert thought the war had taken twice as long as it should.[121]

Badoglio, in his book on the campaign, did not give the number of casualties, possibly because that might have seemed to devalue the war. Mussolini in private once said that victory had been won too cheaply with only 1,537 Italians killed: he would rather have had more so as to make it look more significant.[122] Some estimates of casualties were even smaller, even under a thousand, and this was out of a mobilised force of 800,000 men.[123] On the other hand the officially admitted financial cost of setting up the empire was about 40 milliards of lire or twice the total annual revenue of the state, and officials were at pains to maintain that the effort was perhaps as large as that put into the whole of the First World War, when 600,000 Italians had been killed.[124]

Whether or not the effort had been worth while, Mussolini was pleased with the results. Success had converted a war which was by his own reckoning immoral into something right and good.[125] Not only had he defeated the League of Nations and a coalition of fifty-two powers who applied sanctions against him, but it could be pretended that the rest of the world admired him for it,[126] and far from arousing dismay at home, the war of aggression eventually proved hugely successful with public opinion. This explains why Renzo de Felice can call the war Mussolini's "political masterpiece".[127] What the Duce could not see was that, apart from undoubted gains in prestige and propaganda, the conquest by itself was worth little until he had pacified Ethiopia and found the resources for its reconstruction. He did not yet realise that, by increasing Italy's maritime vulnerability,[128] a distant empire would become a huge financial drain on an already heavily unbalanced budget; nor that it would weaken Italy in relation to both Germany and the western powers; nor that, by antagonising members of the League, he was giving up his options in foreign policy. Some of his foreign supporters, moreover, deserted him as they saw that behind the propaganda he was just a bloodthirsty autocrat and aggressor.[129]

Many people later,[130] and some earlier,[131] recognised that what could be superficially portrayed as a great achievement might be in fact a potential disaster, especially when Mussolini began to act as though, just because he had defeated a poorly organised and ill-equipped army of irregulars, he could defeat anyone. He tried to pretend that as a result of the Ethiopian war his armed forces were for some reason stronger than ever,[132] and that his army was sufficiently motorised for a European war.[133] Perhaps he forgot that African mercenary troops had done most of the fighting on the Italian side—though he later admitted that most of them had deserted.[134] It was rather stated that since the victory was a logical consequence of fascist doctrine and organisation, Mussolini could challenge any opponent anywhere,[135] and had thus proved Italy to be first among nations; Britain and France by comparison were obviously enfeebled.[136] Ironically the same war which forced the democracies into rearmament gave Mussolini the illusion that he could continue without danger along the same path as before. A too easy success encouraged dilettantism and a self-confident attempt to play a much bigger role in Europe, without waiting to provide the resources which that role demanded.[137]

It would no doubt have been hard for Italians to become popular in Ethiopia, but they would have had more chance if only they could have afforded to show magnanimity, and here the whole logic of fascism was against them, with its cruelty, its arrogance, and its insistence on make-believe. As only a small area of the country was under direct Italian control, the proclamation of victory soon looked like a mere propaganda stunt. When the Italian generals reported to Rome that Addis Ababa was surrounded by large enemy forces, they were told to conceal the fact; they were to treat any surviving Ethiopian troops as "rebels" and hence all prisoners were to be shot without trial.[138] Despite the fascist declaration that they never used the odious methods employed by other colonising nations,[139] Mussolini ordered that brute force and even savagery should be preferred to magnanimity; his instructions were not only to execute prisoners, but again to continue using poison gas and "a systematic policy of terror and extermination", and ten people should be killed in reprisal for every one man lost. The viceroy, Rodolfo Graziani, later declared that only on orders from Rome and against his better judgement had he behaved harshly, but hundreds of villages were burnt by his soldiers and the survivors were executed on mere suspicion, in a policy which makes all the more remarkable the generosity of Haile Selassie after his reconquest of Ethiopia in 1941.[140]

One of Mussolini's least attractive decisions was to kill off the young Ethiopian intellectuals on the assumption that without them the country would be more easily governed.[141] One Italian journalist, unable at the time to refer to such matters publicly, noted in his diary what was happening, how mock trials were held where the accused understood nothing and could not be understood, and how petrol would sometimes be poured over prisoners to burn them alive.[142] Some prominent citizens surrendered on the promise of a pardon only to be shot out of hand, and Mussolini approved of this, though much damage must have been done to Italy's good name by such behaviour.[143] Haile Selassie later recalled that the first generation of Ethiopian elementary-school teachers was systematically exterminated and the development of the country consequently set back for decades.[144]

Convinced that they had to deal with an entirely barbaric community, the fascist administrators were officially encouraged to ignore local traditions. They were ordered to smash the equestrian statue of Menelik, the most famous of Ethiopia's past emperors, and blow up the imperial mausoleum where the national heroes had been buried.[145] Graziani had instructions to impose the ideals of fascism, which meant direct rule and a refusal to govern through local headmen,[146] even when over so large an area this might signify no government at all. Yet in the general euphoria at Rome the government assumed that such problems, like military

ones, were easily solved. To show the majesty of empire everyone, including foreigners, was ordered to give up handshaking and
use only the fascist salute.[147] Graziani lectured the Ethiopians
with condescension, pointing out in public speeches that Italy had
come to impose her highly developed civilisátion on the brutish
traditions of a primitive feudal society. He told them he was going
to put an end to the arbitrary injustices of the previous regime,
and congratulated them on their good fortune in falling into such
noble and generous hands. He added that their incorrigible men-
dacity and ignorance made it unlikely that they could profit from
the new and progressive culture for which he stood, but if they
resisted he would inexorably destroy them and their possessions
by fire and the sword.[148]

Mussolini, for imperative reasons of publicity, announced in
December 1936 that all of Ethiopia was pacified,[149] though opposition was growing and even spreading to Eritrea. Graziani
sometimes felt like the commander of a beleaguered garrison with
the enemy closing on him.[150] He became harsher in his repression, taking advantage of the fact that the Ethiopians were without
their leaders, without new supplies of arms, and divided against
themselves.

The worst excesses occurred in February 1937, after an attempt
had been made on Graziani's life. In all probability the would-be
assassins were former members of Graziani's police who had a
grievance, and certainly the official assumption that there was a
widespread plot possibly backed by British agents was quite un-
true.[151] Whoever was responsible, Italian soldiers and militiamen
ran wild for several days, looting and killing indiscriminately, and
foreign observers saw blood streaming down the streets. Obviously it was a panic reaction, but executions continued even
after the soldiers had been brought to order, and Graziani once
specified—though sometimes he said the opposite—that the kill-
ings were in revenge and at his express orders. Telegrams from
Mussolini confirmed that "all suspects must be executed immediately", and in any village where resistance was encountered "all
adult males must be shot."[152] Fascist "moderates" such as Federzoni, Grandi, and Volpi associated themselves with Mussolini in
sending congratulations for these reprisals,[153] but foreign observers were appalled by cruelties which seemed to serve no political purpose whatsoever. Ethiopian sources, not always in agree-

ment with Italian, reported that perhaps thirty thousand were killed, including people who were hundreds of miles away and must have been innocent.[154]

Italian newspaper correspondents meanwhile sent home stories of Graziani's humane and generous treatment of the rebels.[155] Only later could they tell the different tale of how the viceroy incited his men to further acts of severity as the months went by. When weapons were found in the most famous Ethiopian monastery, its population of three hundred monks and a hundred deacons was executed,[156] and Mussolini confirmed once again that "the maximum use" should still be made of mustard gas for destroying villages.[157] So tens of thousands of homes were indiscriminately destroyed and official reports show that there continued to be anything up to two hundred executions a day: the officials preferred to use black troops for these mass daily executions as they feared that Italian soldiers might refuse to obey.[158]

Public opinion in Italy was not allowed to know what was happening. Only the more senior fascist officials at home were aware that a colonial war was continuing and even spreading after September 1937; only they knew of the heavy financial implications for Italy of this unexpected development and the loss of respect for Italy which it entailed.[159] Foreign embassies and newspapers reported the disappearance of the Ethiopian intelligentsia and the fact that Graziani's government had little authority outside the main cities,[160] but this did not leak out in Italy. Moreover some foreign journalists, for example Evelyn Waugh, helped the concealment by reporting Graziani to be an amiable Christian gentleman,[161] and others were given plenty of tangible encouragement to tell a more favourable story.[162]

Italy's administration of the new colony was defective from the start. The minister for African affairs found his Italian civil servants to be unruly and disobedient,[163] and police reports informed Mussolini about the misconduct of fascist adventurers who were mainly concerned with the provision of jobs for their relatives and clients.[164] When Farinacci was sent out to investigate, he reported that fascism had done the impossible by making the warring tribes of Ethiopia band together against the invader; and he concluded that, at no greater cost than applying principles of elementary justice, the Italians could have had an easily governed colony, whereas instead their prestige was declining to almost zero and more casualties were being recorded than during the war itself. Instead of obtaining an income from their colonies, Italians had to foot an enormous bill which made nonsense of the economic arguments for colonialism.[165] Even though the government altered the figures so as to minimise the deficit, between 1936 and 1940 the Ethiopian enterprise continued to use up the reserves which were badly needed elsewhere.[166]

By the end of 1937 it was clear that Graziani had failed, so he was brought home. Mussolini did not want to give him too many honours, but allowed some of the usual crowd scenes which the party was so good at organising, and these quite convinced Graziani that Mussolini must be jealous of his popularity.[167] The new viceroy was the Duke of Aosta, a wiser and more moderate man, but he found it hard to choose a different policy, and harsh police methods did not come to an end.[168] Italy did many things for her empire in the five years before it collapsed, spending a great deal of money there and leaving behind some notable public works, but she got little benefit in return and reaped hatred for her injustices when they became generally known. Never was Ethiopia under firm control. A vast amount of propaganda about the glories of empire cannot conceal the fact that the Italian army remained encamped there amid a hostile population which was just biding its time to rebel.

6

TOWARDS THE AXIS

Mussolini's colleagues and some of his enemies were ready to admit that he had real gifts as a politician, but it was domestic administration which he understood, and he had begun by thinking of foreign policy as primarily something to help him preserve and increase his power at home. Subsequently this was almost reversed: as soon as his domestic authority was unchallenged he turned more and more to foreign affairs, partly as a means of extending his power still further. But here his knowledge and capacity were more limited, as were also the means at his disposal. Some people went so far as to call him inexpert in the field of foreign policy because he could not be relied on to show finesse, patience, and flexibility but on the contrary took pleasure in wilfully accentuating international differences as a weapon of internal politics or for psychological self-indulgence. Certainly he seems to have been concerned less with making rational calculations of national interest than with dazzling and fascinating his fellow citizens, playing up their collective vanity and their loose ideas about national glory, because this helped him think that fascism was serious and important.

With his instinct for publicity Mussolini was thus quite ready to manufacture foreign enmities so as to keep up excitement or to have a scapegoat for the sufferings which such a policy entailed. A paper enemy was made in turn out of Germany, then France, Yugoslavia, Switzerland, and England; and without this kind of artificial safety valve, wrote Lord Perth in Rome, "public opinion might become dangerously introspective and critical of the internal doings of the regime." All this was well known among foreign diplomats, who usually adjusted their attitude accordingly and did not take Mussolini's posturing too seriously.[1] It was also well known among his own staff. The director of press services was told to launch a verbal attack on more than thirty different countries including Guatemala in the single year 1934, and wondered if this was exceptional.[2] In his search for power and notoriety, Mussolini went so far as to say that he would like Italy to be hated rather than liked or ignored. He also thought that the humiliation of other nations could be a proper objective of Italian foreign policy. Yet this was dangerous as well as foolish, because he could overreact if he found Italy's or his own prestige called in question, and in such moments could gratuitously take up a position from which it was hard to retreat without loss of face.[3]

The Duce's foreign policy was not usually without rhyme or reason, but sometimes its main impetus came either from the desire to cut a figure, or else from the wish to make a nuisance of himself in the hope that someone would buy him off. He liked to alternate provocation with sweet reasonableness, threats with conciliation, so as to conceal the lack of strong principle, but also because of a sensible intention of keeping as many lines of conduct open as possible.[4] It was not abnormal for his ambassadors to be left without much idea of whether he wanted to be conciliatory or provocative,[5] and it is safe to assume that he sometimes did not know himself. Even the most senior officials in the Rome foreign office sometimes had to guess what official policy was and be ready to pay the penalty if they guessed incorrectly.[6] Another quirk of behaviour was Mussolini's preference for acting not just through official channels but through private envoys who, though often quite junior and inexperienced, might have secret orders to work behind the back of the Italian ambassadors and in direct contradiction to the official policy of the foreign office.[7] This was part of the Duce's passion for spies and secret information. But apart from being risky and wasteful, it was bad for morale in the diplomatic service, and bad because of the reputation of unseriousness which it gave to fascist foreign policy.[8]

If there were any restraints on Mussolini's exercise of foreign policy, these came less from the foreign office than from the party,[9] and not even this had much noticeable effect after his intuition and political judgement had apparently proved so successful in Africa. Victory in Ethiopia may not have brought much in the way of solid benefits, but he found it useful for convincing public opinion and his colleagues that Italy was now universally esteemed and even given pride of place in the outside world.[10] An altogether new assertiveness made itself felt, for instance when the young expert on foreign policy, Mario Toscano, declared on be-half of Italy a "right of priority" in the Mediterranean,[11] or when it was said that she had a right to demand a reduction in the dues payable in the Suez Canal,[12] and even a right to force the British out of the Mediterranean so that their ships could come there only by Italian permission.[13] Federzoni, by now an elder statesman of the regime, protested that by "an inexorable law" Italy must ex-pand and impose a new equilibrium of power in accordance with her interests.[14] Bottai and other intellectuals continued to justify pugnacity and assault as qualities which were essentially fascist, and emphasized that the Ethiopian war showed the Italian army to be invincible.[15] Italians were said to have proved now that they were more intelligent than other peoples, more mature politically, and they "had in their blood an inextinguishable desire for domin-ion, to lay down laws and to lead others". In Africa they had learned that fighting was likely to be more effective and perhaps cheaper than negotiation. Their new watchword was *"Roma doma"*, "Rome dominates", and it could be said quite openly that too many countries round the Mediterranean did not belong to Italy.[16] As Germany was finding her national formula in racial-ism, Italians were finding theirs in Roman imperialism. Four large marble maps now set up on the wall of the basilica of Maxentius marked successive stages in the conquests of the ancient Roman empire, and Italians enjoyed the implication that history might repeat itself.

Mussolini's own statements were deliberately confusing and contradictory. In several interviews for the foreign press he de-clared that Italy was a satisfied power with no further imperial ambitions,[17] but these particular sentences were excised before being quoted in the Italian press. To Italians he said rather that another war would soon be necessary and "the whole economy of the country must be bent to this inevitable end".[18] Another of his cryptic phrases became memorable from being painted on count-less houses up and down Italy: "whoever has iron has bread, and if the iron is well-tempered, he will find gold as well".[19] In pri-vate he explained that victory in Africa was the first stage in a planned policy; he had no intention of giving the Italians peace; his own genius, as he called it, discerned a destiny which provi-dence had forced upon his shoulders and which he must follow to the end. He would first consolidate Italian domination of the

Mediterranean and persuade Greece and Turkey to place themselves under his aegis. Then, as he concluded after reading a book about Napoleon, he would have to fight Britain,[20] and he became furious if anyone hinted that this might not be so easy. Giuseppe Bastianini, who in June 1936 became deputy foreign minister, had to confess that Mussolini was now impervious to argument, and the only course was to go along with his views in the hope that he would change his mind or forget. Bastianini added that, having abolished free discussion inside party and parliament, *il capo* quite sincerely had come to think of himself as infallible, and his conquest of Ethiopia as far greater than the conquests of Napoleon.[21] To Alessandro Lessona, minister for African affairs, Mussolini said, "you must all understand that I am not to be contradicted, because it only raises doubts in my mind and diverts me from what I know to be the right path, whereas my own animal instincts are always right".[22]

Mussolini set up a special ministry of propaganda in June 1935, and it was laid down that propaganda was "one of the chief tasks of a state". The fascist idea of propaganda was defined as telling the objective truth about fascism, confounding the lies of its enemies, and clearing up the "ambiguities" which were bound to surround "a movement of such amplitude and vast historical meaning".[23] Sometimes, of course, when propaganda became almost an end in itself, the ambiguities were on the contrary deliberately accentuated, and it is hard to know whether Mussolini was trying to confound the enemy, or his colleagues, or Italian public opinion, or whether sometimes he may not have confused himself as well. To take one instance, he liked to tell foreigners that he could mobilise eight million Italians if necessary and had no need for a black colonial army in addition,[24] but what he told his ministers was that he wanted a black army in Ethiopia as a means of dominating the whole of Africa.[25] In May 1936 he tried to impress party leaders by speaking of a million Ethiopian soldiers backed by a local metallurgical industry in East Africa to make munitions, and told them he meant to conquer the Sudan and link up Libya with the rest of his African empire, thus by-passing the Suez Canal which was now proving so expensive.[26] Sometimes more realistically he mentioned 300,000 as the size of this black army, but sometimes the propaganda for imperialism preferred to multiply the number to two millions.[27] It is doubtful if the correct figure mattered at all to him or anyone else. The main purpose was to sound impressive.

In the middle 1930s propaganda put special emphasis on the spread of fascism abroad; it was said that only fascist Italy could realise the true unity of Europe; that Rome and Moscow were the only alternatives, and that no other state, certainly not Germany, could compete in the contest for leadership of the world revolution.[28] When the fascist encyclopaedia listed other countries which had copied fascism, the names included Brazil, Portugal, Poland, Rumania, and the Greece of General Metaxas. Thirty-nine other states were said to have flourishing fascist parties, including Belgium, Holland, Spain, Norway, Sweden, Switzerland, Hungary, Canada, Australia, South Africa: and in all these, "fascism as an ideal force is animating a new civilisation". Fascist institutions were also being copied in still more countries, a fact which proved that this was "the best and most fitting model for the existing historical moment". In Britain, not only Oswald Mosley but Lloyd George and Bernard Shaw frankly recognised the value of fascism, so it was asserted, and Churchill, in a strongly anti-nazi speech, once referred to Mussolini as "the greatest law-giver among living men".[29] It had to be admitted that fascist parties abroad differed from each other, being either pro-Jewish or anti-Jewish, pro-socialist or anti-socialist, and there was some vague intuition that this raised a problem about what fascism really meant, but no solution to this conundrum was immediately apparent.[30]

Mussolini looked on Italians living abroad as a seed-bed of fascism, especially the many millions in South America. Secret service funds were used for supporting political parties there,[31] and the hope was expressed that South America in general might look to Rome for leadership in its inevitable contest with North America.[32] High personages were sent out there to talk about fascism, and free holidays in Italy were given to the children of emigrants, but this was a one-way traffic and barren of results, partly because the assumption was made that Italy was a proper subject of interest for other people without there being any reason for Italians to be interested in other countries. The emigrants living in Argentina and Brazil continued to lose their Italian identity as

French, Spanish, and Anglo-Saxon culture overwhelmed them, and it was a grave disappointment that they showed so little concern for the primacy of Rome.[33]

A more serious effort was made in the United States. Fascist Italy had for a time been dependent on loans from North America—J. P. Morgan, for instance, lent over a hundred million dollars to Italy in 1926 on the assumption that fascism created the conditions for profitable investment. Moreover remittances from Italo-Americans were an important item in the Italian balance of payments. A major contribution to victory in Africa [34] was said to be Mussolini's achievement in persuading President Roosevelt not to apply economic sanctions against Italy, and thereafter it was hoped that the Americans' strong ethnic links with Italy would prevent the United States from siding too exclusively with France and Britain. In this cause a good deal of money was spent, and the English-language edition of Ciano's diary omits several names of American newspapermen who received special attention.[35] But the fascist leaders lacked much understanding of the North American situation. In 1934 Italian money supported the candidature of Fiorello La Guardia for mayor of New York despite his anti-fascist sentiments,[36] and not only were John L. Lewis and the AFL backed as champions of "fascist syndicalism", but there was delight that Roosevelt was aping fascism, as they believed, and taking up the *manganello*, or big stick, of his presidential cousin.[37] From the very first it was assumed that the New Deal must be fascist because it relied on authority rather than the outmoded practices of liberalism. The Duce thus praised "the intensive cult of dictatorship to which President Roosevelt is dedicating himself", and was delighted that the three western democracies had thereby been reduced to two.[38]

Though detailed accounts are usually lacking, subsidies were sent from Rome to foreign fascist organisations, for instance to the Rexists in Belgium, to Jacques Doriot in France, and to a smart Swiss deputy who persuaded the gullible Mussolini to pay him large sums of money for doing absolutely nothing.[39] Some of the French nationalists were full of praise for Italian fascism, and at one moment were in touch with the Italian government about setting up deposits of arms near the frontier.[40] At critical moments Mussolini spent quite a lot on the French press. In September 1935 he sent a million lire to the Italian ambassador in Paris, mentioning five newspapers in particular to be cultivated, and at the end of 1938 at least one weekly Paris magazine still had a regular subsidy from the Italian consulate general.[41] It was the more disappointing that the French never produced what could be accepted as a serious fascist party.[42]

More promising were the Irish Blue Shirts, led by General Eion O'Duffy, who dropped hints that he intended to assume power by a "march on Dublin", and there were grounds for thinking that Ireland was readier than other countries for the expansion of fascism.[43] In England Ambassador Grandi set out to stimulate interest in Mussolini. Within a few days of arriving in London in 1932, he wrote to describe how almost every evening he had to explain to an admiring audience what fascism meant. He reported that even H. G. Wells was pro-Fascist, and he was also working on the "Duke of Wales",[44] but Grandi's letters are so full of self-praise and so full of admiration for Mussolini's "genius" that they are rarely convincing. "The Ambassador of Mussolini in London takes pride of place over everyone", he reported, though he was anxious for Mussolini to believe that his own thoughts were rather on the happier memories of 1921 and 1922, when he led his armed bands wreaking havoc in the Italian countryside.[45] According to Grandi's own account, fascism had a formidable future in England, and he was advising the English Fascist Oswald Mosley to take revolution into the streets of London.[46] He admitted that he had little confidence in Mosley, but was nonetheless supporting British fascism to the tune of about £60,000 a year.[47] Mosley later denied this, but there is other evidence that British fascism was subsidised from Italy.[48] Everyone in England was said to be hanging upon Mussolini's every word, anxious for his praise, determined to mend their ways if he chided them. Grandi added that he was glad to find himself in a world where even respectable journalists, while not obvious Fascists, could be persuaded to write favourable articles on Italy in return for a small monthly payment.[49]

One trouble with British Fascists was that, though they adopted the black shirt and the Roman salute, they were British patriots first; they opposed Italian claims on Malta, and also erred by copying anti-semitism and other nazi aberrations.[50] Nevertheless Mussolini's agents, having to justify themselves and their salaries, reported improbably from London that there were up to half a million Fascists in Britain, in other words many more than there had been in Italy when Mussolini came to power, and all of them watching Rome and feeling Mussolini's influence. Most Englishmen, and most true English intellectuals, announced Luigi Villari, supported Italy against Ethiopia.[51] Mussolini was quite capable of basing policy on this blatant falsehood. One major flaw in fascism was that it told journalists what to write and then found that it liked to believe their eulogistic stories. When Mario Appelius in China was threatened with dismissal for not following his colleagues in writing that the name of Mussolini was on everyone's lips, he mildly protested that very few Chinese had ever heard of the Duce or even of Italy for that matter, but then purged his tactlessness by reporting that every Japanese schoolboy knew all about fascism.[52]

The ideals of pan-fascism sometimes overlapped with those of Italian irredentism, particularly by stressing Italian rights in Corsica, Tunisia, Switzerland, and Malta. Within a few months of coming to power Mussolini had tried to exploit discontent with French rule in Corsica,[53] and he continued to subsidise the movement for Corsican autonomy, arguing that Italian was the language of Corsicans, and hoping that he could create a groundswell favoring separatism and union with Italy.[54] Similarly in Tunisia, where perhaps as many as 100,000 of the population were Italian by birth or ancestry, a lot of money went secretly or openly in support of *italianità*, and criminal intimidation including killing was also employed.[55] As for Switzerland, especially in Canton Ticino and to a lesser extent in the Grisons and Valais, where there was an Italian-speaking population, the Swiss authorities freely allowed Italian cultural activities, and fascist propaganda encountered the barren soil of indifference rather than provocative opposition. Mussolini keenly resented that German influences continued to advance in what he called "Italian Switzerland", and secret subsidies were paid to withstand this advance, but the Fascists increasingly realised that theirs was a losing cause unless a major European war revived the chances of annexing this area to Italy.[56]

Also in Malta there were Italian claims against the British, who had ruled this strategically vital island for over a hundred years.

Mussolini from the very beginning used Italian cultural associations as a means of spreading the cause of Italian fascism; though some of his consular officials warned him that the Maltese were indifferent to both fascism and Italian nationalism, he preferred to listen to others who told him the opposite.[57] Within Italy the press showed little interest in the issue until the British in 1932 began to encourage the Maltese language as an alternative to Italian in schools and the law courts; it was this question of language, as the Fascists admitted, which then made a hardly existing problem into a matter of national prestige. The same Mussolini who made the Italian language compulsory for the Greek population of the Dodecanese islands was outraged that Maltese should be made compulsory in Malta; [58] it was said to be an essentially Italian island and Maltese a non-language.[59] Eventually an active campaign was launched for the annexation of what Grandi called "the Italian gem of the Mediterranean", and the Italian foreign office began using secret service funds to influence the island's elections. Whether there was ever much local support for fascism is hard to say, but Malta was included in Italian guide books as part of Italy and, in the last days of the fascist regime, was given a bogus "representation" in the Italian parliament.[60]

These objectives of irredentism and pan-fascism would in time lead Mussolini to an alliance with Hitler, but during the first half of 1935 there was little sign of this. After signing his alliance with France in January 1935, Mussolini boldly spoke of destroying Germany if Hitler continued his militarist policy,[61] and staff talks were held with the French to prepare for possible war against the Nazis.[62] Hitler countered in June 1935 by apologising for the murder of Dollfuss and promising that he did not intend to annex Austria.[63] When France imposed economic sanctions against Italy, Mussolini found he needed German coal and munitions,[64] and Germany did in practice help him economically, though less than was sometimes said.[65] Hitler could only gain from the war in Ethiopia, because it weakened the "Stresa front"—the association of Italy, France, and Britain formed in April 1935—and allowed German industrialists to supplant Italy in many markets of central and south-eastern Europe.[66] Simultaneously Hitler was secretly providing money and arms to the Ethiopians for use against Italy, perhaps hoping that this would help to prolong the war and make the Italians yet more obliged to seek the friendship of nazi Germany.[67]

Unaware of this, Mussolini in January 1936 informed Hitler that the sanctions had created a definite breach between Italy and France, and hence, although he was not ready to permit an *Anschluss*, he would recognise that Austria was a satellite of Germany and no longer of Italy.[68] Some of his advisers were telling him that it would be a colossal error to side with Hitler, but others, especially on the brutal wing of fascism, were insistent that Austria was expendable and that Italy together with the Nazis could dominate Europe for a hundred years.[69] Probably Mussolini was of two minds, because he continued to play a double game and assure the French that he was still on their side if the price was right.[70] But the press, obviously on orders, became more pro-German,[71] and the Duce sent word to Hitler that, although fascism could not play its cards openly yet, nevertheless Germany and Italy had a partnership dictated by destiny, a *Schicksalsgemeinschaft*. As he used this word he hit his fist on the desk and added, "I am very strong, Italy is much stronger than people think", and he declared his former friendship with France and Britain would never be restored.[72] In later years Mussolini tried to make out that, even as early as April 1935, he had secretly been aiming at a reconciliation with Germany,[73] though this was just another of his historical fabrications. The reconciliation is more properly dated in or about January 1936. Hitler was thereby enabled to take advantage of the divisions caused by the Ethiopian war, to defy the rest of Europe, and to reoccupy the demilitarised Rhineland. The Germans realised that Mussolini was trying to get back to "the pendulum position", as the German ambassador in Rome, Ulrich von Hassell, called it, and hence was already more than half way to accepting an *Anschluss*. When they hinted that Italy still seemed to be keeping a foot in both camps, Mussolini laughed and said that he was now on the German side but was just pretending otherwise to the British and French.[74]

While the Nazis and some of the British realised that Mussolini could be gulled by even gross adulation, most French politicians refused to sink so low: one of them had coined the wounding phrase *César de carnaval*,[75] which Mussolini found hard to forgive. The Fascists had for some time been trying to persuade themselves that, because the French birth-rate was falling, France must be incurably decadent. They tried to forget that the Italian birth-rate was simultaneously falling, because for Mussolini it was a decisive point that France was "losing" three hundred people a day by putting the pleasures of life before the duties of multiplying and fighting for the fatherland.[76] He was upset to find that Italians still admired the French, and Bottai dutifully echoed that this francophilia was "a grave moral vice." For some years fascist leaders had been protesting about how many Italian students preferred attending French universities.[77] Likewise it was insufferable that the French continued to write histories of the First World War without recognising that Italy saved them from defeat.[78] Mussolini had himself once been an enthusiast for French culture, but times had changed and fascism now turned to develop the different theme that French literature was finished, that Proust and Valéry were out of date, Gide and Mauriac boring, that what was lively in French art derived from Italian futurism.[79] Either Italians would overcome their inferiority complex towards France, or else they would not deserve the mantle of leadership which fascism was bestowing on them.

Mussolini still knew very little about Britain or America or the other English-speaking countries. His attitude to the British was based on a few platitudes and generalities: as he pronounced in 1935, they had not progressed since the Edwardian age and so had nothing to teach him.[80] He had "a mathematical certainty" that neither Britain nor France would ever declare war on Italy, because of their decline in population,[81] and they could therefore be provoked with impunity. Early in 1936 he asked the director general of statistics to work out details of this decline, and then announced that, since 11 million people in Britain were over fifty years old, here was proof positive that they would never fight another war.[82] The fact that there were 2 million more British women than men told in the same direction, and he calculated that there would soon be only 30 million people in the British Isles, "all of them very old": here, he explained, was a fact of fundamental significance.[83] Taking it into account alongside the figures for alcoholism and sexual perversion, fascism could safely assume that Britain was finished and her empire about to disintegrate.[84]

Whenever it became clear which way Mussolini's mind was working, the journalists and place-hunters competed to reinforce his arguments, and this particular topic is a good example of how far propaganda could be exaggerated as political differences with London became more acute. One expert announced that there were 7 million spinsters in Britain because they were too ugly to get married; [85] another view was that the British population would soon be down to 20 millions or would even disappear entirely in a few decades, unless the monarch intervened and permitted polygamy.[86] Medical specialists gave it as their opinion that the practice of birth control was chiefly to blame because it caused sterility among English women, and Dr. Cucco, a specialist from Palermo and one-time member of the fascist Grand Council, found from his researches that contraception also led to conjunctivitis, nervous asthma, dyspepsia, bad memory, insomnia, excitability, and a ceaseless anxiousness and irritability: his learned thesis was favourably reviewed by the medical press, by the Vatican newspaper, and by the royal academy.[87] Another doctor thought that the fatal decrease in births among the British, like their notorious cowardice and unwillingness to fight, was due rather to the mutilating operation of tonsillectomy,[88] and here too was another comfortable assurance that this decadent people was unlikely to hit back if attacked.

The fascist leaders did not have much experience of the outside world. Mussolini continued to think of the British as a people who put on evening dress when they took tea at five o'clock.[89] Achille Starace, who after 1931 came second in the hierarchy, was unwilling to believe that Eire was a separate and possibly friendly country. But a half-knowledge of English literature was used by the professors to demonstrate that the British were no less decadent than the French. Virginia Woolf was evidence of a loss of masculinity, Galsworthy's *Forsyte Saga* of narrow materialism, Chesterton and Belloc of the nation's drunkenness. The reading of Samuel Pepys was recommended by Guido Piovene so as to be able to understand the avarice, the social conformism, the sensual vulgarity which existed behind the mask of every Englishman. One student discovered the typical Englishman in Dr. Jekyll and Mr.

Hyde, another found him in the Bertie Wooster of P. G. Wode-house, who "was not the invention of a novelist, but rather the ordinary type of Englishman as he has emerged from generations of repressed Victorians." [90]

The propagandists were anxious to correct certain historical misconceptions, among them those which had been invented by Gibbon and other similarly partisan writers.[91] It was a misconception to say that there had ever been friendliness between Italy and England. Italy had not only rescued Britain and France from defeat in 1918, but was generally recognised to have surpassed them and become "the first nation in the world".[92] With the aid of such authoritative texts as *1066 and All That*, an interesting picture was built up of Britain as an effete country corrupted by wealth and power, undermined by puritanism, ruined by the Jews and psychoanalysts, and by the national habit of eating five meals a day. In Scotland the aristocracy was said to maintain its feudal position by the help of private armies, while at the other extreme the British workman could not afford even one meal a day, and tens of thousands of people in London were dying of hunger each year.[93]

Propaganda, whatever the Fascists said, came to mean the art of using myths to supplement or replace reality, and in fascist Italy, where the realities were unsubstantial, myth-making became the one essential art of government, more important than statesmanship or far-sightedness or even effective administration. Propaganda laid down that France and Britain were weak and unable to retaliate. Their air forces were inferior to those of Italy, and the defence of Paris or London would be impossible, so that war against Italy was unthinkable for them.[94] Italy was strong, while France no longer counted at all.[95] As for Britain, Mussolini in 1937 spoke derisively of "the fat underbelly of the democracies", whose people were cowardly and pacifist.[96] In such belief he was strongly influenced by the casual vote of an Oxford undergraduate society in 1933 against fighting for king and country, and eventually he persuaded himself that this vote represented the firm opinion of British youth in general, Close associates found that he could not be argued out of such a view,[97] but preferred to believe Grandi and Villari, who told him that the British ruling classes were not only corrupt but thoroughly frightened of war and convinced that Italy could beat them. The Italian ambassador in

London—partly because he did not like to reveal that he had so narrow a circle of acquaintances in England, mainly among the appeasers, and partly because he was pestering Mussolini to give him a title and knew he had to keep in step—sent information that proved to be seriously misleading.

A war against Britain had for some time been advocated in certain fascist circles,[98] and Mussolini began to speak of this with some confidence after the successes of 1935. It was his view that seven weeks would be enough to bring victory.[99] He believed, or at least said, that he now had air command of the whole Mediterranean, and not only was strong enough to destroy the British fleet in Alexandria, but had a silent bombing aeroplane which could fly from Italy to London without being perceived.[100]

In June 1936 Mussolini appointed the thirty-three-year-old Galeazzo Ciano as foreign minister. Ciano was the son of a naval war hero ennobled by fascism who had attained position and enormous wealth as a politician and financier.[101] The son had not been a zealous Fascist in his youth, though in later years managed to alter this fact by fabricating suitable credentials.[102] Everyone agreed that he was tremendously ambitious; most allowed him charm and some intelligence, though he was not popular in the party or outside it. Apart from his marriage to Edda, Mussolini's daughter, Ciano's chief claim to office had been his success running the propaganda department (1933–1936), and particularly the campaign against Britain. His first task as foreign minister was to complete the work begun by Grandi, namely to make the foreign office thoroughly fascist, and to initiate Mussolini's new policy of linking up with nazi Germany, for, though he later tried to minimise his own contribution, the axis between Hitler and Mussolini was in large part his handiwork.[103]

The decisive step in creating this axis took place when Ciano travelled to Berlin in the autumn of 1936 to persuade Hitler to move more towards Italy and away from Britain. For this purpose he took with him copies of confidential British documents collected by Grandi, who was secretly in favour of a German alliance and for this purpose was apparently being provided with British cabinet papers by a pro-fascist member of the British parliament.[104] Mussolini had been disturbed by the victory of the popular front in France, which was too obviously a challenge to his doctrine that Europe was going fascist. He was therefore ready to accept German rearmament and Hitler's claim to colonies; in return he was hoping for a more formalised friendship. Hitler seized his chance and told the Italians that he would be prepared for war against the democracies in three years' time: his own ambitions were only in eastern and northern Europe, and he would leave the Mediterranean entirely to them. Knowing that the Duce was open to flattery, he took care to remark—or at least Ciano quoted him as saying—that Mussolini was "the first statesman in the world, to whom no one else could even remotely be compared". After such a handsome acknowledgement, the way was clear for Mussolini in November to proclaim that a Berlin-Rome axis was in existence.[105]

By much reiteration Mussolini's collaborators tried hard to convince themselves, in 1936 and 1937, that they held a balance of power in Europe, since in defiance of a wealth of obvious facts it was said that they possessed one of the most powerful armies and air forces of any country, and at the highest possible technical efficiency.[106] Foreign military observers were said to be greatly impressed with the Italian military manoeuvres of 1936, though this was a very long way from the truth.[107] When the German war minister spent three days examining Italy's armed strength, he too was said to have admired their discipline and their advanced equipment,[108] though unknown to them his private conclusion was that Italy was very weak and she would be probably more useful as an enemy than an ally.[109] By this time the general staffs and police forces of the two countries had begun to exchange information, though Hitler ordered his representatives to mistrust the Italians and not give away too much.[110]

To balance this growing proximity to Germany and to cover himself in the Mediterranean, Mussolini in January 1937 made a "gentleman's agreement" with England. It collapsed almost at once, partly because Mussolini was reading secret documents which revealed, to his astonishment, that Eden thought poorly of him, and also because of stories in the British press about the indifferent fighting qualities of the Italian army. Mussolini became more angry than his colleagues had ever seen him and publicly commented on the "desolating puerility" of such an ignorant people. Nearly all British newspapers were at once banned from Italy for four months, and the Italian press was ordered in retaliation to stress any unfortunate incidents they could discover during the coronation of King George VI: graphic accounts were soon describing the hospitals in London overflowing with casualties as protesting crowds demonstrated against the monarchy and the Anglican Church. Such an exaggerated reaction suggested to foreigners that, if the capacity of his army was such a sensitive point, something must be seriously deficient in Italian military preparations.[111]

In September 1937 Mussolini at last visited Germany and was skilfully persuaded by the Nazis that they were militarily invincible. Dazzled by parades and by the Krupp factories at Essen, he reached the climax of his tour when he addressed what was said to be a million Germans on the Maifeld. The speech was given in a torrential downpour and was understood only with difficulty,[112] but he himself was enormously impressed by the carefully staged theatricality of the occasion and did not guess that the enthusiasm might be in any way artificial.[113] Mesmerised by the flatteries of Hitler, he was equally an easy victim of those Italian journalists who wrote of his "apotheosis" in Berlin and of how he talked to three million Nazis in perfect German. In city after city these Italian visitors found evidence that Hitler had produced a new type of German, no longer the fat, pallid, bespectacled stereotype of former years, but vigorous, healthy, and red-cheeked. This was obviously going to be the winning side. And what was even more attractive, Hitler cleverly kept up Mussolini's illusion that Italy was an equal partner in the axis, or even possibly the superior partner.[114]

At the end of 1937 three facts reflected a new sense of pro-nazi euphoria. One was the beginning of Mussolini's campaign against the Jews.[115] Another was his clamorous withdrawal from the League of Nations. Membership in the League had been increasingly unwelcome as his movement became more totalitarian, and he could not like any international body where fascism could be freely criticised and free speech was still the rule. The decision to leave it was discussed by the Grand Council for no more than two minutes, and the unanimous approval included the votes of Grandi, Federzoni, Volpi, and Bottai; for they like everyone else had by now been taught to believe that not Geneva but Rome was becoming the centre of decision-making in Europe.[116]

The third event was Mussolini's signature of a tripartite pact with Germany and Japan against communism. This was a deliberate move towards what Ciano thought would be an inevitable war against Britain. It gave Mussolini the exquisite happiness of feeling himself at the centre of the most formidable political and military combination that had ever existed, and few people had ever seen him so gleeful.[117] Japan had until recently been for him one of the greatest threats to civilisation and the white races,[118] but this attitude changed almost overnight—so suddenly indeed that a consignment of armoured cars, on the way to China for use against Japan, had to be ordered to wreck itself in the South China Sea.[119] Before many months had gone by, Mussolini was the proud recipient of the imperial Japanese Order of the Chrysanthemum.[120] The alliance of the Second World War was well on the way to becoming a reality.

7

CIVIL WAR IN SPAIN

The wearisome civil war dragging itself out in Ethiopia through 1936 and 1937 was made more difficult to fight when Mussolini, losing interest since he could no longer afford to report the situation in the newspapers, helped to start another civil war in Spain. Since 1931 he had been financially supporting a number of different opposition parties in Spain,[1] because the very existence of a left-wing government there was another public challenge to his doctrine that fascism was the central theme of the century. Hoping for a monarchist restoration and for commercial privileges granted to Italy at the expense of France, he sent arms for one military coup, though when it failed he quickly congratulated the republican government at Madrid on putting it down.[2] Again in March 1934 he signed an agreement with two Spanish monarchist parties, giving them money and arms to overthrow the government, and he did this without his own foreign-office officials being consulted or even informed. As he confidently, and without irony, told the Spanish negotiators, the case of Austria was proof that his word could be relied upon whenever he promised to help.[3] When this coup also collapsed, he continued to send a monthly subsidy to Primo de Rivera in 1935 and 1936.[4]

The rebellion of General Franco in July 1936 came to Mussolini as a surprise,[5] and when first asked to give help he refused.[6] Only when he heard that the Germans had agreed to assist did he send Franco a dozen transport planes; this grew gradually, despite his repeated promises of non-intervention, into a full expeditionary force.[7] Military opinion, notably that of Marshals Balbo and Badoglio, was against such intervention on the grounds that the Italian armed services wanted time and all the money that could be spared for a major programme of reorganisation and recuperation after their efforts in Africa.[8] On the other hand, Ciano showed what was described as childish delight at the idea of fighting in

Spain.[9] Mussolini moreover believed Franco's assertion that the war could be won in a few weeks without much effort, and perhaps was encouraged by his own irresponsible propaganda about Italy's war capacity.[10] Later, when Russia sent military help to the Spanish government, it was possible for the Fascists to generate more enthusiasm by calling the war a crusade against bolshevism, but in fact they decided to intervene long before bolshevism had been any danger: [11] their original motive was rather to assert the authority of fascism and of Italy through the Mediterranean. One personal reason given by Mussolini for fighting was his secret wish to toughen up Italians and make them a more warlike people.[12] Possibly there was some thought of getting bases in the Balearic Islands, and the propaganda industry also invented strange geopolitical notions about the vital strategic role of Spain in "controlling or paralysing the English channel".[13]

If Franco's rebellion became a major civil war, this was in good part owing to the help he received from Germany and Italy, while the republican government in Madrid was supported by Russia, by France, and by an international brigade which included many Italian anti-Fascists. Franco complained that he had asked for equipment only and the arrival of large numbers of Italian troops had been almost forced upon him.[14] Another objection by the Spaniards was that, as in Ethiopia, the Italian divisions contained far too many untrained soldiers, because Mussolini was once again determined to win glory for the fascist party militia of which he was commandant, and had no idea that these units were highly inefficient. Some artillerymen had never fired a gun before; there were battalion commanders who had had no training for sixteen years and knew no modern arms at all; and one fascist general described his men as mostly scum, who for publicity reasons were called volunteers, though many had been forcibly drafted from among the unemployed as a kind of outdoor relief organised by the party.[15]

At the beginning of 1937 the Fascists still thought the war would soon be over, and when the Italian ambassador in Madrid, himself a good Fascist, sensibly warned against such easy optimism, he was indignantly recalled after only two months in his post.[16] Mussolini preferred to rely on the advice of unofficial emissaries who, as was now almost normal, were sent to spy secretly on the Italian embassy. Roberto Farinacci, who was one of those sent to investigate, also took a message asking Franco if he would accept an Italian prince as king of Spain. Franco was indignant at the suggestion, as he also was indignant when the Italians criticised him for conducting the war with excessive brutality. When Farinacci's hostile comments about Franco's generalship came to the notice of the Spanish police, this did not contribute to the popularity of the Italian expedition.[17] Nor did Mussolini's determination that the blackshirts should snatch the chief honours of the war. The Duce in fact encouraged his generals to push too far ahead too quickly without regard for Franco's general plans and strategy, whereas the Spanish authorities resented the independence of the Italian generals, and understandably did not want Madrid to be captured by alien troops.

As a result of these differences, and of the lack of training and amateurishness of the general staff,[18] General Mario Roatta led the Italian expeditionary force to defeat near Guadalajara in March 1937. Franco had warned them against over-confidence, but Mussolini was anxious to stake the prestige of his army on arriving first at Madrid. Defeat therefore came as a most bitter blow, especially after so much boasting about the unconquerable fascist spirit, and above all since the victorious enemy were not regular troops but a scratch army of irregulars including many anti-fascist Italian exiles. To increase the fighting spirit of his men, Roatta had told them that the enemy would torture and kill any prisoners, but this was hardly very encouraging and many deserted while others became so demoralised that they had to be withdrawn from the front.[19]

Only under the impact of defeat did Ciano realise with what irresponsibility so many untrained men had been sent to Spain. He tried to put the blame on the militia for having officers who had never exercised command before. He reported to Mussolini that, unlike the anti-Fascists of the international brigade, the Italian soldiers lacked initiative, as they also lacked fanaticism and hatred for the enemy, and were terrified of the enemy's tanks. He particularly explained—and it was an alarming thought—that the proximity of the anti-fascist exiles was threatening to undermine many years of political indoctrination by the regime.[20]

Mussolini rather put the blame on lack of cooperation by

Franco, though this did not prevent him pleading for Spanish reinforcements to come and rescue the situation.[21] He tried to persuade the Germans that the defeat was of no importance, while in Italy he announced that it was no defeat at all and only described as such by malicious foreigners. Privately he knew that he would be unable to withdraw his army until they had won a clear victory, so as to erase the memory of what had occurred.[22] Nor could he prevent some Italians from learning through the foreign press about what had happened, and anti-fascist criticism sometimes began to be heard inside Italy itself.[23] The German general Von Thoma, who was observing events in Spain, took careful note of the weakness thus revealed in the fascist military system; worst of all, as he later recalled, was the fact that since the propagandists needed to establish that the battle of Guadalajara had been no defeat, Mussolini was obliged to keep his incompetent generals in their commands, instead of sending them back to the obscurity they merited.[24] This kind of flaw vitiated the whole fascist system.

Franco did what he could to prevent the press saying too much about the battle of Guadalajara,[25] but privately he could not conceal some degree of satisfaction, and among his generals some were openly pleased about the humiliation of the Italian army, because they resented the bad behaviour of the Fascists and their condescending attitude.[26] Franco told the Germans, perhaps exaggerating so as to please them, that the Italian divisions were tragically incompetent and a real liability; he would be glad if they withdrew altogether, as the quality of their army was markedly in contrast with their presumptuousness.[27] Mussolini's official and unofficial representatives in Spain confirmed that the domineering and provocative conduct of the Italian officers showed up badly in comparison with the correct and helpful attitude of the Germans. Though he was giving more help to Spain than the Germans were, he was earning little gratitude and even making new enemies.[28]

Hitler for his part was more calculating in support of Franco. He wanted economic concessions in return, and wanted to try out new aeroplanes and anti-tank artillery under combat conditions. Where Mussolini needed a striking military success, the Germans were not unhappy to see the war prolonged so as to cause the maximum turmoil in Europe, and for that reason were glad to see

Italians becoming ever more bogged down. Mussolini would have liked to have more German troops in Spain, but Hitler preferred to let Italy bear the brunt of the risks and the expenditure, realising that as time went by Mussolini would become more deeply enmeshed and at odds with the western democracies.[29]

As the war continued into the summer of 1937, Italian submarines, pretending to be Spanish, successfully sank a good deal of neutral shipping in the Mediterranean, probably not realising that the British had broken the Italian naval cypher and knew who was responsible. The Fascists took little account of the indignation caused in the outside world by submarines which could not afford to surface and rescue the crews of torpedoed merchant vessels.[30] More Italian soldiers were despatched to Spain, this time with better preliminary training, but still without much enthusiasm for a war which was not easy to explain or justify. By the end of the year some of the generals were anxious to pull out altogether, especially when further desertions began to be registered and when public opinion in Italy became slightly more open in its criticism.[31] Mussolini could not afford to agree. After Guadalajara the reputation of fascism was pledged on scoring a triumphant success, and Franco thus knew that the Italians would be forced to give him all the military stores he required, usually for no payment at all.[32] Mussolini urgently begged the Spanish generals to move faster and be more ruthless in finishing the war, but they were anxious not to leave too many scars on their own society. Mussolini's enthusiasm for them diminished noticeably and sharp words became more frequent, but he had let himself be caught in a situation where circumstances were largely beyond his control.[33]

A preponderant part was played in the Spanish war by SIM (Servizio Informazioni Militare), the military intelligence organisation which had been General Roatta's special concern. Placed under the immediate orders of Ciano, SIM had been hoping to use Spain, like Ethiopia, for developing new techniques of chemical warfare: they were ready, for instance, with poisons and also with bacteria for starting epidemics behind the enemy lines.[34] Though in all probability such substances were not used, SIM succeeded in one major coup when it was ordered to assassinate Carlo Rosselli. This man was one of the foremost anti-fascist exiles and had distinguished himself fighting against Mussolini in Spain. His murder and that of his brother took place near Paris in June 1937, and the Fascists tried to put the blame on the French or on the Communists.[35] In fact it was a deliberate political assassination ordered by the Italian foreign office:[36] Mussolini denied that he knew of the murder in advance, but he said this only when he realised that it had been a political mistake.[37]

Neither Mussolini nor Ciano ever showed much interest in humane considerations or international law, for fascism prided itself on being realistic and surgically unsentimental. Although propaganda was directed against the "homicidal sadism" of the Spanish republican forces,[38] fascist doctrine decreed that neutral ships could be sunk and without warning; Ciano ordered that the water supply of enemy towns should be cut off; and Mussolini said that any Italians taken prisoner in Spain should be shot, since "dead men tell no tales" and so no one would know about it.[39] Also the bombing of non-military targets was deliberately ordered, because Ciano and Mussolini hoped that civilian populations could be terrified into submission: to make sure, the under-secretary for air, Giuseppe Valle, personally led the first such bombing attack.[40] The decision to bomb Barcelona in February 1938 was evidently taken by Mussolini on the spur of the moment without consulting anyone, and certainly without bothering to ask Franco's permission. The Spanish commanders were horrified and asked him to stop at once, but terroristic bombing raids by Italian planes continued, and Mussolini expressed himself as delighted that they were making Italians hated abroad, for it was all part of his plan to give his fellow countrymen a reputation for pugnacity and ruthlessness.[41] Even the Germans were shocked, or pretended to be, and at last there were protests from the Vatican at the use of such a weapon against a Catholic population; so Ciano tried to convince people that Franco was the one to blame.[42]

The fall of Madrid, which fascist newspapers had announced as imminent in July 1936,[43] took place at the end of March 1939, and brought this horrible war to a close after half a million people had died. Italians were led to believe that their army had scored a triumphant military success which covered them with glory,[44] and it is quite true that Italian help was essential for Franco's victory. But others thought that Italy by her intervention obtained no direct advantage—and this at great cost.[45] One positive result was that Spain remained fascist. A hypothetical one was that Russia did not get bases in the western Mediterranean. Yet another, less positive, was to create an almost irreparable breach between Italy and France, which dangerously reduced Italy's options in foreign policy to the same extent as it increased her subservience to nazi Germany.[46]

Italy lost in Spain only about 3,000 soldiers,[47] but in other respects Mussolini confessed that the war had "bled his country white".[48] The monetary cost was put at between 12 and 14 milliards of lire, in other words twice as much as Italy's annual military budget.[49] A quarter of a million Italian rifles were left behind in Spain when the Italians went home, as well as nearly 2,000 pieces of artillery and more than 750 military aircraft, which together amounted to a third of Italy's available armament.[50] (Some of this Italian equipment was subsequently sold secretly by Spain to Yugoslavia.) Mussolini had at first intended that Franco should pay the full cost of all materiel, but then found he had no option but to write off half the debt, and in the end wrote off most of the rest. For some time he hoped at least to get concessions in the Spanish mines and in the steel complex of Sagunto, but Franco obstructed this. In sum the war can be said to have been a very heavy burden on the far from flourishing Italian economy.[51]

The supreme disillusionment was Mussolini's discovery that his intervention in Spain had not even brought him the gratitude which he thought was his due. He had hoped that Franco would join the axis, but before the war was over he had to admit that Spain was crushed and impoverished to the point where she would have to stay neutral in the next clash of mighty opposites.[52] Nor was Italy given preference over Germany, or even over England. The Germans contributed less to Spain in terms of expenditure but got a great deal more out of it.[53] Moreover the Germans had had no scruples in trading simultaneously with the opposite side in the Spanish civil war,[54] because their reasons for intervention had been partly economic, and by the end of 1938 they were bringing out of Spain over a quarter of a million tons of various ores each month.[55] Germany and Italy both tried to keep secret from each other their own economic involvement in Spain,[56] but the Germans were far more efficient in knowing what they wanted and how to get it.

8

THE COLONIES,
1936–1939

Fascism lived on dreams of future prosperity, and the easiest and most illusory of these dreams were woven out of colonial prospects and aspirations. To stir up enthusiasm for the new empire which Mussolini on 9 May 1936 had proclaimed to be in existence, Italian journalists were set to work describing the vast mineral wealth of East Africa.[1] One mining engineer said this was nonsense, but his remarks were deemed unpatriotic, and most reporters preferred to speak of mountains of iron ore waiting to be exploited by Italian technology.[2] There were always some financiers and companies and journalists who did very well for themselves in this field by exploiting the gullibility or corruption of the fascist administration. Nevertheless as the years 1937 and 1938 went by there was very little hard fact to show for all their speculation, and in any case Italy did not possess enough mining engineers to exploit even her own domestic mineral wealth, let alone that of Africa.[3]

On the assumption of having to prepare for a major war, Mussolini laid down in February 1937 that they should plan for the empire to be economically self-sufficient, though in peacetime it would be expected to furnish Italy with raw materials and to import Italian manufactures.[4] This paradox was never clarified and perhaps he never noticed the contradiction. He wanted Ethiopia to develop its own industries, even heavy industry, and some Fascists fooled him when they suggested that East Africa might not only earn foreign currency for Italy by exporting elsewhere, but become a great centre of industrial production for the whole African continent.[5] Italian exporters, on the contrary, though they were glad to see inflated colonial budgets that would pay for goods from Italy, were anxious that Ethiopia should not be allowed to develop to the point of becoming self-sufficient or of being able to compete with Italy in other markets.[6]

Though some individuals gained, the profits were not generated locally but came directly from the Italian taxpayer, as thousands of millions were spent in the empire which might have been more profitably spent in developing the depressed areas of Italy itself.[7] In this sense fascist Italy was more generous than any other colonial power, and the results in Africa were sometimes imposing, even though expenditure was directed more to political advertisement than to community benefit or to a working economy.[8] Large numbers of unemployed were drafted from Italy to build hotels, hospitals, schools, and upwards of four thousand kilometers of asphalt road, but costs were as much as ten times what they were at home, and many of the roads, either because they were badly built or because they were too expensive to maintain, were soon abandoned.[9]

The fascist authorities had assumed that the agricultural possibilities of the empire were almost inexhaustible,[10] and that in a few years this fact would create a real economic asset for Italy.[11] When foreign newspapers were sceptical, an attempt was made to draw a fictitious picture of great prosperity already achieved.[12] Nevertheless, although many relevant statistics were confused or concealed, exports from Ethiopia were declining in 1937 and 1938, and in some cases ceased altogether.[13] By the end of 1937 Mussolini was acknowledging in private that his calculations had gone radically wrong.[14] Partly this was because a multiplicity of state controls made economic life difficult. Partly it was the widespread refusal by Ethiopians to accept the new paper currency instead of the familiar Maria Theresa *thaler* which alone they trusted. Partly it was that labour shortages and heavy government expenditure resulted in everyone, from domestic servants upwards, earning five times what was normal in Italy, which raised prices on Ethiopian goods so that they could no longer compete in the export market. Other obvious reasons were the lack of security and the fact that many agricultural labourers were drafted to make roads, so that some plantations closed down altogether.[15]

The government claimed that they freed 2 million slaves in Ethiopia and transformed perhaps 4 million other serfs into free workers, with guarantees and assistance such as many European countries did not allow even to their own nationals.[16] Yet these facts are in doubt, and it is clear that a kind of slavery was brought back again when forced labour was instituted in agriculture, the mines, and public works. Just as earlier in Somalia, local headmen were constrained under threat of punishment to produce a quota of labourers, and although there were regulations about giving these conscripts good food and medical help,[17] little check was made on this.

Mussolini decided from the first days of his new empire that its exploitation could not be left to free initiative, but should be state planned.[18] His other axiomatic preconception was that there would be mass colonisation by Italians, who might take about half the land for themselves, and this point was said to be not open to discussion.[19] Already in 1936 the army confiscated some of the more fertile areas,[20] and eventually the law once again caught up with practice: the categories of land that could be taken included estates belonging to the ex-emperor or to rebels, or on which tax had not been paid, or which were uncultivated, or even where the government thought the land could be cultivated more efficiently.[21] It was admitted that this was a highly delicate matter, since the Ethiopians felt very strongly about questions of land possession,[22] but the practice was justified as being less harsh than the brutal principle of spoliation which was allegedly adopted by the British in their colonies.[23]

One journalist who claimed to know about such things, after a quick visit announced that there was ample room for millions of Italians in East Africa, and this optimistic assertion became part of fascist orthodoxy, though it does not seem that even at this late date (in 1937–1939) any scientific study was made of its workability and cost.[24] Such a study might have drawn attention to the fact that Italians had shown almost no desire in the past to emigrate to colonial territory. It might also have stressed the need to wait until East Africa was pacified—except that public opinion could not be allowed to know that the war was still continuing. The Germans soon learned from their confidential agents that the process of colonisation was falling far short of expectations. At the end of 1936 there had been 146,000 Italian workers in East Africa, but by June 1939 the number had dropped to 23,000, and in May 1940 only 854 agricultural families were said to be working over this great area.[25]

Mussolini set great store by police reports and private delations of corrupt practices in the large imperial bureaucracy, though his interest was far less in remedying corruption than in ferreting out stories which allowed him to set fascist leaders against each other and make them frightened of his secret sources of information. No doubt invention and sheer malice coloured many of the reports he received about corruption, but it is indisputable that, not having to bother with normal methods of accounting, the chief colonial proconsuls, De Bono, Balbo, and Graziani, had been able to award huge contracts to their own friends and clients without competitive tenders and without any effective supervision from Rome. Mussolini did not mind much about minor peculation among subordinates: his first interest was to see that scandals remained secret, and his second was to use his private knowledge as a kind of threat so as to compel loyalty and obedience. Since public criticism was not permitted, fascist *gerarchi* knew that they had a guaranteed immunity from the courts so long as they kept in with the party and with Mussolini himself.

One unsavoury scandal erupted when Alessandro Lessona, the minister for Africa, accused some colonial governors of corruption on a grand scale, and in particular said that De Bono had deliberately ignored cheaper contractors in order to give a virtual monopoly of public works to a concern with which he was financially involved. Possibly Lessona was acting here as an interested and perhaps injured party, but police reports confirmed that there were strong grounds for suspicion, and also that roads and airports in East Africa were costing twenty times what they would in Italy. In February 1937 De Bono in self-defence wrote a letter to a Roman newspaper, and this letter, most unusually, brought some of the unsavoury details to public attention: he calculated that Mussolini would never let anyone near the top of the fascist hierarchy be found publicly guilty of a major criminal offence, and hence that no reply to his letter would be permitted. He was right, and so kept his public reputation intact.[26]

As a result of this method of contracting, a few powerful individuals and companies took over the economic life of the Italian colonies. Working in conditions of monopoly or near-monopoly, they could name their own price. If they knew how to enlist or buy the support of a minister or a fascist party secretary, they could obtain permits to build hotels and other public buildings even where there was no demand for them. The propagandists of course had to put out the contrary story that Italy brought to Ethiopia for the first time ever an efficient and thoroughly honest civil service,[27] but the viceroy in June 1938, reported that a quarter of his colonial civil servants were corrupt and most of the rest incompetent placemen.[28] Farinacci, no mean judge, was horrified to see so much outright robbery, so little control or permitted criticism, so much monopoly, and such vast sums of money getting into the wrong hands; he found that two years in Ethiopia was enough to take an unscrupulous man all the way from pauper to millionaire.[29] What became known as "the African mentality" eventually spread to Italy itself, and signs of individual wealth suddenly became more obvious: it is likely that by 1939 the obvious enrichment of party leaders began to sap the confidence of ordinary Italian citizens in the fascist regime.[30]

The Italian educational system had no long tradition of training colonial civil servants, so administrators came mainly from the party or the army. Because of this lack of trained personnel, it was probably rash to insist on the practice of "direct government" in a country which had known almost nothing except indirect rule and local autonomy. Fascist appointees were in any case usually looking for a more lucrative and high-sounding job than that of district commissioner; yet without a large class of local commissioners the fascist system of direct rule could not work, and even the attempt to abolish slavery might have taken a century or more.[31] The minister Lessona laid down that fascism as an authoritarian system demanded centralised rule, and as a result found, as Mussolini was to find, that orders were not carried out, indeed that "usually people did the opposite of what they were told".[32] The existence of five different police forces in the empire, each with a different ministerial allegiance, suggests that the fascist tendency to bureaucracy and to the creation of private empires got completely out of hand. All manner of parasitical offices were set up, often overlapping each other, and providing the finance and the "clientelistic" retinue for many a minor fascist *gerarca*. Among these offices were the capillary ramifications of the party, also of the corporative system, which hardly worked in Italy let alone in the completely alien conditions of Africa. All this helped to reduce the effectiveness of administration, slowing up decisions and depriving individual officials of responsibility for actions taken.[33]

In the development of fascist racial policy, the problem of the Jews was given the most publicity, but some people at the time thought that the Jewish question was less important, as it also came later in time, than the problem of black people in the empire.[34] Mussolini did not think much about racial matters until the conquest of Ethiopia, yet there was already a trend of policy towards some kind of apartheid,[35] and one of its champions, the celebrated anthropologist Professor Lidio Cipriani, maintained that racial doctrines were implicit in fascism from the very beginning. Cipriani believed in Italian racial superiority, which he defined as biological and unchangeable; it was his view that Italy was not in Africa to raise the standards of colonial peoples, nor even to impose her own civilisation, because the natives were incapable of receiving it, but by inherent right of supremacy. The native-born population had "an irreducible mental inferiority", and Cipriani paradoxically added that this might even be contaminating for the white races despite their unchangeable biological superiority. Africans were incapable of progress, he explained, and hence it was useless to talk to them of parliaments and self-government. By measuring cranium capacity he satisfied himself that they were like children whose infantile joys were in simple pastimes, and hence their schooling should not aim higher than the memorisation of a few basic facts.[36]

This was not a widely accepted view in Italy until after 1935. Previously some people, on the contrary, had been able to argue that the lack of racial or religious intolerance differentiated Italians from Anglo-Saxons.[37] A lack of racial prejudice was also indicated by the earlier practice of *madamismo*, where civilian and military personnel at all levels would regularly have black mistresses, and this was even officially welcomed and legislated for.[38] But official attitudes changed suddenly in 1935 when large numbers of Italian soldiers and workers upset the sex balance in East Africa and the birth of many mulatto children created quite unexpected social problems. In their contacts with the local population the soldiers were now instructed to develop a precise consciousness of their superiority: they could respect the natives and even like them, but not be sentimental or fraternise.[39]

The policy laid down by the minister for African affairs in

August 1936 had as its basic rule that whites and blacks must live separately, so that places of public entertainment could not be frequented by both, and there should be no familiarity, above all no *madamismo*.[40] One law of April 1937 imposed penalties of up to five years in prison for any Italian citizen living with a black "subject", and forbade legitimation or even recognition of half-breed children. Another law in June compelled whites and blacks to live in different areas; and in July Italians were forbidden to drive buses carrying "subjects" or to travel on the same public services.[41] The reason given, to preserve the purity of the race, was entirely hypocritical, because fascism never dared to legislate against having sexual relations with African women. The real sin was living alongside the natives as equals and thus damaging the reputation of the master race. White women guilty of racial crimes, *a fortiori* of sexual crimes, were treated more harshly than men because theirs was an additional offence against white masculinity: in one bad case Mussolini took the law into his own hands and ordered the offenders to be beaten before being sent for five years to concentration camps.[42]

To relieve a critical situation, one emergency measure was the organising of prostitution on a fairly large scale by the government. At first Italian women, after a short period of instruction, were sent to East Africa, but in April 1938 Farinacci had to inform Mussolini that 90 per cent of them were pregnant and this was creating difficulties.[43] On the highest racial principles it was thought better not to allow native women in government brothels, and Italian women were now also excluded as it was found that their presence lowered the whole ruling class in native estimation, so a search went out for white but non-Italian prostitutes. Eventually a consignment of French women was selected by an experienced lady in Marseille and despatched to East Africa, but the authorities in French Somalia unfortunately would not let them proceed beyond Jibuti.[44]

In 1938, when an international conference was called by the royal academy to discuss Africa, the Italians were by now ready to propound the fascist doctrine of racial superiority. Fascism, said the former minister of education and colonial governor, Count Cesare De Vecchi, did not intend to assimilate other peoples but to govern them, basing itself on their scientifically proven biological imperfections, and dogmatically rejecting the democratic idea of the evolution and emancipation of colonial peoples.[45] A former minister for Africa then put forward what seems to have been the main contention of the conference organisers, the idea that Africa belonged by right to the nations of Europe; instead of being regarded as colonial territory, the continent should be considered an extension of Europe. The distinguished lawyer Gaspare Ambrosini tried to maintain that this proposal, coming from "the genius of Mussolini," was unanimously accepted by the whole conference: though its foreign members had not in fact been consulted and perhaps did not understand what he was saying.[46]

Another Italian voice at this conference was that of a former journalist and governor of Somalia, General Maurizio Rava, who summed up the fascist conviction that it was wrong to regard natives as equals. They should be treated with kindness, as one would treat children, on the supposition that they were inferior physically and morally. It would be entirely wrong, he argued, to let them think that in the future they could ever become on a par with whites; this had been the great error of the British in India when they opened the Indian civil service to the local population. Rava challenged the belief of Sir James Frazer that local cultures had any value, because its implications were insidious and dangerous. The natives should be given elementary education, and a few could be taught trades and professions at a low level, but nothing more. One reason he gave was that, in schools where whites and blacks were educated together, the latter for some reason often came out at the top of the class, and this gave them a sense of pride which could only spell trouble.[47]

Teaching Italians that they were a superior race was a task imposed on the Fascist Party, and the lesson was not always easily learned.[48] Some difficult illogicalities could be discerned in fascist racial legislation. For instance, alongside talk about purity of race, the legislators insisted that this was nothing like nazi racialism. Scientists argued that half-breeds, being "against nature", were especially subject to disease and rightly outlawed from Italian society,[49] yet those born before 1937 were exempted from the discriminating laws on the grounds that they were no danger.[50] Laws punished concubinage savagely, but not sexual relations with natives, and hence interbreeding continued to increase alarmingly.[51] Another law, of June 1939, introduced the penalty of up to three years' imprisonment for any act harming the prestige of the race,[52] and any crime had its penalty automatically increased by one quarter if it could also be construed as diminishing Italian prestige. Heavy fines were levied against Italians who did manual labour for a native, though no similar law could apply to the professions because government policy was to keep higher-paid jobs as a white monopoly. Films for native audiences also had to be censored lest they might see anything offensive to the prestige of the Italian race.[53]

Mussolini's original plan for Libya was that it should become an area of intensive Italian settlement, and some estimates assumed that a thousand miles of North African coast would be peopled preponderantly by Italians as a basic means to achieve Italian control of the Mediterranean.[54] In the first ten years the Fascists nationalised half a million acres of the best agricultural land for this purpose, but only 1500 families came to settle. Here was presumptive evidence, as Mussolini himself admitted, that Libya might never become a colony of settlement,[55] but a new attempt was made in the middle 1930s, with the long-term aim reduced to bringing in only about 25,000 colonists. Marshal Balbo, the governor of Libya from 1933 to 1940, tackled this problem with his customary verve and with some humanity. He brought the area of nationalised territory up to a million and a quarter acres,[56] and in return did much to improve the material condition of the population, providing educational and medical services, finding new supplies of water, and organising expert agricultural advice. After wholesale confiscation of tribal property in Cyrenaica, the social structure of the tribes had also to be destroyed so as to ensure the final defeat of the Senussi. Inevitably, and despite legal safeguards, the bedouin suffered, because this policy required most of them to be driven off their territory in the hope that they could be turned into a reserve of cheap labour in settled village communities; the nomadic bedouin were nobody's friend, and it was not much consolation when Balbo told them that he had delivered them from bondage and backwardness.[57] Nor could he protect them against sharks such as the exiled murderer Amerigo Dumini, who illegally seized large areas of their land and then used influence and blackmail to force the government to buy him out.[58]

Eventually in 1938 a convoy of settlers led by Balbo in person sailed from Italy with 1800 families in seventeen ships. A tremendous publicity boost was given to this event—too much, indeed, for Mussolini, who could not bear any of his lieutenants getting that amount of limelight and who ordered a sudden clamp-down on all news about it.[59] In true fascist language the settlement of these 1800 families was called "one of the greatest mass transmigrations that history recalls."[60] New villages had been built with such names as Garibaldi, Marconi, and D'Annunzio, each village having its fascist party headquarters and a church. Farmers were given some fifty acres if they were white, ten acres or less otherwise, since the needs of the Arab population were said to be smaller. They were provided with seed and stock, told what and when to plant, and the government guaranteed to buy their produce. But the war came too soon for the experiment to show if it could have worked, and the basic problems of even this minimal settlement had not been solved when the colony was lost for good.[61]

Against the policy of domination enunciated by De Vecchi and Rava, Balbo worked half-way towards a degree of assimilation of the Arab and Berber population of Libya. He set up a fascist branch of the party for them, together with a blackshirt youth movement, and when speaking in public was courageous enough to stress that, unlike the East Africans, these were peoples of ancient civilisation whose intelligence and traditions would not allow them to remain premanently at a colonial level.[62] Mussolini visited Libya in March 1937, and the importance given to this occasion is indicated by the size of the conscripted retinue of journalists—more than three hundred of them—and in their collective presence he melodramatically laid claim to the title of protector of Islam. Many Libyans had fought for Italy in Ethiopia, and Balbo asked the Duce to reward them by the gift of Italian citizenship. This suggestion was praised as being an altogether new departure in European colonialism and proof that fascism was following the example of ancient Rome by assimilating subject peoples rather than dominating them,[63] but any intelligent observer must have seen that it was utterly at variance with the equally fascist principle of racial discrimination and subjection.

Members of the Grand Council were in a quandary when they found that Mussolini wanted both racial exclusivism and rights of

Italian citizenship for the Arabs. They decided to compromise: to give only second-class rights, and just to a few carefully selected local notables. At the same time the four Libyan provinces were declared part of Italian national territory, and this had a genuine psychological value, since it could be used to reinforce Mussolini's new claim that he could cut the Mediterranean in two by controlling both sides of the straits of Sicily.[64] But there were legal difficulties in defining the rights of second-class citizenship and reconciling them with the racial laws. Only a few thousand Arabs were prepared to detach themselves from their own traditions sufficiently to ask for Italian citizenship, and not many had their request granted. Once the newspaper headlines had made their point about Mussolini's progressive and generous policy, not much more was heard of the doctrine of assimilation.[65]

The title of protector of Islam occurred to Mussolini because the Italian government, having replaced the Turks in Libya, could by a stretch of the imagination claim to have inherited the authority of the caliph. On the other hand some elements in fascism regarded colonialism as a Catholic crusade and thought of Islam as the religion of barbarian peoples threatening to submerge the spiritual values of the west.[66] Mussolini had to steer carefully between contradictory attitudes: on the one hand he prized the Catholic Church as a means of extending Italian influence in Africa;[67] on the other his own religious latitudinarianism allowed him to back any established church, provided it was obedient. He built and restored mosques at government expense, and in 1935, to obtain Arab support against Ethiopia, set up an Islamic theological school in Tripoli, while Balbo as governor frequently consulted the Moslem authorities and forbade the sale of alcohol during Ramadan. Propaganda was further served by a powerful radio station at Bari broadcasting to the Arab world, and by 1939 Mussolini was, after Dante, the Italian most translated into Arabic.[68] But whether or not this painstaking friendliness won fascism much support is doubtful; the long war against the Senussi had not been forgotten.[69]

In Ethiopia the religious situation was more complex. As well as protecting the many Moslems there, Mussolini, by virtue of succeeding to Haile Selassie as head of state, claimed that his government had a quasi-religious status in relation to the Coptic Church, and used this argument to sever the connection which the Copts had maintained with the monophysite patriarch in Egypt. At the same time he tried not to offend the Catholic authorities and hinted that perhaps the schismatic Coptic Church could be persuaded or pressured into submitting to the Catholics of Rome. He also expelled some of the Protestant missions from the empire, since on this issue Catholic exclusiveness was reinforced by his own conviction that Protestantism was altogether too liberal a force in educating the younger generation. [70]

In the field of education, Fascists admitted the desirability of producing the skilled artisans, farmers, and people needed to perform some of the low-ranking jobs in the colonial administration. Apart from this, though in Libya a few richer citizens were allowed to send their children to the Italian schools of Tripoli, the general doctrine was one of separation. It was specified that education had to be "essentially practical" and had to avoid any attempt to Europeanise. Preferably it should be confined to an elite, in case too many people started refusing menial jobs and adding to the social problems of a growing urban proletariat. [71] Special textbooks were prepared for the colonies. Emphasis was placed on Italian history, but not the mid-nineteenth century, since it would be dangerous to teach natives about the conspiracies and revolutions of the Risorgimento. Children would learn to read through such phrases as "I am happy to be subject to the Italian government"; "Italy governs her colonies wisely"; "The Duce loves children very much, even Arab children." [72]

In the Dodecanese Islands of the Aegean, conquered like Libya from the Turks in 1912, Italy ruled over a Greek population, but Mussolini was anxious to make them Italian and fascist, because he wanted Rhodes as a naval station and a base for the expansion of Italian influence in the Near East. Italian thus became a compulsory language in the schools, and Greek ceased to be the language of instruction even for Greeks. Other steps were also taken to instil in the population an Italian patriotism, for instance by insisting that everyone should salute the flag each evening. [73] The government also made an unsuccessful attempt to attract Italian farmers, and for a time it was vaguely hoped that the existing population would either emigrate elsewhere or otherwise adapt to being the hired labour of Italian colonists.[74] Local customs, at least in the early years, were respected: for instance, divorce was allowed to the 80 per cent of the population who were Orthodox Christians, as polygamy was for Moslems, but steps were taken to secure the independence of the Orthodox community from the patriarch of Constantinople just as the Copts had been separated from the Egyptian patriarch, and eventually all the confessional schools were nationalised.[75] The governor, until the racial laws were introduced, used to attend the major festivals of the Orthodox and Jewish communities, and in 1928 he set up, partly at government expense, a college for training rabbis, since it was hoped this would help the dissemination of Italian culture throughout the Levant.[76]

Policy changed when, in 1936, Count De Vecchi became governor of the Aegean Islands and at his own request was given full military and civilian powers, which allowed him the supreme pleasure of being able to legislate almost at will. His task was to make the islands an integral part of national Italian territory, introducing a fascist and totalitarian spirit, and Mussolini said he did not mind if some rough measures were used.[77] But De Vecchi, just as earlier in Somalia, employed the fascist methods of bludgeon and castor oil to such effect that even the Duce was moved to anger at his incompetence and inhumanity.[78] Though successive governors tried to stimulate agriculture, an excess of regulations almost defeated this purpose, and it did not help when they tried to link up the islands with the Italian market and discourage existing trade links with nearby Turkey and Greece. The elective basis of local government was of course replaced and Italian laws and administrative practices increasingly introduced. Here, too, complete confusion reigned when the policies of assimilation and subjection were applied simultaneously. On the one hand all Greek newspapers were abolished so as to bring about cultural assimilation, while on the other hand the racial laws were applied to stop intermarriage.[79] De Vecchi lived in great splendour, building himself a magnificent and costly palace in Rhodes. When the claxon sounded announcing the arrival of his enormous limousine, all other vehicles had to stop and, under threat of imprisonment, citizens were required to get out and stand to attention making the fascist salute as he passed.[80] Such were the methods by which this arch-Fascist thought to inculcate respect and bring back the glory that was Rome.

Mussolini had established in 1934 that Italy's historical destiny lay in Africa, and from this precept he eventually gave more practical shape to his grandiose vision of a large colonial empire stretching from the Indian Ocean to the Atlantic, an empire in which millions of Italians would settle and so solve Italy's main economic problems. Superficially it was a far from unattractive idea, and probably contributed not a little to the popularity of the fascist regime. But once Ethiopia had been conquered, once the propaganda value of imperialism had been tapped, Mussolini lost interest. Probably he had no idea about how to develop the colonies which had cost him so much to obtain. Perhaps he realised that there was no way of profitably exploiting the empire except by defeating France and Britain and making them pay for any developments.

Although his ministers had to inform Italians that Mussolini personally and every day guided the course of imperial policy,[81] in fact he left these ministers for months on end in ignorance of what he intended, or whether he intended anything.[82] Sometimes newspapers were told to play down the empire, whether because he was disillusioned with the results, or because propaganda required heroic deeds and not ordinary administration. With his sensitivity to public opinion he must have known from continual references in the press in 1937 and after that Italians showed little interest in colonial development once the excitement of war had passed.[83] Most people in the end seem to have found the imperial idea an illusion. Far from making new friends and loyal subjects for Italy, the empire created new enmities. Far from solving Italy's economic problems, it helped to make them insoluble; nor did this very considerable transference of capital to the empire justify by its results any goodwill which may have inspired it.

What was perhaps the main economic argument, namely that large numbers of Italians would settle in the colonies, had proved quite unfounded. Mussolini had laid out a fortune on the basis of mere guesswork, yet the Italian population of New York City was still ten times that of the entire Italian empire. Another assumption had been that empire meant commercial advantage and a profitable source of raw materials. But Italy's imports from her colonies in 1938 were little more than 2 per cent of her total imports, and it could be said that she had spent ten times as much on administering these territories as the total volume of trade with them.[84] Far from being self-sufficient, as Mussolini had ordered, the colonies had to import half their food and all industrial requirements. Italy exported to East Africa in 1938 goods to the value of over 2 thousand million lire, nearly twenty times as much as she received; with Libya the proportion was about eight times; and this gap in the balance of trade was widening from year to year.[85] So topsy-turvy were the economic calculations that, whereas Italians had counted on abundant supplies of coffee from the empire, the year 1938 saw the beginning of a serious coffee shortage in Italy at the same time as many coffee plantations in East Africa were going out of business.[86]

Individual fortunes were no doubt made out of such a one-sided commercial activity, but Italy lost. Mussolini had been hoping, for example, that the colonies would strengthen national self-sufficiency and assist Italy's balance of payments, but on the contrary they made the deficit worse, because the steep rise in Italian exports to the empire was of goods which might have been sold elsewhere for foreign exchange. Another factor was the high cost of freight to East Africa, and ships for this purpose had to be taken off the more profitable transatlantic routes.[87] In addition, quite apart from the continuing military expense, which was kept secret, the cost of organising and exploiting the empire was over a thousand million lire in hard currency each year, in other words more than one-tenth of the total foreign reserves available in 1938 and 1939.[88] Some Fascists continued to call it an investment which in the end would prove rewarding,[89] but this again was guesswork, and Felice Guarneri, who as minister of foreign trade was the one man who knew the whole truth, told Mussolini that the empire was swallowing Italy itself.[90] Guarneri recognised that Italy could not continue such a rate of expenditure for more than a few years. He knew, and was exasperated by the fact, that it was an essential dogma of fascism not to count the cost. Moreover he knew, because from January 1936 onward the responsibility was placed on his shoulders, that expenditure was disproportionately directed towards the grandiose and flamboyant, rather than to projects designed to produce practical results.

What may seem surprising is that so little of the money was allocated to the search for oil, even though petroleum products were the main weakness in the Italian economy, and though Libya, as soon as a free economy returned, was to prove one of the great oil-producing countries of the world. It is the more surprising in that Libya had been known since antiquity as a producer of hydrocarbons,[91] and yet only a few minor soundings were made there in twenty years of fascism. Probably there was a deliberate policy of waiting to see what other countries could find in Algeria and Egypt before diverting capital from less important but more showy things. Foreign oil companies were quite sure that oil could be found in Libya and were ready to contribute the techniques and equipment which Italy lacked, but even after it was known that this was a very promising area for exploration, the Fascists refused the offer; they had gone to immense trouble to build up the illusion of Italian "primacy" in science and technology,[92] and could not risk the loss of face in letting people think that only foreign companies could do the job.[93] They wanted the profits for themselves, but without the burden of investment.

Another problem was that fascism had set up a state hydrocarbons agency, the AGIP, with special privileges against competition from private companies. AGIP not only had found it far more profitable to develop the commercial side of its work, buying and distributing oil from Rumania, Iraq, and Russia rather than finding its own sources of supply, but had also played on feelings of national pride so as to obtain further laws making it unprofitable for foreign capital and foreign firms to search on a large scale in Italian-controlled territory.[94] AGIP each year imported increasing quantities of oil into Libya at considerable cost, and yet undertook only very small-scale drilling operations there.[95] Studies undertaken by fascism on the North African economy discussed at some length esparto grass and sponge fisheries, but hardly mentioned the possibility of oil, and AGIP carried out much bigger drilling programmes in Ethiopia than in Libya.[96]

The official story described Italy's colonial policy as "the most interesting spectacle of the century" and perhaps the most noble contribution which fascism had made to the world.[97] Its originality was said to lie in being based not on egoism or exploitation, as were those of Britain and France, but on social justice and sacrifices made by the mother country.[98] But, as so often, there were contradictions between what was said to impress the world at large and what was designed to bolster fascist morale. On the one hand it was stated that the native populations in Italian territory were not kept in a state of inferiority and separation as elsewhere,[99] and their interests were the prime concern of government; on the other hand Italy's "civilising mission" was to keep the natives in their place, helping them but not letting them govern themselves, not letting them suffer the disadvantages of too much higher education, but acting rather in the interests of the civilised world to keep the barbarians of the empire in subjection.[100]

Probably the most notable contribution of fascist Italy to colonialism was the theory and practice of apartheid. "It would be ridiculous and absurd", said Cipriani, "to push backward peoples along the road of progress", because Africans were incapable of understanding civilisations other than their own, and this was why fascism rejected the "squalid" and "wicked" idea of assimilation practised by France. According to a leading ministry official, Italians had "the biological qualifications of a dominant people and hence the right to colonise less evolved regions", whereas France, like Portugal and Holland, was creating a half-breed society which was morally wrong and socially inexpedient.[101] The British, too, were beginning in neighbouring colonies to favour the native peoples, but this could not succeed because it was a return to anachronistic liberal ideas of the nineteenth century which fascism had superseded. Italians, on the other hand, were bound to expand across central Africa simply because they had colonists and surplus manpower, while other countries had not.[102] Such views, though amply illogical and of already proven inaccuracy, passed without criticism in Italy. Not even the regime's intellectuals were permitted freedom to study colonialism objectively; paternalism and racialism were accepted as dogmas beyond serious discussion, and as a result the positive achievements of Italy in Africa, and the dedicated service of many Italians, turned to dust.

9

1938:
ANSCHLUSS AND MUNICH

Mussolini liked to create a sense of false security by repeating that fascism did not mean war,[1] and equally liked to create enthusiasm at home and panic abroad by stressing that the very essence of fascism was to be combative and martial. He relied on instinct and luck to keep a proper balance between these alternative poses. His more belligerent statements either were intended to frighten foreigners, or more usually were for domestic consumption to convince Italians that he was a superman who knew how to make himself and themselves properly respected. Occasionally if foreign newspapers quoted him in an interview as saying that he wanted peace, this particular reference might be cut out before the interview appeared in the papers at home.[2] There was of course another implicit contradiction here, and Mussolini himself as well as the commentators occasionally found difficulty in resolving it. To be on the safe side they used to make the unexceptionable assertion that he was ready to fight but would prefer peace. Sometimes, however, eloquence carried them too far and they wrote, not very plausibly, that he had done far more than the League of Nations or anyone else to save Europe from war.[3] Fascist journalists, whenever they were left without instructions, usually adopted the non-committal formula: anything others could do, Mussolini could do better, in war as well as peace.

Nevertheless the general tone which came to dominate the official press through 1938 was one which exalted military values. More and more, fascism spoke of militarising the nation so as to make other countries afraid of challenging Italy too directly.[4] Perhaps this was bluff, and if so one can see the reason for it; but it would have been misguided, for at the same time as it forced other countries into retaliatory action, it deceived the Italian people and the fascist leaders themselves into a dangerously belligerent intoxication. The party secretary, Achille Starace, used to say that war

to him "was like eating a plate of macaroni," [5] and this quintessen-
tially fascist remark was differentiated only in its vulgarity from
the advocacy of militant action by the conservative nationalists,
with their views about national greatness and the universally recognised qualities of Italian valour. The nationalists, some of
whom may not have been so keen on fascism as in the 1920s, continued to preach about the prodigious qualities of the Italian race,
the "ethical genius of their leader," and the spiritual primacy and
divine mission of Rome. [6] Federzoni, who later blamed fascism for
the belligerent policy which led their country to disaster, at the
time publicly praised it, and used his very considerable authority
as a senior statesman—he was president of the senate and president of the royal academy—to perpetuate the absurd and hazard-
ous legend that Italy's military machine was in a state of perfect
readiness for whatever might befall. [7]

A test of the country's military strength might have seemed
close at hand when Germany in March 1938 invaded and incorporated Austria, so effecting the *Anschluss* which Mussolini had
promised to prevent. The creation of a weak and independent
Austria in 1919 had been Italy's one substantial gain from the
First World War, and Mussolini well knew the danger of permit-
ting a powerful German state to reverse this gain and become
his immediate neighbour with a common frontier on the Brenner
Pass. In June 1934 he had stood out against an *Anschluss* by moving troops to Italy's northern frontier, and in 1935, as well as
continuing to subsidise the government of Vienna, he secretly
agreed with the French on joint military action if ever this were
necessary to support Austrian independence. His magazine *Gerarchia* in April 1935 protested that Italy would be "an insurmountable obstacle" to German ambitions in this vital area, and bravely
added that the German leaders were "terrified" of the Duce,
whose military strength they knew to be perfectly adequate for
the task of stopping them. [8]

Mussolini was badly informed about other countries, and underestimated the strength of anti-Italian and pro-nazi feelings in
Austria. [9] In 1936 and even in 1937 he was still calling it a vital
Italian national interest not to have the Germans on the Brenner, [10] but as we have seen, the Ethiopian war, by losing him
French support, propelled him into a major change of policy. It is
also likely that the sheer monetary cost of bolstering Austrian in-

dependence was proving too much for him.[11] He therefore secretly agreed with Germany that he would give up his protecting role at Vienna and, while trusting Hitler's promise that the Germans did not want a complete *Anschluss*, assured them in return that he would concentrate on southward expansion in the Mediterranean.[12] Nevertheless, because he did not want to confess openly that he was backing down from one of those "immovable" positions he was so fond of, he let Italians continue to think that he could and would stop a German invasion of Austria.

Although the Germans had undertaken to do nothing without reciprocal consultation, in March 1938, giving Mussolini only a few hours' notice, they marched into Austria and confronted him with an accomplished fact. His refusal on this occasion to rush troops to the Brenner Pass won him the permanent gratitude of Hitler, but the real test of his skill was in how far he managed to disguise from his own people the obvious fact that the most solid plank in Italian foreign policy had just been thrown away. In the Grand Council and parliament he courageously contradicted earlier statements and tried to maintain that the disappearance of Austria was in the interests of Italy,[13] and he even denied that he had ever either directly or indirectly undertaken to defend this buffer state.[14] One argument used was that, after the liquidation of Austria, no difference remained to divide Italy from Germany, and indeed that, since Austria was the sick man of Europe, her disappearance would be the best guarantee of peace.[15] Alternatively it was said that the *Anschluss* had been always inevitable and would help Germany and Italy to defend European civilisation against barbarism.[16]

Though in public he put on a bold front, in private Mussolini knew that Italy's most secure frontier was now entirely vulnerable. He was angry because any Italian able to read behind the headlines could observe his impotence and submissiveness to Germany; also because Germany now threatened Italian influence in the Balkans; also because the German-speaking population inside Italy's northern frontier might enter into Germany's irredentist ambitions. Only a few people were allowed to know of his displeasure, but in fact he came to the point of saying that, if the Nazis tried to push him any further, he would organise a world-wide coalition and crush Germany for the next two centuries.[17] As he was presumably reading some of the secret dispatches written by foreign ambassadors in Rome, he must have realised that many Italians were critical of him, and police reports would have confirmed that discontent was vocal and open.[18] An event that brought Hitler within a hundred kilometers of the Adriatic Sea revived the nationalists' fear of Germany, and the severance of many trade links with Austria was having a sudden and disastrous effect on commerce in Trieste and north-eastern Italy.[19]

Though events in Ethiopia and Spain had shaken many people's faith, there continued in Great Britain and America to be a fair amount of support for Mussolini. Even Churchill, up to at least October 1937, was prepared to accord him some admiration as an anti-bolshevik,[20] and many other politicians were ready to support a policy of appeasement if that would prevent an Italian alliance with Hitler. This was particularly true of British conservatives, and their help, especially that of Neville Chamberlain, the prime minister, was enlisted by Mussolini in forcing the resignation from the foreign secretaryship of Anthony Eden, who had been moving into the anti-fascist camp. Grandi, in London, by his own account had almost daily contacts for this purpose with Sir Joseph Ball, a conservative politician who was close to Chamberlain, and whose name was another of those omitted from the English-language edition of Ciano's papers,[21] but Grandi's report seems to be not entirely accurate.[22] One of the go-betweens through whom the Italians kept in touch with Chamberlain behind Eden's back was Guy Burgess who, unknown to either party, was photographing messages and passing them to the Soviet Union.[23]

With Eden out of the way, Mussolini was able to make another reinsurance agreement with Britain in April 1938. Like the agreement of January 1937 it had little practical effect, though Mussolini did seem to make an important concession when he agreed to guarantee the *status quo* in the Mediterranean. He knew that public opinion in Italy was not favourable to his axis with Germany,[24] and therefore was sensibly anxious to keep open an alternative line of possible action,[25] but on both sides this agreement was half-hearted. On the Italian side it was hard to revise the constantly reiterated concept of the British as enfeebled, anti-fascist, and anti-Italian. Many people in Britain, for their part, had been convinced by recent events that Mussolini was an enemy of peace.

Some of the conservatives agreed with Eden and now also Churchill that any policy of appeasement was both wrong and unworkable, while the leader of the parliamentary opposition, Clement Attlee, spoke contemptuously of this bankrupt and "tottering dictatorship" whose friendship was no longer worth purchasing.[26]

Though greatly impressed with Hitler's military machine, Mussolini had good reason to treat the Germans with caution. He had been deceived by them over Austria and made to look foolish. He knew that they were tapping the telephone of his ambassador in Berlin.[27] Clearly they were regarding Italian fascism with some condescension,[28] and were being obstinately unenthusiastic about some of the doctrines which Mussolini had called the greatest products of the century.[29] The Fascists were still hoping to persuade others that theirs was the true doctrine and nazism only a copy, even a bad copy, just as they also tried to insist that Hitler was a lesser man than Mussolini. Sometimes it seemed to them that fascism might be profoundly different from nazism, and they were astonished and annoyed when an exhibition of fascist art in Berlin flopped because some of their prized pictures were thought by the Nazis to be thoroughly decadent.[30] Catholicism was one of the biggest points of difference, because Mussolini ruled over a Catholic people and would not follow Hitler along the road to paganism. Italians also resented the growing disparity in strength between themselves and the Germans, and repeatedly but ineffectually demanded to be allowed a fully equal say in the affairs of the axis.[31]

On the German side, Hitler too had his doubts. Ideally his preference would have been for an alliance with Britain.[32] He had not wanted the Italians to emerge too successfully from the Ethiopian war, and was not entirely displeased at their military reverses in Spain.[33] The Nazis had still not forgotten the "treachery" of 1915–1918 when Italy deserted the Triple Alliance and fought against Germany; they disliked the brutal way in which the Fascists had persecuted the German-speaking population of northern Italy, as they also disliked Mussolini's attempt to defend Austrian independence between 1933 and 1937.[34]

Hitler's private conversation rarely touched on Italy or fascism. While he admired Mussolini and continued to do so, he was fairly sure that fascism would never make heroes out of Italians, and sometimes he spoke of them with an almost hostile scorn, as a people who never could become warlike and could not possibly understand the meaning of the contemporary revolution which he saw himself as leading. Though a temporary alliance with them might be useful, ultimately he felt that national socialism stood alone in possessing the real secret of the future, and some of his followers continued to wonder if Italy as an ally would not be more burden than help in the event of war. Some in Hitler's circle sneered at the pretentiousness of the Duce, for example when he posed on horseback brandishing the "sword of Islam." And sometimes there was ominous talk of the possibility of one day having to make war against fascist Italy.[35]

Nevertheless, in the absence of alternative friends, these two countries and regimes needed a closer relationship with each other. Even though sceptical of Italy's military capacity, Hitler saw the political and psychological value of a formal treaty between them. Mussolini for some time continued to resist any advances, in part because he had learned to distrust the Nazis, but more because he still retained enough independence of judgement to know that Italy would never carry much weight unless she kept at least some freedom of action; yet if faced with a choice he would rather be number two to Germany than number three to Britain and France.[36]

The possibility of a treaty was discussed in 1937, and again in May 1938 when Hitler visited Rome, but inconclusively. The two leaders on this latter occasion had only one serious talk together, when they spoke of war in general without agreeing when or against whom. Mussolini argued persuasively that the British were a declining people who could be relied on to give way to axis demands.[37] He also tried to impress his visitors with well-rehearsed military displays, remembering how he himself had been so tremendously impressed in Germany the previous year. When the flatterers said that the reception put on for the Germans was fully equal to that given to him at Berlin, he corrected this insufficient praise and insisted that he had done better.[38] He had, it is true, made a good impression personally on his guests, but it is unlikely that they did not notice the painted cardboard and imitation trees along the processional routes or the antiquated military equipment in the parades they had been obliged to watch.[39] The truth was that the German army leaders knew perfectly well that the Italian army was worth little,[40] but Italian support was needed for other reasons than military.[41]

Hitler's visit nonetheless brought the two countries much closer together. Whereas Mussolini had so far shown occasional impatience and even some hostility towards the Nazis, immediately afterwards he took steps to bring round to the cause of the axis such prominent Fascists as Balbo and Bottai, who had been less than wholeheartedly enthusiastic.[42] Batches of fascist leaders were sent to visit Germany, and the foreign office began to issue statements about the "affinity of destiny" between their respective nations,[43] while among the more extreme Fascists a much stronger note of pro-nazism reflected a substantial change in attitude. There was even praise of Himmler and of the SS as an elite force which Italy should copy to defend the integrity of the race. The First World War, which until now Italians had viewed as a great patriotic struggle against Germany in which hundreds of thousands of Italians were killed, had to be given a new character, and one Fascist shocked the orthodox by daring to say that it had been "undeservedly" lost by the Germans.[44]

Early in 1938 Mussolini was saying that war against Great Britain would be inevitable, and the idea was so intoxicating as to weaken his better judgement. He had been convinced, especially by the failure of the British to stop his troops going to Ethiopia, that their rearmament was pure spoof and they were not intending to fight. His deputy in the war office, General Alberto Pariani, perhaps trying to conceal many sins of omission, assured him that Italy would complete her current programme of rearmament by the spring of 1939 and be ready to attack not only Britain but France and Switzerland as well.[45] Mussolini acted as though he believed this foolish remark. He said he would not need any help from Germany for such a war except her benevolent neutrality. His plan was to take the British entirely by surprise and attack them in Egypt, because he had been assured that their soldiers would not fight in the African heat.[46] They were afraid of him, he said, and indeed their fear of war was greater than that of any other country in the world.[47] By mid-September 1938 he spoke as though the war might be imminent, and Pariani told him that it would be over quickly because of the large quantities of poison gas which Italy had in store.[48] Perhaps this is why he now talked of having absolute proof that he could "liquidate" France and Great Britain forever, and Ciano not only agreed with him, but spoke in much the same sense to the British ambassador himself.[49] Pariani meanwhile drew up with Marshal Balbo a plan for a quick occupation of Egypt, and tried not to make too obvious in his report that the necessary preparations would require another three or four years of munitions production.[50]

At the end of September the war clouds dissolved when the leading statesmen of Europe came together at Munich, but the price of peace was that the Germans annexed a large part of Czechoslovakia. This conference was a considerable success for Mussolini: it met only because the British appealed for him to use his influence with the Germans, and hence he seemed to hold the scales between peace and war. Since he disliked the Czechs as francophile democrats, he had secretly given Hitler advance notice that he would support the German claim,[51] and the latter then settled with him that at a certain point in the discussion Mussolini would relieve the deadlock by producing his prearranged compromise, and Hitler would accept it. Mussolini thus emerged from the conference with the reputation of being a more reasonable and benevolent dictator than Hitler, even a more effective politician, and so earned the momentary gratitude of immense numbers of people throughout Europe.[52]

Mussolini at Munich was noticeably ill at ease with having to submit publicly to discussion, because this was not at all the fascist style of procedure, yet he basked in the admiration bestowed on him by Hitler and returned home to meet the most rapturous applause of his whole lifetime. Some people thought that he was disconcerted by this applause, which was unusual in not being officially organised, and no doubt by temperament he would have preferred applause for his militant speeches rather than for his success as a peacemaker.[53] But the reception contributed to give him further illusions of grandeur. He later would recall with some complacency how Chamberlain and Daladier at Munich had licked his boots and how he had saved Europe from destruction.[54] Forgetting his earlier claims to have on several occasions altered the course of world history, he boasted to the fascist leaders that for the first time in seventy years Italy had taken a preponderant and decisive share in international politics.[55] One senior official in the Italian foreign office extolled it as a great moral victory and a perfect example of fascist political wisdom, though the same person in retrospect condemned it as a purely theatrical gesture in which Mussolini threw away Italian interests for the benefit of Germany alone.[56]

The immediate results of pacification at Munich were more than satisfactory. One was that Britain and France at last recognised the Italian annexation of Ethiopia. In a secret speech on 25 October to party leaders, Mussolini announced that the decision at Munich spelt the end of the League of Nations and the end of communism in Europe. Italy, he told them, had reached a situation of incomparable world prestige, and everyone else would now be obliged to accept that nothing could stop the march of fascism. Nevertheless, the cheering on his return had obviously been in favour of peace; in other words it confirmed that neither the axis nor his talk of war were popular, and foreign consuls in Italy confirmed this. The British ambassador thought that at last people might be beginning to lose their belief in Mussolini's infallibility; the Duce was turning Italy into a German satellite and this was resented; his laws against the Jews were "almost universally unpopular in Italy, even among most Fascists". According to the ambassador, when a news film about Munich was shown in Rome, pictures of Mussolini were greeted with no applause at all, though the king was hailed ecstatically: in a police state, perhaps the applause offered in the anonymous darkness of a cinema provided the best index of public opinion, and already some of the fascist leaders were worrying that passive resistance and even open disregard of the plethora of government regulations were growing.[57]

After meeting Daladier and Chamberlain, Mussolini came away reinforced in his view that there was little to fear from France or Britain as an enemy, and he tried also to convince himself that there was nothing to fear from Germany as a friend: Italy, he insisted, was now "the decisive factor" in Europe, and hence Hitler would have every interest in ensuring that Italian needs were satisfied.[58] At the end of October Joachim Ribbentrop, Hitler's foreign minister, arrived in Rome with another request for a formal treaty. Mussolini evaded this by saying that an alliance virtually existed already, while a formal engagement might forfeit the element of surprise which they would need for their war. But clearly he now saw the axis as not just for defence, and the Germans seized their chance, proffering the bait that it was Italy's turn next to extend her frontiers as compensation for what Hitler had already won in Austria and Czechoslovakia. So as to sound more impressive, the Germans added the blatant falsehood that they had two hundred divisions ready to fight and as many again in reserve. What they now wanted was a clear decision by Mussolini that he would work towards an aggressive war against France and Britain. In the meantime each party would agree what conquests in particular they had in mind.[59]

Though he liked public support, Mussolini was not much interested in following public opinion; the challenge he liked best was to manufacture it, as a true journalist knew how. In 1935 he had brilliantly created popular enthusiasm for the Ethiopian war, and he now felt equally sure that he could do the same for the axis by holding out to Italians a prospect of glory, riches, and power. In November Ciano brought parliament cheering to its feet by repeating, as a counter-falsehood, that fascism was absolutely ready for war.[60] *Critica Fascista*, a more measured periodical than most, exclaimed that Italians had no use for the normal canons of international law: they were "thirsty for expansion and grandeur" because they were "a people destined to command"; and Germany, far from being a menace, would guarantee them against being attacked in the rear while they proceeded to satisfy their ambitions in the Balkans and the Mediterranean.[61]

The director of *Critica Fascista*, Bottai, later looked back to these months as the deplorable period when Mussolini capitulated to the entirely non-Italian spirit of nazism.[62] But Bottai did not object very forcibly at the time. On the contrary, as minister of education he signed a cultural agreement with Germany in November. This was part of a set policy to diminish the teaching of English and French in Italian schools and instead to increase the very small amount of German. As a result of this agreement, a good deal of Italian money was diverted to boosting German culture and ideas.[63]

Meanwhile the regimentation of the nation continued along

what anyone could see were essentially nazi lines. The army, the militia, and then the police had to copy the German goose step, and Mussolini cannot have been taken seriously when he justified this by saying that the goose was a Roman bird which had once saved the city against invasion by the ancient Gauls.[64] Dazzled by the lively and multi-coloured uniforms used in Germany, in a deliberate spirit of emulation he indulged his own love of dressing up. At the end of 1938 he put the Italian police into something much more resplendent; and journalists too, just like the German journalists who had accompanied Hitler to Italy, were given an appropriate livery with a peaked cap. All civil functionaries of the state, including professors and schoolmasters, ended up with uniforms, and one minister recorded that he had to possess ten different ones for different seasons and occasions; another was said to have twenty-four. This was a way, declared Mussolini, of making Italians into a military people and was thus a logical conclusion of fascist doctrine. In consequence the armed forces had to go short. The fascist order of priorities, being based on the needs of propaganda, saw civilian uniforms as more important than military ones, just as there was more point in making miniature rifles and machine-guns for schoolchildren than real ones for the army, because it was easier (and perhaps as important) to give the illusion of militancy than to provide the real thing.[65]

So little interested was Mussolini in the wishes or the policy of other countries, that his ambassador in Paris was given no instructions at all and was obliged to avoid the French foreign minister as much as possible: only two telegrams were sent to him in four critical months of European history, one of which was about finding a French governess for Ciano's children.[66] The Fascists were humiliated to find many Italians, despite fifteen years of the regime, still reading so many French books. Nor could Bottai's friends understand the perpetuation of such "historical illusions" as that France had helped the unification of Italy in the nineteenth century.[67] There were elements of inferiority complex here, as also in Mussolini's anxiety lest Frenchmen were not taking him seriously. His orders were that the organs of propaganda should be turned peremptorily against France. When told that the French thought him to be their enemy he was pleased, since he liked being hated but could not bear being condescended to or merely tolerated.[68]

In November he suddenly decided to repatriate the best part of a million Italians who were working in France. Not only would these men be needed for the army in wartime, but their return would make a series of good newspaper headlines. Italian emigrants had similarly returned to help Italy fight the First World War, and it would surely be embarrassing if fascism had a lesser call on their loyalty than the much-despised liberal Italy of 1915–18.[69] Some people in the foreign office chafed at having to take responsibility for such an absurd decision, especially as to bring back so many workers would contradict the fascist thesis that domestic overpopulation made colonial expansion vital for the country. The bureaucratic machinery for this huge transmigration was set up at considerable cost, but a year later only 50,000 emigrants had returned, many of whom were unable to find the houses and jobs which they had been promised. Mussolini's interest, once again, was more in the psychological value of the announcement than in its practical execution.[70]

Fascist foreign policy now concentrated on deliberately creating "an insurmountable abyss between Italy and France", and on 5 November the press was ordered to step up agitation favouring Italy's acquisition of Nice and French Tunisia. Several days later, when a new French ambassador arrived in Rome, Mussolini was annoyed that some Italians at the railway station by their spontaneous applause took the edge off the cool reception which had been ordered. He told Ciano not only that he would make the ambassador's life difficult but that he was now determined to work towards the annexation of Corsica.[71] When Ciano was addressing parliament on 30 November, some of the deputies stood up and shouted "Tunisia, Corsica, Savoy, Nice". The shouts, which of course were said to be spontaneous, had been organised by the Fascist Party to annoy the French.[72]

If Mussolini was subsequently annoyed about this parliamentary demonstration, it was when he realised his mistake: because such behaviour not only tied him more closely to Germany, but united France from left to right against Italian pretensions and frivolously negated a lot of expensive propaganda.[73] However, he could hardly have expected anything else. He knew perfectly well that the party of Corsican independence, which for some years he had tried to create, was a fiction.[74] Possibly in his post-Munich euphoria he had momentarily deluded himself that French morale would crack under fascist combativeness, and it was the more upsetting to find that his intended victims took this parliamentary outburst not too solemnly. *Candide* wrote that, if Italy claimed Nice and Corsica, the French had an equally valid historical title to Sicily, and outside the Italian embassy in Paris there were cries of "we demand Venice for our honeymoon couples". When Paris newspapers retaliated further by publishing unsavoury details about Mussolini's private life which Italians were not meant to know, only with difficulty could he conceal his chagrin.[75]

Among those who observed him closely, Mussolini could seem to be losing his political touch.[76] He had been given a splendid chance to capitalise on the reputation he had made at Munich and to continue holding the scales between the rival power-groups of Europe. Instead he was propelling himself towards a position where he would have no choice but to serve Hitler. After trying hard to burn his bridges with the west, he continued to provoke the French into solidarity against him, forcing the British to rearm and move away from appeasement; so doing, he deprived himself of the cheaper and more effective alternative of diplomatic manoeuvering. Having made public territorial claims on France, fascism would never again be able to accept friendly relations with Paris until the French salved Mussolini's dignity and made concessions, even though his lack of diplomatic finesse made such concessions quite excessively hard to obtain.[77] In earlier days he had tried to keep open a degree of choice in foreign policy, but now he was acting as though determined to cut off any chance of retreat.

IO

GROWING TENSION

Neville Chamberlain, who had no instinct for and little knowledge of foreign affairs, continued to hope for a while that the interests of Italy and Germany were so divergent that Mussolini could be appeased by kindness. He did not sufficiently appreciate that the Duce was encouraged by appeasement to assume that the west, perhaps deluded by his martial attitudinising, was in a state of panic and could be pushed even further. Left-wing opinion in Britain, on the contrary, was becoming even more stridently hostile to fascism, and Churchill was coming to think that, though France and Britain evidently had to deal with a dangerous and unpredictable man, there might almost be some advantage in having Italy as an enemy because she would be a leaden weight on the German economy.[1] Due note was taken in London of Mussolini's remarks about preferring to live one day as a lion that a hundred years as a sheep, but according to Lord Perth, the British ambassador in Rome, Italians "were becoming tired of perpetual roaring and would prefer to graze in peace".[2]

Ambassador Grandi in London was either unable, or did not dare, to keep Mussolini properly informed. Not only were his sources of information limited by his social tastes but he was in a false position, because in London he liked acting as an anglophile, while at Rome he thought it expedient to be more germanophile and to say that the British would not be a serious obstacle to fascism. No doubt he knew that he was being spied on by the fascist police;[3] fearful for his position in the hierarchy, he went out of his way to make the kind of comments which he thought Mussolini wanted. For instance he had once reported that forty million Englishmen were enraptured by Mussolini, whom the British ruling classes thought to be "the greatest statesman the world has ever known".[4] He gave no indication of knowing that the British prime minister, about the most pro-Mussolini of anyone in Lon-

don, did not care a rap for the Duce except to stop him from allying with Hitler.[5] Most British politicians, Grandi wrote, were
inept and corrupt.[6] He was glad to imagine that he had deceived
them into believing in his friendship, whereas his own preference
was for an alliance with Hitler,[7] and he dutifully obeyed Mussolini when instructed to make a pro-nazi speech in London.[8] In
private he went further and insisted that, since the British army
presented no danger, fascism could safely contemplate war against
France.[9]

Early in January 1939, in view of the European war which now
seemed to him inevitable, Mussolini made up his mind to sign a
military pact with Germany.[10] Before telling Hitler, however, he
invited Neville Chamberlain to visit Rome, taking care to make it
clear in public that the British were inviting themselves: he valued
the chance to remind Italians that, though he himself went abroad
only to Germany, British ministers were begging to come and
see him for the eleventh time since 1922.[11] When Chamberlain arrived on 11 January, some observers thought that Mussolini
showed possibly more attention to him than he had to Hitler two
years earlier.[12] Probably he hoped to give his guest the impression
that Great Britain could only lose if she tried to resist the armed
might of fascism. But on the contrary the British took home the
conviction that the military façade of fascism was only skin-deep
and that Italian public opinion would be against war. Appeasement was obviously less attractive to Chamberlain once he
had seen fascism at close quarters, and on his return to London he
decided to open secret discussions with the French on the hypothesis of a possible war against Germany and Italy.[13]

Mussolini claimed to despise the British premier as a man of
peace and compromise, and their encounter in Rome reinforced
his neurotic assumption that anyone who carried an umbrella
must by definition be feeble and unmilitary.[14] He was all the
more confident that democracy must be an ineffective method of
government if it produced such a leader. Contempt for democracy
and for both Roosevelt and Chamberlain contributed to make fascism underestimate the British and Americans as a factor in world
politics,[15] and this was one more reason for seeking an alliance
with Hitler. But for the moment he made no public statement of
policy. Indeed there were some signs that the newspapers in Italy

were being left without guidance or direction, almost as though Mussolini did not know his own mind,[16] and of course this was much more noticeable and embarrassing than it would have been in a democracy.

The one constant theme from which Mussolini could no longer back down was his animus against France. Corsica, Nice, and Tunisia were more obvious and perhaps easier targets than Malta or British Somaliland. Since the assumption was that fascism had nothing now to fear from an Anglo-French alliance, the army was casually instructed to exclude Britain from their war hypotheses, and at the same time public opinion was told that hostilities against France were inevitable and French defeat certain.[17] Irritated by what he took to be the French pretence to intellectulal superiority, he explained in private that the French respected only those who had beaten them in war, and his intention was to beat them and then take his revenge by wholesale destruction and levelling some of their cities to the ground: [18] the prospect evidently gave him satisfaction. When books critical of France did not sell fast enough, the propaganda ministry was told to buy up all available copies and distribute them free, while other pro-German books had to be made even more pro-German before the censor would approve them.[19]

In February 1939 Mussolini read to the Grand Council a memorandum which he had written so that it would remain in the archives as proof of his vision for the future, and as he had never before given them a document on foreign affairs, it was clearly a major statement of policy. The main message was that they were prisoners in the Mediterranean, and Corsica was one bar of the prison, as it was also a pistol pointing at the heart of Italy. Britain was practising a policy of encirclement, and along with Greece and Egypt should be deemed an unfriendly state blocking Italian expansion. While Germany checked any potential enemies in Europe, Italy should prepare to "march to the ocean" and assert her authority at Gibraltar and Suez. He would still like to wait several years before starting a war, because he needed more rearmament; in particular he wanted twice as many submarines as he had and a black army in Ethiopia, but was confident of one day acquiring an imperial outpost on the Atlantic, and this could be done only with German assistance.[20]

Ciano had been told about his document the previous day but was not consulted about it. This was not unusual. Indeed, why Ciano was retained as foreign minister is hard to say, except that he was the Duce's son-in-law and, like Starace in domestic policy, he did what he was told. Ciano did not allow other ministers to know much about foreign policy, and he himself had only a marginal influence in formulating it,[21] nor was he allowed by Mussolini to know some of the vital facts, for instance about Italy's military capacity or lack of it. The main function of this young, inexperienced, and irresponsible minister was to protect Mussolini from having to see foreign ambassadors, and to execute any policy the Duce might choose. Whatever he said later, at the time Ciano wanted close ties with nazi Germany and war against England, though he was quite aware of what was at risk. Against anyone reluctant to ally with Germany he could call for disciplinary action.[22] No doubt he lacked the inclination or the judgement to be entirely consistent in his political views, but he did not intend to question Mussolini's certainty that the Germans would win the next European war, and was determined to be with them on the victorious side.[23]

Ciano had a better education than most other fascist leaders, and was more at home than they were in Roman society and the world of diplomacy. He was something of a playboy, and at least one ambassador found him hard to take seriously, for he did not seem able to concentrate his attention for more than a few moments.[24] Others considered him an amusing conversationalist when he was really trying, but for most diplomats he was essentially a lightweight. In fascist circles, though he was envied as the Duce's son-in-law, two years in office had not made him more admired or liked. He was not a hard worker. His juniors appreciated his easy informality, but not the fact that he jibbed at long memoranda and was sometimes reluctant to receive foreign representatives. To some people it seemed that his appointment was putting an end to a long tradition, an end to that careful sense of responsibility which in the past had given such a high reputation to Italian diplomacy.[25]

Other minor criticisms were made of Galeazzo Ciano's lapses of taste and his bad manners, and it was in character when at the coronation of Pius XII he scandalised onlookers by strutting down the nave of St. Peter's giving the fascist salute and waving to the crowds on each side.[26] His idiosyncratic behaviour made Hitler refer to him as "that disgusting boy". But the Germans were chiefly alarmed by his lack of discretion,[27] and his notorious inability to keep secrets was one reason why they seldom let Mussolini into their confidence. One of Ciano's girl friends used to pass important facts immediately to the British ambassador,[28] and his favourite haunt, the Roman golf club, was well known to journalists as about the best place in Europe for leaks of information. His other weakness, as his friends agree, was exhibitionism and vanity. Since he loved public attention he used to travel with a whole court of photographers and journalists, and because he could not abide contradiction he preferred to be surrounded by second-rate people who would at least laugh at his jokes and flatter his self-esteem.[29]

Though he sometimes deluded himself to the contrary,[30] Ciano was altogether less subtle and less clever than Mussolini, and yet by keeping more contact with the outside world was on some occasions able to show more moderaton and common sense. He was not someone who would stand up strongly for his own opinion in the inner councils of fascism, though he compensated by hectoring foreign diplomats from smaller countries whom he thought he could bully.[31] To the Duce his outward demeanour was utterly deferential and obedient as to a clearly superior being, copying the latter's deportment and mannerisms, even his handwriting.[32] Ciano's private diary, in which some entries were evidently written for others and especially Mussolini to see, mentioned praise from his father-in-law as the greatest satisfaction in his life, and even the sound of the Duce's voice on the radio could move him to tears. Mussolini, though to all appearances so self-confident, needed this degree of flattery, and of course it contributed disastrously to insulate him from the truth.[33]

Ciano would have liked to be designated the heir apparent to Mussolini as his own father, Admiral Costanzo Ciano, had been before him, but when he asked the Duce who would succeed to the leadership of fascism, the oracular reply was, "Let the person take power who knows how to dominate men and things".[34] Finding himself allowed so little real authority, he set about getting it by stealth, building up a clientele in the fascist leadership, intervening in appointments, and insisting that the chief of police and other key officials should visit him regularly. At certain moments, especially when Mussolini was ill or more than usually unsure of himself, Ciano had real power and, if he had possessed stronger personality or convictions, might have wielded an important influence on events. On one occasion it seems to have crossed his mind to have Mussolini poisoned,[35] but only the thought, not the deed, was in character. As time went by, he was treated more distantly by his father-in-law; instead of being received every day, he was asked more rarely to the Villa Torlonia and was accorded something of the same remoteness and indifference as all the other ministers.[36] The Duce, as well as raising the possibility that Ciano had Jewish blood, used to criticise his falsetto voice and above all the fact that, by bad behaviour in public and boastful habits, he might be making the regime look ridiculous, which was something Mussolini rightly feared above everything.[37]

Hitler's view of Ciano was contemptuous and this was a serious weakness in the axis, but he had a genuine liking and some admiration for Mussolini, which was reinforced by a deep gratitude for the way the Italians had let him invade Austria and Czechoslovakia without asking for anything in return. Though he sometimes laughed at the Duce,[38] the Führer looked upon this man alone as an equal and sometimes spoke of him, whether seriously or not, as a genius.[39] Other Germans thought that no one else had such a capacity to influence Hitler, and although this exaggerated trust proved to be a mistake, even in defeat Mussolini remained the Führer's friend, the only man in his whole lifetime to whom it could be said that the German leader had behaved with trust, more or less honesty, and some magnanimity.[40] By exercising his powers of fascination, Hitler drew Mussolini under a spell until fascist Italy became little more than a tool in German hands, possessed of no more than a marginal capacity for moderating nazi ambitions.[41]

Mussolini, on the other hand, perhaps because he knew his opposite number mainly through staged monologues, thought of himself as the more intelligent as well as the senior of the two.[42] It perhaps never occurred to him that Hitler might be duping him by flattery into dropping his guard. The Duce claimed to admire

Churchill and even Stalin more than he admired Hitler, and used
to say that the Führer was too schematic for a real statesman, too
anxious to reduce complicated problems to something simple. He
therefore would have liked the politics of the axis to be run from
Rome, or at least said so in retrospect.[43] According to Grandi his
desire to belittle Hitler became almost a mania, and he would say
"the fellow has no intelligence, no dynamism, no political flair",
or else sometimes wrote him off as a dangerous fool and "a horrible sexual degenerate".[44]

On the half dozen occasions when these two national leaders
met each other, the world thought that they were taking major
decisions, but it is doubtful how much real communication there
was or how much they understood each other. Mussolini took
trouble over foreign languages, because he needed to read foreign
newspapers and liked to impress visitors—even Gandhi was given
a few hurriedly learned words in some Indian tongue.[45] To the
very end of his life he took German lessons, and let it be known
that he was studying for two hours a day. He spoke the language
slowly but not badly, though it is probable that he understood
little when Hitler was in full flood, and yet was too proud to
admit that he needed a translator. Once again the pose was more
important than the reality.[46]

It is to Mussolini's credit that, when the four most prominent
statesmen of western Europe met at Munich in September 1938,
he alone spoke another language than his own, and he could
address some words to each of the other three in their own
tongues. His French was good if not always correct, and he even
brought into written Italian a number of Gallicisms which,
though startling to the purists, had perforce to be accepted henceforward as proper usage by the dictionaries.[47] He let it be understood that he not only spoke Spanish but knew Latin and Greek, a
minor falsehood which his children found diverting.[48] His English
was also said by the flatterers to be moderately good,[49] though
others found it unintelligible and did not like to tell him so.[50]

But though he studied the languages of other countries, he
never spent enough time studying their basic interests, and rarely

showed that he knew this might be a mistake. In earlier days Italian ambassadors had often been recalled from foreign capitals to advise in Rome, but in the 1930s this practice lapsed. The more astute and ambitious diplomats realised that it was less important to report objectively on foreign countries than to concentrate on the kind of information, true or false, which would be acceptable. He himself knew that this was happening, but scarcely tried very hard to stop it, and in any case he came to think that journalists were better providers of the kind of information about other countries that he needed.[51] Italian diplomacy thus had to act on an insufficient basis of accurate knowledge, especially as Ciano copied Mussolini and sometimes refused to read dispatches. If they wanted to influence policy, ambassadors learned to use more roundabout methods. One of them described how he used to wrap information in "homeopathic pills, or make ironic comments on the facts he wished to convey, or even pretend to deny them, as that might be the best way of bringing them to the attention of the minister".[52]

One or two of the older ambassadors were courageous enough to stick by their own opinions, but independence of mind was discouraged and after 1937 its open expression had become very difficult indeed. On leaving for their foreign postings they were sometimes not even given a general directive about policy. If Mussolini ever saw them when they returned on leave, it was his habit not to ask for information about their accredited countries but to give it, because he thought it more important to impress them with what he had learned through journalists and police spies. Raffaele Guariglia in France and Augusto Rosso in Russia were kept in the dark for months or even years at a time, and Rosso privately arranged with Dino Alfieri at Berlin to exchange information so as to make up in part for this crippling deficiency. Count Luigi Vannutelli in Brussels said that he had no idea at all from official communications whether he was meant to be conciliatory or the reverse, and did not dare to ask.[53]

In London, Grandi knew enough about fascism to behave with adequate circumspection. He used to write long though not very helpful reports, and seemed to realise that his future career depended on not giving offence. On one occasion he showed a momentary independence and an unfascist sense of humour when, on learning that Mussolini had sent private agents to talk secretly to the British government, he informed the British police that they were impostors who should be arrested. But at really critical moments he preferred to keep silent so as not to compromise himself, and sometimes thought it wiser to ask the British foreign office rather than Rome for information about Italian policy.[54] His successor in London, Giuseppe Bastianini, warned Ciano that British military preparations were more serious than Grandi had evidently allowed people to think, but realised that his reports were not read, and when he returned home from London he found that no one in Rome showed much interest in his views.[55]

Even in the crucial post of Berlin the Italian ambassador knew that the reports he made to Rome were unread or at least unbelieved.[56] Ciano knew nothing of Germany, and neither he nor the successive Italian ambassadors in Berlin could speak German. He and they had to converse with Ribbentrop in English,[57] and lack of communication was accentuated by the fact that the two foreign ministers strongly disliked each other. Ciano flattered himself on being much cleverer than Ribbentrop and able to dupe the Germans almost at will. In the same vein he used to boast that he had made history by standing up to Hitler.[58] But it was all fantasy. Both Mussolini and Ciano, by their overconfidence and vanity, refused to accept information and advice which would have greatly assisted the conduct of foreign policy, and the Italian intelligence services were too ill-equipped to fill the gap.

In the absence of adequate intelligence it came as an unpleasant surprise when, in March 1939, a messenger arrived to say that Hitler was invading Czechoslovakia, thus upsetting the balance of power in Europe just as he had done earlier with the *Anschluss* and again at Munich. Mussolini was disconcerted to be treated just like anyone else and made to look foolish by being caught unawares. Moreover the invasion was in patent defiance of his arbitration at Munich, and was proof that the Germans had a strategy of their own which they were keeping secret from him. Since he had assured other Fascists that Hitler would not act in this way, he was personally affronted by this blatant proof that he was as much in the dark as everyone else.[59] His colleagues had never seen him so depressed, and they too were inclined to regard it as the saddest day for Italy in a hundred years.[60] All they could do in protest was to complain to the Germans that "it had been Mussolini's turn to move, but he had been thrust aside". For one moment Mussolini talked of invading Croatia to redress the balance, and he recklessly added that if the Germans tried to stop him he would fight them too.[61]

When another meeting of the Grand Council took place on 21 March, members were left to guess even so basic a matter as whether Italy was yet an ally of Germany, but some of the members must already have made up their own minds: at all events a careful account of this meeting, evidently written by one member, was in the hands of the German ambassador within hours. Mussolini spoke to say that they now had no option but to stand by the axis because Germany was so much stronger than other countries, and there must be no further question of negotiating with the democracies to see if a better offer was forthcoming. Bottai found this statement entirely contradictory, but of course everyone at once accepted it, including Bottai, and including also the foreign minister, who two days earlier had been saying that they should desert Germany and join the western democracies. Grandi was another who spoke in favour of siding with Germany against the British. Balbo was brave enough to expostulate that "licking Hitler's boots" was a contemptible attitude, but his was a lone voice, and the others preferred to take refuge in the comfortable doctrine that Mussolini alone had all the information and must know best.[62]

A few days later the Duce made a defiant public speech calling for more guns and aeroplanes "by whatever means and whatever it costs", even if it meant "bringing all civilised life to a halt." This much applauded speech spelt out for Italians in general that the Mediterranean was their vital space to be claimed by right of arms since "my will knows no obstacles".[63] Some years later Mussolini was able to confess that on occasion he himself had suffered from the national vice of rhetoric when caught by the glamorous vision of military victory,[64] but at the time he was the captive of his myth. After any such pronouncement he was enslaved by his own words, especially when whatever he said was multiplied by the newspapers. Bottai's magazine stood with all the others in proclaiming the certainty of war, the necessity of the German alliance, and the inevitable defeat of France and Britain.[65] Industrialists, Alberto Pirelli for example, publicly supported the new policy,[66] and a whole chorus of demands went up for victory, for conquest, for recognition of Italian leadership in the world.[67]

What the Duce was talking about, and perhaps genuinely intended, was a war against France, a war which he thought he could win on his own provided that the Germans helped him with munitions. Hitler, on the other hand, tried to restrain him on the pretence that Germany was not ready. The Italians had rather been assuming that, since Britain would be unprepared until 1941, war should be precipitated quickly before the British and Americans were ready, but of course they gave way to German advice.[68] In private the Italian military leaders were by no means so confident about such a war as Mussolini was, and perhaps his belligerent words had just been another attempt to impress either the Germans or the fascist leaders.[69] The Germans, however, were not impressed and were determined to ensure that Mussolini, while remaining tied to the axis, did not start some foolhardy war on his own which might upset the timing and the objectives of the quite different policy which Hitler now had in mind.[70]

For some months the Italians had been asking for military discussions with Germany. Hitler reluctantly agreed to these, though he was determined to avoid any commitment or even any frank discussion. What he wanted from his partners was in the first place a promise to keep the Balkans a neutral area for the supply of raw materials, and in the second place that they would cooperate with German plans by preparing a diversionary attack in North Africa, or against Corsica, or possibly to eliminate the British base at Gibraltar.[71] He was, however, determined not to let them know his own operational plans: detailed information was to be given to them only if it seemed really important for him to learn in exchange what they intended. Already the Germans knew, presumably through whomever was their confidential agent in the Grand Council, that Mussolini was worried about domestic opposition after he had let Austria and Czechoslovakia be invaded without getting compensation; they also could presume that he would be alarmed that the rapid increase in German power was dangerously altering the balance of forces to Italy's possible disadvantage.[72] So some pacificatory move in Italy's direction was required.

At last on 4 April military discussions began at Innsbruck between Generals Keitel and Pariani, although Mussolini was so anxious to keep all the threads of policy in his own hand that Badoglio, the chief of general staff, was not even allowed to know that the talks were taking place. Pariani explained to Keitel his idea of a war against the French, a war which he hoped would be a straight duel and preferably confined to Africa. Keitel replied by pointing out that a war against France was bound to implicate England, which in turn would involve Germany and hence would lose the element of initiative and surprise on which Hitler was counting. As both parties were so cagey, there was no possibility of their agreeing at this meeting to make joint plans for the war, but they reached a general agreement to put off hostilities for several years.[73] The degree of mutual mistrust is indicated by the fact that the Italians kept entirely quiet about the fact that, even while these discussions were proceeding, their troops were moving to attack Albania: either they feared that the Germans might try to stop them, or else it was intended to make the point that Italy could also have her own secret plans. The supposition must be that Mussolini wanted these military talks only in the hope that, without giving away his own weakness, he could learn enough of German intentions to decide whether or not to commit himself to a military alliance.

II

THE INVASION OF ALBANIA

By the late 1930s, the Fascists had come to regard Albania as virtually an Italian protectorate—what Mussolini called "an Italian province without a prefect".[1] He had worked hard at excluding other countries from the Albanian economy, and tried to claim for Italy an exclusive right to all mining operations there, as also over fishing in the Adriatic and a monopoly of banking. When Germany offered to help Albania with mining finance, in particular with sinking the oil wells which Italy needed so badly, she was warned off. Italy made continual "loans" to Albania with no suggestion of repayment, and indeed without Italian money King Zog could not possibly have paid his civil service or army. The officers in the Albanian army were mostly Italians, and other Italians were highly placed elsewhere in the government.[2]

King Zog, though kept in power by Italian money, would have liked to encourage other countries to invest in Albania and reduce the economic dependence on Italy, but only the Japanese were determined enough. Italian journalists visiting Albania were surprised to discover that Japan could undercut a great variety of Italian goods, and only about a third of Albanian imports in 1938 came from Italy, yet Mussolini was having to use Italy's scarce foreign currency to keep the Albanian economy from collapse and to make these purchases from Japan possible.[3] Though Albania had an entirely agrarian economy, not enough cereals could be produced for its own consumption, so Italy had to send food to keep the population alive.[4] All this made Albania an economic adjunct of Italy, but only as a burden on the Italian exchequer and with few of the rewards which fascism had hoped for.

In the spring of 1938 Ciano secretly proposed a new policy, namely that as compensation for letting Hitler take Austria, Italy should annex Albania and turn the Adriatic into what would be almost an inland Italian sea. Mussolini eagerly agreed and casually remarked that he would fight for it if necessary. The date was fixed for a year ahead, in May 1938.[5] When he visited Albania for Zog's wedding in April 1938, Ciano studied the situation and wrote a long report explaining that this potentially rich country could take at least another two million inhabitants and needed only Italian settlers and Italian intelligence to make it flourish. The Italian diplomatic representative in Albania, Francesco Jacomoni, then got secretly in touch with various brigand bands in the mountains, and a plan was agreed upon by which these men would descend into the towns at a given signal and provoke a crisis from which they should be able to obtain a popular manifestation in favour of union with Italy. Mussolini accepted this plan in full knowledge that it might mean "setting fire to the powder keg of Europe".[6] He simply took Ciano's word for the assumption that Albania could become a profitable complement to the Italian economy. So far, in their years as the protecting power, the Fascists had in fact done nothing to make a geological survey of the country, nor had they even taken the basic step of building a proper road between its two main towns; the economic information on which policy was now decided had to be taken on trust.[7]

In June 1938 Ciano imparted his project to Volpi, the president of the Italian confederation of industrialists, who had large economic interests in the Balkans. Volpi was delighted and hoped that Italy would invade Turkey as well as Albania. The army staff were also informed so that they could prepare a plan of attack.[8] Apparently the Germans had learned of the scheme before the Italian army did, and so Ciano's diplomatic denials were not treated seriously.[9] The Grand Council was not informed until October. By that time a number of Albanians, observing how easy it was to tap fascist funds for themselves and their families, were encouraging the Italian government with further inventions about the economic resources which their country was supposed to possess. Ciano had also improved his project by finding an assassin who, for 10 million lire, was ready to kill Zog and thus make certain of starting a revolution.[10] Another possibility was to involve Hungary by offering her an outlet on the Aegean at the expense of Greece, and this appealed to Mussolini because, as he saw it, the larger the international complications the easier an invasion might be. Alternatively, perhaps Salonika could be offered to the Yugoslavs if only they would agree to distract Zog's attention at the crucial moment.[11] The existing strongman in Yugoslavia, Stoja-dinovich, was being backed by Rome in the hope that he would set up a fascist dictatorship in Belgrade, and his cooperation might therefore be especially welcome.

A more detailed plan was ready by the first week of February 1939, that is to say before the Germans invaded Czechoslovakia. There was need for hurry, because some former exiles had been allowed to return to Albania, and they might in time be able to organise a patriotic movement of resistance against any Italian coup. Also Jacomoni found it expensive to continue paying the armed gangs and the local politicians in Tirana, who of course increased their demands as the time for action came near.[12] Though he undertook to ensure that the revolution would look like a spontaneous movement of the Albanian people, Jacomoni begged that Italian soldiers be ready to land quickly and with fur-ther lavish funds to pay the revolutionaries. King Zog, too, was allocated an extra grant to give him a sense of false security.[13] No doubts were likely to be expressed by anyone in Italy, except that King Victor Emanuel, perhaps because he disliked the deposition of another king, made one of his rare political interventions by raising the obvious point that Mussolini was undertaking great risks for an almost negligible gain.[14] Opposition could of course be expected elsewhere in Europe because Albania was a member of the League of Nations, and also because Mussolini had publicly undertaken to avoid territorial changes anywhere round the Medi-terranean. But Ciano gave an assurance that the independence and integrity of Albania would not be touched. Italy's policy in this area, he said, was just to guarantee law and order at Tirana.[15]

The invasion was timed for the first week of April so as to coin-cide with the birth of a baby to the Queen of Albania, and Good Friday was chosen as a date when such action would not be ex-pected. But in the middle of March Mussolini was shaken by news of Hitler's move into Czechoslovakia, particularly since he feared that the Germans might be preparing to advance south-wards towards Croatia with the possible objective of obtaining a port in the Adriatic. That would have ruined plans for bringing the Balkans under Italian control. Mussolini's first reaction was to halt the attack on Albania so as to tackle this more urgent threat. Ciano's view, on the other hand, was that they all the more needed compensation for Germany's successive annexations, and to conquer Albania would raise morale and popular confidence inside Italy. For a few days Mussolini dithered, but on 24 March Jacomoni was ordered to go to King Zog and demand a formal Italian protectorship over Albania, explaining that the advance of Germany into the Balkans made this absolutely necessary.[16]

The chief of general staff was informed on 29 March that Albania was to be invaded: it was too late for him to object, though he was far from happy about what he heard. The operational commander, General Guzzoni, was told only on the evening of 31 March, and so much of a novice was Mussolini about the planning of military operations that the air force received their orders only two days before the invasion.[17] The official histories were later to claim that the expedition was a splendid example of fascist organisation, and this piece of counterfeit was afterwards used to prevent an enquiry which might have shown up some of the radical flaws in the regime. But General Guzzoni had to mobilise his expeditionary corps during a hurried railway journey down to Brindisi, and conscripts were given only a few hours' notice, nor was any time allowed for instruction in the weapons which many of them had never seen before. Some of them had to join motorcycle companies when they had never ridden a motorcycle, others were allocated to signals' units when they did not even know the Morse code. Even though Italian contractors had built the port installations where most of the troops were to land, the naval commanders had apparently not been told that the main harbours could not take deep-water ships. Radio communications were so defective that the senior air force officer had to fly to and fro between Albania and Italy carrying messages to explain what was going wrong. He reported with astonishment on the lack of unity of command, and added his view that, if only the authorities had remembered to use air reconnaissance first, not a single shot need have been fired because they would have seen that there was no opposition at all.[18]

As it was, the lack of preparation and training, the excessive hurry, and the absence of coordination between army, navy, and air force all showed up the clumsy mismanagement which so often characterised fascism. Jacomoni's armed bands, which by his own account he had paid handsomely, might as well not have existed and perhaps did not. Guzzoni, by the hesitancy of his advance against no opposition, gave critics the chance to assert that the Albanians were bravely resisting the forces of fascism, and this weakened the Italian story about the local population welcoming delivery from Zog's tyranny. Ciano's chief assistant, Filippo Anfuso, after describing how the foreign minister flew briefly over the battleground with other ministry officials to qualify for his campaign medal, commented that "if only the Albanians had possessed a well-armed fire brigade, they could have driven us back into the Adriatic".[19]

So many people were aware of the bungling that Mussolini had to make a frank statement to the fascist leadership, explaining that the expedition had nearly failed because the organisation and the people at his disposal were so defective.[20] It probably would not have occurred to him that he might himself have been at fault, but in view of later events it is important at least to establish that he no longer can have had much doubt that the military machine in his hands was a feeble one. It is possible that many of fascism's senior officials only now realised the inefficiency of the system. They had suspected bluff, but had not realised how much there was, and it was a shock to the foreign office that the army could with difficulty mobilise only a few thousand men despite all the boasting about a military and militarist nation. Ciano commented in his diary: "There has been a lot of cheating in the sphere of military supplies, and it is a tragic mistake, because it has deceived even the Duce. General Valle says that there are 3,006 effective aircraft, whereas the naval information service reduces this figure to 982. The difference is too large. I have told these facts to Mussolini, because on such a matter, however much it pains him, one must be absolutely frank to prevent this kind of thing being repeated." [21]

Meanwhile the propaganda machine went into action to cover up what had happened. Respectable historians, who after the fall of Mussolini told a very different story, at the time applauded it as a splendid act of aggression.[22] According to official accounts it would remain in history as a classic masterpiece of efficiency, organisation, power, courage, and political sense. Colonel Emilio Canevari, perhaps the best known of the military commentators, enthusiastically reported the brilliant attack by non-existent motorised formations "in close contact with the air force", and explained that all observers had been impressed by the clockwork precision of a carefully studied and brilliantly executed attack; apparently nothing was improvised, everything had been prepared minutely, and under Mussolini's personal direction the three armed forces had operated as a perfectly coordinated unit.[23]

Put this way, the news was good for morale, which was one of the chief objectives of the operation, and was particularly welcomed by the operational commanders who might have feared courts martial and were delighted to find that fascism expected no better of them. Grandi wrote to Mussolini hailing him as a second Augustus, as a national hero who, without faltering, had started Italy on a path of attack which would lead them through the Balkans to the conquest of the Orient. According to Grandi the Duce had incidentally defeated Britain as well, because Greece could henceforth be occupied by Italy at will, and so he had established a "complete dominion over the eastern Mediterranean".[24] This was lethal adulation to such a man as Mussolini, who proceeded to assume that he now controlled the whole Balkan area and had effectively loosened the bars of Italy's Mediterranean prison. Newspapers and magazines took up the praise. He had restored the equilibrium of the axis at a stroke and had greatly increased Italian prestige and military strength, as well as opening up unknown economic riches which he would surely know how to exploit. "By union with Albania, the Italian empire has become a formidable power in Europe". Nor would this be the last country which Italy would annex; on the contrary it became a cliché of the regime that Albania was the spearhead of an Italian penetration which would somehow irresistibly proceed towards the mysterious East.[25]

Ciano, at the same time as he continued to promise that Albania would remain an independent state,[26] got a group of local citizens to style themselves a "national constituent assembly", and within five days of the troops' landing, this body expressed the unanimous wish of the whole population for the king of Italy to become also king of Albania in a personal union of crowns.[27] Ciano in private liked to say that local opinion would actually have preferred himself as king, but either modesty or Mussolini restrained him.

In effect, though no real independence was permitted, the country was allowed to keep its own name, its separate flag, its language and stamps. Mussolini later thought he had been wrong to allow even this degree of freedom, because he realised, as did others, that there was little truth in the pronouncements about Albanians welcoming with joy their new union with Italy.[28] But the Fascists at the time were full of self-congratulation over the magnanimity with which Italy gave Albania freedom as a completely equal partner in the greater Italian empire,[29] even though the constitutionalists found difficulty in formulating the status of a nation which was equal though subordinate and yet almost identical. Since the racial experts now discovered that the hitherto much despised Albanians were another Nordic race like Italians,[30] more civic rights were accorded than to the Greek inhabitants of the Aegean Islands, who were themselves one degree better than the "Italian citizens" of Arab Libya, who were a long way above the black "subjects" of Italian East Africa; but it was specified that none of these various groups was exploited, since all "participated in common advantages for a common end conformable to the traditions of ancient Rome".[31]

It was in character that Mussolini did not worry excessively about the reaction of other countries to what he had done. He knew that the Germans would have at least to say that they approved, though in fact he had thwarted Hitler's wish to keep the Balkans neutral. In France he had to spread the very different story that his attack on Albania was a move against Germany. The Italian ambassador to Greece, who asked for instructions about what to say, was left without any because there was nothing to be said.[32] One small problem was that the presence of many Moslems in Albania complicated Mussolini's policy of claiming the protectorship of Islam, so he made amends by announcing that he would build a mosque in Rome, until the Vatican protested that this desecration of the Holy City would violate the concordat of 1929.[33] Most offended of all were the British, who saw what had happened as a typical example of totalitarian brutality which put an end to hopes that Mussolini might be less of a gangster than Hitler.[34] Only the previous year Italy had promised Britain that she would not alter the *status quo* in the Mediterranean, and Churchill now made a deliberately insulting comparison with the way Italy had similarly broken faith with Germany in

1915.[35] Mussolini retorted that the British had no interest at stake, and he could not think them so unrealistic as to believe in the sanctity of treaties.

These minuscule events in Albania thus marked an important stage in the process by which a coalition gradually built up to destroy fascism, if necessary by force of arms. A few days after the invasion President Roosevelt made his first really serious intervention in European politics to arrest the progress of dictatorship: he invited Hitler and Mussolini to give an assurance that for ten years at least they would not attack twenty-nine named countries. More important still, Britain and France took a major step against the axis when they now guaranteed Greece and Rumania against aggression. Mussolini replied that he attached no importance to this guarantee, since Greece was in his view entirely dependent on the good graces of Italy.[36] But ten days later the British announced the introduction of compulsory military training, a fact which marked a fundamental change in their foreign policy, and they followed this by making a pact with Turkey. Mussolini had proceeded on the assumption tha the England of Neville Chamberlain would never answer back and never contemplate being embroiled in a war on the continent. It was now his turn to protest against what he called an aggressive policy directed against Italy.[37]

The Fascists did not remain long enough in Albania to provide an entirely fair test of the effects of the conquest on either the Italian or the Albanian economy. Mussolini had assured his colleagues that Italy would gain greatly, especially as he hoped to raise an army of 200,000 men among the Albanian mountaineers, and the glib talk of transplanting two or even three million Italians to settle in the waste areas of this desolate land was repeated.[38] In preparation for such a development the Italian taxpayer once again had to foot the bill as resources were poured across the Adriatic, and, just as in Ethiopia, prices shot up in Albania by 30 per cent during the first six months of Italian occupation. Food still had to be sent there from Italy, and most other things too.[39] Italian exporters gained considerably, because Albania was brought inside the Italian customs union and the percentage of Italian imports into the country rose dramatically. But what the traders gained,

Italy lost. Albania in 1939 provided Italy with 140,000 tons of oil, but this was a tiny fraction of national consumption; it could still have been provided without an expensive policy of conquest, and in any case Albanian oil was sulphurous and cost much more than oil available elsewhere.[40]

Jacomoni, who was put in charge of Italy's Albanian administration at Tirana, was an intelligent and on the whole moderate politician, though corrupted by the regime and strangely subservient to Ciano. A considerable bureaucracy grew up to administer the ample money which he and various institutions were given to spend on development. Ciano still thought of the invasion as very much his own personal war, and treated the country almost as a kind of family property, renaming one of its towns after his wife, and making sure that he was repaid not only with a campaign medal but with luxurious hunting lodges and game reserves.[41] Evidently he had large secret funds at his disposal for miscellaneous expenditures in Albania, and the police uncovered a network of corruption which involved him and his friends: in this case they deviated from normal practice and thought it prudent not even to tell Mussolini.[42]

A number of adventurers came to Albania just as they had to Ethiopia, and fascist leaders developed a keen interest in securing jobs for their friends and concessions for contractors under their personal protection. Incongruous marble palaces were built for the Fascist party, the fascist youth movement, the fascist social services, and these were sometimes linked in people's minds with the fact that Mussolini's private secretary was closely involved with the marble mines of Carrara.[43] At all events it reflected an odd idea of priorities in a country which was so poor and undeveloped.

A great amount of power fell into the hands of a specially created ministry for Albanian affairs under Zenone Benini, one of whose main jobs was to apportion the available money in various directions. Being the real type of authoritarian Fascist, Benini was very generally disliked, especially as he was under pressure to get results quickly for propaganda purposes. By his own testimony, millions were spent on reclaiming land just because this provided the right sort of news, even where other land was available which would cost far less to cultivate. Mussolini identified the "battle against malaria" as one major priority, though some expert advice called this just another fraudulent piece of publicity. But the chief reasons why Benini and Jacomoni failed to produce adequate results were, first of all, that corruption and lack of financial accountability characterised the economic and financial life of this petty Balkan empire, and secondly that fascism made its first priority the starting of yet another war in the Balkans which would ruin all they had done.[44]

12

THE PACT OF STEEL

Along with the political axis between Italy and Germany went a drawing together of the two national economies. As early as 1933, representatives of Italian industrialists had been meeting with their German counterparts, and after May 1937 such meetings became regular, with the express aim of "eliminating harmful and useless competition" in export markets.[1] Dr. Hjalmar Schacht, the man whom the Italian minister Guarneri referred to as "the terrible president of the Reichsbank", was a past master at exploiting bilateral arrangements with a weaker partner. Under his "clearing system" Italy found herself with a large frozen credit balance and no way of liquidating it save by further imports from Germany, but German goods available against such frozen balances could be expensive, and their quality declined as German rearmament got under way and required the best materials for itself. What Guarneri wanted above all was coal, whereas Schacht and his successors were also anxious to send manufactured articles. Somehow the government at Rome was persuaded to agree that a certain proportion of German products which they particularly required should be paid for in hard currency outside the clearing system, and it took time before the Italians realised that this would become an intolerable burden for them.

In return for German machinery, chemicals, and coal, Italy exported great quantities of fruit, vegetables, hemp, silk, rayon, and sulphur; but here, too, by applying a rigid system of controls, Schacht had been able to force down the price of Italian agricultural exports. He was helped when sanctions, and the Italian rejoinder of "counter-sanctions", severed many economic contacts with the west. Another disadvantage for Italy was that, after the *Anschluss*, traffic with Austria was greatly diminished as Austrian trade was re-routed towards the Baltic rather than the Adriatic, and in consequence Germany became an almost exclusive market for some Italian products. In the Balkans, too, Italy found in Germany her most determined and most unscrupulous competitor. Many complaints were made of unfair trading, but they did not prevent Italy's becoming more and more subservient to the economy of the Reich.[2]

One symptom of this dependence was an economic agreement signed in December 1937, by which the Italians promised to maintain a high level of imports of finished goods from Germany despite their cost, and to help pay for these they agreed to send a first batch of 30,000 agricultural labourers to Germany, with more construction workers to follow during 1938.[3] There was some minor displeasure in Italy at sending labour out of the country, because it not only looked undignified, but was a public indication that fascism, despite its claims, had not been as successful as nazism in solving the country's unemployment problems. It also appeared to signify an acceptance by Italy that she was and would remain an agricultural country, and that her workers would remain agricultural and semi-skilled workers, just so that German labour could be released for the more skilled and more rewarding tasks of industry. Italians could now begin to see what their allotted role might be in the new order of a nazified Europe. Eventually there were to be 350,000 Italian workers in Germany.[4]

The most vulnerable point of Italy's economy was her dependence on imported fuel. In 1932 she had obtained 59 per cent of her coal from Britain, but in 1936, as a result of the League's sanctions, this proportion fell to only 1 per cent; Russia provided four times as much as Britain did, and both France and Belgium increased their coal exports to Italy in 1936, but the great bulk, upwards of 7 million tons a year, henceforward came from Germany.[5] As soon as the Italians adapted their factories to the special qualities of German coal, they found that the change was, for technological as well as political reasons, almost irreversible, and the Germans worked hard to increase this dependence, even when they knew that they would be unable to keep up supplies.[6]

Here was a serious problem for Italy, because when German rearmament came into full swing there would be only a limited margin to spare for increasing her coal supply. Also the existing railroads and railway trucks would be quite insufficient for wartime requirements when German coal, now mostly coming by sea from Rotterdam, might well have to be sent overland. By February 1939 the situation was seen as "truly tragic", because Germany was already falling short of her promises, with the result that some Italian war industries had only a few days' supply of coal, and production was seriously affected. Indeed some industries and gas-works were, or pretended to be, on the point of closing. A new agreement guaranteed Italy 9 million tons of coal a year, but a few months later this looked like an optimistic target.[7]

In May 1939 the axis between Germany and Italy was going to be formalised by a treaty, the Pact of Steel, which bound Italy to Hitler's policy of war. In trying to explain Mussolini's motives for thus trying his own hands one must not overlook the possibility of some degree of sheer inadvertence. There were also undoubtedly elements of both conscious bluff and self-deceit. He told his own generals in confidence that he would never make war,[8] and he may possibly have meant this at the time, because he presumably knew Italy's weakness and so would have preferred to use stealth rather than force if this were possible. Yet at the same time he was telling the Germans that he intended to fight the French and was confident of beating them,[9] just as earlier he had told them that he could defeat the British, and he may have been himself inveigled into overconfidence by this constant beating of the drum. He had learned the useful, if dangerous, lesson that a great deal could be achieved by mere words without the need for deeds; yet warlike words, unless used with the greatest discretion, could bring nearer the war that he told other people he would never fight. Probably he was already enslaved by his own myth, unable to drop the self-imposed mask of a fire-eating warrior and having to act as though he believed in it.

The Italian attack on Albania the month before provides a commentary on Mussolini's predicament. First it shows that he had already deceived himself about the efficiency of his armed forces, and it also shows that he could not afford to learn from the experience because the lesson would have implied acknowledging what was wrong and repairing any deficiencies. He decided callously and light-heartedly on a minor war for what seem purely sentimental reasons and without any thought of long-term consequences, but when Britain reacted by offering military guarantees to Turkey and Greece, he accused them of aggressive "encirclement", and this in turn became a reason for allying with Germany.[10] He succeeded in persuading some subsequent historians that such calculated encirclement of Italy was proof that the British were warmongers, indeed that they alone and certainly not the Italians wanted war in 1939.[11] Just possibly he persuaded himself that he was acting in self-defence against an aggressive Britain when he capitulated to Germany and so pushed Hitler one stage nearer to a much more serious war.

In 1938, though there had been several suggestions for an alliance between the two countries, the Italians had been reluctant to tie themselves formally, but now the Germans took their chance. In the middle of April 1939 Göring came to Rome to discuss the consequences of the Albanian enterprise and to allay some of Mussolini's anxieties by giving another assurance that Germany had no ambitions in the Balkans. He also brought the telling piece of information that the Germans had a long-range bomber in quantity production which could be used against England. Mussolini, suitably impressed, agreed that a European war was unavoidable and it was a question merely of choosing the right moment. But Göring knew from what had happened in Albania that Italy must at all costs be prevented from taking any initiative, so suggested aiming at not earlier than 1942 or 1943. As further bait for the trap he pretended that Hitler was planning nothing against Poland.[12] Mussolini admitted that he had no particular plans for war during the next two or three years, but so as to sound more incisive he added that he was ready whenever necessary to occupy the Balearic Islands "with the utmost speed", and was secretly supplying arms to the Arabs for a revolt in the Middle East against Britain. He tried to impress his visitors by putting on an anti-aircraft exercise and blackout in Rome, but it was not a success.[13]

The next step was a meeting between Ciano and Ribbentrop in Milan on 6 and 7 May. Ribbentrop was hoping for a non-committal pact of friendship, but had orders to avoid any obligation which would allow the Italians to drag Germany into war. Mussolini was still uncertain: up to 5 May he was privately hinting that a good offer from France might prise Italy loose from the axis, and even on 6 May it was evident to the Italian foreign office that nothing sensational was about to happen.[14] But once again he was caught by his own propaganda. He had arranged for the police

and the Fascist Party to organise a very special popular acclamation for Ribbentrop in order to quash rumours about Italians
being hostile to nazism, and he was therefore mortified at statements in the French press that the German minister had been
badly received.[15] On a sudden whim he determined to teach a lesson at the same time to both the French and the bourgeois citizens
of Milan who were letting him down.

Within a few hours, and apparently without consultation inside
the foreign office, Italian policy was given a new direction. Until
now it had been generally assumed that, notwithstanding all the
belligerent words, Italy had to remain "the needle of the balance"
in Europe, on the grounds that she would be lost if ever she failed
to keep an equilibrium of power.[16] But late on 6 May a telephone
call from Mussolini to Ciano in Milan ordered that an alliance be
signed at once with Germany. Mussolini always liked to think
that such sudden, sensational decisions would excite and fascinate
people and would be taken as characteristic of his particular genius. Speaking in private, Ciano allowed that he was not quite
so pleased with what he was ordered to do because it had obviously been a cursory last-minute decision. Still, he acted his
allotted part. In order to impress Ribbentrop he once again insisted that Italy would before long be obliged to fight France so
as to impose a respect which at the moment was lacking, and
this would preferably be without German help. He also raised the
possibility of invading Greece and perhaps other Balkan states.
But he qualified this by the hope that Italy would have another
three years for preparations, and here Ribbentrop, perhaps with
some relief, said the Germans fully agreed.[17] In asking for what
was an offensive as well as a defensive alliance, Ciano was entirely
contradicting what he had been saying two days earlier, but he
took refuge in the hope that Mussolini must always be right. It
was all a propaganda stunt, he assured a colleague, and would
have no practical results.[18]

So casually was all this done that the Germans were left to draft
the actual treaty, and their text was accepted on all substantial
points without discussion, even though Ciano saw at once that it
was dynamite.[19] Mussolini was so anxious to correct any impression in Berlin of Italians being untrustworthy that he did not wish
to appear to haggle over safeguards and qualifying clauses. Nothing, for example, was included in the treaty about having no war

for three years: the Germans deliberately omitted this proviso because they were already planning their attack on Poland. Mussolini was so sure of himself, or so careless, that he failed to notice it had been left out. Though Hitler had already hoodwinked him over Austria and Czechoslovakia, he still thought of himself as the shrewder negotiator, and only later did he see that Ribbentrop had completely outclassed him on one of the few occasions when diplomacy was a matter of make or break for fascist Italy.

The Pact of Steel was signed in Berlin on 22 May, but a few days earlier Mussolini made a public speech announcing that a treaty would shortly create an indivisible communion between the two states and peoples. A claque had been carefully rehearsed to start a wave of applause as he announced this fact, but the crowd in Turin obstinately refused to take up the applause and the claque found itself embarrassingly isolated. Later in the speech Mussolini, perhaps adapting to the tone of his audience, remarked that nothing in Europe would at the moment justify war: at which point, though the official text makes no reference to applause, the cheers were deafening and protracted. Mussolini ordered the prefect immediately afterwards to alter the official account and the sound recording so as to put the applause where he had intended it to be.[20] To him this was a vital point. When the foreign press picked out for approval his casual phrase about no war being in sight,[21] he was most disconcerted lest public opinion or the Germans might see it as a sign of weakness on his part.

Once the treaty was signed, Italy found herself committed to fight with all her forces and no time limit if ever Germany should become involved in war. The pact was unconditional and applied even to an aggressive war started by Hitler. The one possible safeguard was article 2, which said that both sides would consult each other if international events threatened war, but this was virtually cancelled by another clause which specified that, if there were no time to consult, support would be immediate.[22] Mussolini did not bother with such details. His view had always been that pieces of paper made little difference to the march of events, and one could always find an excuse to default if need be. Ciano naively accepted as good coin a declaration repeated to him in Berlin that the Germans had no intention of attacking Poland, and he suddenly began to imagine that his brilliant diplomacy might have guaranteed peace for the next four or five years.[23]

There was jubilation in Italy, or at least in the official press, at the news that "the two strongest powers of Europe have now bound themselves to each other for peace and war," [24] and perhaps some Fascists assumed that Germany would thereby be compelled to pull all Italy's plums out of the pie or her chestnuts out of the fire. In parliament the deputies were summoned to suspend their session and march to the Palazzo Venezia to applaud the author of this master-stroke; but though Starace fretfully tried to bunch the parliamentarians into disciplined marching order, many of them managed to sneak off along side roads. [25] Some leading Fascists were not entirely happy with what had happened. [26] The king once said, and possibly spoke truthfully, that he was informed of the details only after the pact had been signed. [27] Certainly there was a breach with constitutional practice, because all treaties had by law to be ratified by the king, whereas article 7 said that this one would be effective immediately upon signature. But there was no one who could make this kind of criticism in public. No one sent in their resignation, let alone abdicated.

Subsequently, when the new policy turned out disadvantageously, others among the Fascists found various implausible excuses for it. Mussolini himself pretended that he had meant the pact to be only defensive. [28] Villari put out the story that the Duce, suddenly realising that the Nazis had ambitions for world power, was intending to restrain them and make them less dangerous by binding them to a treaty. [29] It was also said, again erroneously, that a secret clause in the pact excluded any war before 1943 and that Hitler was pledged not to fight sooner. [30]

Somewhat late in the day, on 30 May, a document known to history as the Cavallero memorandum was sent to Berlin to record that Italy wanted no war for the next three years and to have this vital qualification in writing. The document, which was widely circulated to all high functionaries in Italy, was in other respects a bellicose statement of intention. It explained Mussolini's view that war against the "plutocratic nations" was inevitable and Italian policy should be based on that fact. His aim was, in the very first moment of hostilities, to seize Balkan territory as far as to the Danube, and especially to put Greece, Rumania, and Turkey *hors de combat* as a penalty for their presumption in accepting guarantees from Great Britain. This would be done even if they proclaimed their neutrality, because the Balkans were part of Italy's living space and would be required for the provision of food and raw materials.[31]

After reading this memorandum, none of the higher officials in Italy could have been in further doubt about Mussolini's aim. Some of them in later years confessed or pretended that the evidence of his aggressive intentions came as a very unpleasant surprise.[32] But the motto of fascism was "believe, obey, and fight", and no one who repudiated this motto or who rejected fascist imperialism would presumably have remained in high office. Perhaps, on the other hand, they had learned by now that fascism was mostly bark and no bite, and some of them must have known that no actual plan to occupy the Balkans had ever been seriously considered. But their chief hope must have been that peace was secure for the next three years. This period would suffice to create a black army in Ethiopia and to replace their antiquated artillery, and also to shift the industrial complex in Italy from the vulnerable north to the south. According to Mussolini, more time was also needed to step up his anti-Jewish campaign. Another even more eccentric excuse was that, in order to get more foreign exchange, he would like to wait until he could launch an international exhibition in 1942 to celebrate the twentieth anniversary of the march on Rome. He needed time to foster movements for independence in Corsica and Brittany, as well as to stir up Eire, India, and the Arab world against Britain. He had great hopes for accelerating the "destruction of morals" in the west, and for inciting all the colonial peoples outside his own empire to rebellion; but this would all need several years to prepare.

Far from encouraging the Germans to put off their war, Mussolini's belligerent remarks in the Cavallero memorandum may well have encouraged the opposite, but what is clear is that a difference of opinion over timing existed from the start. Ribbentrop and Göring said later that they could not recall Mussolini expressing any wish to delay, or else they had given it little importance in view of his ostentatious determination to occupy the Balkans and fight France single-handed.[33] Hitler, on the other hand, would certainly have noticed the discrepancy. He repeatedly asked the Italians for private discussions all through the summer of 1939, and it was Mussolini once again who found excuses.[34] Perhaps the

Duce hoped that events would be taken out of his control if he said nothing. Possibly he feared to engage in consultations just because, by article 2 of the treaty, any talks might be taken as binding him to war, whereas he wished to feel free to join Germany or leave her as circumstances might dictate. Whatever the explanation, he did not want consultations or a joint strategy, and correctly feared that Hitler would interfere with Italian plans if the two of them ever met face to face.

Mussolini's continuing mistrust of Germany was fully justified, because the very day after signing the Pact of Steel, that is to say before the Cavallero memorandum arrived to stress the need for delay, the German generals were told that they must prepare to invade Poland. Perhaps Hitler had been waiting until the pact was signed before taking this decision. He specified that any mention of war against Poland be kept entirely secret from the Italians. In any case he was reading so many Italian secret documents that he knew that their security could absolutely not be trusted.[35] Mussolini's job, as the Germans saw it, was just to neutralise Britain and France in the Mediterranean. His active participation might even be unwelcome in the kind of war they now had in mind, because it would help to spread the conflict, whereas they were hoping to attack Poland without France or Britain being involved.[36]

The Germans had a fairly clear view of Italian military deficiencies. General Brauchitsch and Marshal Göring had visited Italy during April and May, and were not impressed with what they saw. The two allies continued to have discussions at a technical level, though the Italian staff officers showed a perplexing evasiveness.[37] In May representatives of the two air forces agreed that, if war broke out against France, the Italians would have charge of those areas south of the 45th parallel and Germany those areas above the 47th,[38] but this was the nearest the two allies came to agreement on any practical policy. A somewhat inconclusive meeting of the two naval staffs was held at Friedrichshafen in June, when the Italians let out that they were thinking of an invasion of Egypt. The Germans were certain that Mussolini was not strong enough to carry out such an attack, but what chiefly worried them was that he had colonies and other prestige targets in mind, and was not thinking of helping Germany by threatening France.[39]

In general the two countries agreed that they should exchange information about munitions, for instance about standardising fuels for aircraft, about new weapons and new techniques of production; but very little seems to have been done about technical cooperation in actual practice. The Germans refused to let the Italians have one of their new Junker planes for dismantling and study, and they backed down on an earlier promise to provide anti-aircraft guns. Strict instructions were also issued against letting the Italians have information about any weapons in process of development.[40] On the German side there was no enthusiasm for a unified command or for agreeing in advance on basic strategy, but the Italians too showed little wish for genuine military talks or for the appointment of liaison officers between the two forces.[41] It is as though each side were anxious to keep open a line of retreat in case the other should involve them in some ill-advised war; in other words, as if Italy and Germany had wanted a treaty mainly for its propaganda value, so as to frighten others and to encourage their own peoples, but without intending a real alliance. They both concealed fundamental facts, they both had mental reservations, and neither put a great deal of reliance on the other.

13

THE ARMED FORCES
AND PREPAREDNESS FOR WAR

Among the vital facts which Mussolini kept secret—not only from the Germans but from many of the concerned Italian officials themselves—were those relating to the unreadiness of the armed services, whose lack of serious preparation dated back long before 1939. It is ironic and almost paradoxical that Mussolini—though his inconsiderate actions forced other countries to rearm, and though he continued to insist that Italy should have the foreign policy of a great power and the capacity to fight an aggressive war—nevertheless neglected to make the military preparations required by his vision of Italy's role. In 1931 he had warned his collaborators that war might be possible any time after 1935,[1] and statements continued to be put out that the armed services were perfectly organised and endowed with all the latest equipment, yet the war against Albania found Italy with her army disorganised, strategic plans almost non-existent, and an armament in general antiquated and sometimes quite useless; and far too little had been done to build up an industrial potential capable of producing the munitions that the foreign policy of a great power would have required.[2]

The Italian army in the Second World War mobilised 3 million men,[3] but since 1934 the propagandists had been asserting that more than twice this number were ready and trained to arms.[4] Mussolini in August 1936 went one better and declared that he could mobilise 8 million men in a few hours and by a simple order.[5] In the usual fascist manner this figure was pushed up to 9 million, then to 10 million,[6] and in 1939 the army somehow produced a semi-official grand total of 12 million men.[7] Fascist writers therefore proceeded to maintain that Italy possessed one of the most formidable armies in Europe, supported by a navy and air force which had reached perfection, and repeated that they had "little or nothing to learn" from Germany or anyone else in military matters.[8] As some of the generals subsequently explained, the armed services had gradually been corroded by the spirit of fascism, its corruption and profiteering, its inefficiency, and above all its habit of relying on rhetoric rather than substance.[9]

Another example of reliance on mere words was that, to impress foreigners, the legally prescribed period of military service had been made longer than the one in France, even though it was well known that not enough uniforms and equipment were available, so that the various laws on military service—like so many other fascist laws—could not be applied.[10] After returning to civilian life, conscripts were under legal obligation to return for periodic spells of military training, but in practice there were far too few instructors or junior officers, and examples are known of soldiers being given no military training at all between demobilisation as a lieutenant in 1918 and being recalled to command a battalion in June 1940.[11]

By another confusing piece of legerdemain, in 1938 the composition of army divisions had been reduced from three regiments to two. This appealed to Mussolini because it enabled him to say that fascism had sixty divisions instead of barely half as many, but the change caused enormous disorganisation just when the war was about to begin; and because he forgot what he had done, several years later he tragically miscalculated the true strength of his forces. It seems to have deceived few other people except himself.[12] Some of the less principled elements in Italy's military establishment welcomed the change, because more divisions meant more promotions and more generals, so much so that Farinacci complained that the army with all its superabundant gold braid looked like a Mexican one. The number of senior officers had to be kept secret after 1938 for fear of criticism, and Federzoni was improbably informed that there were more generals than subalterns.[13] Fascism introduced the idea of promotion for political as well as for military merit, and indeed Mussolini acted as though he genuinely believed that fascist principles were more useful than military training for his commanders.[14]

One military concept developed by fascism was that of "the lightning war". The generals concocted this idea at least by 1933, knowing that a very short war was all that Italy could contemplate, and Mussolini, characteristically making a virtue out of necessity, then seized on the *guerra lampo* as something typically fascist and dramatic. The under-secretary for the army, General Federico Baistrocchi, who well knew that the idea was quite unrealistic, said in public that a lightning war was not only possible but certain and easy.[15] Mussolini stressed the same point in March 1938, when he needed to divert attention from his failure to support Austria. In a much applauded speech, he said he was equipping the army for a quick war, and added that, as he himself intended to assume the supreme command, he was now spending most of his time personally supervising the process of rearmament. The chiefs of staff took the hint and confirmed that they were ready for such a lightning war: they knew this had to be said if they wanted to retain their posts, so they repeated that Italy was as strong as any potential enemy, and the genius of the Duce would infallibly bring them decisive victory by land and sea at the very beginning of hostilities.[16]

Expecting a war of quick movement, the Fascists went on to claim that they had all the most modern weapons, and that an advanced degree of motorisation was their answer to the problems of defence.[17] When this piece of pretence failed to convince enough people, the military experts went almost to the other extreme and warned against excessive motorisation.[18] Sometimes the police used to lend their vehicles to the army to be painted a different colour for military parades, and then had them painted back again.[19] So unserious were preparations that Marshal Graziani, when he unexpectedly found himself chief of army staff in 1939, commented brutally that Italy was still stuck at the stage of the Macedonian phalanx. When he remonstrated, Mussolini told him not to bother because the army was intended for show rather than for real action.[20]

For purposes of propaganda, Mussolini let it be known that he possessed three armoured divisions, and it was sometimes said that they included 25-ton tanks and equipment which was the most advanced anywhere.[21] But in fact these armoured divisions existed only on paper. Foreign observers knew perfectly well that, apart from a few experimental prototypes, there was nothing bigger than the 3.5-ton armoured car copied from a similar British vehicle and which had proved a dangerous liability in Spain. These armoured cars were very fast, but carried nothing bigger than machine guns, and could be penetrated by small-arms fire. They had no radio and almost no vision. According to the commander of one "armoured division", they preferably had to be guided by infantry walking ahead, who as a result often suffered more than the enemy from their fire. Nevertheless production continued, though they were almost worse than useless except for transporting ammunition.[22]

General Mario Caracciolo, who was in charge of technical services, at one point took drawings to Mussolini for various possible types of medium tank; after listening to him, Mussolini pointed to a drawing and said, "Make this one". Hundreds of millions of lire were thus committed by a complete amateur who trusted his own intuition and could not resist a dramatic gesture,[23] but the system was such that no one else could have taken any decision. When the first light-medium tanks began to come off the production line in 1940, they were already out of date and the army recommended stopping manufacture, but they went on being produced throughout the war because nothing else was available.[24] At the end of the war the chief of staff admitted that Italy still lacked anything which could seriously be called a tank.[25]

Mussolini in October 1936 coined his famous phrase about having "eight million bayonets", but in 1939, after three further years of rearmament, Italy still did not have enough bayonets for the 1.3 million rifles which was all that the army could muster.[26] These rifles, moreover, were of a design introduced as long ago as 1891, yet they were not to be replaced during the entire war. Likewise most of the artillery used in 1940–1945 was obsolescent materiel dating back to the First World War, and some of the best guns in the Italian army had been captured from the Austrians in 1918.[27] The army staff had repeatedly requested a major programme of renovation, though Mussolini pretended that they had never done so. At one point indeed he had agreed to what they were asking, but the money was never forthcoming, and still in 1938 Italy was making only some four or five pieces of artillery a month.[28] New models were finally put into production at the end of 1938 in a programme which aimed to reach a total of 450 guns a month by 1943,[29] but in fact never in the Second World War did production rise much above 200 guns a month, whereas at the end of the First World War Italy had been producing over six times as many.[30] Fascism prided itself on its efficiency and drive, and despised the pre-fascist liberal Italy as pacifist and inefficient, but these comparative figures tell a very different story. When war broke out in 1940, Italy had almost no anti-aircraft artillery at all,[31] and this despite formal assurances given to parliament and to the supreme commission of defence.[32] No one bothered much about anti-aircraft defence until the German attack on Poland at last taught fascism something about the realities of modern war.[33]

Each of the three services had its separate spy and information network, and some of the officers in command have put on record that no other country had such chaos in this field. They each competed against each other, even planting false documents and arresting each other's agents.[34] About the air intelligence, which seems to have been far the most costly,[35] little is known, but army intelligence (SIM) had by 1939 become a kind of supernumerary political police in addition to the four normal civilian police services. SIM spent a lot of its time collecting newspaper cuttings, or in small-time spying on other fascist departments, or in profitable smuggling on behalf of either its own officers or girl friends of the Duce.[36] The head of army counter-espionage, Colonel Santo Emanuele, seems to have been working as much in the private interests of Ciano as of the regime, and Ciano kept him in office despite the protests of his superiors and others who thought him thoroughly inefficient and corrupt.[37] According to General Cesare Amé, who was head of SIM, Mussolini forgot or at least omitted to tell them about the likelihood of war, and so left them without any possibility of preparing for it.[38] It seems that the Duce preferred his secret agents to concentrate on finding out information about his colleagues rather than about the enemy, and as a result they apparently had no informer in Malta or even, though this is barely credible, in Great Britain.[39]

The Italian air force was very largely a creation of fascism and in many respects a characteristic product of the regime. A considerable influence was exercised on Italian military thinking by the celebrated theorist of air warfare General Giulio Douhet, a man who paid only nominal allegiance to fascism, but who produced for Mussolini the welcome idea that wars would henceforward be settled by bombing planes during the first days of fighting; in other words, war was something which even a poor country such as Italy could undertake without undue apprehension, so long as resources were properly allocated. Money should not be wasted on anti-aircraft defence, for instance, or on air-raid shelters, or even on fighter planes. On the other hand Douhet thought that poisons, bacteriological warfare, and lethal gases would play a large part and be used massively against civilian populations.

Douhet specifically argued that the aerial defence of British towns would be impossible, so that a strong Italian air force could utterly destroy London "from the very beginning of hostilities". He also argued that British sea power was out of date as a serious implement of war.[40] Some knowledgeable people challenged these views, but in general the experts preferred to accept without second thoughts the kind of belief which they knew Mussolini wanted to be true. They assumed that the next war would be decided by massive air attacks "as soon as war was declared or even earlier". One serious hypothesis was that, flying through artificial smoke screens, a force of 300 planes using bombs of poison gas could kill up to 5 million civilians in the first week.[41]

Another strong influence on the development of the air force was the personality of Marshal Italo Balbo, who was minister for air from 1929 to 1933—the only period when Mussolini was not personally in charge. Balbo was a dynamic character and brave flyer, but he also had the authentic fascist characteristic of overvaluing the newsworthy and the spectacular. He eagerly sought the renown which came from leading formation flights across the Atlantic, and for the same reason pushed the air force into an excessive preoccupation with competitive records. By 1935 Italy claimed most of the international records for flying, and this was a great achievement. The chief of air staff informed parliament that they had been won with ordinary machines. It was his further boast that Italy no longer needed the help of foreign technology in this field, and indeed that Italian planes were not only "the best in the world" but in wartime would be able to control the whole Mediterranean. Such statements were, as they were intended to be, greeted with enormous enthusiasm, and the authorities proceeded to draw the conclusions that the Italian air force was second to none, and that Italy must be impregnable.[42] With his love of phrase-making, Mussolini once talked of blacking out the sun with the sheer numbers of his aircraft, and later he spoke of having won dominion over the air.

But these claims were wrong. In fact Italy's ordinary military planes had derived surprisingly little benefit from the impressive records and prestige flights. Balbo and his under-secretary, General Giuseppe Valle, needed to overpraise Mussolini, and of course they assured everyone that Italy's brilliant position was due to the genius of the Duce himself.[43] But foreign experts were not so impressed.[44] Douhet himself, before he died in 1930, realised that Mussolini was being deceived by his own fascist propaganda.[45] The Duce too, even before 1930, knew through police reports and the deputy head of air staff about some scandalous maladministration in the air ministry, and it was clear that entirely false information was being presented to the public.[46] Occasionally a hint of criticism even reached parliament or the press,[47] only to be drowned in the ritual chorus of approbation.

But Valle, when he was promoted chief of air staff in 1934, made a secret report to demonstrate that Balbo, his former chief, had falsified the figures. Subsequently Francesco Pricolo, the next air force general to hold this post, pointed out that Valle too had juggled with the numbers of aircraft, and commented that the Italian air force, instead of leading the world as Mussolini said, was in fact "at the level of a Balkan state". Almost half the planes which Pricolo inherited had to be written off as useless, which according to his own figures left not much more than a thousand effective machines in all.[48]

The fascist leaders were always secretly telling tales against each other to Mussolini, and one must be careful about assuming without corroborative evidence that such tales were true. Balbo gives the impression of having been more honest than most of the others, and certainly he was a better organiser and far more energetic. In 1932 he asked Mussolini for the job of minister in charge of coordinating the whole of national defence, and he drew up a proposal to spend about four times as much as before on the navy and air force, mainly by cutting down on the public works so beloved of fascism. Such an appointment would have been welcomed by some military leaders,[49] but not only inter-service rivalry made it difficult. More important, Mussolini was deeply jealous of the popularity of this much younger man, and realised the dangers for his regime if anyone else stole too much public attention: on one occasion the Duce dismissed the editor of a paper which printed a photograph in which Balbo rather than himself was the most prominent feature.[50] He was also a little afraid of the person whom he called "the one person capable of killing me."[51] Whatever the reason, no one was given the job of coordinating the armed services, and Balbo was eventually banished to Libya where he remained as governor until his death. The armed services remained firmly uncoordinated, because it was another of Mussolini's phrases that they were already fully integrated under his own personal direction and needed nothing more.

Just as the fascist bosses liked to accuse each other of various failings, so they were able to accuse the air-force generals of corruptly deceiving Mussolini about the strength of the air arm. Yet Mussolini was air minister as well as head of government, and said not only that he spent most of his day thinking about military matters, but was closely supervising every aspect of aircraft production and air-force activity.[52] One under-secretary for air reported that he never once saw Mussolini turn up at the ministry.[53] Nevertheless a progress report was made to him every week, so one must assume that with a little probing he could have discovered the true facts if he had wanted to. There is little doubt that Italy had all the technical expertise to produce good planes. If military provision was insufficient, the reason must be sought in politics and the overconfidence generated by propaganda. In other words, the responsibility lies with Mussolini himself, a man who took decisions on the assumption, for example, that he had a bomber which could fly all the way to England without being heard, or that he had the right planes and bombs to destroy the British fleet in a single day.[54] It was Mussolini who failed to keep himself informed, who failed to take responsible decisions, and who failed to resist the temptation to find in newspaper headlines a means of concealing unpalatable truths.

A certain lack of seriousness can be seen even in the famous aeronautical experimental station which he set up in 1935 at Guidonia. This had been made to look very imposing; it possessed the second supersonic wind tunnel to be built in Europe and was said to be one of the great creations of fascism, typical of fascist dynamism, and a great contribution to Italian prestige. Such prestige, interestingly enough, was said in this context to be a political and military fact because it was the same as making oneself feared.[55]

Whenever there was money to spare, it went towards prestige rather than towards an integrated, long-term programme of research which was much more expensive and had less calculable and less immediate results than those of propaganda. Hence none of the main technological developments of the period—automatic flying equipment, gyroscopic instruments, high octane petrol, anti-icing devices, retractable undercarriages, and the variable pitch propeller—was made at Guidonia. The fine buildings and installations were highly praised in the press, but the results were meagre.

Another commentary on fascism was the story of aerial torpedoes. The navy acquired a Norwegian patent from which they developed a good aerial torpedo which even the Germans decided to buy from Italy, but the air force showed a strange lack of enthusiasm, perhaps because they feared that such a weapon would lead to the development of a separate naval air arm. So the declaration of war found Italy disastrously backward in what was to be a vitally important weapon for the Mediterranean and one for which Italians had done some of the preliminary work.[56]

Nevertheless, it was part of the logic of fascism to reiterate that Italy, solely because of Mussolini's determination and vision, had the finest air force in the world, with the best planes and equipment.[57] By implication and sometimes explicitly, it was held to be far superior to the R.A.F., and a single Italian squadron could with fair certainty destroy any British fleet which came in sight. This gratuitous overconfidence was a dogma that survived even the initial experiences of the war,[58] and it came fatally in the way of any serious attempt to discover and remedy flaws.

When the Second World War broke out, figures were given to show that Italy had 8,530 planes,[59] but the air ministry privately admitted in April 1939 that there were only 3,000 front-line aircraft, and the naval information service reduced this to under a thousand.[60] On further investigation the figures turned out to be 454 bombers and 129 fighters, nearly all of which were inferior in speed and equipment to contemporary British planes.[61] When Mussolini received intimations of such discrepancies he expressed shocked amazement. Some people began to comment that he feared the truth so much that he no longer wished to hear it. He can hardly have been intending to bluff foreign observers, because they had their own means of knowing that the official figures of the air ministry were nonsense, and indeed the British were quite sure that the efficiency of the Italian air force was growing less, not greater; the intention was to bluff Italians, and unfortunately it succeeded.[62]

Mussolini's only excuse was that the air staff must have purposely deceived him, seemingly to cover up either inefficiency or corruption, and though this was denied by the accused, there is evidence that planes were flown from one aerodrome to another in order to make any real census difficult.[63] But the deception was much more his own. For example Mussolini tried to keep his end up with the Germans by telling them he was manufacturing 500 planes a month, though in fact monthly production was 150 in 1939, and rose to only 300 at its peak. Production had been much higher in 1918, and one must record with some astonishment that Italy produced more aeroplanes in the First World War than in the second.[64] This was no credit to the vaunted efficiency, military qualities, and airmindedness which Mussolini claimed for himself and for fascism.

The navy was probably the best equipped of the armed services and the least corrupted by the regime. Nevertheless Admiral Domenico Cavagnari, the under-secretary and chief of staff at the outbreak of the war, was an ardent Fascist, with the reputation of being a politician rather than a sailor and of having been promoted because of his political views.[65] By his own confession, running the naval ministry took him no more than two hours a day.[66]

The admiralty had set out to possess the fastest ships in the world, and once again one is tempted to think that this was because world records made good headlines. The decision discounted the fact that speed had to be earned at the expense of armoured protection, of seaworthiness, and above all of range of operation. The Italian navy was very strong on paper and quite excessively fast, but it could not function more than 500 miles away from base, and the rate of fuel consumption in its high-velocity marine engines made some of its units unusable under conditions of war.[67]

The Italian navy in 1939 had as many as eight battleships either built or a-building, making up a third of the entire tonnage of the fleet, and once again it is clear that reasons of prestige came into this particular proportion. They were fine ships and acted as a powerful threat, but in practice only two of them were involved in any serious engagement during the entire Second World War, and this one operation, off the coast of Calabria on 9 July 1940, lasted for only a few minutes. Mussolini was to claim on that occasion that he had destroyed half the British naval strength in the Mediterranean, but he said this just to impress the Germans, who were not impressed because they knew that very little damage at all had been done on either side. The Italian air force, which was always glad to diminish the role of the navy, claimed that not a single shot fired from these vastly expensive battleships ever hit an enemy vessel during the entire war.[68] A good deal of expert opinion would have preferred a concentration on small craft. Alternatively, if the money had been spent on aircraft carriers or on assault craft for attacking Malta, a very different story might be told about the war against Britain and France. Mussolini later tried to pretend, quite untruly, that he had made repeated attempts to persuade the navy not to build these battleships.[69]

The decision to have no aircraft carriers was taken by Mussolini himself as air minister in the mid-1920s, and the reason he gave was entirely inaccurate, namely that Italian land-based planes could cover the whole Mediterranean. He was delighted to think that he had stolen a march on other countries by realising ahead of time that carriers had been rendered obsolete by the rapid development of bombing planes, and the air force supported him in this eccentric view because they feared that the existence of carriers would mean that the navy would get an independent fleet air arm. The admirals at first protested, but Mussolini in 1936 ordered them to drop any further discussion of the matter, and they therefore dutifully argued that aircraft carriers would be useless. It was for Mussolini to decide, said Cavagnari, and in deciding against them "he is naturally right". Moreover the Duce's leadership had given Italy the privilege of being the one nation in the world with a dynamic concept of naval power.[70] When events proved this opinion to have been wrong, Mussolini pretended that he had always wanted aircraft carriers and had been argued out of this by the experts;[71] but by then it was too late and the war had been lost.

A particular strength of the Italian navy was its possession of a larger fleet of submarines than any other nation. This, and in particular its midget submarines, constituted a highly effective force, but on very little evidence people had assumed that submarines would effectively paralyse the action of large battleships, and also that in wartime they could move to the Atlantic and blockade the British Isles. Italians were told that their submarines were better than any others in the world and that because of them England had lost her dominion of the seas.[72] But Mussolini was interested as always more in the propaganda-value of numbers than in effectiveness or modernity, and design was still based on the obsolete tactics of the First World War. By all accounts Italian submarines were far too slow in submerging, with too limited an offensive capacity, and not adapted to the transparent waters of the Mediterranean. One result was that in 1940 a tenth of Italy's operative fleet was sunk within the first three weeks of war. Only after this, and reluctantly, did the Germans begin to let Italy have information about new equipment and techniques, and radical modifications to Italian submarines then became necessary.[73]

These facts of course did not prevent the admirals repeating that the Italian navy was the best anywhere. They called it a superb fascist creation, one of the most splendid monuments to the regime, which made Italy invulnerable to any attack. As they accepted fascist claims about Mussolini having made Italy self-sufficient in food, they maintained that the navy would not need to be tied down to convoy duties but would go over to the attack from the very beginning of a war. Even the naval ratings were said to be the best of any, and this was another guarantee that the Italian fleet would not stay in port during the next war as much as it had in the first. Naval excellence was of course ascribed personally to Mussolini himself.[74]

The fascist admirals and generals singled out one point in particular for praise, namely that since the regime was by definition authoritarian and centralised, it had been able to develop a special structure of command and a unity of direction in Mussolini's hands which the democracies were not thought able to provide.[75] Theory apart, however, in practice it was one of fascism's more obvious deficiencies that there was little coordination and only a somewhat threadbare central authority. In particular the lack of cooperation between navy and air force was a major flaw in the Italian war machine. Almost no technical or tactical plans were worked out before the war for combined operations between the services, nor indeed did they know much about each other, so that each went its own way, with results that might have been guessed.[76]

Once again, foreign intelligence services knew what the Italian public, and perhaps even Mussolini himself, did not know, that serious deficiencies marred the vaunted efficiency of the Italian navy.[77] The Germans must have been aware of this as well as anyone, and apparently saw little point in helping their ally. They deliberately said nothing to the Italians about radar or about new echo-sounding devices that were to be indispensable for naval warfare; above all they said nothing about the new techniques of night-fighting, ignorance of which was to be perhaps the most serious lack of all in the Italian navy. The Germans knew that Italian technical knowledge had not kept abreast of what was being developed elsewhere, and indeed that the Italian fleet was in no position to sustain an offensive war against any great power.[78] This was an almost insuperable problem. One incidental result of the sanctions enacted against Italy in the past years had been that, because of lack of fuel, the navy had cut down on practice operations. In fact they entered hostilities without any operational plans, and their first coordinated exercise was on 9 July 1940 after war broke out, when for the first time they met the British in action.[79]

Mussolini had been hoping that he had successfully sealed off the narrow straits of Sicily and so had prevented enemy ships moving through the Mediterranean. He did this by "discovering" the island of Pantelleria, and he boasted that he had overridden the experts when in 1937 he decided to fortify this island and so block the channel.[80] He was wrong, because not brilliant intuitions and phrases but serious planning would have been necessary to bar the central Mediterranean. When war came the admiralty charts of these important straits were still seriously defective and a hydrographical survey had to be begun under very difficult conditions. Also the admiralty found themselves with far too few mines to carry out Mussolini's project, and only mines of an obsolete type which were easily swept, so that an important potential advantage was thrown away.[81]

Though Mussolini put an exaggerated trust in his fortification of Pantelleria, he assumed that Malta would be untenable by the British in wartime.[82] The British as early as 1935 and 1936 had prepared detailed plans to attack naval bases on the Italian main-land,[83] and they put these into action five years later with devas-tating success, but the Italians on the contrary decided that it was not worth bothering about Malta. The navy in November 1938 suggested a contingency plan for a possible invasion, but Musso-lini did not allow them to develop it. Either he thought that hostil-ities would be too short, or else he assumed, accepting the doc-trines of Douhet, that air attack alone would be sufficient to make Malta surrender.[84] The consequences of this decision were grave.

One superficially plausible excuse advanced for the failure to modernise the armed services was that Italy lacked sufficient money and industrial resources. Mussolini was reluctant to use such an excuse because it would have seemed a confession of weakness, and it would moreover have invited the obvious retort that he should have chosen a foreign policy more within his means. The truth in any case is different, namely that he omitted to mobilise the undoubted industrial resources available in the country. One leading industrialist told him that Italy had the ca-pacity available for producing ten times as many tanks and thirty times as many guns as were being made,[85] but Mussolini did not even set up a ministry of production to investigate this possibility. Serious shortages admittedly existed, but more important was that the available money was wasted or spent on other things. An im-mense amount of steel and concrete had been used in grandiose fascist buildings, and this process continued well into the Second World War. Great sums of money were allocated to sports sta-diums, barracks, and motorways. A good deal was spent also on the armed forces, but far too much on sumptuous parades or on comfortable quarters for senior officers, and this at a time when the artillery consisted of museum-pieces.[86]

Mussolini's ministers have described him as having only a su-perficial knowledge of economics, and he never understood the complexity of economic problems, or at least he pretended not to see the difficulties lest they interfere with his politicial aims.[87] If anyone expostulated, Mussolini had a conventional reply about fi-nance never being a real problem; political decisions should be taken and then the money would come.[88] He also had another well-worn remark about never having refused any additional grant that the military had asked for: when he said this he seemed to believe what he was saying,[89] and it is true that Badoglio and the senior military establishment sometimes flattered him that it was nothing less than the truth.[90] Nevertheless repeated projects had been put up to him year after year for increasing the military budget. Sometimes these requests had been public,[91] sometimes only private, but until the Ethiopian war they had no effect. General Pariani, the chief of army staff, said he made at least twelve requests for extra allocations of money, and got nothing until the middle of 1938.[92] Normally debates on the military budgets were accorded only one or two hours of parliamentary time each year, and sometimes no discussion at all was permitted.[93] Parliament was regarded by Mussolini as a rubber stamp which had no part in the grant of supply or in constructive criticism.

Mussolini subsequently gave as an alternative explanation for the deficiencies that he had not known how much was lacking. But he himself served in every case as the minister concerned, and innumerable reports were sent to his office from the under-secretaries, as well as others from the chiefs of staff, from the supreme commission of defence, the war production commission, the national council of research, and the army council. From the very beginning he had also insisted on being president of the autarky commission and of the national council of corporations. It was one of the great boasts of fascism that everything was centralised and coordinated under the supreme personal direction of the Duce, and perhaps it never occurred to him that such a hierarchical structure might leave him less well informed and less able to impose his will. Other observers, for example the British and German military attachés at Rome, were not deceived about Italy's military capacity, though their sources of information were negligible in comparison.[94]

Another explanation sometimes given is that Mussolini had no intention of fighting any war. This may possibly have been true up to the early 1930s, but his attacks on Ethiopia, Spain, and Albania tell a different story, and he later deliberately declared war on France, Britain, Greece, Russia, and the United States. It might be nearer the truth to say that he thought other countries were bluffing in the same way as he was himself, and therefore that military problems like financial problems would solve themselves without much need for close and serious attention. Equally plausible is the partial explanation that his sense of showmanship had seized on the dangerous half-truth that in a totalitarian society it was less important to do things than to seem to do things, and in the process he himself confused myth with reality. At some moments he certainly realised how fundamentally inefficient his regime was, as witness his desperate remark that he was the most disobeyed man of the twentieth century,[95] but for most of the time it looks as though he genuinely deluded himself that fascism meant efficiency and hence all was well.

One fundamental point was that the regime could not afford to encourage criticism and indeed usually prevented it altogether. As Ciano said, "You must not contradict Mussolini because it only makes things worse", and a general who warned him not to fight was dismissed on the spot.[96] In other countries the chiefs of staff would have corrected some of the mistakes, but Mussolini deprived the general staff of any power, and preferred keeping it as a purely consultative body, because this gave him as head of government greater authority and enabled him without an intermediary to send orders to each of the three services separately. Mussolini tried to persuade his more ignorant colleagues that the Italian general staff was as good as that of Germany or anywhere else, but in fact it hardly existed at all, having a peacetime strength of only some half dozen middle-rank officers, and usually met only two or three times a year to discuss quite minor matters.[97]

No doubt Marshal Badoglio, chief of general staff, could have been much more helpful, if only by resigning in protest when he realised that there was so little behind the bluff, but Badoglio enjoyed a vast salary from fascism in return for very little real responsibility or hard work, and wealth and position mattered to him excessively.[98] Despite his position, he did not bother to attend the main army manoeuvres of 1937 or 1938, yet in 1939 expressed surprise at discovering that almost all the artillery were still horse-drawn.[99] That such a man should simultaneously have been appointed in 1937 to succeed Guglielmo Marconi as director of the national council of research is a good indication of the mediocrity which, apparently by careful and deliberate thought, was imposed on every branch of administration. A man of stronger character might have confronted Mussolini and at least placed the main military facts firmly before him, but his colleagues knew that to ask Badoglio to show that degree of courage or principle would be a waste of time. Although without doubt he knew about the deficiencies, he was never prepared to stand up to the Duce, and had been appointed to high position for this very reason. His excuse for not resigning was that resignation would do no good. Evidently he persuaded himself that the government would either stop short of war or else muddle through.

Not only mediocrity, but also deceit and falsehood lay at the heart of fascism and were essential aspects of it. Mussolini, when he signed his military alliance with Hitler, knew perfectly well about most of the deficiencies in military preparation,[100] but had to pretend otherwise, because the whole edifice depended on him giving his collaborators the illusion that he had foreseen and discounted everything. In public he enjoyed the continuous sycophantic applause for his magnificent work in bringing the three armed forces to a state of perfection with all the most modern equipment. He encouraged the chiefs of staff to repeat continuously that Italy had the best armaments in the world and that the Duce, who carefully supervised every aspect of rearmament, had made the country's military organisation ready for anything, until Italy could be said for the first time to be stronger than either France or Britain: above all it was the fascist spirit and the professional capacity of the services which gave Italy an edge over other countries.[101] Ciano himself, though he knew about the bluff, was also its willing victim, and had been so brain-washed by propaganda that in his private diary he could without irony compare the dynamism of fascism with the sluggishness of the Japanese.[102]

The main weakness was obviously at the top, with Mussolini himself, whose preference for deceit and mediocrity was aggravated beyond repair by fundamental mistakes of policy. From 1935 onwards he moved increasingly towards a situation where he was provoking the enmity of two of the most powerful nations in the world, and yet, though foreign policy was altered in the direction of war, surprisingly little change was made in military potential to meet this deliberately provoked challenge. Mussolini personally presided over the various planning committees, but he refused to let them discuss policy. The major decisions were made by himself alone, trusting his own instinct, after listening to some of the facts but almost never to advice. The supreme commission of defence met only once a year up to 1939. Nor do its minutes suggest that there was much, if any, criticism of Mussolini's views. Its secretary, General Umberto Spigo, says that he tried to persuade Mussolini to extend its competence beyond mere technical and industrial matters to questions of military policy, but Mussolini refused. He never allowed it, for example, to take up the paramount question of what type of war to prepare for, or how to alter the structure of the armed forces to meet any particular challenge, and Spigo eventually came to feel that the nation was rudderless. The general staff were not informed about the kind of war he had in mind, but were told that they should not bother their heads over matters of high policy that did not concern them.[103]

Mussolini also presided over a special commissariat for war manufacture set up in July 1935, but to the post of its executive director he appointed General Alfredo Dallolio, a man over eighty who was physically ailing, and any request to find someone more energetic was pointedly refused. This body, too, was given no executive authority, and the three service ministries still continued to work on their own when ordering supplies, with duplicated administrative staffs and competing against one another for scarce materials. Dallolio was fully aware that Mussolini's boasting about Italy's military readiness was entirely deceitful, but as a disciplined soldier he saw his job as obeying orders, not criticising.[104]

Forecasts about the size of the army should have been determined not by numbers of people in certain age groups, but by the capacity of industry to supply them, and if this rule had been followed, Mussolini would probably have talked not of 8 million soldiers but of 3 million or less. But there is little evidence that the criterion of industrial capacity came much into his thoughts. He was simply relying on fighting a short war, where such things would not matter. He told the supreme commission of defence that he hoped to fight so short a war that he could send the factory workers to the front.[105] Many industrial leaders must have known that Italy was unprepared for war, but evidently decided that Mussolini was playing his own secret game of bluff and they should therefore keep silent.

This was a major discrepancy in planning. Thus, though Mussolini set up an aircraft experimental institute, he was less concerned to create the industrial capacity to utilise its findings. Another miscalculation was over the provision of raw materials. For instance, although he had won what he proudly called the "battle of wheat" and claimed Italy would be self-sufficient in food, he omitted to remember that three-quarters of the necessary fertilisers for Italian crops came from abroad and supplies could not be relied on in wartime.[106] Italy's total imports normally required an average of forty-four cargo ships arriving each day, three-quarters of them coming through the Straits of Gibraltar, and possibly it was hoped that even in wartime these would continue to arrive under neutral flags. When at the last minute it was discovered that most imports would have to come by land, nothing had been done to provide the extra railway track or goods wagons that were required.[107] This was a failure of imagination, but also a failure of planning and technological education.

In a totalitarian society, even science and technology had to be fascist, and this too had an important share in Italy's failure to make ready for war. Articles had been written in the press from quite early days about "fascist science".[108] It was claimed that the fascist revolution by its very authoritarianism had created the most favourable climate for scientific research.[109] As a minister of education said in parliament, a limit should be placed on intellectual freedom and pure research, since the best science ought to be politically slanted towards training the new generation for the national needs of tomorrow.[110] The intellectuals of the regime rallied round this theme, and a celebrated academician was able to pronounce in 1933 that the whole scientific world of Italy was at last permeated through and through by the fascist mentality, so that it was now properly disciplined for the service of the state.[111]

Mussolini's chief instrument for this process was the Marquis Guglielmo Marconi, the great pioneer of radio communications, who was an early member of the Fascist Party and was given the task of activating a national council of research in 1936. Mussolini created this body as an organ of the state endowed with ample funds, and announced that he intended to use it to bring the problems of scientific research to the very forefront of national policy. He gave it considerable powers over other research organisations and, at least in theory, over production in factories. Marconi explained that the council would coordinate science and technology for national needs, acting as a permanent organ of consultation to which the government could resort for anything to do with science or research. It would also make periodic reports to the government about productive capacity and about various commodities which were important to the national interest. As well as trying to prevent duplication of research, it would have the particular aim of emancipating Italy from foreign patents and foreign companies.[112]

The great encouragement fascism gave to scientific research, one of the boasts of the regime right up to the end, was said to have placed Italy in the lead for scientific discoveries and their practical application.[113] Mussolini said he was confident that he was doing all that was necessary in this field.[114] He was praised for having carried out an immense revolution by adjusting the whole nation to a new belief in technology. Scientists under fascism were taught to despise the free-thinking world of liberalism where science was demonstrably inferior, and an example of this inferiority was said to be the work of Albert Einstein. Italians should rejoice that Mussolini had saved them from the danger of free experimentation where research "invariably gives inconsistent and antagonistic results".[115] They should be proud to know that fascism was by its very nature bound to produce more men of genius than could be found in the purposeless, free-for-all environment of democracy.[116]

The results, however, were not commensurate with expectation, because once again Mussolini's rhetoric had lulled him into a false sense of optimism. The army chief of staff boasted of Italy being ahead of the rest of the world in technology,[117] and on this assumption there was presumably no urgency to improve existing methods. Though leaders of industry sometimes hinted that too little was being done for research,[118] the Fascists preferred to rely on the kind of rhetorical assertion that said Italians were cleverer than other people and better inventors.[119] The result was that, despite all the encouragement given to research institutes, the number of patents continued to be minimal, and the number actually adopted by industry in preference to foreign patents was still fewer.[120] By 1942 it had to be admitted that the national council of research had failed in its main task.[121] But no one dared suggest in public that the whole fascist idea must have been wrong, or that something about authoritarianism and reliance on official directives made scientific investigation difficult.

One example may be cited, that of research into radiolocation. The fascists claimed they had invented this technique but had not continued with production simply because it cost too much.[122] Certainly in 1934 and 1935 Marconi had been working on short-wave direction-finding equipment for ships, and as he was both president of the research council and also on the grand council of fascism, one can assume that he had all the money had authority he needed; nevertheless he did not pursue these researches with his usual single-minded concentration. The naval authorities continued with experiments, but not very satisfactorily,[123] and they were entirely caught by surprise when they ran into British radar at the battle of Matapan in 1941.[124] In his last months of life Mussolini, searching for an alibi, traced the beginning of the decline in his fortunes to the fact that Marconi, before his death in 1937, had refused to impart the secret of a death ray which he had brought to perfection.[125] This pathetic and garbled story is an oblique commentary on the achievements of a great scientist whose work was confused and misdirected by politicians who placed the search for power above scientific truth.

14

NEUTRALITY OR
NON-BELLIGERENCE?

It was a recurrent theme in Mussolini's mind that he must alter the character of Italians to make them more disciplined, strong, silent, and perhaps also less intelligent.[1] He was proud of his country, yet some of his acquaintances doubted whether he was a real patriot and thought he was more likely exploiting patriotism for personal reasons of his own.[2] One of his earliest lessons in public life had been that the recipe for keeping Italians happy was "3 per cent fun and 97 per cent drum,"[3] and he therefore set out to force them to obey, to make them believe whatever he said and march at his command without question.[4] The Spanish war was a deliberate exercise in making Italians a martial people; after Spain he sought another war for the very same reason, and when he said as much to members of the Grand Council they broke into applause.[5] Yet this was hardly disinterested patriotism, and he could be very contemptuous of what he called such a race of sheep, who for their own good had to be kept "lined up in uniform from morning to night, and given stick, stick, stick."[6]

Perhaps Mussolini thought sometimes that he had succeeded in changing the national character. At all events the journalists competed in assuring him that he had, and his military organisation of Italian youth was by their unanimous voice said to be one of the finest triumphs of the regime in preparation for the great trial of war. Accordint to Curzio Malaparte's magazine *Prospettive*, and Bottai's *Critica Fascista*, the new sense of discipline and militarism was a product of the greatest and perhaps the only real revolution that had ever happened in Italy.[7] As the minister of propaganda informed parliament, a main ingredient in this revolution was the purging of school textbooks, as well as the prohibition of foreign influences in children's literature, and the insistence that education should be organised round the ideas of heroism, fighting, and sacrifice. Even in elementary school, children were drilled with

miniature rifles and machine guns, and this was welcomed as a
properly formative influence on national character.[8]

By May 1939 Mussolini was ready to submit the new generation of fascist youth to the supreme test. Though he was privately
telling the Germans that Italian rearmament needed another three
years of effort, he half hoped for a small war on the cheap before
then, and could not forbear from keeping up a provocative and
belligerent pose. He warned the British that he would fight if they
tried to stop Germany invading Poland,[9] and insisted that no one
would be strong enough to prevent him occupying the Balkans as
soon as any major war broke out. Plans were produced to attack
Greece, a project which was said to be not difficult.[10] Mussolini
also had a scheme for breaking up the kingdom of Yugoslavia and
making Croatia into a puppet state or an Italian province. It was
important to be ready to assert Italian claims to predominance in
the whole area of the Danube and the Balkans, taking advantage
of German preoccupations with Poland. Though the western democracies had guaranteed Greek independence, he was satisfied
that they would not be able to halt the armies of fascism, nor was
he worried by the prospect of war against the United States.[11]

Early in June Mussolini received the first of several invitations
to join Hitler for a meeting to discuss the possibility of war in
Europe. No reply was sent to this request from Berlin, partly
because the Duce feared that Hitler might veto his plans for the
Balkans, partly because he did not believe the Italian ambassador
in Berlin who sent a warning that, if Rome refused such a discussion, the Germans would decide things on their own.[12] Mussolini
continued in private to be disparaging about the Germans, calling
them not really a military nation since they were too eager for the
pleasures of life, and he still tried to behave to Hitler as to an inferior who should take advice from a man of greater experience.[13]
Fearing that his colleagues might be beginning to doubt his policy
of bluff, the Duce went still further and at the end of July explicitly told the Germans that, if or whenever Hitler decided on war,
Mussolini would be found behind him one hundred per cent and
ready to mobilise at a moment's notice.[14] This precise statement,
despite the rider that Italy would still prefer delay, can only have
encouraged Hitler to fight, and Mussolini was so anxious to ap-

pear strong that apparently it never occurred to him that such a naive piece of braggadocio might increase the chances of war.

After having told both the British and the Germans that he was ready to commit Italy to war over the Polish question, it is strange that the Duce did not accept Hitler's reiterated requests for talks, so that the Italians might be able to influence German decisions before it was too late. Two valuable months went by, and only about 6 August did he realise that his ambassador in Berlin was right and Germany might be on the verge of starting a war in which Italy was expected to fight. Though he tried to keep up appearances by telling people that the British were enfeebled and their empire was about to collapse,[15] on 10 August Ciano urgently travelled to Salzburg to put the case for peace, and there learned that war against Poland had already been decided. He was greatly shocked and complained about the lack of warning or consulations. But the Germans were relying on the Italian promise of a hundred per cent support.[16] After listening to Hitler, Ciano ended his opposition, and instead of making it clear that the failure to consult Italy absolved his country from any obligation to join the war, made no protest and so by tacit admission once again gave the Germans an impression that Italy was ready to fight.

Hitler played his cards well in neutralising Italian doubts at Salzburg. He grossly flattered the Duce and expressed his own pleasure in living at a time when there was another statesman apart from himself who would stand out as truly great in history.[17] He explained that the best thing for the axis would be to liquidate neutral states in Europe one after the other, just as Austria, Czechoslovakia, and Albania had already been invaded; each partner to the axis should cover the other in turn as they took their pick. He mentioned Yugoslavia as a special target for Italy;[18] but obviously he needed Italy only so as to keep the British and French preoccupied in the Balkans and Mediterranean while he attacked in the north. Realising that Italy would intervene only if it looked like a short and easy war with lots of pickings, he told Ciano that the defences of Germany were so good that France and England were powerless to stop him, and in any case he was sure that an attack on Poland would not involve the west.[19] He carefully made clear that he did not really need Italy's help, though he suggested that the Italians might see it as being in their own interest to intervene.[20]

Ciano did not dare make the obvious rejoinder because he knew that Mussolini was of two minds; indeed the Duce had not gone himself to Salzburg precisely because he was torn both ways and wanted to postpone a decision. Once back in Italy, however, Ciano tried to persuade Mussolini to make it clear to the Germans that Italy had no obligation to fight in a war about which she had not been consulted. Mussolini at first agreed, but then said that honour obliged him to fight if Germany fought, adding that he wanted his part of the booty in Croatia and Dalmatia.[21] Yet he was also riled by the communiqué put out unilaterally in Berlin which said that he and Hitler were in entire agreement about policy.[22] He seems to have been changing his mind almost every day. No doubt he still hoped that Germany's differences with Poland would be solved peaceably, preferably by another Munich conference in which the Poles would give way to his own arbitration.[23] At the same time he recognized that the western powers might be ready to fight, and therefore told Ciano to detach Italian policy from too close an identity with Germany; on the other hand, in case the democracies gave way, he had to remain nominally on the German side "because we too must have our share of the plunder." Italy must therefore be ready to take Yugoslavia, though any more serious war might be impossible at her present stage of rearmament.[24]

Mussolini swung to and fro, fearing the anger of Hitler, fearing an attack by Germany if he was too explicit in his pacifist sentiments,[25] but quite unable to admit that Italy was not strong enough to fight. Some of his colleagues thought that he should separate his responsibility more clearly from Hitler's, on the pretext that Germany had already broken the terms of the alliance, but he replied that it would be cowardly not to march alongside Hitler. Their rejoinder to this was that, as he well knew, Italy was militarily weak. Ciano even suggested that he might be better placed as the "natural leader in Europe of the crusade against Germany,"[26] and the British, after supplying him with documentary evidence that the Germans were reneging on their agreements, raised the possibility that to fight alongside Germany might risk forfeiting the empire whether the axis won or lost.[27]

It came as a great and not entirely welcome surprise when Hitler made his pact with Stalin on 23 August. Mussolini, despite what he later claimed, had at one stage encouraged Germany to make such an agreement, but had never expected negotiations to succeed so well.[28] He saw clearly enough that the nazi-soviet pact altered the whole balance of power in favour of the axis, but he might now be pushed into a war in the same camp as the Communists, against whom fascist propaganda was strongly directed.

Without a clear lead from the Duce the fascist hierarchy divided on this issue. Bottai, for example, one of the more intellectual Fascists, showed that he was also intellectually irresolute and opportunist: on the one hand he had to admit that anti-bolshevism was the essence of fascism; on the other hand he hinted that fascism and communism might have a close common interest against liberalism and capitalism, which meant that Germany, Italy, and Russia should possibly unite against the rest of Europe.[29] Mussolini himself was not entirely out of sympathy with this view, but on reconsideration sided with Balbo and Ciano who, besides criticising the German alliance with Moscow as being against the letter and spirit of the Pact of Steel, held firmly to the realisation that neutrality was the only sensible policy for Italy, and could not stomach the cynicism with which some other Fascists were swinging away from their earlier denunciation of bolshevism.[30]

This was a critical moment for Mussolini because he could hardly delay much longer before the war might begin and deprive him of any chance of taking a conscious decision. He was frightened that the British might attack Italy if he gave up neutrality, but also frightened that otherwise the Germans might do so.[31] On 25 August he told Hitler that he was ready to fight, but only if Germany would provide the munitions he was lacking.[32] On 26 August, when he informed his senior officers that they must prepare for war at very short notice, their answer was that Italy's capacity for any major engagement was negligible. Many army leaders had up to the last moment, in the best traditions of the "fascist style", been insisting that all was well and they were ready to fight all comers, but faced with this latest order they realised that they would no longer be able to conceal the results of their negligence and inefficiency.[33]

One military commentator after the August manoeuvres of the army reported in confidence that Italy's war capacity was less than it had been before the First World War; the so-called motorisation could now be seen as just a joke, he said, the armoured divisions existed only as a name, and morale was abysmally low. The same commentator, in typically fascist double talk, informed the public that the army had the best equipment in Europe, while its morale and professional capacity were excellent.[34] Farinacci, one of the fascist old guard who still had the courage to tell Mussolini the truth, wrote to him in private that the condition of the army was catastrophic and its fighting spirit simply non-existent. "It is a merely toy army, without the least serious training," Farinacci explained.[35] Mussolini dropped hints of possessing a secret weapon, but it is hard to know what he was referring to unless it was to Marconi's supposed death ray or to the poison gas which the military leaders were still intending to use on a large scale.[36] He knew perfectly well that the lack of industrial capacity, as well as of uniforms and munitions, was such that conscripted recruits had usually been trained for only a small part of the eighteen months prescribed by law. According to Farinacci, out of misplaced national pride little attention had been paid to new developments and techniques in other countries, while the under-secretary in charge of the army, General Pariani, went on talking about armoured divisions even though he knew that they did not exist and that his miniature tanks would be entirely useless under modern conditions of war.[37]

Torn between desire and realism, Mussolini at one point drafted another telegram telling Hitler once again that he was ready to fight, but his staff delayed sending it, and a few hours later the Duce changed his mind.[38] In a futile gesture to placate his ally he ordered the Venice film festival to award its top prize to a German entry; he had done exactly the same before the Munich conference in 1938.[39] More seriously, another way of postponing a choice was to work out the supplies required from Germany without which Italy could not move, and on 26 August, after a hurriedly summoned and short meeting, a long list was formulated, including 6 million tons of coal, 2 million of steel, 7 million of oil—in sum an estimated 17,000 train-loads of material. The actual amounts were fixed with the precise intention of being beyond Germany's capacity to provide, and Mussolinin inter-

vened personally to increase some of the suggested figures by between 50 and 200 per cent,[40] despite the knowledge that an exaggerated list would inevitably show Hitler that Italy was acting
irresponsibly and in bad faith.[41] The Germans had not expected
such an unsubtle evasion, and Hitler commented simply that "the
Italians are behaving to us just as they did in 1914".[42] He had
been counting—or at least he said so—on Italy's positive support
as a matter of course, and Mussolini's action allowed him to say
subsequently that, if only Italy had stood firm at this point, Poland would have accepted the German ultimatum: in other words,
Italy's dithering brought about a world war.[43]

Mussolini was anxious not to make a public acknowledgement
that Italy did not have the force of which he had so often boasted.
He was unwilling that the world should know how two wars in
Africa and Spain had used up his resources, since this was the
very opposite of what he had been claiming. He also feared the
comparison with the Italian tergiversations of 1914 and 1915
which was bound to be made if, after continually announcing his
solidarity with Hitler, he deserted the axis as soon as a real war
broke out. One of his familiar propaganda clichés had been that "a
great country cannot remain neutral", but now his gift for phraseology enabled him to coin the more acceptable concept of "non-
belligerence" instead of neutrality. Most unusually, he asked the
cabinet on 1 September to confirm this non-belligerence, as he
thought it prudent to make his ministers share the responsibility
for something which might provoke adverse criticism. In the
meantime, though the press was told not to report the fact,[44] he
devoted his energies to an attempt to mediate and so prevent the
war which he now had every reason to fear. This was worth a try,
though in practice it proved to be too late to obtain another easy
success such as he had experienced at Munich a year before.

Until 1 September the Fascist Party machine, presumably because it assumed Mussolini believed all the things he said about
the glories of war and the strength of Italy, wanted intervention
on the side of Germany.[45] Party newspapers proclaimed that no
nation in Europe was morally and materially better prepared for
war than Italy. They scented victory, the long-awaited moment
when Italy would impose on the world her own grandeur and her
imperial ambitions. Youth leaders welcomed the idea of war as

"like a gigantic sporting event", as the culminating moment of the whole fascist revolution.[46]

On the other hand, despite what Starace and the party said, there is no doubt that the overwhelming majority of ordinary people in Italy favored peace, and the chief of police made the fact clearly known to Mussolini.[47] Neutrality was wanted even by some of those who knew that it might be taken as yet another example of Italian unseriousness and untrustworthiness.[48] De Bono noted in his diary that to remain neutral would mean a serious loss of face, and he blamed the professional bluffers, of whom he said Mussolini was the chief, for landing them in such a situation.[49] Grandi seems to have advocated formally denouncing the alliance with Germany, but Mussolini vetoed any discussion of this point, arguing that Italy had a promising role as a mediator, and to denounce the alliance would deprive her of the one cheap success which might still be available.[50]

The Duce's confusion became more acute in the first few days of September as propaganda tried to conceal reality. He attempted to act in such a way that, if war did not break out, he could pretend that he might have fought; or alternatively, if Britain declared war on Germany, that he would not be thought fearful if he stood aloof. It was announced that Italy, with twelve million men trained to arms, with a hundred divisions and innumerable submarines, and above all with Mussolini's own genius, was ready for an offensive in the true fascist style.[51] But when a partial mobilisation was carried out in September, it proved a major disaster, since not enough uniforms were available, there were insufficient feeding facilities and barrack-room space, and organisation was chaotic.[52] The Italian people were told that they were strong and feared, and that Mussolini was master of the situation.[53] But reluctantly he had to agree in private that only ten divisions were properly equipped, and that, even though he was minister for air, he had little idea of even how many planes Italy possessed.[54]

When the Second World War began in September 1939, Mussolini did not enjoy remaining on the sidelines. Deeply impressed by the apparently easy German successes in Poland, he once again brought up the project of attacking Yugoslavia, until Ciano dissuaded him.[55] Alternatively he went on hoping that Italy could insert herself as a mediator in the war by heading a bloc of neutral nations.[56] With luck the main combatants might all exhaust themselves and leave him to make the peace, in which dangerous illusion he recklessly ordered Ciano to stoke up the fires of war.[57]

A politician of stature might have exploited this magnificent opportunity to sway the balance of power, but Mussolini could not seem to act decisively or make up his mind, and some people thought that he was going through a crisis of moral paralysis as he had done after the murder of Matteotti in 1924.[58] When he was asked in which direction fascist Italy was moving, he replied that the pilot should not be disturbed,[59] and so obviously disoriented was the regime that some historians have concluded that the king could have easily dismissed him.[60] The idea of a decisive German victory was quite intolerable to the Duce's jealous mind, and both he and Ciano were prepared to hint that they might eventually join the war against Hitler.[61] He could just conceivably have fought on either side, but neutrality was out of character and also dangerous, since after preaching war for eighteen years he would lose all credibility if he now posed too obstinately as the champion of peace.[62] The point was taken by the journalists, who went on with their parrot-wise invocation of war as the natural objective of fascism.[63] Italy, wrote the venerable Giovanni Papini, would soon recapture her former position as the dominating force in Europe, fulfilling her divinely appointed function of leadership for the edification of the human race.[64]

Not many of these journalists can have realised the delicacy of Mussolini's position, because they can hardly have known how completely unable Italy was to contemplate a serious war. But Mussolini knew it and for this reason, even after Britain, France, and Germany were at war on 3 September, armaments production continued in Italy on the assumption that a war was years away and in any case would last no more than a few weeks. There was consequently no need even now for serious industrial mobilisation. The target date of 1943 was repeatedly confirmed by Mussolini, though the experts thought that 1943 might even be overoptimistic, since steel production at the end of 1939 was barely enough for ordinary peacetime needs, and there was now official confirmation that the armed forces were inferior to those with which Italy had begun war in 1915.[65] After the unfortunate experience of actual mobilisation, Mussolini came close to acknowledging that modern warfare was very different from what he had imagined, and hence agreed that 1 million rather than 8 million or 12 million soldiers should be the target figure for his army. He was still unable to tell his general staff when, where, or whom he was planning to fight, but tried to make them think that for security reasons he was keeping these powerful secrets locked in his breast. His order was that they had to be ready with plans for any war that seemed feasible, and showed no sign of knowing that this was an impossible request.[66]

One index of the Duce's intentions was the fact that the sale of armaments to other countries did not stop in September 1939. Orders poured in from France and Britain even more than from Germany, and when the military authorities protested that weapons should be kept for Italian use, they rarely obtained much satisfaction. Early in 1940 there were projects to sell 600 planes to France, 400 to Yugoslavia, and 400 to England.[67] Not many of these were ever delivered, but the sale of aircraft abroad continued through the subsequent years of war despite military needs at home. Forty planes were sent to Finland, to be used against the Russians, who also possessed Italian arms. The very first anti-tank gun produced in Italy went abroad, despite objections from the army. Weapons were sent to South America, to Bulgaria, Rumania, Portugal, Brazil, and to both sides in the Sino-Japanese conflict. In 1940, the year Italy came into the war, twenty-three different countries received military equipment from Italy.[68] If foreign currency was so badly needed as this, Italy was clearly in no position to think of entering the war herself.

Instead of concentrating on rearmament, Mussolini, with an eye to keeping public confidence in the regime, continued his policy of public works. In particular he did not stop building the gigantic showpiece designed to celebrate the twentieth anniversary of fascism, the world exhibition planned for 1942. Great pride was taken in the fact that work on this was not stopped, though it took enormous quantities of cement which the defence services badly needed.[69]

At the end of 1939 Mussolini ordered into operation an earlier plan to fortify the Alpine passes. This massive folly, which involved building what he hoped would be impregnable fortifications along Italy's entire northern border, was one of the biggest engineering works undertaken by fascism, and the fortifications were most complete along the frontier with Germany. These defences against a German invasion were still being built as late as 1942, presumably at least in part with steel rods imported from Germany.[70] It made no difference that the collapse of the French Maginot line showed such fortifications to be a waste of resources, because Mussolini's head was full of slogans and metaphors which convinced him that a frontier could be hermetically sealed.[71] Nor did it make any difference when his allies complained of such an unfriendly act: he simply answered that the agreements made with the various building contractors had to run their term.[72] When the Germans invaded Italy in September 1943, this Alpine barrier delayed them only a few hours.

The strain of these months of paralysing indecisiveness was such that Mussolini became seriously ill. Some assumed that his ulcer was returning. Several people referred to him as being slightly out of his mind.[73] The chief of police thought that perhaps there was a recurrence of syphilis for which he should take a cure, and Ciano agreed that the incoherence of the leader was bewildering for anyone who had to work with him.[74] Since at one moment he feared that Germany might win too soon, at another that she might lose, his visitors went away with contradictory impressions which added to the general confusion in Rome.[75] At a Grand Council meeting on 7 December, when Balbo raised once more the possibility of fighting on the same side as Britain and France, not one member spoke against it.[76] Though Mussolini could say that the alliance with Germany was a question of honour for Italy, he could also remind people that they were simultaneously bound by a pact with England, and he even recalled that the pact of non-aggression with Russia of September 1933 had not been denounced.[77] Equally perplexing, he tried to encourage anti-German feeling in Japan.[78] Still worse, when by mistake he heard of the German plan to invade Belgium he informed the Belgians, and the Germans knew from intercepted telegrams that this had been done, with feelings that can be imagined.[79] Perhaps he did not know that the head of Italian counter-espionage was working for the Germans [80] and might be reporting on his behaviour.

Hitler needs no justification for having consequently treated Mussolini with the greatest reserve. The more they saw of the Duce's conduct, the more the Germans regarded him as feeble and unreliable—*butterweich* was the current word in Berlin.[81] They assumed that he would do all he could to pursue his goal of imperialism and hence would join the war as soon as, but not before, Germany attacked successfully in the west; at the same time the fact that Italy had little offensive capacity and would rely heavily on imports of munitions from Germany made her alliance not particularly attractive.[82]

15

MUSSOLINI CHOOSES WAR

As the year 1940 began, though Mussolini's indecisiveness did not cease, he was attracted more and more to the idea of war. He admitted that Italians might well turn out to be too much in love with peace and quiet, but he intended to treat them as sheep who for their own good should be kicked into fighting.[1] Already they had been taught to think that fascism was essentially a military revolution and Italy "the most warlike nation in Europe"; now they would have to learn in addition that Mussolini was by instinct and vocation a great military leader.[2] War, he reminded the country, should be regarded as "the normal condition of peoples and the logical aim of any dictatorship."[3] Those of his colleagues who wanted peace became more subdued as they realised the direction of events, while others, for instance Marshal Graziani, who was chief of army staff and hence fully aware of Italy's military weakness, saw a possible chance to displace Badoglio as chief of general staff by irresponsibly advocating active intervention.[4]

Mussolini warned his ministers on 23 January that Italy could not remain neutral for ever without relegation into the second class of European powers;[5] yet when she fought, her victory would be assured, since the island of Pantelleria had by now been made impregnable and effectively cut the Mediterranean in two. He was still confident that the Americans would never fight and that British naval power in the Mediterranean would collapse as soon as Italy entered the war.[6] The democracies were for the thousandth time said to be decadent and pacifist, lacking in the strength, and resolution, and the sheer administrative efficiency necessary for real fighting.[7] In Mussolini's view, as neither France nor Germany were strong enough on their own to turn the phoney war into something serious, Italy could now plan to intervene in the summer of 1940 with decisive effect.[8] Several days later he changed his mind and said it had better be the second half of 1941.[9] Obviously he was picking out these dates with a pin; neither was based on a rational calculation.

But the prospect of intervention and actual fighting was greatly flattering to his ego. He hoped that, as he was obviously the more intelligent of the two dictators, the Germans would let him take over the political direction of the war,[10] and in this mood on 3 January he wrote a strange letter to Hitler, the first communication between them for four months. In this letter he repeated that Italy would not be able to fight a long war, but would first help Germany as a neutral by providing food and raw materials, and then intervene at the most critical and rewarding moment. What he chiefly advocated was that the Germans should fight Russia, because it was in the east that the Germans would find their living space and nowhere else. In the west they would be well-advised to make peace, especially as there was a danger— here he contradicted himself—that America might intervene and prevent them winning. This letter illustrates the incoherence and variability of Mussolini's views. It shows his pretentiousness and self-esteem, and perhaps also his wish that the Germans should not emerge too successfully from the war.[11]

In February, when the supreme commission of defence met for its annual conference in secret session, Mussolini took pains to ensure that discussion was confined to merely technical and uncontroversial points,[12] but some unwelcome facts emerged incidentally. Reserves of raw materials turned out to be lower than they had been in September, which indicated that valuable months had been wasted. Industrial capacity, in a period of expansion as the rearmament programme developed, was sometimes lying idle for want of basic commodities. A further problem was raised in the discussion of how, in wartime, Italy could import the 22 million tons of goods which would be her minimum annual requirement. Badoglio and General Soddu frankly explained that, if this problem could not be solved, no major war could be undertaken.[13] The minister of exchange, Raffaello Riccardi, while agreeing with this general conclusion, attacked the general staff for presenting rearmament programmes that were impossible to implement when reserves of gold and foreign exchange were so low. Badoglio replied that the military had to specify what munitions would be required for whatever policy that Mussolini imposed; it was not their job to decide policy, nor to say if the resources of the country were sufficient. Riccardi then spelt out some of the facts as he saw them: in wartime, Italy would not be able to export freely and so could not build up further purchasing power; tourism would stop; already the price of imported coal had almost doubled in six months and no more coal or oil would be forthcoming without prompt payment.[14]

Mussolini, presiding over this conference, moved with a sure touch through the forest of documents, summarising with great skill, but it was noticed that he avoided working out any of the sums in detail.[15] His optimism was impressive. When lack of raw materials was mentioned, he agreed that Italy was in difficulties, but stressed that France and Germany would wear each other down without either being strong enough to score a decisive victory, and this would give Italy a much greater relative strength.[16] He was ready to spend all the remaining foreign reserves, because at some point he was determined to fight, though that would be only when he was certain that he could sway the balance.[17] Oddly, he reproached those in charge of foreign exchange for not having realised that war was likely and for not having built up greater stocks,[18] but lack of money was not ultimately important in his view and would not stop him from redrawing the map of Europe.[19] People had always warned him that there was no money, yet the bills had always been paid in the end, and it would be the same in the future.

With similar logic Mussolini routed the other pessimists. They had always grumbled that Italy lacked iron, yet the mines of Elba were still producing, he said, and in an emergency he could collect half a million tons of scrap inside Italy. He glibly announced that steel production could be doubled in 1940 to 2.5 million tons and eventually reach 4 million tons a year.[20] Though he accepted that there was some difficulty about textiles because the vital imports of wool and cotton were drying up, the synthetic *lanital* made from milk—despite the objection that it smelled unpleasant and did not wear well—was in his opinion a decided success; he said nothing about the impossibility of importing enough milk to make it.[21] He agreed that farmers were managing to conceal perhaps three-quarters of the produce which by law should have been handed over to the government food stocks, but was strangely confident that the existing production of meat and cereals would suffice for wartime needs.[22] When told that some key factories had only a few hours' supply of coal, he replied, inconsequently and also incorrectly, that "within a few years" Italy would produce six times as much coal as at present, and he trusted that great efforts would be made to build up stocks over the next few months.[23] Some of his listeners knew perfectly well that he was deluding himself all along the line, yet he wound up these four days of debate with a great show of confidence.[24]

Despite what was said in private by the experts, Mussolini continued on occasion to act as though Italy were militarily and industrially ready for war.[25] He did this even though he knew that only ten divisions were ready to fight and though he was reminded that these were very much smaller than divisions in the French and Yugoslav armies.[26] After a tour of army units, De Bono reported to him that some soldiers possessed only one pair of boots, one shirt, and some did not even have a single pair of trousers.[27] Nevertheless, because of the Duce's self-confidence, not one major decision was taken during these months of non-belligerence to increase the strength and the provision of the army.[28] Mussolini was by temperament more concerned with the public relations aspect. He ordered a strict supervision over the publication of photographs so as to give the illusion of a well-drilled and well-prepared army,[29] but nothing was done to set up an adequate liaison with the German general staff and no plans were prepared for attacking Malta or Egypt. In the naive belief that a "lightning war" was possible without careful preparation, the armed forces were simply told to be ready for war against France, against Britain, or against Yugoslavia, or in North Africa, or indeed even against the Germans.[30]

It is just conceivable that Mussolini might still have fought against Germany if she ever looked like losing,[31] but hardly that he would have remained neutral indefinitely, and the likelihood always was that he would support his ally so long as she continued to be successful. Early in March the British cut off supplies of German coal which until now had been allowed through the blockade, and this came as a challenge to his complacency and self-importance. "It is not possible that I, the Duce, should become the laughing stock of Europe," he exclaimed; "I am being humiliated right and left; but as soon as I am ready I will make the English repent, and my intervention will be a signal for their defeat." [32] Apart from this very genuine concern about looking ridiculous, the possibility that Germany might attack Italy if he remained neutral still worried him a great deal, and the Nazis carefully treated him to their usual mixture of veiled threats and gross flattery. [33] More and more, said Ciano, Mussolini was feeling the fascination of Hitler in that deep layer of his personality which yearned for glory on the battlefield. [34]

An important moment of choice came on 10 March, when Ribbentrop arrived in Rome with the news that the Germans were ready to attack in the west with over two hundred perfectly equipped divisions. [35] After a brief reflection, Mussolini said later that evening that he would undertake to enter the war as soon as conditions were right. [36] He was seen to be nervous, because until now he had been merely playing with the possibility in the abstract. Persuaded by Ribbentrop's arguments, he agreed that the British were not to be feared and he could easily defeat their navy. He was still sure that the Americans would never enter the war. With some effrontery he tried to persuade his German ally that "almost the entire civilian life of the Italian people had been sacrificed to the production of armaments." [37]

His determination was confirmed when he met Hitler at the Brenner Pass on 18 March. The Germans repeated at this second meeting that the war would be won during the summer. They were not asking Mussolini for help, because they did not need assistance, though he might be able to supply the last ounce of strength which would turn the scales. They explained that he should remain neutral if he was content with a second-rank position in the Mediterranean, but otherwise the Germans would allow him the privilege of sending troops to join in the attack on the western front. Mussolini was impressed and flattered. After the meeting, however, he suddenly realised that he had let Hitler do all the talking when there were so many things he had himself intended to say, and it was not right for a dictator, especially the senior of the two great dictators, to remain silent. [38] Hitler in fact was deliberately deceiving the Italians about his own plans and about the strength of the German forces, realising that his ally had insufficient information to check what he said.[39] The deceit was mutual.

On 31 March Mussolini drew up his plan of action. He still thought it "very improbable" that the Germans would ever launch a major attack in the west, though on second thoughts he crossed out the word "very".[40] He underlined another phrase about "protracting as long as possible our existing attitude of non-belligerence", because he was still determined to wait until there was no conceivable doubt about the outcome. The armed forces were informed that they would have to remain on the defensive when war broke out: Corsica, he thought, was hardly worth taking, as it would in any case fall to Italy at the peace settlement; an offensive might possibly be launched against Yugoslavia, but only in the event of revolution first breaking out there; no attack was to be made on Malta, Bizerta, or Egypt. The one land offensive was likely to be against Sudan and Somalia. Apart form this, only the navy would be expected to fight, and the order to Admiral Cavagnari was nothing less than to take the offensive everywhere—a mysterious command which ruled out any concentrated attack and must have been received with considerable perplexity. In a phrase which Mussolini had coined in January, the idea was that Italy should fight "a parallel war", not with Germany but alongside her; the objective was not to help in defeating France, but to take advantage of nazi victories so as to establish a dominant position throughout the Mediterranean and obtain "a window on the Atlantic Ocean".[41]

So little urgency was there that Mussolini's elaborate orders of 31 March were given to the leaders of the three services only on 9 April, after which the chiefs of staff did not meet again for another month.[42] His instructions were received by them with general pessimism. The army staff said that, from their point of view, very little action was possible even in the case of a complete French collapse. The air staff could not understand the reasons for participating in the war if the enemy was not to be attacked, especially as intervention would also result in holding up vital imports of raw materials. The naval staff pessimistically reported that their situation was worse than in September 1939 and the

British had ample power to bottle them up if they chose to do so. Far from being able to attack in East Africa as he had been ordered to do, said Graziani, the situation there was much graver than the public had been allowed to know, because Ethiopia was in general revolt against Italy and large areas were entirely out of Italian control; if the British attacked, they could capture Eritrea without difficulty.[43]

Badoglio tried to reassure his colleagues by saying that, even though preparations were abysmally defective, Mussolini could be relied on to make the right decision at a moment when only a minimal effort was needed for victory. He repeated that no plans were to be made for any attack, not even for some hypothetical eventuality, because Italy would intervene only when Britain and France had collapsed. For the same reason Mussolini had no intention of requesting or accepting German help; the Italian war effort had to rely exclusively on Italian resources, nor should there even be any contact with the German general staff, because any German appearance in the Mediterranean might be fatal to Mussolini's aspirations and his idea of a purely parallel war. To make mobilisation less burdensome, they would now reckon on calling up only 800,000 men because equipment was scarce. No mention at all was made of Malta at this meeting. When the air force complained once more that they could not prepare for war without a clearer idea about which enemy and what kind of campaign, there was no response. The Duce's precise orders were that they should remain entirely passive, and above all they should regard the Germans with the very greatest reticence and detachment.[44]

On the other hand Mussolini had asked the Germans to inform him when they planned to attack. But the latter had no confidence at all in his discretion and he was told only on 9 April that Germany had begun its occupation of Denmark and Norway.[45] They had already advised him against attacking France on the Alpine frontier and had asked for Italian troops to help then instead on the western front, their aim being to outflank the French Alpine fortifications by a move through the Vosges and the Rhone valley.[46] As Mussolini gave some encouragement to this idea, the Germans worked out the operation in some detail,[47] but Mussolini and Badoglio let it drop because they wanted to remain independent and assumed that, once the Germans had broken through in the west, Italian troops would be able to win cheaper and more prestigious victories on their own elsewhere.[48] A number of people subsequently argued that this failure to join the Germans in attacking through "the Burgundian gap" was a major mistake in policy,[49] because if they had, Italy would then have had a sure military success.

Many in the fascist leadership knew enough of the true facts to be greatly frightened by the prospect of war. Subsequently it was said, with exaggeration, that nearly everyone in Italy, including some who thought the risks minimal, was still against fighting. There was thought to be some opposition from the king, from the Church, from finance and industry.[50] The chief of police was certainly pessimistic about Italy's ability to wage war. Marshal Balbo spoke without restraint against war even to the British ambassador, and Marshal De Bono thought Mussolini must be going off his head.[51] Ciano himself told many people, including foreign representatives, that he was against joining the Germans,[52] and some of the military leaders, including the Duke of Aosta, made similar views known.[53] Yet fascism, by stressing the virtues of authority, had eroded any sense of personal responsibility and denied the usefulness of criticism or disagreement. No one was sufficiently opposed to what was happening to be ready to resign from any influential or lucrative position.

Grandi, for example, though he was inwardly unhappy about the possibility of war, was more interested in keeping his various jobs and preserving the illusion of solidarity. According to some people, Grandi only pretended to be an anglophile and was converted to intervention against Britain by Germany's military success.[54] He, just like Badoglio and the king, could not resist Mussolini's argument that victory might cost little and would bring them wealth, power, and glory. As president of the lower house of parliament, on 27 April Grandi made a violently belligerent speech to say that future generations would hold the Fascists responsible if they did not realise that a thousand years of history pointed towards fighting for Italian liberty against France and Britain. To the tremendous acclamation of the deputies, he hailed Mussolini as the man who had taught them to be warlike, who had given them the certainty of victory and courage to risk everything on a single throw. All the representatives in parliament, he exclaimed, would obey Mussolini with enthusiasm and absolute dedication.[55]

Public opinion may have wanted peace, but fascist leaders and journalists, whatever their private views, thus thought it expedient to beat the war drum when they spoke in public. Many of them became crudely bellicose out of sheer conformism. One after another they repeated the leader's remarks about the armed forces being perfectly ready for war, and about victory being certain for the very reason that Mussolini was leading them.[56] De Vecchi and the under-secretary for home afairs, Buffarini Guidi, clamoured for war.[57] No newspaper or magazine could afford to sound a discordant note. They all announced with one voice that the world of liberalism was collapsing and Italy was seizing her rightful position in the world.[58] Mussolini was later able to say that, if there was any criticism of his policy in May and June of 1940, it had been criticism for delaying too long and risking that Germany might win without Italian support.[59]

For as long as he could, the Duce continued to play it both ways. He was not good at making up his mind in such a difficult situation. He was naturally worried that the spell which he had cast over Italians might be broken if he did not choose the moment correctly and enter the war so as to pick up an easy victory, yet so long as there was some chance of a negotiated peace he preferred to keep open the possibility of a settlement in which Italy might play a leading part. As was his wont, he tried to cover his indecisiveness by speaking in different senses to different people, and some of his speeches had to be censored before publication.[60] He knew that his choice might settle the future of Italy perhaps for centuries, but let it be known that he would decide with a calm mind and the patience of Fabius.[61] He had to take into account that in the First World War over half a million Italian soldiers had deserted, yet, even if the material in his hand was fallible, it was still humiliating to stand with his arms crossed while others were writing history.[62] He told some people that it was stupid not to want war, since only war could regulate the relations between different peoples. Then he stressed again that he would fight only when he had a mathematical certainty of winning.[63]

At the end of April the possibility was raised once again of an attack on Greece or Yugoslavia to coincide with Hitler's offensive on the western front. The Germans were now ready to allow this if it was the only way of getting Italy to act,[64] and Ciano, who always had great visions of Italian expansion in the Balkans, asked the Italian ambassador in Athens to investigate the possibility of first assassinating the king of Greece.[65] The army was less enthusiastic. But then came news of the failure of the British navy in the Norwegian campaign, and this seemed to confirm that the Italians might have an easy time in the Mediterranean.[66] On 10 May the Germans invaded Holland and Belgium and once again invited Mussolini to make up his mind. The Germans' quick advance was a startling fact, and it seems that they may also have tried to impress him with half-truths about their success in splitting the atom.[67] On 14 May the Duce woke up the chief of air staff in the early hours to say that, as France was on the point of collapse, the Italians just had to do something, and it was no time to think of a minor campaign in the Balkans when the whole of the west was collapsing.[68] By 20 May he was told that the end of the war was in sight [69] and he might well arrive on the scene too late.

Mussolini did not announce his declaration of war until 10 June. His mind was virtually made up by 13 May [70], though he still wanted to make doubly sure and needed time to gear up popular opinion. He publicly ridiculed those who were still praying for peace and warned anyone who opposed the idea of war that they might be shot as traitors.[71] Even if the French were to offer him Corsica and Tunisia, even if they offered double what he had been asking, he was now determined to refuse, because what fascism now needed above all was war and the prestige of victory.[72]

When they saw what was happening, the fascist leaders rushed—as Ciano expressed it—to acquire pre-dated credentials for wanting to fight.[73] Bottai joked about founding a new party, that of the interventionists in bad faith, but he and his various magazines nevertheless led the intellectuals of the universities and the royal academy in acceptance (whether sincere or insincere) of this new belligerent mood.[74] Ciano himself, as one might expect, became almost overnight an advocate of war, and the leading industrialists, though with private reservations, spoke in the same sense.[75] Mussolini was jesting when he said that he found himself the only pacifist left,[76] but was entirely correct in sensing a huge swing in public opinion to the belief that Germany would win soon and Italy had better join her quickly.[77] German victories in Norway were given as proof that democracy did not work.[78] Crowds of students in Milan marched through the city to the offices of the *Popolo d'Italia* singing the hymns of the fascist revolution and calling for war.[79] In public, at least, few if any doubted now, and a greater increase than ever before was reported in membership of the Fascist Party.[80]

In whipping up enthusiasm, the propaganda machine, especially with the aid of lessons learned from the Nazis, moved with considerable efficiency. Mussolini as usual felt that this was the most vital aspect of policy. He knew how important it was not to disillusion those who were watching him; the secret of his success was that he had always to succeed, always to keep the public eagerly at their windows year after year looking at the spectacle he put on for them, and this was the task on which he probably spent most of his time and energy.[81] A German general who regularly visited him noted that almost always a representative of the ministry of propaganda was waiting in his anteroom, usually the minister himself.[82] Every day the Duce continued to pass many hours reading the newspapers and drawing up his never-ending stream of orders to the press. A large bureaucracy had by now grown up in response to this paramount need to embellish the news. If any crowd listening to Mussolini dared to be unresponsive, officials knew that they had to make up for it by reporting wild enthusiasm, but usually the "applause squad" mobilised by the police and the party made this unnecessary.[83] The militia could quickly produce a noisy mob of hooligans to parade against some foreign embassy or to organise a "spontaneous parade" of students, and for this purpose there were plenty of "propaganda-fed, out-of-work opportunists whose only ideal is to glorify their own existence in the name of patriotism at the expense of the state".[84]

The word "propaganda" had not acquired its full connotations by the time of the seventh edition of Panzini's dictionary in 1935, but was accepted in the title of a government ministry in that year, although soon afterwards it was realised that there was need to counter the pejorative implications that the term had picked up:[85] in 1937 the ministry's name was therefore changed to "popular culture". Some of the more honest journalists recognised that the enormous amount of paper devoted to publicity was largely useless except to stoke "the furnaces of half the world".[86] On the other hand some flatterers in the press preferred to deny that Italians were being fed any propaganda at all, since their intelligence and good taste put them above such things.[87] But in fact the ministry, under its various denominations, absolutely controlled the press, radio, screen, and stage, and all these were manipulated in a single direction. No journalist could obtain work who did not have a license from the minister, and all the recognised journalists of the regime were now employed directly by the ministry to build up the great superstructure of illusions designed to push the Italian people into battle.

The war bulletins of both belligerents were generally and easily slanted. The press was now under orders not to refer to any possibility of a negotiated peace, because the public had to be made to feel that war was inescapable.[88] Virginio Gayda, the main official spokesman, had announced on 21 April that "the whole Mediterranean was under the control of Italy's naval and air forces, and if Britain dared to fight them she would at once be driven out";[89] in private he used to say that of course he did not believe what he was obliged to write.[90] Mussolini's paper on 14 May stirred up enthusiasm by issuing a warning that at any moment there might be a landing on English soil, and repeated that Italians should be proud that it was they who in 1935 and 1936 struck the first blow at the decadent west.[91] Other papers very generally dwelt on the theme of Italian superiority and the imminent destruction of France and Britain.[92]

Such propaganda was evidently still thought to be much more useful than any purely material preparations. At all events by the end of May there was still nothing like a chiefs of staff organisation, and indeed until 1941 the Italian "supreme command" existed only in name and served merely as an advisory body.[93] The Duce simply trusted his own powers of improvisation. Nor had he even worked out a possible strategy in advance. No doubt this was in part a result of the Ethiopian war, which had given him the idea of trusting his own instinct and natural genius for military strategy. In his view the secret of German success lay in the fact that Hitler ran military affairs personally and did not allow his generals much say: Mussolini meant to do the same.[94] To impress the other *gerarchi* he announced that with the help of a single secretary he could personally exercise the powers of supreme commander along with all his other jobs:[95] this, of course, was said while he was still expecting easy victories which would contribute to his own personal renown. Only after Italy had been defeated everywhere did he manufacture the quite different story that he had never exercised the powers of supreme command and had reluctantly taken up a purely nominal position only after being begged to do so by others.[96]

The Italian constitution provided for the king to be at least in name the supreme commander. Mussolini intended to alter this fact, but, to his annoyance, Victor Emanuel agreed only to a form of words which delegated the royal powers temporarily to the Duce. Not until a few days before war began was this vital question settled. On 29 May it was agreed that Mussolini would be in effective command and give orders to the three services through Badoglio, with a small higher command of not more than about twenty officers to help him. He decided that this body would stay in Rome since the British could be relied on never to affront the papacy by bombing the holy city.[97] He then announced that he assumed command of all the troops in action on all fronts.[98] But it was far too late to secure a real collaboration between the three services, and indeed there was just a single liaison officer to keep each in touch with the others. To judge by the available documentation, such a point had little or no interest for the new generalissimo. In his eyes the one important fact was that he had now achieved his greatest ambition, that of leading his country in war, and according to Ciano he had never seemed so happy.[99]

Subsequently both the king and Badoglio insisted that they had strongly opposed entry into the war, and Badoglio said he had told Mussolini that it would be suicide.[100] Possibly the Duce was correct in his cynical comment that Victor Emanuel was worried about the huge personal fortune which he had deposited in London.[101] But the king, as well as being greatly avaricious, was a patriot and not averse to extending his kingdom. Though he was more level-headed than Mussolini and knew that dangers lay ahead, he made no serious move to keep Italy neutral and probably was quite content to accept Mussolini's judgement that the war would soon be over and won.[102]

As for Badoglio, he certainly made some objections but did not resign, nor did any of the other generals and politicians who later claimed to have realised that the decision to fight would mean national suicide. Badoglio was advised by some of his friends to give up his post, especially as he was notoriously pro-French, but he did not do so and did not even stand up to Mussolini with any strength or determination.[103] He had shown himself to be a reasonably good Fascist and accepted the doctrine of "believe, obey, and fight". Probably, too, like the other military leaders, he was confident that Mussolini must have adequate information about the proximate victory of Germany, and hence that all must be well.[104]

At the last minute, President Roosevelt on 26 and 27 May tried to persuade Mussolini to remain neutral, pledging that Italy would be allowed to attend any peace conference with a status equal to that of the belligerents. To this the Duce made a cold reply, since the prospect of victory was by this time quite irresistible, and he spelt out that if the United States decided to help Britain and France it was no concern of his. Any attempt to buy Italy off with concessions would be "indecent and immoral".[105]

Badoglio spoke of Mussolini as now being in a kind of frenzy. The final decision between peace and war was taken without consulting the cabinet or the Grand Council and perhaps without asking anyone at all. On 28 May Narvik fell and the Belgian army capitulated, while on May 30 the British evacuation from Dunkirk began—events that made the Duce accelerate his intervention lest he be excluded from "the victors' banquet".[106] He had the face to say that it would be immoral to hit the French when they were already defeated, and the press therefore was told to distort the news so as to exaggerate the strength of the enemy and make a fascist victory seem less of a walk-over.[107] His subsequent view was that if he had waited one single further day he would have forfeited any right to make claims on France, and indeed that if he had not intervened precisely then, he would have risked more than he would ever have done from premature intervention.[108]

In August 1939 the Germans had wanted Italy to fight, but in June 1940 they were of a different mind. By now they had won on their own, and in any case they felt that it would weaken their thrust into France if they also had to support an attack on the Alpine front. They realised that the Italians, apart from intending to fight a different war altogether, might possibly hinder any German attempt to make peace with France and Britain. Hence the German army seems to have tried to prevent Mussolini declaring war at all.[109] Hitler later looked back on Italy's intervention as something which helped the British more than the Germans, whereas by staying neutral she might have continued to be of considerable assistance to the German war effort: "our Italian ally has been a source of embarrassment to us everywhere", was how he put it.[110]

Mussolini's euphoria was entirely due to his conviction that the war would be over in weeks.[111] When his military leaders complained that the armed services could last at most two or three months, he replied grimly that this would be more than enough for his purposes "so that I can collect my booty".[112] He needed only "a few thousand dead" to give him the right to sit down without lack of dignity at the table of peace, and this phrase about several thousand dead was repeated on several occasions.[113] It is reminiscent of his brutal remark about 1500 Italian casualties in 1941 being "too few" for the loss of the Italian empire, as 1,537 deaths had been too few for its capture in 1935–1936.[114]

Fascist mismanagement allowed Italy to enter the war lacking any close understanding with her ally and in what was called the worst possible economic conditions.[115] Her army was still weaker than at the start of the First World War, munitions were ludicrously inadequate, and foreign exchange was almost exhausted.[116] But this did not prevent the propagandists' saying that preparations were perfect.[117] Mussolini confirmed to Hitler that the country was in a perfect state of readiness, its army organised down to the last detail under his personal supervision, superbly equipped with the finest weapons, and prepared to take part in the invasion of England or be sent wherever else the Führer might desire. He repeated that over 8 million soldiers were available if necessary; already he had seventy effective divisions and he would produce twice this number if Germany could help with equipment.[118] In fact, fewer than twenty divisions were ready to fight, and only about a million men could be called up because the necessary clothing and barracks accommodations were still lacking, not to mention weapons.[119] Mussolini knew these facts, but as he privately confessed, "if I had to wait until the army was ready I would have to stand idle for years, whereas we must fight at once and do the best we can".[120] Although several armoured divisions existed in theory, their full complement between them was seventy light-to-medium tanks of doubtful efficiency and no heavy tanks at all, while the artillery was still that of the First World War, and the very few anti-aircraft batteries in existence had no more than a thousand rounds each—enough for twenty enemy air raids.[121]

After so many years of speaking about "a lightning war", it is hard to credit that the Italians had still devised almost nothing that could be called a plan of operations. Mussolini's intention, however, was to declare war, not to make it. He wanted his armed forces reserved for future events once Germany had won, and hence his orders were still to remain strictly on the defensive. Unless in retaliation, there was to be no bombardment of France, Corsica, or Tunisia.[122] He wanted the French to be able to concentrate all their strength on wearing down the German forces, and expressed positive pleasure that they were doing this to good effect, since he did not want his nominal ally to be too fresh or strong when peace returned.[123]

Propaganda meanwhile repeated the familiar patter about Italy commanding the Mediterranean. It was said that, since Malta was only twenty minutes' flying time from Sicily, at any moment Italy could deal a mortal blow at the British Empire,[124] and it is almost certainly true that with adequate preparations Mussolini could have taken Malta and cut off the central Mediterranean.[125] The island's air defences at the time consisted of only three obsolescent Gladiator planes which had a maximum speed of 250 m.p.h.,[126] and there were only eight British submarines in the Mediterranean while Italy had over ten times as many.[127] Yet not until 5 June does Malta seem to have been mentioned in the discussions of the chiefs of staff, and on that occasion the navy said it might be unwise to launch any attack on the island.[128] From the fact that no plan for such an attack was already prepared we can assume that Mussolini had all along intended not to fight seriously, but to keep his own forces intact while relying on the Germans to win the war on his behalf.

Though after the war they sometimes tried to conceal the fact, the military commanders were content at the time to concur with this attitude and trust the judgement of their supreme commander. From private papers of the Istituto Superiore di Guerra it appears that they began the war on the following assumptions: that Malta should be disregarded, as it could be neutralised at once and occupied at any subsequent moment without difficulty; that consequently British air attacks on Italy would be impossible; that the central and eastern Mediterranean was under Italian domination, so that enemy ships could no longer pass through the Straits of Sicily; and, finally, that this would release most Italian submarines for use in the Atlantic, where they would effectively destroy the illusion of British naval supremacy.[129]

Similar optimism and improvidence was apparent in Italian policy towards the Balkans. The army had plans drawn up for a possible attack on Yugoslavia, but once again were suddenly told at the beginning of June to drop the idea, since Mussolini had decided that he needed the Balkans more for the raw materials they could provide, and since, furthermore, he was fairly sure that at the peace settlement Italy would get everything she wanted without having to undergo the risk and the expense of actual fighting.[130] Ciano, in one of his visits to Albania, casually ordered the generals to make dispositions once again for a war against Greece, and this without consulting the chief of staff in Rome.[131] As General Santoro commented, to think that preparations could be switched at such short notice was entirely typical of fascist ideas about war; it was typical of the uncertain direction, the contradictory orders, the lack of vision, and the inability to make real preparations which characterised the regime.[132]

16

AN UNCERTAIN START

Mussolini would have liked to avoid altogether the formalities of declaring war, as he had in his dealings with Ethiopia, Spain, and Albania,[1] but he was dissuaded by the traditionalists in the foreign office. Fascist propaganda then made a great deal out of what was called the splendid popular reception given to his speech of 10 June 1940 announcing that hostilities were about to begin. In fact, however, the large crowd summoned on that day to the Piazza Venezia was dispirited and unwarlike, and the news seems to have been greeted with more bewilderment than enthusiasm. The witnesses of this fact are too many for it to be denied.[2] It would probably be wrong to talk of strong domestic opposition to the war, though something can be read into the fact that sales of the Vatican's *Osservatore Romano*, the one newspaper which remained more or less neutralist, had risen in previous months from 60,000 to 200,000 a day.[3] All the other periodicals and journals, including of course those which represented the pre-fascist school of Italian nationalism,[4] were unanimously for intervention, though they hardly constitute a fair index of public opinion. Some applause for the declaration of war was organised by the usual claque, but though there is not much evidence that anyone thought of defeat as possible,[5] many people were clearly unhappy about fighting an already defeated France. What Roosevelt called the "stab in the back" was too obvious.

There was, and remained, some confusion about why Italy was at war. For months and even years people went on debating whether this was a glorious fascist initiative or whether it was wanton aggression by the democracies,[6] but so long as Italy was victorious the first alternative was the more attractive. Fascism had always called war something good and noble which aroused the best qualities in people and stimulated them to poetry and heroism.[7] Only blood, Mussolini had once said, can turn the bloodstained wheels of history. While fascism was by definition belligerent and revolutionary, the democracies were by contrast unheroic and pacifist,[8] and Mussolini recognised this difference when his new version of international law prescribed that aggression was not only proper but desirable wherever the past had to be buried.[9] The war, in other words, was at first thought of as being consciously willed by fascism as something necessary for Italian ambitions; Fascists were ready to fight because they had prepared for it deliberately and Mussolini had taught them to be brave and virile; whereas the democracies were foolishly unprepared because they did not accept Mussolini's doctrine that war was something normal and desirable.[10]

Nevertheless, as soon as the fighting started to go badly the contradictory doctrine was propounded by official spokesmen, such as Volpe and Toscano, namely that fascist Italy alone in Europe had consistently held out an olive branch and left no diplomatic possibility unexplored to avoid war.[11] Mussolini himself came to adopt this view and to argue that fascist Italy had not wanted to fight,[12] that the British had provoked the war "with criminal and premeditated intent", had first begun the arms race in the hope of pushing Italy and Germany into bankruptcy, and had then scorned Mussolini's persistent attempts to preserve peace.[13] Whether Toscano and Volpe realised that these views were inconsistent with earlier fascist claims is not clear.

A similar contradiction can be found in the various attitudes adopted towards Winston Churchill. In the opinion of Luigi Barzini, Senior, the famous journalist who passed as an expert on Britain and America, Churchill was an incompetent, a born loser, and in accepting this view Mussolini greeted the news of Churchill's appointment to the post of prime minister with sarcastic indifference.[14] On the other hand Luigi Villari, another authoritative foreign correspondent, developed the interesting theory that Churchill in secret letters to Mussolini had begged the Italians to enter the war and take over the Balkans, the argument being that the British wanted Mussolini at the peace table to exercise his well-known moderating and restraining influence on Hitler. Villari added in 1956 that, even though this correspondence had unfortunately not yet been found, the facts were beyond doubt, and amongst other things they explained why the Italians deliberately did not fight as hard as they might have done against the British.

His interpretation of events was accepted by a number of other fascist sympathisers who maintained that the British therefore had an obligation to Italy which should be discharged in the peace settlement.[15]

The final decision to fight was quite precipitate. If Mussolini had only waited four more days, he might have saved one-third of Italy's merchant marine, which was caught without warning in neutral ports, but he thought that there was no time to be lost, and also that these 212 ships would soon be free to sail home in the triumph of victory. For the same reason factory managers were told to finish off only those munitions which could be utilised in the next few weeks,[16] and the training of pilots was actually reduced so that instructors could go to the front for the quick final blow.[17]

Hitler assumed that the Italians had everything prepared to attack Malta, or Corsica, or in North Africa, and was astonished to find them with strict orders to remain entirely on the defensive.[18] But Mussolini had no plans to fight, only of preserving the idea that he was on the point of launching some great offensive. He thus offered the Germans an imaginary armoured division which he said was ready and could leave at once.[19] Not only did he take no serious action against Malta or Egypt, but he did not even trouble to transport many reinforcements or supplies to his troops in North Africa, because he assumed the war would be over before such action would be required.[20] Dr. Goebbels was embarrassed in having to explain such apparently culpable inertia to the German people, and the Berlin correspondent of Mussolini's personal newspaper noted a strong feeling there against Italy's behaviour.[21]

Mussolini's calculation, however, was almost right, for on 17 June, only a week after he had declared war, the French requested an armistice. But instead of pleasing him, the unexpected mention of an armistice made Mussolini extremely angry, because it had never occurred to him but that he would proceed to Paris on Hitler's coat-tails as a conqueror.[22] With mixed feelings he sent out an order on the same day to suspend hostilities before there had been any time to attack French territory,[23] and he knew this would not seem very heroic.

It is probable that more thought had gone into what demands should be made on a defeated enemy than on preparing an offensive. At least one map was printed showing Corsica, Savoy, Nice, Tunisia, the Sudan, Somalia, even Cyprus and Crete as Italian. Mussolini assumed that the forces of the axis would now proceed to occupy the whole of French territory as well as the ports of Algiers, Oran, Casablanca, and Beirut, and also that they would take over the French fleet and air force.[24] With these prospective acquisitions in mind he went on 18 June to Munich for a meeting with Hitler, but then came a second disappointment when he learned that Germany wanted a not too punitive settlement so as to stop the French armed services from defecting en masse to the British. Most of Italy's territorial ambitions were accepted, except that the occupation of mainland France should stop at the Rhone, with perhaps a strip of territory linking Italy with Spain. Mussolini was given a virtually free hand to take over immense areas in North and East Africa, but was barred from incorporating the French navy and air force.[25]

Only a few hours after the Germans had approved most of his demands, Mussolini surprised his ministers by going into reverse and saying that he would make almost no claims at all on France. This was a dramatic and important decision. In retrospect one can see that Italian occupation of the Tunisian port of Bizerta would have completely changed the course of the war in North Africa, because Italian supply convoys could then have remained out of range of Malta-based aircraft. Mussolini in this way casually gave up what Marshal Giovanni Messe, one of the most distinguished Italian soldiers in the war, called the one chance in all of modern history for Italy to obtain real mastery in the Mediterranean.[26]

Subsequently Mussolini himself developed the legend that at Munich the Germans forced him to give up his claims to North Africa,[27] but there is little evidence for this, and Hitler in fact was surprised that the Italians had not carried out the terms of their verbal agreement.[28] One possible explanation of Mussolini's change of mind is that he was simply embarrassed at not having done enough to earn such colossal acquisitions of territory. Perhaps he saw moderation as a way of winning French friendship in a German-dominated Europe, or at least a way of preventing a Franco-German liaison at Italy's expense. Just possibly, in the absence of interpreters, he had misunderstood Hitler's language at

Munich and thought that the Germans wanted him to be more moderate. Whatever the explanation, however, he quite obviously had no thought at all that the war might go on for long, and just assumed that North Africa would fall to him automatically as soon as the British surrendered. Once again he was a victim of his own propaganda, which was already announcing that the democracies had been decisively beaten and had no hope of recovery.[29]

Mussolini's irresolution and confusion is indicated by the sequence of events. On 17 June he ordered the cease-fire with France, and a few hours afterwards the French were asked to send plenipotentiaries to discuss the armistice.[30] On 18 June he was in Munich with Hitler. On 20 June he suddenly went into reverse again and told his generals that, since the German army had reached the Rhone, Italy would have a splendid chance to retrieve the situation by taking advantage of the French collapse and attacking at once in the Alps. Badoglio and Ciano opposed this because Italy could gain no conceivable credit from fighting an already vanquished enemy. But Graziani, the chief of army staff, replied that his forces were ready to attack the next morning, and Mussolini therefore confirmed that Italian prestige and the need to assert Italian interests against Germany imperatively demanded some invasion of French territory.[31] Negotiations were by now proceeding for an armistice, but the newspapers were instructed to conceal this fact.[32] Even though Mussolini's personal paper had already run headlines on 18–19 June to announce that France had admitted defeat and asked Germany and Italy to make peace,[33] it was hoped that people's memories were short. Three days later a full-scale attack commenced against the French.

The main effect of this action was to confirm the total inefficiency of fascism. Only a few hours were allowed for moving a large army from defensive positions in the Po valley for an offensive in the Alps. For publicity reasons Mussolini was determined to use his few tanks, even though they were of no use in mountain terrain,[34] and he took no account of the fact that the air force had no bombs suitable for destroying the massive enemy fortifications.[35] Nor did he think it necessary to give his troops the proper clothing for a mountain war, and hence there were more cases of frostbite than of wounds from enemy action.[36] When progress was slow, a desperate attempt was made to persuade the Germans to carry out an air-drop of Italian troops behind the French lines so as to justify bigger Italian claims in the armistice, a proposal which the German army turned down with derision.[37]

The results were unimpressive. Italian newspapers were ready with headlines for the occupation of Nice, but they could not be published because no headway was made beyond the environs of Menton.[38] Propaganda overcompensated by attributing the fall of France to this last-minute Italian intervention, calling it a splendid victory ranking among the finest pages in all Italian history, with enormous casualties making it "among the most titanic enterprises of all time".[39] It was also claimed apologetically that French resistance was keener against the Italians than it had been on the northern front against the Germans.[40] But though some people may possibly have accepted this kind of solace, the truth was very different. The French admitted to 37 of their soldiers being killed and the Italians to 631 in the whole Alpine campaign. The Italian attack, in other words, was a very minor affair and it succeeded in capturing only thirteen small villages.[41] As Ciano commented, luckily the armistice came in time to save appearances before the facts became generally known, and some combatants thought that the armistice barely saved Italy from a French invasion.[42] Mussolini, as usual, after sending people casually to their deaths, put the blame for his discomfiture on the soldiers and on the Italian people in general for not being worthy of him; even Michelangelo, he grumbled, needed good marble before he could make his statues.[43]

After failing to beat an already beaten enemy, Mussolini did his best to make the French recognise themselves as well and truly defeated by the might of fascist Italy. He was determined to reduce them to the status of a second-class nation, since he thought that Italy's welfare would depend on France remaining permanently "in a state of subjection".[44] No pity should be showed to this defeated enemy: France would have to pay the costs incurred by Italy in the war, and probably accept reduction in size by one quarter to a population of some 34 millions.[45] There was talk of a possible Italian annexation of Toulon and other parts of the French Mediterranean,[46] and also of confiscating many Italian works of art in Paris museums.[47] The newspapers were told to begin speaking of France as a second- or even a third-rate power, and also to write against the teaching of the French language in Italy; preferably they should avoid running articles which showed any sympathy to France or French culture.[48]

With one enemy out of the way, Mussolini was stung to learn that the Germans might be considering a compromise peace with Britain, for this would cut across his vision of a diarchy in Europe between the two axis powers. He was always alarmed by the thought that Hitler might be ready to share power with either Britain or France, and hence was now anxious for the war to continue.[49] His considered view was that the British could be easily vanquished if only Hitler made up his mind to sacrifice half a million German lives in the attempt.[50] To stir up flagging enthusiasm at home, the propaganda industry broadcast with renewed zeal that Italy had an absolute mastery of the Mediterranean and could exercise her control down into the Indian Ocean.[51] As time went on, these claims became yet more extravagant. The Italian air force was once again said to be decidedly superior to the R.A.F., and sometimes was quite simply called the strongest air fleet in the world.[52] Potential enemies were warned that not only did Italy now possess all the raw materials needed for her war effort, but fascism had a new style of fighting which would soon astonish the world.[53]

On 7 July Ciano arrived in Berlin with his usual train of secretaries and attachés dressed in their most resplendent uniforms. One of his tasks was to insist with Hitler that Italian troops and planes should have at least a token share in the invasion of England. Under cover of this demand, and tacitly admitting the gross error of three weeks earlier at Munich, he also put up Italy's demands for Nice, Corsica, Malta, Tunisia, the Sudan, Aden, and possibly other parts of Central Africa across to Lake Chad and beyond.[54] The Germans, on the other hand, had strong feelings about Italy's unhappy and unhelpful share so far in the war, and Hitler suggested that they should now wait for the share-out until Britain had been defeated.[55]

From press reports some idea can be obtained of what the Fascists were hoping to get out of the war now that they had time to think about war aims. They started with the claim to absolute predominance in the Mediterranean basin, an economic unity comprising 200 million people who, it was said, were ready to accept the discipline and leadership of fascist Italy or even to become part of Italian national territory.[56] Malta, of course, would fall to Italy, since the experts had convinced themselves that the Maltese population was racially and linguistically Italian.[57] Cyprus might also be annexed, or possibly it could be given to Greece in exchange for Greek territory surrendered to Italy.[58] By general consent it was thought that Palestine should be "restored" to the Italians, since the Roman Church had traditionally been guardian of the holy land and Victor Emanuel had several ancestral claims to the throne of Cyprus and Jerusalem.[59] Apart from some outright annexations, Italy hoped to establish a large lira-area which would look to Rome in the same way as northern Europe would be subject to Berlin: the Italian sphere of influence would probably include Algeria, Morocco, Spain, Portugal, Greece, Bulgaria, and Turkey.[60] Syria, Asia Minor, and possibly also the petrol countries of Iraq, Iran, and the Gulf could all become more distant parts of Italian "living space".[61]

How far these demands were generally shared cannot be known. There was, however, virtually unanimity in saying that the destiny of Italy lay above all in Africa, where her claims to primacy were considered incontestable and where immense areas were waiting to be made fertile by hard-working Italian peasants. Italian predominance in the Red Sea would probably mean her occupation of Aden, Perim, and Socotra, as well as the nearby British and French colonies on the African coast, while at least some areas in the Sudan would have to be taken from Egypt in order to provide a link between Libya through Ethiopia to Somalia, thus opening a land route to the Indian Ocean. Gibraltar and Suez would both belong to the Italian rather than the German living space.[63]

Ever since he coined his phrase about obtaining "a window on the ocean", Mussolini had hoped to win some kind of outpost on the Atlantic coast of Africa. Another phrase spoke of Africa being "complementary to Europe", and both these figures of speech had been incorporated into fascist dogma so as to make the bulk of Africa part of Italy's vital space.[64] Apart from Egypt, South Africa, and possibly Liberia, the rest of the continent would be divided among the victor powers, and even Egypt would come under Italian influence.[65] Kenya and Nigeria were now singled out in particular for annexation to the Italian empire.[66] Further-more it remained a principal dogma of fascism that millions of Italians should settle in the colonies wherever the climate was suit-able, and there was talk of a new railway being built from Tripoli through central Africa to replace the line from the Cape to Cairo.[67]

As various aspirants for Mussolini's favours outdid each other in bidding up Italy's ambitions, it was an easy step to go further and talk of rescuing India from the British, also of liberating Australia and New Zealand, as well as excluding the Americans from the markets of the East, and the easy assumption was made that a maritime state such as Italy would surely acquire a much greater say than Germany in the wider trade routes of the world.[68]

There was more reticence over Italian ambitions in Europe. Corsica, Nice, and possibly Savoy would be fair game. One view was that Switzerland would split up and part of it go to Italy.[69] Mussolini by now accepted that the Italian-speaking Swiss had no wish to change their nationality, but, supported in this case by the king and Ciano, he nevertheless wanted to annex the southern cantons up to the watershed of the Alps.[70] He also of course had ambitions in the Balkans, for whose populations he always af-fected a considerable contempt. He was still reluctant to see the different Balkan states as real nations in their own right, and this area too was thought of as ripe for annexation, or at least as part of what was frequently called, in an obvious copy of nazi doctrines, Italy's living space.[71] Occasionally claims extended as far north as Hungary and Rumania,[72] in part because wartime requirements of oil had to be met very largely from the Rumanian oil fields, but the Germans made it clear that the Danube basin and the Black Sea area were on the contrary reserved for nazi control.[73]

All the earlier dreams of expansion became more explicit as soon as French opposition was removed, and it was believed im-portant to act before the Germans put up counter-claims of their own. When Mussolini at last ordered preparations for a serious of-fensive, his immediate target was Yugoslavia, because he had always claimed this country to be an invention of the Treaty of Versailles and to have no right to exist in a Europe remodelled by fascism. The Germans would far rather that he had concentrated on attacking Egypt and Suez, and also suggested the possibility of landings in Crete and Cyprus, but they realised by now that there was little chance that he would contribute in any major way to winning the war, since he was interested only in picking up bits and pieces.[74] Though Hitler was prepared to agree that Italy could eventually have Yugoslavia, he pointed out that if this happened too soon it would damage axis strategy, since Hungary might use the occasion to attack Rumania and the Russians to march on the Dardanelles.[75] But Mussolini paid little attention to such a warning, and throughout the summer of 1940 he continued to set the stage for a large-scale attack on Yugoslavia. Yet ironically this single major attack prepared by Italy during the whole course of the war [76] was never carried out and cannot have been entirely meant seriously, as one can see from the fact that Mussolini continued to demobilise part of his troops, and evidently had no intention of doing anything until Hitler invaded Britain.[77]

The Duce wanted people to think that he was taking his new duties as commander-in-chief very seriously, and insisted on personally reading all military telegrams and making all the important decisions by himself. He would not let anyone else draw up the daily war bulletin, for in this realm of propaganda the biggest concentration of effort and his own special talents were required.[78] Each day he had a precise list of instructions for the press, particularly on the choice and lay-out of headlines, and on what to include or exclude from the news: usually the minister of propaganda came in person to fetch these from his office.[79] Photographs of himself for the papers were also carefully selected each day to show him only confident and aggressive. For the same reason, when he had to review the troops he liked to run down the line at the double, because he was not interested in inspecting them so much as in their deriving confidence from observing his own physique and martial bearing.[80]

An essential part of Mussolini's technique of government was to seem a superior being. Ever since 1933, DUCE had preferably to be spelt in capital letters, and it became normal practice for even senior admirals and generals, when admitted to the presence at Palazzo Venezia, to run the twenty metres to his desk before saluting: the Germans thought this extremely odd.[81] When he decided on a campaign, whether against France or subsequently in Africa, Greece, or Russia, he liked taking the main decisions on his own and consulting the chief of staff only two or three weeks before fighting was due to begin, for the latter's task was mainly administrative and not thought to be of great importance. After three months of exercising supreme command, he convinced himself—not without reason—that the general staff was quite useless, and he could easily omit to consult or even inform them if on a sudden whim he decided to dismiss a general or in other ways interfere with their dispositions.[82]

An exaggerated concentration of power now lay in the hands of one man, and this affected more than just the armed services. In general he slowed up the machinery of all other branches of administration by choosing to decide utterly trivial points. According to the chief of police, it was the small details of administration rather than the big decisions of policy which mainly interested Mussolini, probably because here at least he was not paralysed by doubt. For instance, he alone could decide when the traffic police should change into their white summer uniforms, or when the military band on the Lido should begin its series of Sunday concerts.[83] From 1939 onwards this psychological quirk became more noticeable and more dangerous. Thus on 21 April 1940, when the whole fate of Italy was in the balance, Mussolini found time to discuss and authorise the felling of a tree stump on the Via dell' Impero.[84] On 16 May, since he had to approve details of the Rome opera season, he demanded the inclusion of *Tannhäuser* rather than *Parsifal*, and no doubt this was because of some intricate theory about its effect on public morale.[85]

No man could have emerged unscathed from the degree of adulation to which Mussolini, a willing victim, subjected himself. Thus in these same weeks of 1940 a series of crowded public lectures was held with the title *Lecturae Ducis*, a reference to the *Lectura Dantis* for the exegesis of Dante in medieval Florence, and the parallel was typically arrogant. Various fascist leaders in turn would on these occasions interpret one of Mussolini's better-known speeches in what became almost a religious ceremony organised by the semi-official School of Fascist Mysticism at Milan.[86] The propagandists were ordered to write their articles in the light of the rule that "everything which happens in Italy comes from the Duce and carries his unmistakable sign".[87] They in turn informed their readers that all over the world, whether in England, in the Congo, in Detroit, or the Polynesian Islands, "the first thing anyone says to you is 'talk to us about Mussolini', because they would all like to have such a man themselves".[88] As well as being commander-in-chief and prime minister, Mussolini was still head of five different ministries himself—namely interior, colonies, and the three service departments—and none of the nine other cabinet ministers would act without his express consent. When he was warned that concentration of power beyond a certain point would mean inefficiency, he was quite unmoved, and the result was that inefficiency, incompetence, and mismanagement were all too evident. Whenever he left Rome on a tour of inspection the consequences could be paralysing, because no one would decide even quite small matters in his absence.[89]

One thing which puzzled and annoyed the Germans was Mussolini's continued insistence on taking part in the invasion of England. Once again they urged instead that he should concentrate his small resources on North Africa which they, unlike himself, saw as a key sector in the war.[90] But Mussolini preferred what he thought to be the easier and more glamorous task of assisting the German conquest of Britain. British power in his opinion had to be destroyed because this was the one surviving country to come between him and his dreams of African and Mediterranean expansion. Englishmen must therefore lose their empire and maritime strength; they must bend their pride "under the heel of Rome", by which was intended an Italian army of occupation based in London.[91] Like the French, the British would be forced to pay in hard cash for the damage they had done to the world, and future generations of Italians would then be taught a pitiless and permanent hatred of this alien and contemptibly moderate people.[92]

Against the advice of the Italian air force and of the Germans, three hundred planes were by Mussolini's express wish sent to Belgium in October 1940, along with a veritable army of journalists, to assist in the bombing and capture of London. They would have been far better occupied in Malta or Libya. Subsequently, when the political situation changed, there were good propaganda reasons for stating that no Italian plane ever bombed London [93] and perhaps this is true, but Italian planes were said at the time to be having a decisive effect in razing London and other cities to the ground in one of the most decisive and beautiful actions in all history.[94] It was reported officially that the superiority of Italian planes was unequivocably confirmed in the Battle of Britain.[95] But in fact the Italian machines, as their own pilots had to admit, were completely unsuited to this entirely unexpected kind of war- fare, since they lacked the requisite range, instruments, and ar- mour, and their excellent pilots had received no adequate instruc- tion in the work they were now asked to do. General Kesselring, the German commander, has recorded that Italian planes were ob- solescent; he therefore confined their use to less dangerous zones of conflict and after a few weeks sent them all back to Italy, so putting an end to this expensive folly.[96]

When victory did not come as soon as he had been expecting, Mussolini judged that it would be psychologically wrong to admit his disappointment. On the contrary, on 22 September he tried to impress his entourage by expressing his hope that the war would continue for a good time yet, and added that a long war would, for some esoteric reason, be to Italy's advantage: his listners won- dered what he could possibly mean.[97] Fighting, he confessed, was "the only beautiful thing worth the pain of living," and only through battle could Italy achieve the pride of place for which she was destined.[98]

Even after the Germans asked him to withdraw his useless planes from Belgium, statements continued to be made about the fascist air force dominating the skies of the Mediterranean,[99] and just possibly Mussolini believed them. The journalists tried to please him by repeating that the Italian air force was the best in the world, in the same way as it also had to be repeated that Ital- ian admirals and generals were better than their opposite numbers in Britain, just as Mussolini was of course an incomparably finer politician and war leader than Churchill.[100] The Duce himself pa- thetically tried to convince the Germans that his planes were in fact the best anywhere, and the figures he gave Hitler for aero- plane production were double the real number [101] because he had little appreciation of the fact that accurate figures were necessary in planning strategy: in his view, on the contrary, what was needed was just to impress people and then leave the walls of Jericho to fall of their own accord. As he had built no aircraft carriers, it was announced that the course of the war had shown carriers to be quite useless,[102] until carrier-based planes dealt a crippling blow to the Italian navy on 11 November. Mussolini had rather concen- trated on building battleships, and it was these capital ships which he now had to recognise might have been largely a waste of money.[103]

Mussolini's invasion of Greece in October 1940 exemplified this improvident and disorganised attitude to the hard facts of real life. Two weeks before the invasion he began another large-scale demobilisation which shows once again that his plans were entirely unserious. Without first consulting the chief of general staff, he sent half the army home,[104] and once begun it was impossible to halt this process until 10 November; so when he suddenly decided to attack Greece, 600,000 trained soldiers were being disbanded at the very same time as 100,000 new and largely untrained recruits were urgently called up for what was going to be Italy's most difficult and costly campaign of the whole war. Mussolini did not mind, because he was oddly convinced that fascist soldiers could walk through Greece with no difficulty at all. This was a country only one-fifth the size of Italy, and her army was, for no reason at all except blind parochial pride, much despised in fascist circles. Any doubters were informed by Ciano that the enemy leaders had been bribed not to fight and that at most one bombardment of Athens would be enough to make this craven people capitulate.[105]

On 15 October Mussolini summoned a group of ministers and generals and announced to them that they had two weeks to prepare and start an invasion in the very difficult mountainous country of northern Greece. The minutes of this meeting reveal the assumption that the opposing Greek army would be only 30,000 men, though the true figure was to be about ten times that number. The meeting was told that the Italian attack had been "prepared down to the smallest detail," and Mussolini clinched his arguments by stating that Bulgaria would probably enter the war against Greece, though he had absolutely no evidence for this and in fact the Bulgarians had no intention of fighting. He had forgotten to summon to this meeting any representative of either the navy or the air force, though what was being discussed was a seaborne operation for which command of the air was essential. There was no one present to draw out the implications of the fact that Albania had only a single port where heavy equipment could be landed, and this was cluttered up with ships unloading marble for fine fascist buildings. The general in charge of the expedition stated that one division could be disembarked in a single day at a harbour where the navy later said that a month would be needed.[106]

No one at this council of war stressed the vital point that by 28 October the rains might well have begun, or that it would already be freezing in the mountains, which made winter equipment absolutely essential; and in fact many roads were already impassable by the end of the month. No one mentioned that demobilisation was still proceeding, and perhaps everyone simply forgot such a fundamental detail. Mussolini allayed any remaining doubts by saying that he took full responsibility and his generals need not be worried by the number of casualties. He concluded after a bare hour and a half by saying that they had examined the problem from every angle and there was nothing more to be said. It was most unusual for him to stage this kind of discussion, and he did not do so when he decided to attack Ethiopia, Spain, Albania, France, or Russia. On this occasion he evidently wanted to share out the responsibility with others in the fascist leadership, taking advantage of the fact that the leaders he had chosen were not the sort of people who would dare to contradict him in front of their fellows.

Public opinion in Italy was sometimes encouraged to believe that an aggressive Greece was attacking peace-loving Italy.[107] For several weeks after the invasion began Mussolini also managed to conceal from the Italian people that the expedition was a complete flop. The newspapers instead described how the Greeks were welcoming the Italian troops and gratefully accepting the imitation bronze busts of the Duce and other gifts distributed by fascist agents.[108] But soon the Greek army was pushing into Italian Albania, and in the whole of twenty years nothing did more harm inside Italy to the myth of fascism. So many Italians knew what was happening that at long last the propaganda machine proved ineffective. The idea of a parallel war alongside nazism had to be renounced and Mussolini was eventually obliged to take the humiliating step of begging the Germans to come and rescue him.

Almost at the same time his army in North Africa suffered a serious defeat. The Germans had on several occasions urged him to concentrate his forces in a drive on the Suez Canal, and after

much prodding Mussolini finally on 26 October ordered an unwilling and indeed terrified General Graziani either to begin an attack or to be dismissed.[109] He later blamed Hitler for failing to
send armoured support to be employed in Africa against the British,[110] but the truth is that the Germans had offered such help on
several occasions in the summer of 1940 and had been turned
down flat. Mussolini trusted to what he called his infallible animal
instinct which told him that the war was going to be over soon,
and assumed that in the general collapse Italian troops would
reach Egyptian soil without German assistance and so be able to
claim more of "the booty". In his view it was important not
to bring the Germans into North Africa; indeed it was important
to keep them out.[111] Graziani had nearly a quarter of a million
soldiers in Cyrenaica, but without proper equipment and training
such an immense force was easily routed and largely taken prisoner in the first weeks of 1941 by 30,000 more mechanised British
troops. From now onwards the Germans assumed the direction of
affairs, and when General Erwin Rommel in February was sent to
retrieve the situation, Mussolini ceased to be a war leader in any
meaningful sense. His attempt to go it alone had failed.

17

THE LOGICAL CONCLUSION
OF FASCISM

From the very beginning of hostilities Italian journalists strove manfully to create enthusiasm and confidence in inevitable victory. By their account France and Greece had succumbed to the might of Italian arms, and German help had been a secondary matter.[1] True to the formulae of the regime, they welcomed judgement by battle as an entirely proper test by which the real quality of the nation and of fascism could be assessed. They were confident that Italian brains and organising capacity were bound to bring success, and this would still be true even if enemy forces were ten times as numerous and a hundred times as well-armed. Italians could rest assured that they would win just because they were the most intelligent people on earth, the most balanced, the most imaginative and cultured, and also the bravest and most robust.[2]

Moreover Italians could have the extra confidence given by the knowledge that Mussolini had brought out the very best in the national character and won them a head start over other nations. Fascism, wrote the academician Gioacchino Volpe, was something altogether new in human history; it heralded a new civilisation based on an altogether new idea of man, while the Duce himself was universally recognised to be the greatest national leader of modern times, and Italians were fortunate in being able to profit from his judgement and wisdom whenever the meaning of contemporary developments was in doubt.[3] Such ideas became more urgent, more shrill, and even more lunatic as defeats in Africa and Greece forced the propagandists into a corner. The whole world, wrote the *Critica Fascista* reassuringly in 1941, was coming into the orbit of fascism and gradually adopting its ideas, candidly recognising the intellectual superiority of Italians in every field of human intelligence, and this was one special reason why they were predestined to triumph.[4] Any one of the achievements of fascism, declared the magazine *Lo Stato*, would immortalise a regime for centuries; there was nothing else of comparable greatness in all human history, and it was inconceivable that it should not emerge victorious in war.[5]

The democracies on the other hand were condemned to defeat because they looked to the past and were at least a century out of date. Here was another of the familiar doctrines and assumptions of fascism which, by its very exaggeration as an instrument of war propaganda, became one more cause of Italy's defeat. Not only were liberal democrats thought unable, because of their parliamentary constitutions, to take decisions firmly and quickly, but they were essentially unwarlike; their educational system was not geared to producing the courage and discipline needed for battle, and their economic system would prove quite unable to switch from competitive individualism to organised war production.[6] The democracies believed in empiricism and utilitarianism, whereas fascism had a superior *forma mentis* which pinned its faith to rationalism, idealism, and ideology. Between two such attitudes, between the empirical and the logical, the second was bound to win.[7] What was more, the ordinary soldier in Britain, unlike his counterpart in Italy, had little knowledge of and no confidence in the cause for which he was compelled to fight.[8]

Fascist intellectuals unanimously and increasingly condemned the corruption as well as the general backwardness of English life. They condemned it equally for its individualism, its internationalism, and also for its anti-clericalism. Whereas Italians, on the other hand, accepted the more solid values of religion and nationalism. If Italy was destined once again to be acknowledged as the main centre of European culture, it was because Italians had learned from Mussolini what the democracies, by definition, could never learn, namely that individuals had duties towards the state and the community.[9] Such were the opinions of the best brains in fascism. Alessandro Luzio, Volpe, Costamagna, Bottai, Sergio Panunzio, and Francesco Orestano, these were high priests of the cult, all of them university professors of competence and repute, all of them better men intellectually and morally than most of the party hacks who used political influence to obtain academic preferment.

The war aims formulated by individual journalists and intellectuals were not merely territorial, because by victory fascism would earn the right to force its ideas on the rest of Europe.[10] Some writers went to the point of demanding for Italy a recognition of her "universal primacy" as an instrument of God in laying down the world order of tomorrow.[11] But even the more moderate insisted that the defeated nations be forced to change their ways of thinking and their democratic procedures: democracy was too dangerous, and authoritarianism would therefore have to be imposed on friend and foe as they all proceeded towards "the supreme goal, the fascistisation of the world".[12] According to one view, Anglicanism would also have to give way to Catholicism,[13] and of course other countries must be made to accept the crusade against the Jews. Even neutral countries, for instance the United States, would have to recognise the leadership of Italy in the field of culture, and the minister of education called for the use of force to compel the recognition of Italy's cultural superiority, so that other countries could by imitation be elevated to higher standards of thinking and behaviour.[14]

The end of democracy and liberalism would also bring with it the end of national independence for small nations, because fascism, at least as long as it was winning, taught that the rights of small peoples had to give way to the vital necessities of the big powers,[15] and Mussolini thought that all the smaller European states would entirely disappear with victory.[16] According to Mario Missiroli, who had been an ornament of liberal journalism before fascism and was again to be so after it, there was room for only two living spaces, those of Germany and Italy, which, since they were the two countries which had created modern civilisation, had a right to force their views on everyone else.[17] Indeed Italy would share with Germany the direction not only of Europe but also of European dependencies in Asia and Africa. Because nations could no longer be regarded as equal, and because Italy in particular had a mission among other peoples which gave her a right to use force to impose her own way of life, the principles of international law, said the diplomat Giuseppe Bastianini, should be changed to fit these new facts of the world situation.[18]

All this held out the prospect of a bright economic future for the victors, or at least the propagandists had to say so, though Mussolini himself was half hoping for conditions of greater austerity as being more consonant with the rigorous ideals of fascism.[19] The confederation of industrialists, under the lead of Count Volpi, could now envisage reorganising not only Africa but also Europe with an eye to controlling markets and sources of raw materials.[20] The aim was for both Italy and Germany to be industrialised states at the centre of two big living spaces which would depend on them for manufactured goods. Fascists criticised the "false political pride" which impelled small Balkan states to make bicycles, sewing machines, and typewriters, since for such manufactured commodities they should rely on Italy.[21] (A similar false pride was detected by the Germans in Italy itself for wanting to become an industrial power instead of relying on her ally for manufactures,[22] but such a view was thought in Rome to be unfair.) Italians had to be reassured that the new order in Europe would guarantee them abundant jobs for a century or more.[23] The losers would of course have to pay reparations, and British oil interests in the Middle East were seen by Mussolini as one possible indemnity, because a victorious Italy would have the right to appropriate as much oil as she would need.[24] With luck the whole of Europe would increase its standard of life if the axis powers succeeded in imposing economic reorganisation and properly exploiting the raw materials of Africa and the Middle East.[25]

This dream of future prosperity, like so many other aspects of fascism, was developed and exaggerated to create belief and enthusiasm rather than to make people actually do anything, and there was little intention of accepting present sacrifices unnecessarily when victory would bring so much gain at so little cost. Thus in Italy itself the war had much less effect on the system of production than in other belligerent countries. Mussolini had said that to win the war he would totally sacrifice civilian needs to military,[26] but in fact productive capacity was switched to war purposes far less than in 1915–1918, in the same way as the cost in lives was to be much smaller.[27] Part of the paradox of Mussolini's situation was that, at the same time as he needed the reputation of being a great war leader and organiser of victory, he also by instinct saw the usefulness of creating the impression that he could win easily and without great disturbance to the ordinary life of the nation. Perhaps he knew that his tenure of power would last only so long as he could provide the illusion of bread and circuses.

Churchill's technique was quite different when he offered people tears, toil, and bloodshed. Mussolini rather preferred to keep the appearance of normality and wherever possible make the war seem painless and easy. Hence he made no order for general mobilisation,[28] and newspapers were told to play down the fact of casualties.[29] He admitted that this was no way to win a war, but thought that the major need was to keep up morale.[30] Some Italians, on the other hand, were shocked to find so little disturbance of ordinary civilian life, and after being preached at for so long about the superb discipline and idealism of war, were disillusioned to learn of far more serious and dedicated attitudes adopted in other belligerent countries.[31] But fascism continued to think it a matter for boasting that so little was demanded from Italians and that there was no general mobilisation.[32] To put this differently, resources were considered to be less usefully spent in war production than in fuelling the great propaganda industry which was trying to convince ordinary citizens that all was well. The monthly supplement of Mussolini's personal paper, the *Popolo d'Italia*, weighed over 1.5 kilograms in May 1940, and its issue of November 1942, the month of defeat at El Alamein, was still over a kilogram despite all the talk about paper shortages.

Such an order of priorities helps to explain how the fascist government never—not even at the most critical moments of the war—lost sight of the need to prepare for a post-war economic struggle against Germany. Strong vested interests decided not to convert factories too wholeheartedly to munitions production, as it was important to keep skilled labour for civilian goods even if underemployed on short time. As newspapers reported with pride, the government was preparing to take advantage of the post-war boom, by ensuring that factories would be ready to start production at once, and by keeping unused ships in good repair, as well as by building up stocks of raw materials so that Italy would arrive first on the international market; it was even hoped that the war would not come to an end prematurely before these preparations were complete.[33]

The Germans of course knew that Mussolini was neglecting to

mobilise manpower and resources for the war. They were not pleased to discover that large stocks were being accumulated and many factories were meeting peacetime requirements, at the same time as Germany was being insistently called upon to help Italy with extra supplies. They sometimes wondered why, if he had not wanted to fight whole-heartedly, he had entered the war at all, and when they asked why so many cars were still on the streets when naval vessels were confined to port for lack of fuel, it was not a convincing answer that going to work by road saved time and thus increased production.[34] Fascism deliberately chose not to fight a total war. Statements made by three ministers in May 1942 show that, since they assumed that the war was bound to be won, they gave a high priority to amassing reserves so as to be ready to meet competition when all was over. As Rome and Berlin were expected to be the two big centres of finance and trade in Europe, government departments were shrewdly working to ensure that the country was in a position to take advantage of such a splendid position.[35]

As Mussolini was at first expecting only a short war, he intended to keep public confidence by the avoidance of severe food rationing. For the same reason, official figures were fabricated to show that the food situation was getting better, even when it was becoming much worse.[36] A ration card was issued at the end of 1939, but it affected only a few commodities and in any case was very generally disregarded.[37] Journalists exulted in the fact that, while Britain suffered acute shortages, Mussolini had worked a miracle to make Italians the one people in Europe with plenty to eat and even able to export food to Germany.[38] Early in 1941, when Italian soldiers in the frozen mountains of Albania lacked boots, any citizen in Rome could buy as many shoes and leather bags as he could afford: [39] rationing of these goods was avoided on the grounds that Italians on average could afford only one pair of shoes every second year and no new bureaucratic machinery was needed to enforce such an absolute minimum.[40]

Only in October 1941, after sixteen months of war, did bread rationing begin; the "battle for wheat" and self-sufficiency in cereals had so often been trumpeted as one of the great victories of fasicsm that no deficiency in flour could be lightly admitted. Mussolini in the end agreed that he might have waited too long before rationing bread, but excused himself by blaming shortages on farmers who were illegally turning their produce onto the black market. Clothes rationing, too, only began in October 1941. On second thoughts the Duce thought that bread and clothes rationing would be good for Italians as it would help to bring them discipline and a proper sense of austerity, and he thought that he therefore might well retain it after the war was over.[41] But in fact it did more than anything to bring indiscipline because the ration laws were disobeyed, and indeed it was officially admitted that disobedience was necessary for the working of the economy, since the black market, unlike the government, was at least efficient.[42] People who could afford to eat in restaurants and buy luxury goods, or who could live in holiday hotels and dine at the smart Roman golf club, found little difficulty in indulging themselves. Nor apparently did the leading fascists ever lack for much.[43]

Extravagance could also be seen in the continued construction of public works which, as always, were useful to Mussolini because, as well as providing jobs, they also provided him with striking headlines for the newspapers. In November 1940, no doubt because he needed to show that he was not put out by military reverses, he decided on a gigantic programme of public building. When asked by the minister in charge how this could be reconciled with the war, his orders were to act "as though the war did not exist". The first priority would be motorways, and also navigable canals which, though existing traffic admittedly did not justify them, would be useful in the post-war world as a link with trade routes through the Adriatic to the Near East. These grandiose proposals were accepted in parliament by acclamation and with very little debate after members had been told how important it was to show that fascism could carry on the ordinary life of the nation at the same time as fight a war.[44]

In May 1942 the minister of works boasted that Italy was doing more public building than the other belligerents, putting up prisons, a big observatory, several bridges over the Tiber, and spending more than ever before on public housing. In September the minister of culture, with an eye to post-war Olympic games, decided to spend several million on improving the winter sports facilities at Cortina d'Ampezzo.[45] Of course this used scarce construction materials and was highly inflationary, but no one could express such criticism in public. Action started on several of the canals, as well as on prospecting for a tunnel under the Straits of Messina,[46] and Mussolini ordered that this should continue even though there was no money and no prospect of finishing the work. Perhaps he was moved by the unemployment consequent on his failure to call up eight million soldiers, but probably his main motive was to provide some relief from news of defeats and to make the war seem less burdensome. When a deputation of industrialists from Brescia asked for improvements in their local railway, he agreed at once, to their delight and perhaps surprise, but as soon as they had gone he told his officials to take no practical action.[47]

As government expenditure increased, corruption of officials seems to have become greater or at least was less easily concealed. To give one example, reports by the secret police on the minister for foreign exchange, Raffaello Riccardi, suggest that this old-time Fascist may have been connected with fraudulent practices over export licences and currency deals.[48] The lack of public criticism allowed such bribery and graft to flourish far more in an autocracy than where the press was free to investigate, and Mussolini accepted minor corruption among his underlings as a means of blackmailing them into absolute submission. This became much more noticeable in the late 1930s with all the government contracts for rearmament. In wartime the manner in which these contracts were allocated often got quite out of hand. One senior police officer has recalled how the term "fascist leader" became almost synonymous with "thief",[49] and how the police were under orders to ignore the sometimes very substantial dishonesty in high places.[50] At the end of 1941 some leading Fascists made efforts to reduce the now notorious profiteering in the high echelons of the party, because at last it was realised that the reputation for dishonesty was damaging the regime.[51] But in practice little seems to have been done,[52] and some of the more scandalous instances of graft, for instance in the family of Mussolini's mistress Clara Petacci, were by superior orders removed from official police cognisance.[53]

In the spring of 1941 the Germans moved into the Balkans and North Africa to retrieve the military defeats which Mussolini had so rashly invited. A few days sufficed for the conquest of Yugoslavia and Greece, and then Rommel, after recapturing the whole of Libya in April, took the war into Egyptian territory. Hitler in June launched his attack on Russia, and Mussolini automatically followed suit. By now he had lost all independent power of decision or initiative. He was also deluded into assuming that this new campaign would soon be over and that a now much greater quantity of "booty" would be shared only among those who sent troops to help Germany on the eastern front. He himself, though in retrospect he tried to deny the fact, had so often affected to despise the Russian revolution and the Red Army that he had few doubts about a quick victory.[54] When this assumption proved erroneous, however, he tried to put himself in the right by pretending that he had opposed Hitler's invasion of Russia,[55] even though he had long since advocated just such a war, and already before the Germans started their invasion he was preparing troops to support it.[56] He insisted on sending an expeditionary force to the Russian front despite the fact that his tiny armoured cars were no match at all for the huge Russian tanks, and despite the more fundamental objection that his forces were already stretched to breaking point in the Balkans and North Africa. His own worry was not this but rather that Italian troops might not arrive early enough on the Russian front to take part in the triumph of victory.[57] Meanwhile the propagandists adapted as best they could to his fluctuating moods by welcoming the despatch of soldiers to Russia as both inevitable and beneficial.[58]

The German general staff opposed sending Italian troops to this distant field of battle, since they saw it as the very height of folly to extend commitments still further while so many soldiers were tied down elsewhere.[59] Some Italian staff officers agreed with this view,[60] but the new chief of general staff, General Ugo Cavallero, compliantly supported Mussolini's reading of the situation.[61] As speed was thought to be vital, the expeditionary force was equipped with careless negligence. Planes were sent into sub-zero temperatures without de-icing equipment.[62] The so-called motorised divisions were sent, too, though in fact they were still largely without transport, and some of these nominally mechanised troops had to cover a thousand miles on foot.[63] The phrase "motorised divisions" had been simply a phrase for publicity purposes, but Mussolini, as so often, forgot this, and then was quick to blame the Germans for not providing trucks to save his men from destruction.

The Duce particularly needed to have Italians on the eastern front because, as with the invasion of Britain, he was obsessively determined to be in force wherever Hitler was going to win the war.[64] When the Germans notified him in October 1941 that Russia was as good as defeated, a batch of journalists was dispatched to be present at the march into Moscow.[65] The press in Rome put out that Russia was losing because these "half-breed Mongols", as Canevari called them, were "racially inferior"; they lacked the initiative and drive of fascist soldiers because, unlike Germans or Japanese or Italians, they had for centuries been forced to obey as slaves.[66] Perhaps Mussolini believed this. At any rate, fascist racial doctrines had from the very beginning gratuitously assumed that the Slavs, when matched against the heirs of ancient Rome, would not even put up a fight.[67]

Not content with sending one army to Russia, the Duce was soon preparing a second expeditionary force which he pressed on a reluctant Germany, explaining to his unwilling generals that the more men he had on the eastern front, the better he would be placed to make big demands at the peace conference.[68] Fascism was intending to strike at the heart of communism and restore a "White Russia" once again.[69] For this somewhat remote cause, tens of thousands of people were sent haphazardly to useless deaths. Mussolini blamed everyone but himself. He later tried to make out that, with a fraction of the men who had frozen or starved to death in Russia, he could have easily won the war in North Africa, and that it was Africa rather than Russia where the axis should have found its real living space.[70]

In this way Mussolini contradicted himself repeatedly, perhaps without realising it, as he struck one pose after another in an attempt to preserve the one single unchanging but fragile piece of fascist dogma, that "Mussolini is always right". In fact, however, by December 1941 he was no longer judging rationally, and when he expressed pleasure at a setback for the Germans on the Russian front, or when on other occasions he wondered if it might not suit him best for the Germans to be defeated, these must surely have been symptoms of minor derangement.[71]

Furthermore, with hardly a moment's hesitation he followed the Japanese attack on Pearl Harbour by an equally rash declaration of war on the United States. Luigi Barzini and other experts on American affairs had flattered his prejudices by insisting that America would never fight, while others had even argued that American capacity for munitions production was virtually non-existent,[72] and Mussolini himself, who had still done nothing to repair his total ignorance of American affairs, was wont to assert that participation by the United States could have absolutely no effect on the war, because her military capacity was negligible.[73] He had been warned that others thought differently,[74] but a German victory was now his one hope, so presumably he thought he had no option but to join the Germans and Japanese, and find arguments to make this new war look plausible. At any rate he trusted as usual to instinct, and trusted also that some kind of dramatic move on his part would confirm among his entourage the belief in his omniscience and infallibility.

Perhaps in his growing remoteness from reality he had not realised how unwelcome a shock his announcement of war against America would be to the Italian people.[75] He told his uncomprehending ministers that, although the war might now last as long as five years, nevertheless the United States could contribute little to the allied cause,[76] and the propagandists dutifully embroidered on this opinion by pretending that war against America would be universally welcomed as a war of liberation.[77] A well-worn doctrine of the fascist intellectuals was that America must not be allowed to impose her semi-barbarism on the true representative of civilised values, fascist Italy,[78] and it was now argued that the gradual mixture of races in the United States made Americans every bit as decadent and enfeebled as the Soviet Union.[79] So effete were Americans thought to be, that a single bombardment of New York was said to be enough to bring them to their knees,[80] the very same supposition that had erroneously been used in monotonous turn about Barcelona, London, and Athens.

Russia and Africa were the two fronts where Italy suffered her heaviest defeats, but because of Mussolini's careless presumption, the greatest number of her soldiers was concentrated in the Balkans, and for long periods twice as many casualties were recorded here as on the African and Russian fronts. Left by the Germans to carry out garrison duties over an enormous area, more than half a million Italian soldiers were eventually needed in 1942 to hold down the civilian populations, as fascism inadvertently but inexorably brought into being a nationalist and communist opposition in one Balkan country after another. Mussolini's simple-minded invasion of Greece in October 1940 could thus be seen in retrospect as depriving him of any chance of winning the larger war. Moreover it was from what they saw as members of this army of occupation that many Italian soldiers learned the futility of fascism, and some of them turned instead to communism as a more plausible and effective answer to contemporary problems.[81]

Fascist leaders of course continued to sing their own praises for the "new order" which they were bringing to the Balkans,[82] but the almost complete lack of local support was hard for them to bear with aplomb, and they gradually moved from moderation to excess, from idealism to a cynical disregard of all humane values. In 1942 Mussolini ordered the use of terrorist methods, as he saw his enormous army increasingly hemmed in by local movements of insurrection.[83] Orders were issued to be ready to use poison gas to clear whole areas of their inhabitants, and the fascist party secretary, Aldo Vidussoni, advised the extermination of a million people so as to make the occupation easier.[84] These fierce measures were not adopted, but some units of the Italian army desperately resorted to systematic terrorism and wholesale shooting of hostages. Drastic orders were given for people to be executed without trial, for monitory reprisals, and also for the relatives of anyone involved in armed rebellion to be shot. Some of the worst excesses of fascism happened in these two years when the regime was put to the test of having at last to go beyond talk and apply in practice its ideas about living space and the new order in Europe.[85] Just as in Ethiopia, where similar terrorist methods had been used in 1936–1938, the practical implications of fascist doctrine were becoming explicit.

As the full nature of fascism and its logical consequences became clearer to ordinary Italians, they displayed an instinctive revulsion against the small gang of people who had clumsily landed the country in such a sorry plight. It was the war, and especially defeat in war, that effectively lost fascism much of the popular support it had so far enjoyed,[86] and soon this change of mood could be referred to obliquely in public.[87] At the end of 1942, defeat in North Africa removed some of the last lingering hopes. Yet Mussolini seems to have retained a good deal of his own personal popularity,[88] because the public had been taught to revere him alone and to ascribe any mistakes to his accomplices. His fascinated concentration on the technique of propaganda was to this extent a success.

Mussolini, on the contrary, was contemptuous of the Italians for being so utterly unserious and for letting him down after all his disinterested efforts on their behalf; he had tried to make them great, he said, but all he found around him was excrement.[89] In this mood he expressed himself as glad that his own people were suffering from the war, because it might toughen and improve their character.[90] If there had been half a million deserters in the First World War, he commented, this time there were fully a million shirkers of their duty, and six millions more who would rather endure defeat than suffer in their pockets. Some of these traitors were unfortunately among the elite of the fascist party. He concluded that the time had come to use brutal methods against such people, but unfortunately the machine at his disposal was too feeble when the problem was so huge.[91]

The ministry of propaganda did what it could to cover up deficiencies and preserve as long as possible the illusion that the war was as good as won. In 1942 newspapers were instructed to emphasise that Italy had taken a "preponderant" part in the Italo-German alliance, and a last-ditch attempt was made to reveal fascism as a great seminal force in the world with constructive answers to all contemporary problems.[92] Mussolini's speeches were translated into at least twenty-five languages, and likewise the "Mussolini law code", though it ran to well over ten thousand pages, was laboriously translated during the war into German, Spanish, and French, so as to establish the Duce as the supreme law-giver of the century. His *Doctrine of Fascism* had also been published lavishly in eighteen different languages, but all available copies were recalled and destroyed in April 1940 when the author had second thoughts about certain crucial phrases. Shortage of paper never seems to have been much of a problem in this pivotal branch of the administration. One of Mussolini's empty speeches was printed in a million copies by the propaganda ministry, and when the twelve-volume edition of his speeches was destroyed by bombing, a new issue was quickly prepared. More than a hundred thousand copies of a work about the mythical Italian armoured divisions had still been circulating throughout occupied Europe in a dozen different translations during the winter of 1940–1941,[93] for what purpose it is hard to say.

As defeat became more likely, fascist war aims were made to seem more moderate and idealistic. Italy was now said to want a peace without national hatreds, without revenge, and a new world where armaments would be abolished, frontiers broken down, and colonies given independence.[94] Mussolini thought sometimes of making a separate peace with either Russia or the western democracies, but while he was making up his mind he continued to pretend that the war must go on to the bitter end, and as a last resort Italians were encouraged by being told that nothing was lacking for the war effort, not iron, not coal or oil; arms were apparently available in such superabundance that the enemy could never have as many, and the morale of Italians was said to be quite unbreakable because they were a race fit to dominate the world.[95] Furthermore they were assured yet again that other countries, including Britain and America, were acknowledging the victory of fascism by themselves adopting its beliefs and behaviour.[96]

This kind of message was repeated and amplified by the 890 writers and journalists who in 1942 were listed as part-timer employees on the payroll of the ministry of propaganda.[97] These men, along with those employed by the foreign office and other departments, diligently published article after article throughout the war proving that victory and prosperity were just round the corner. As time went on they must have found it a difficult and perhaps sterile activity. As some of the Fascists themselves had to admit, the rhetoric and the sheer implausibility of newspaper and radio bulletins reached a saturation point, where they were no longer persuasive. So many fascist claims had proved false that the public can hardly have believed stories about British and Americans wanting to reduce Italy to the level of a purely agricultural country, or to close her universities, to impose forced labour on her, and carry off Italian works of art as plunder of war. Still less can it have been believed that the allies intended to execute hundreds of thousands of Italians and transport all their children abroad.[98]

This was a stern test for the fascist technique of propaganda. Its practitioners had been taught to go on building up the stakes in order to make today's news more dramatic than yesterday's and today's adjectives more superlative, because, if they ever flagged, the public might lose the necessary degree of tension. Either way the danger was that people might cease to believe, and the large number of bureaucrats in the ministry had to steer between these two dangers, by being extravagant without going so far that credibility altogether disappeared. In a closed society, as Italy largely was before 1940, success in this balancing act was not difficult once the proper methods had been learned. But after 1940 the war exposed Mussolini to an inescapable public comparison between what he claimed to be true and the hard facts which were outside his control. In other words the multiplication of superlatives, which like the sorcerer's apprentice could not be stopped, was bound at some time to reach a point where the process was patently incredible.

As problems became more complicated and intractable, Mussolini shut himself away in his own private illusions. Unlike Hitler or Churchill he did not even like talking to the army leaders, but preferred to keep aloof and superior, just as he invariably acted to depreciate both generals and ministers in public esteem if they became so well known as to detract from his own personal prestige.[99] Where possible he preferred not to be accompanied by advisers when he spoke to Hitler, with the result that as before he probably did not understand all of what was said to him. He certainly despised the other leading Fascists,[100] and one reason for his sometimes extremely odd selection of these leaders was precisely that he liked to choose unworthy people whom he could afford to despise.[101] He kept them very generally in the dark about his intentions because he had a positive distaste for discussion with them or indeed with anyone else, and perhaps this is a common enough fact among dictatorships everywhere. To avoid any participation with them he had to concentrate everything in his own hand, and ended up inevitably with what his own ministers described as lack of any government at all.[102] The man who first won power in 1922 on a platform of law and order against anarchy, ended by standing for a travesty of law and an institutionalised anarchy, but he concealed this by controlling all the media of information. Not for nothing did he call himself the most disobeyed man in history.[103]

Mussolini had an excellent memory, and liked to impress people by reeling off facts and figures to indicate that he knew everything that was happening. But he was increasingly selective and fallible in his knowledge, and he still preferred to rely on a press-cutting service and an assiduous reading of even local newspapers, since he did not like to acknowledge to prefects and ministers that he needed them for information. Apart from listening each evening to the BBC news bulletins, an act which for other Italians was treason,[104] he paid close attention each morning to voluminous reports by the various police services, though much of this material was worthless gossip, as he well knew. Certainly these reports did not deserve the great deal of time he devoted to them even on the most busy and critical days of the war,[105] and for the most part they were just a self-indulgent voyeuristic intrusion into the private lives of his various subordinates.

The numerous hierarchy of fascist leaders, at local as well as national level, knew that, because of their own mediocrity, they could exist only in the shadow of this man and without him they would be nothing; they had therefore needed to build up the great myth of the Duce as someone who was always right, who was far-seeing, omniscient, and beyond criticism.[106] But in 1942 and 1943 they were in danger of being swept away along with the very myth which they had spent their active lives in self-interestedly perpetuating. More and more of them began to criticise Mussolini in private, to throw doubts on his mental condition, and to blame him for ruining the country.[107] Even Ciano, until now the much-favoured son-in-law, secretly arranged a meeting with Cardinal Montini to explain his opposition to the war and his eagerness in adversity for the consolations of religion.[108]

Just as Mussolini liked to see himself as alone, without any superior and even without real collaborators, so the Duce also came to think of fascism as something which, as it had begun just with himself, would also finish with himself;[109] this was almost to say that fascism was not the great doctrine of the future, as he had once tried to maintain, but just a miscellaneous rag-bag of ideas covering what was essentially a personal desire for power. In his isolation he was more and more out of touch with real life, and began to compare himself not only to Napoleon but to Jesus Christ.[110] It was noted that even on the few occasions when he visited the soldiers in the field, he rarely if ever went near enough to the front to observe the reality of battle, nor did he like visiting the victims of bomb damage to see what war meant to ordinary people who were ignorantly compelled to fight it. He always had a horror of death, and according to Ciano he had commanded in three wars without ever seeing a single casualty. As Ciano also explained, Mussolini, at the same time as being squeamish, was more cruel and blood-thirsty than was generally believed, and could now be expected to commit any outrage so as to cling to the last vestiges of power.[111] The Duce spoke of making a mysterious terroristic attack on England, or of the use on a large scale of a poison gas which would kill every living thing, and of his even more mysterious death ray.[112] These were the words of a man losing contact with reality.

Mussolini had more than once maintained that war was the ultimate test by which a nation and a leader should be judged, and obviously by this self-imposed measurement he was a failure. Yet he did not confess to any personal responsibility for the war, still less to responsibility for Italy's defeats.[113] The war itself he blamed on the stupidity of France and Britain; the defeats he blamed on the Germans [114] and also on his own generals.[115] Above all he continued to blame the Italian people who, though in public he cynically continued to flatter them as the most intelligent and martial among the nations,[116] in private he contemptuously denounced as immature, superficial, unwarlike, unintelligent, untruthful, and spineless.[117] He grumbled that too few of his fellow countrymen had been prepared to die in what he liked to call "the sublime holocaust of this war",[118] and in a momentary outburst of indignation said he meant "to go on fighting to the last Italian".[119] But if he was prepared for Italy and all Italians to be destroyed, there could be no reason for the war except the mysterious personal gratification of this one man. Not just fascism, but Italy too meant little to him.

The prospect of defeat was a great solvent of old ties and illusions, a great prompter of doubts and questions. It was odd to find that even in 1943, after three years of war propaganda, almost no one seemed to know why they were fighting.[120] The old liberal ideas, which Mussolini had once thought buried for ever, were creeping back until ordinary individuals imagined that they even might have a right to their own personal interpretation of what fascism really meant.[121] Communism, too, that other mortal enemy, was stated in official reports to be making great progress inside Italy and undermining every branch of industry.[122] Public opinion was sometimes said to be still anglophile despite nearly three years of war, and also had less and less respect for the Fascist Party.[123] Though the die-hards desperately continued to repeat that war was something noble and necessary, which preferably should not end too soon,[124] by the early summer of 1943 it was beginning to look as though the great majority of the Italian people might favour peace at almost any cost.[125] When the allies invaded Sicily in July and then the Italian mainland in September, there was little left to hope for. After a slow but relentless campaign, Mussolini was eventually captured by the Italian partisans and executed summarily at the end of April 1945.

Until almost the last moment he had continued to believe that propaganda was the main weapon required, and that his job as war leader was, first, to establish and maintain the myth of his own infallibility, and then to clothe in plausibly realistic garments all the many other illusions he had thought it expedient to create. He had got used to living in cloud-cuckoo-land, where words and not facts mattered, where the army was judged by its parade-ground performance rather than by anything more substantial, where wars were won not by superior munitions and strategy but by knowing how to manipulate the news so as to give the illusion of strength. It was a world where a skilled publicist could fool most of the people fairly easily, where decisions could be reversed from day to day without anyone minding or even noticing, and where in any case decisions were designed to impress rather than to be put into effect. It was an essentially unserious world, where prestige, propaganda, and public statements were what counted; and it is hard to avoid the conclusion that this was the central message and the real soft core at the heart of Italian fascism. Since the Italian people are not notoriously more gullible than anyone else, one must admit that Mussolini gave a virtuoso performance as an illusionist; not for nothing did he once say that the dramatic art was the greatest of all the arts.[126] Yet it was this same virtuosity which more than anything else brought Italy to defeat.

NOTES

CHAPTER 1: FASCISM TAKES OVER

1. OO,* XXXV, 18–19, 32–34.
2. OO, XXXV, 7, 63; Megaro, 164–65; Sarfatti, 218; Rossi, C., *Mussolini*, 84.
3. De Felice, *Mussolini il rivoluzionario*, 273, 307–308; Templewood, 154; Mowrer, 100–101.
4. OO, I, 104; III, 199; and IV, 153–55; Begnac, 129; Malaparte, 245–47; Niekisch, 263.
5. OO, XV, 91–93; Begnac, 360–61; Rossi, *Trentatre*, 340; Ludwig, *Colloqui*, 67; Croce, 2/125; Benjamin, 249.
6. Ercole, *Pensatori*, 400.
7. Coppola, 15, 38, 90–91; Rumi, 186.
8. Federzoni, *Italia*, 206.
9. Salvemini, *Scritti*, 2/142.
10. R.It., Dec. 1925, 712.
11. OO, XVII, 13; XXI, 221.
12. OO, XIX, 130, 146.
13. OO, XIX, 48; XXI, 164.
14. Di Nolfo, 5.
15. OO, XII, 322–23.
16. Coppola, 33–35; OO, XX, 323.
17. OO, XVIII, 437.
18. DDI, 7/1/88–89; Cassels, 45.
19. Saint-Aulaire, 641–43; Steffens, 2/808; Cassels, 52–53; Tamaro, *Due Anni*, 1/36, Albertini, *Epistolario*, 4/1662–65.
20. Borsa, *Memorie*, 420; *"Picture Post,"* 14.8.1943 ** (Wickham Steed), 7–9.
21. OO, XV, 306; XVI, 5; Chiurco, 2/270–71.
22. Tamaro, *Venti anni*, 1/104.
23. NA, Dec. 1953, 401–402.
24. Cassels, 100.
25. DDI, 7/2/270–71; *"The Labour Magazine,"* Oct. 1923, 253–54 (A. J. Toynbee); Barros, 78; Canevari, *Graziani*, 160.
26. Wagnière, 117; Ciano, *Diario*, 1/299; Donosti, 24.
27. Rossi, C., *Mussolini*, 171; Salvemini, *Scritti*, 2/229.
28. OO, XX, 63, 107.
29. Aroma, *Mussolini*, 295.
30. CF, 15.9.1923, 129; *"Gerarchia,"* Oct. 1923, 1252 (Volpe); Cantalupo, *Fatti*, 167; Roletto, 107.
31. *"Foreign Affairs,"* July 1934, 556.

---

* An explanation of the abbreviations used in the Notes may be found in the alphabetical List of Works Cited (pp. 289–310). (When two editions are cited, the pages correspond to the first.)

** When dates are given in full, they are listed with first the day, then the month, then the year. Thus 14.8.1943 = 14 August, 1943.

32. BD, 1a/5/73, 1a/6/119, 478.
33. Susmel, *Corrispondenza*, 56.
34. Grazzi, 8–9; Rumi, 281.
35. BD, 1a/1/540–41; Carocci, 56.
36. Begnac, 365.
37. DDI, 7/4/413.
38. DDB, 3/164–65.
39. Guariglia, *Ricordi*, 39, 113; DDI, 7/5/632.
40. Slocombe, 244–47; Seldes, 321–23.
41. OO, XXI, 411–12.
42. OO, XXII, 149; DDI, 7/4/85; Toscano, *Storia diplomatica*, 99.
43. "*Gerarchia*," Oct. 1932, 880.
44. St.A. 286/087175–77.
45. CF, 1.5.1925, 171.
46. NYT "*Magazine*," 9.11.1924, 7; "*Gerarchia*," Oct. 1925, 627 and Nov. 1925, 697; Dinale, 135.
47. OO. XX. 170–71; CF, 1.12.1925, 443.
48. *Raccolta delle circolari*, 2/44, 113, 462–63, 510; Cantalupo, *Racconti*, 313–34.
49. DDI, 7/8/190; Soffici (Prezzolini), 279; "*Resto del Carlino*," 8.1.1926; Diggins, 100–103.
50. Milza, 47–53; Berselli, 125.
51. OO, XVIII, 275, 432.
52. Rumi, 302–303.
53. BD, 1a/1/292–93; 1a/5/234–35.
54. "*The Times*," 21.1.1927, 14; DDI, 7/3/406 and 7/4/140; RF, 16.1.1927; CF, 15.12.1928, 470.
55. "*The Sunday Times*," 13.6.1926, 10; Runciman, 17.
56. CF, 1.5.1925, 170.
57. Milza, 71, 76; "*Revue des deux mondes*," 1.10.1922, 637 (Hazard).
58. Ebenstein, 218–19; "*The Times*," 28.12.1923, 8; Salter, 226–29.
59. St.A. 30/014431, (22.1.1923); Leto, *Ovra*, 83.
60. St.A., 30/014443; Diggins, 48–49.
61. DDI, 7/3/565.
62. St.A. 30/014439–42; *Guida generale*, 57.
63. "*English Review*," Dec. 1922, 561.
64. "*Edinburgh Review*," July 1924, 7–8 (Major Barnes); "*Dublin Review*," July 1924, 96–100; "*The National Review*," June 1926, 568–71.
65. Seldes, 164–65, Albertini, *Epistolario*, 4/1745.
66. Carocci, 100, 270, 333; BD, 1a/4/139 and 1a/5/49–50; "*The Times*," 1.11.1935, 18.

CHAPTER 2: GROWING SELF-CONFIDENCE

1. OO, XVI, 158–59; XIX, 266; Dinale, 116.
2. CF, 1.6.1926, 205; OO, XXIV, 283; Rocco, 3/781.
3. OO, VII, 81.
4. OO, XXI, 271; XXII, 37, 65, 385–86.
5. Tamaro, *Venti anni*, 2/308; OO, XXI, 122, 363, 386; XXIV, 235; XXXIV, 124.
6. Carli, 95; "*Libro e moschetto*," 3.3.1929 (reproduced in *Eia*, 117–18); Maurano, *Mentalità*, 123; RPI, July 1925, 5; Perini, 392.
7. Pettinato, *Scritto*, 455; Volpe, *Guerra*, 405; RI, Dec. 1925, 712.
8. OO, XVI, 159; XVIII, 439; XIX, 234, 278; XXI, 363.
9. DDI, 7/1/149–50; "*Augustea*," 15.3.1928, 133; LS, Aug. 1928, 457; Panunzio, 40; RPI, Feb. 1925, 5; "*Tribuna*," 5.1.1926, 174 (Coppola); "*Vita Nova*," May 1926, 24–26, 36, 39; Corso, 186; Carli, *Colloqui*, 45, 95, and *Cervelli*, 29–31.

10. Rochat, *L'esercito*, 520–28; *La guerre* (Rochat), 41–42; Canevari, *La guerra*, 1/135.
11. Canevari, *La guerra*, 1/241–43.
12. St.A, 168/049417–79 (Giuriati); *Das Heer*, 3–4; Settimelli, *Mussolini*, 290; Tamaro, *Venti anni*, 2/234, 456.
13. St.A, 263/074466.
14. OO, XXIX, 82; Leto, 145–46; Rochat, *Militari*, 361; Roatta, 21–22.
15. Badoglio, *L'Italia*, 38; Dollmann, *Roma*, 127; Caviglia, 303–304.
16. Volpe, *Storici*, 384–85, 391–95; *Raccolta delle leggi*, 31.12.1934, 5/4246; *"Vita nova,"* Nov. 1929, 937; *"Antieuropa,"* Ap. 1936, 154, and Ap. 1938, 159; Vecchi, 332; *L'Apporto*, 35; R.It., July 1929, 592–93; PM, July 1939, 194.
17. Volpe, *Saluto*, 144.
18. CF, 1.2.1924, 315–16 (Tamaro).
19. St.A, 40/022403, 022436; BD, 1a/1/652 and 1a/4/173–75.
20. Guariglia, *Ricordi*, 139.
21. OO, XXIII, 161; DDI, 7/7/217.
22. *Foglio d'Ordine*, 27.1.1927, 3; 17.3.1928, 2; DDI, 7/5/254–55; Guariglia, *Ricordi*, 53; *Senato*, 3.6.1931, 4137 (Grandi); Ciano, *1937–1938*, 55.
23. Donosti, 15; Begnac, 415, 537.
24. OO. XXIII, 271.
25. DDI, 7/5/454–55; 485; *"L'Italia Coloniale,"* Aug. 1928, 155–56; *"The Times,"* 29.10.1927, 12.
26. DDI, 7/8/149.
27. Legatus, 56; *Italia fra tedeschi*, 43, (Petersen); Carocci, 152; *"Augustea,"* 30.11.1927, 669.
28. DDI, 7/5/578; BD, 1a/2/122, 127, and 1a/3/179.
29. Carocci, 94–95, 100; BD, 1a/3/524–25; DDI, 7/8/515–16.
30. Aloisi, *Journal*, 168; Quaroni, 136, 140; DDI, 7/6/355; *Foreign Relations*, 1931, 1/545; Packard, 67.
31. Quaroni, 108–10; Tamaro, *Venti anni*, 3/87.
32. DDI, 7/7/93, 99–100; Carocci, 256; Guariglia, *Ricordi*, 151.
33. Barros, 300.
34. DDI, 7/7/519; Payne, *Falange*, 21.
35. DDI, 7/5/295.
36. DDI, 7/4/347; Iraci, 38; Faldella, *L'Italia*, 16; Starhemberg, 106.
37. *Il processo*, 41, 63, 106; Aloisi, *Journal*, 42, 49, 340; D'Amoya, *Declino*, 151–57; Carocci, 175–77.
38. Barker, *Macedonia*, 36–42; DDI, 7/6/131, 514, 518–19, 533; 7/8/233.
39. V.I., Feb. 1933, 134 (Farinacci); OO, XXV, 182–83.
40. DDI, 7/1/79–80; Ludecke, 72–81, 133.
41. DDI, 7/2/238.
42. Cassels, 161, 168–69; Salvemini, *Prelude*, 44–45; DDI, 7/8/438–39, 445–46.
43. DDI, 7/2/318; NYT *"Magazine,"* 9.11.1924, 7.
44. Fest, 265; Ciarlantini, *Hitler*, 19; Donosti, 80; Hitler, *Mein Kampf*, 554.
45. *Italia fra tedeschi*, 24 (Petersen).
46. DDI, 7/2/329–30 and 7/3/30; Cassels, 162–64; Seeckt, 628; *"Storia e Politica,"* 1966, 5/90 (Cora).
47. DDI, 7/5/621–22; 7/6/284, 286; 7/7/414–16; 7/8/493, 500–501, 608.
48. DDI, 7/8/418–19; *Hitler's Secret Book*, 207.
49. DDI, 7/4/18 and 7/5/632; OO, XXI, 319–20; Starhemberg, 94; LS, Jan. 1929, 5 (Signoretti).
50. Guariglia, *Ricordi*, 82; Ginnari, 9; Mussolini, A., *Verso*, 46.
51. Guariglia, *Ricordi*, 76; DDI, 7/8/119.
52. DDI, 7/7/487–90.
53. Guarneri, *Battaglie*, 1/155, 330; Toscano, *Storia dei trattati*, 1/355.
54. DDI, 7/5/166, 175; 7/6/126; 7/8/91–92; Seldes, 264–65.
55. DDI, 7/7/300, 401; BD, 1a/5/59–61.
56. Guariglia, *Ricordi*, 85; Aloisi, *Journal*, 51.
57. Galland, 13–15; Valle, 144; DGFP, C/3/731, 766–67, 802; Petersen, 21–22.

58. *"Affari esteri,"* July 1974, 146–47 (Serra).
59. Mussolini, E., *Mio fratello,* 175.
60. CF, 15.10.1931, 381; OO, XXVI, 84; Donosti, 50.
61. De Felice, *Mussolini il fascista,* 1/563 and 2/26; DDI, 7/2/445–46; Begnac, 505; Litvinov, 66, 110.
62. Di Nolfo, 51, 284; *Senato,* 3.6.1930, 2762, and 3.6.1931, 4150.
63. St.A, 54/026840–54.
64. DDI, 7/5/46, 433–35, 633; 7/6/14–15.
65. *Il Gran Consiglio,* 550; DGFP, C/2/182; BD, 2/6/117; OO, XXVI, 91; CF, 1.12.1933, 442.
66. *"Time and Tide,"* 17.2.1928, 155; Salvemini, *Mussolini,* 403.
67. St.A. 287/087721–27, 087738–42.
68. *"Antieuropa,"* 1929, 1/5–10, 29; 2/124–25.
69. *"Antieuropa,"* Feb. 1930, 851; July 1930, 1178; Aug. 1930, 1258, 1267; Feb. 1932, 107; Gravelli, *Verso,* 23, 219; Ledeen, 77–82.
70. *"Politica,"* May–June 1925, 68/225–26; Feb. 1926, 71/28 and 38–39; Ap. 1927, 78/221; *"Augustea,"* 31.1.1928, 33–35; LS, Jan. 1929, 5; Feb. 1929, 80.
71. CF, 15.3.1930, 102; 15.5.1930, 182.
72. CF, 15.10.1929, 390; 15.5.1930, 191; 15.6.1930, 222; 15.3.1931, 111.
73. *"Antieuropa,"* 1929, 2/154 (Bruers); *"Augustea,"* 15.11.1928, 648 (Rebora); OO, XXII. 172; Ciarlantini, *Vicende,* 175.
74. Longanesi, *Vade-mecum,* 7; *"Lo Stato,"* Mar. 1933, 170, and Nov. 1933, 771; *"Antieuropa,"* 1929, 2/99–100.
75. *"Augustea,"* 31.12.1927, 844; *"Corriere,"* 9.8.1929; CF, 15.1.1929, 33, and 1.2.1933, 59.
76. BD, 1a/6/230.
77. *"Il Primato,"* 1.11.1930, 2 (Maurano): Carli. *Antisnobismo.* 36–39, 73.
78. CF, 1.1.1930, 10; 15.1.1930, 31; 15.4.1930, 149; 1.6.1931, 210–11; RF, 10.3.1927, 3.
79. *"Antieuropa,"* 1929, 8/639–40, and July 1930, 1244.
80. OO, XXIV, 227–28, 235, 282–83; Mussolini, A., *Le forze,* 55.
81. Salvadori, *L'unità,* 128–30; GF, 31.5.1931, 3, and 6.12.1931, 5; PS, May 1930, 362; V.I., Mar. 1930, 319; R.It., June 1929, 500–501; Settimelli, *Mussolini,* 289, 303; Pini, *La civiltà,* 98, 134.
82. De Felice, *Mussolini il duce,* 378–80; BD, 2/1/381.
83. DDI, 7/5/240.
84. OO. XXIV, 281; *"Lo Stato,"* Oct. 1932, 709 (Curcio); Missiroli, *Studi,* 176; Villari, *Italian,* 73.
85. Aloisi, *Journal,* 12, 115; DDI, 7/8/335; Stimson, 268–69.
86. Ojetti, 368, 396; Guariglia, *Ricordi,* 74.
87. Cantalupo, *Fu la Spagna* 42; DDF, 1/1/189; Aloisi, *Journal* (Toscano).
88. BD, 2/1/368.
89. De Felice, *Mussolini il duce,* 377–78, 396–401, 849.
90. Pini-Susmel, *Mussolini,* 3/257.

CHAPTER 3: ITALY AND HER COLONIES, 1922–1932

1. OO, IV, 59, 68; V, 46; XXXV, 16.
2. Bottai, *Mussolini,* 34; CF, 1.12.1923, 235; *"Politica,"* Feb. 1926, 29–31.
3. *"Augustea,"* 24.5.1927, 344–46 (Cantalupo), 15.12.1927, 817 (Appelius), and 15.2.1929, 73; LS, Aug. 1928, 461–62 (Lischi).
4. Mussolini, A., *La lotta,* 46–47; *"Imperium,"* Dec. 1926, 32; RPE, 30.11.1932, 1172 (A. Pirelli).

5. Fortunati, 19; *"Foreign Affairs,"* Jan. 1936, 245–46 (Salvemini).
6. Aroma, *Mussolini,* 73; *L'Impero (A.O.I.),* 271 (Astuto); Capoferri, *L'ora,* 52; OM, June 1942, 235.
7. BD, 1a/2/510; DDI, 7/4/164 and 7/7/109; Guariglia, *Ricordi,* 141.
8. DDI, 7/6/452.
9. DDI, 7/5/164.
10. DDI, 7/5/420; R. Med., Jan. 1925, 25.
11. DDI, 7/6/62; 7/7/89; 7/8/474–77, 487.
12. *"Gerarchia,"* Oct. 1930, 845–48.
13. Longrigg, 132–34; Hess, *Italian Colonialism,* 183; Trevaskis, 10, 19; Lewis, 111–12.
14. Ciano, *Diario,* 1/115; *Africa: espansionismo,* 51–54; RF, 27.4.1927, 1.
15. V.I., Nov. 1931, 631; ACV, 1938, 1/776; *Senato,* 14.6.1929, 649.
16. APC, 3/368–69 (Franchetti); *"Terzo mondo,"* Mar. 1969, 66 (Irace).
17. Guarneri, *Battaglie,* 2/292; *Camera,* 18.3.1938, 4819.
18. DDI, 7/8/454; RSA, Jan. 1941, 44–46.
19. ACV, 1938, 1/722 (Vecchi), 1/722–25 (Rava); Iraci, 113; Rochat, *Il colonialismo,* 148–52.
20. Hess, *Italian Colonialism,* 169–70; Marco, 53–58; Zaghi, 535.
21. *Camera,* 7.5.1925, 1348 (Lessona).
22. DDI, 7/8/447; *Senato,* 27.3.1933, 6074–75 (Di Scalea).
23. BSOA, 1946, 843 (Evans-Pritchard); Canevari, *La guerra,* 1/251–54, 267–69, 377; CF, 15.2.1926, 67.
24. *"Rivista delle colonie,"* Sept. 1924, 351; *Amministrazione fiduciaria,* 50 (Vedovato), 118 (Mondaini).
25. Leone, 2/502–505; *Vita Nova,* Mar. 1926, 45.
26. *La rinascita,* xv, xxi–xxii, 202.
27. Graziani, *Ho difeso,* 29–32; Nitti, *Rivelazioni,* 400; Canevari, *La guerra,* 1/292–95, 301–303; AAI, Dec. 1940, 33.
28. Graziani, *Ho difeso,* 38–39; Gasparotto, 278; Leone, 2/542.
29. Lessona, *Il fascismo,* 5, 29.
30. St.A. 256/070529–30, 070552, 070561.
31. Federzoni, *AO,* 100; RPI, Aug. 1925, 26; Tritonj, 255–57; AAI, 1939, 3/99.
32. Evans-Pritchard, iii–iv, 196, 211; Giglio, *La confraternita,* vi (Graziani).
33. Gregory, 13; BD, 1a/1/700–701; Federzoni, *AO,* 116–17.
34. *Senato,* 12.5.1932, 4978–79.
35. *La rinascita,* 200–206; APC, 6/270–72 (Siniscalchi); Massuero, 107, 361.
36. *"The Banker,"* July 1937, 268 (Lessona).
37. Evans-Pritchard, 198; RSA, Ap. 1943, 248–49.
38. Federzoni, *AO,* 114; Sillani, *La Libia,* 90, 150–51; Lessona, *Scritti,* 75; Villari, *Storia diplomatica,* 7; R.Med., April 1932, 358.
39. APC, 6/272.
40. St.A. 222/057040, 057067–70.
41. *Senato,* 14.6.1929, 655 (De Bono); 12.5.1932, 4996 (Schanzer); 27.3.1933, 6077 (De Bono); Mecheri, 124; *La colonizzazione,* 2/562; Moore, 73–76; Raciti, 70.
42. St.A. 132/036776–77; MLI, Jan. 1973, 10–11 (Rochat).
43. St.A, 256/070769–70; Graziani, *Ho difeso,* 49.
44. DDI, 7/7/348; *"Gerarchia,"* Oct. 1930, 847–48.
45. OM, Oct. 1929, 451; MLI, Jan. 1973, 9–10; Giglio, *La confraternita,* 135.
46. Giglio, *La confraternita,* 133.
47. Graziani, *Cirenaica,* 110; Graziani, *Ho difeso,* 54; Orano, *Graziani,* 16.
48. Boca, 103; Pini, *Sotto le ceneri,* 21; Morgan, 149; Graziani, *Cirenaica,* 117.
49. *Senato,* 12.5.1932, 4980, 4993–95; and 27.3.1933, 6070.
50. Giglio, *La confraternita,* 144; Canevari, *La guerra,* 1/334–35.
51. Pace, *La Libia,* 97.
52. Evans-Pritchard, 188; MLI, Jan. 1973, 32–34 (Rochat); Moore, 172.
53. Graziani, *Cirenaica,* 273.
54. MLI, Jan. 1973, 26.

55. Lessona, *Memorie*, 291; "*Africa*," Ap. 1945, 74 (Evans-Pritchard); Leone, 2/559; V.I., Dec. 1931, 757.
56. Evans-Pritchard, 191; "*The Geographical Journal*," 1945, 228.
57. MLI, Jan. 1973, 27.
58. Aloisi, *Journal*, 46.
59. MLI, Jan. 1973, 36–38 (Rochat); Zaghi, 410; "*Gerarchia*," Ap. 1932, 268–69 (Lessona); "*Lo Stato*," Sept. 1937, 489–90.
60. *Senato*, 12.5.1932, 4982–83; V.I., July 1932, 68; EI, May 1936, 409–10.
61. Marco, 89.
62. *La nuova Italia*, 1/1100–1102, 1112.
63. Ed.F., May 1933, 408–10, 415–16.
64. CF, 15.2.1931, 77; RC, Jan. 1931, 1–2; "*Gerarchia*," Ap. 1931, 277–78, and June 1932, 520; *Africa: espansionismo*, 102–105 (Zaghi), 114–22 (Zavattari); "*Antieuropa*," Mar. 1933, 122, 125–26, 137–39.
65. Mussolini, A., *Tripolitania*, 12; Maurano, *Mentalità*, 132; Ciarlantini, *Antologia*, i (De Bono); CF, 15.2.1929, 72; Massuero, 229; Lischi, 158; "*Vita nova*," March 1933, 215.
66. "*Augustea*," 15.5.1934, 258.
67. "*Vita nova*," Ap. 1931, 308; *Senato*, 18.3.1931, 3374 (De Bono); CF, 1.8.1930, 294.
68. APC, 6/140–43, 153.

CHAPTER 4: THE SHADOW OF HITLER

1. Suster, v (preface by Mussolini).
2. Hoepke, 259.
3. Starhemberg, 92.
4. "*Lo Stato*," May–June 1930, 334 (Renzetti); "*Gerarchia*," Sept. 1930, 709; St.A. 287/087721–29 (Gravelli).
5. St.A. 170/050252–54.
6. St.A. 170/050264–66.
7. Pini-Susmel, 3/299.
8. CF, 1.10.1930, 371; "*Antieuropa*," May–June 1931, 1903; Aloisi, *Journal*, 96; Malaparte, 264.
9. DDF, 1/3/270; Carocci, 30.
10. "*Camicia Rossa*," Mar. 1932, 49–50; Ap. 1932, 74; Mar. 1933, 50; May 1933, 102–103; Mar. 1934, 68.
11. Starhemberg, 21, 94; Aloisi, *Journal*, 50; "*Antieuropa*," May–June 1931, 1891.
12. RF, 16.9.1932, 1; Alfassio, 152–53; V.I., Sept. 1932, 249–51 (Farinacci), Nov. 1932, 506 (Farinacci), and Feb. 1933, 135 (Farinacci).
13. ACV, 1932, 1/285–86; "*Gerarchia*," July 1931, 607; "*Antieuropa*," July 1931, 2048, 2057; "*Augustea*," 31.8.1932, 483.
14. Aroma, *Mussolini*, 48; Aloisi, *Journal*, 109.
15. DGFP, C/1/552; *Trial*, 17/24; Zachariae, 103.
16. "*Vita nova*," Dec. 1932, 1071; Ed.F., Dec. 1932, 949.
17. ACV, 1932, 1/96–98, 254, 272, 353–58, 487–88; "*Politica*," Feb. 1933, 105/5, 74 (Coppola); Orestano, *Verso*, 115, 129–30, 151–52, 196; LS, Dec. 1932, 539; "*Gerarchia*," Dec. 1932, 1075; GF, 30.11.1932, 9; CF, 1.11.1933, 401; Portsmouth, 153–54.
18. St.A. 109/029677A (to his daughter Edda); Mussolini, B., *La dottrina*, 13, 25; OO, XXV, 104, 119–20, 147–48; Faldella, *L'Italia*, 16; Favagrossa, 11; Cantalupo, *Fu la Spagna*, 47.
19. GF, 30.1.1932, 4; "*Politica*," Feb.–Ap. 1932, 15–16 (Coppola); CF, 15.4.1932, 141–42; Gray, *L'Italia*, 13; "*Echi*," 25.4.1934, 454; Camera, 13.3.1933, 8174 (Orano).
20. *Il Gran Consiglio*, 534; OO, XXV, 224; Aloisi, *Journal*, 49–50; Aroma, *Vent'anni*, 150.
21. "*Gerarchia*," Oct. 1932, 878 (Sarfatti); "*Ottobre*," 28.10.1933, 1; CF, 1.3.1933, 92–93 (Paresce); 15.3.1933, 114; Ricci, *Avvisi*, 95; V.I., Ap. 1933, 457–62.

22. Gray, *Credenti*, 236–37; Ciarlantini, *Mussolini*, 20–21, 135; BF, June 1932, 352–56; V.I., May 1933, 521; Lischi, 121–22; *"Vita nova,"* Ap. 1933, 305; RDP, 1933, 187 (Ambrosini); LS, Dec. 1932, 530, Orestano, *Revisione*, 10–12.
23. St.A. 250/068137; Cucchetti, 159.
24. Wiskemann, 21—22.
25. RPI, Aug. 1932, 5–6; Sept. 1933, 5.
26. UF, May 1932, 219–21; Feb. 1933, 67–70; Dec. 1934, 79.
27. St.A. 170/050275; DGFP, C/1/30; Guariglia, *Ricordi*, 135.
28. Rauschning, 47.
29. Iraci, 145; DGFP, C/1/25.
30. Aloisi, *Journal*, 50, 62, 121; De Felice, *Mussolini il duce*, 452.
31. BD, 2/5/238.
32. Melograni, 533, 535; *"Augustea,"* 31.1.1933, 34; V.I., Feb. 1933, 225; *"Antieuropa,"* Jan.–Feb. 1933, 4; RPI, Feb. 1933, 14; LS, June 1933, 291; Ricci, 58–59; CF, 15.8.1933, 314–15; Petersen, 114.
33. Aloisi, *Journal*, 96; Vedovato, *Organizzazione*, 5–6.
34. DDF, 1/3/18; Aloisi, *Journal*, 128; D'Amoja, *Declino*, 261; BD, 2/5/325.
35. Salata, 1/23; Bianchi, *Rivelazioni*, 17 (Grandi).
36. Fd.F., Oct. 1933, 836; UF, June–July 1933, 321–22; RPI, Aug. 1933, 15; CF, 15.8.1933, 309; De Felice, *Mussolini il duce*, 451–52.
37. OO, XVI, 44–45, 48, 82.
38. LEI, Rome 1933, 308–309 (Curcio); LIR, June 1933, 1; RPI, Aug. 1933, 15; *"Augustea,"* 31.3.1933, 162 (Ciarlantini); Volpe, *Il risorgimento*, 416; Vecchi, 22.
39. CF, 15.8.1933, 301–302; 1.9.1933, 322; 15.10.1933, 381, 388; and 1.11.1933, 402; IML, 23.7.1933, 16–17.
40. DGFP, C/1/29–30; C/4/103–105.
41. Guariglia, *Ricordi*, 82, 151–57.
42. De Felice, *Mussolini il duce*, 398–99 (Guariglia).
43. Rauschning, 130.
44. Starhemberg, 26–27, 90–91, 104–105, 108.
45. Aloisi, *Journal*, 134; DGFP, C/1/739, 894–95.
46. DDF, 1/4/540; *Foreign Relations*, 1933, 1/270; Wagnière, 216; BD, 2/5/684, 702.
47. DGFP, C/2/142–43; C/4/105–106.
48. *"Augustea,"* 30.4.1934, 226.
49. St.A. 140/040015.
50. BD, 2/6/245; *"Lo Stato,"* Oct. 1933, 702; LEI, Feb. 1934, 99.
51. BD, 2/6/376.
52. Zingarelli, 144; Braunthal, 174, 178–87, 199 (P. R. Sweet).
53. OO, XXVI, 188.
54. DGFP, C/2/704; DDF, 1/6/60–61.
55. Aloisi, *Journal*, 364.
56. DDF, 1/6/101, 552, 705–706, 763–64.
57. Rintelen, 11; Salvemini, *Scritti*, 3/390–91.
58. St.A. 170/050279; DDF, 1/6/762.
59. Tamaro, *Venti anni*, 3/95; Vergani, 36; Fuchs, 168; BD, 2/6/762.
60. Badoglio, 23; Alfieri, 154; Theodoli, 145–46; Papen, 332; DDF, 1/6/6, 726; Starhemberg, 150.
61. Poncet, *Ricordi*, 247; Dollmann, *Roma*, 99; Cerruti, 147.
62. Aloisi, *Journal*, 198–99; I.I., 24.6.1934, 960; Signoretti, 66; *Les lettres*, 12 (François-Poncet).
63. Meissner, 354; Rosenberg, 39; De Felice, *Mussolini il duce*, 496.
64. OO, XXVI, 136, 185, 189–90, 258–59; Aroma, *Mussolini*, 73.
65. Missiroli, 224, 236; Gambetti, *Cronache*, 137; CF, 15.3.1934, 116; UF, Ap. 1934, 325; IM, 28.10.1934, 22.
66. Scaroni, 92, 100.
67. Ricci, 146.
68. St.A. 20/009434; Ojetti, 440–41.

69. *"Popolo di Roma,"* 29.7.1934 (cit. *Eia*, 234); UF, Aug.–Sept. 1934, 517–18; IM, 28.2.1935, 11–14 (Settimelli).
70. Funke, 29; *Trial*, 17/496; Bojano, 45.
71. *Il processo*, 30–31.
72. OO, XXVI, 358; Schuschnigg, 234–35, 242; V.I., Sept. 1934, 280 (Farinacci); Avenati, 97, 107; Giovannucci, 41, 118; *"Foreign Affairs,"* July 1934, 563 (Grandi); Latinus, 90.
73. *"Gerarchia,"* Ap. 1932, 321; Sept. 1934, 762, and July 1935, 581; OO, XXVII, 21.
74. St.A. 131/036345–47.
75. OO, XXVI, 308; RDC, June 1934, 11.
76. *"Gerarchia,"* Aug. 1934, 636; OO, XXVI, 359, 392, 402.
77. *Leaders of Europe*, 332–33.
78. Schuschnigg, 235.
79. OO, XXVI, 319; Bottai, *Vent'anni*, 71.
80. Acerbo, 420; Starhemberg, 170; DGFP, C/4/102.
81. *"Gerarchia,"* Aug. 1934, 636, and July 1935, 579–81; LS, Jan. 1934, 22.
82. DGFP, C/3/456; BF, Sept. 1934, 708–709; V.I., Sept. 1934, 279; Oct. 1934, 511; Giglio, *Politica*, 42.
83. PS, Ap. 1933, 318.
84. *"Augustea,"* 31.3.1934, 163.
85. *"Vita nova,"* June 1933, 458–59; IML, Oct. 1933, 14; *"Antieuropa,"* Oct. 1933–Mar. 1934, 479–82; *"Augustea,"* 15.4.1934, 194–96; IM, 28.9.1934, 23 (Berto Ricci); I.I., 9.9.1934, 375; *"Il Frontespizio,"* Dec. 1934, 5.
86. St.A. 20/009500–501, 009528, 009531–32; DGFP, C/3/724.
87. OO, XXVI, 232–33; DGFP, C/3/11; Starhemberg, 150.
88. OO, XXVI, 298, 309, 327; *"Gerarchia,"* Aug. 1934, 636, and July 1935, 580–82; Aroma, *Mussolini*, 82.
89. V.I., Sept. 1934, 370–71; Oct. 1934, 516; and Nov. 1934, 647; CF, 1.1.1935, 95; *"Lo Stato,"* Oct. 1934, 674, and July 1935, 530–31; *"Il Rubicone,"* Sept. 1934, 10; *"Antieuropa,"* Oct. 1933–Mar. 1934, 316; PS, Aug. 1935, 241; Papini, *Tutte le opere*, 8/556–58; BF, Oct. 1934, 779.

CHAPTER 5: THE ETHIOPIAN WAR

1. DDI, 7/1/149–50; Hess, 171 (De Vecchi); Funke, 9–10.
2. St.A. 256/070537–38 (Federzoni).
3. DDI, 7/6/163; *Camera*, 7.5.1935, 1349 (Lessona).
4. *"Storia e politica,"* 1966, 5/92 (Cora); R.It., Sept.–Oct. 1933, 127.
5. De Felice, *Mussolini il duce*, 374, 848–49; Guariglia, *Ricordi*, 142–43, 165–72, 763, 769–72; DDI, 7/7/479.
6. Guariglia, *Ricordi*, 144; Aroma, *Vent'anni*, 230.
7. DDI, 7/6/177–79; *Africa: espansionismo*, 71–73; Lessona, 269–70.
8. DDI, 7/7/405–406, 422–23.
9. Graziani, *Ho difeso*, 76; Guspini, 112–13; *L'esercito*, 99; Rochat, *Militari*, 26–27, 31, 46–47, 371; Aloisi, *Journal*, 45.
10. *"Antieuropa,"* Aug. 1936, 175; Bianchi, *Rivelazioni*, 218–21.
11. *"Antieuropa,"* Mar. 1933, 166–67.
12. Tamaro, *Venti anni*, 3/103–104; Funke, 31–32; FO (PRO), 371/18032, 21.9.1934 (Balbo); Aloisi, *Journal*, 226, 239.
13. Rochat, *Militari*, 377–78; Bianchi, *Rivelazioni*, 132–34.
14. *Il processo*, 49, 62; Aloisi, *Journal*, 47–48, 225–26; Conti, *Servizio*, 20–21.
15. DGFP, C/3/524; West, 1/21–22.
16. De Felice, *Mussolini il duce*, 514–19.

17. Ledeen, 118–19, 123; *"Gerarchia,"* Feb. 1934, 95; Jan. 1935, 77–79; and Aug. 1935, 676–77.
18. Aloisi, *Journal,* 272–73.
19. *"Gerarchia,"* July 1935, 579–80; V.I., Feb. 1935, 163, and May 1935, 664; CF, 1.1.1935, 103, and 1.4.1935, 222; *"Lo Stato,"* July 1935, 533.
20. DGFP, C/3/303–304; C/4/102.
21. Bottai, *Vent'anni,* 116; Szembek, 49 (Suvich); Spampanato, *L'Italia,* 150–51, 155, 166.
22. St.A. 120/032693; *Senato,* 28.3.1935, 879; UF, Oct. 1934, 580–81; I.I., 10.2.1935, 198; SIPS (Naples 1934), 151, 162–65.
23. Starhemberg, 217–18.
24. *Senato,* 29.5.1935, 1373–74; Vecchi, *Bonifica,* 98–100; *"Augustea,"* 31.1.1935, 33; CF, 1.4.1935, 213–14; IF, 28.9.1934, 8; Martini, 163–64, 168–70; RDC, Dec. 1934, 13–14.
25. St.A. 120/032671, 032690–91.
26. St.A. 120/032727.
27. St.A. 120/032699.
28. St.A. 120/032738, 032741–42.
29. *"Augustea,"* 28.2.1935, 97–98; and 15.4.1935, 194; RDC, Mar. 1935, 12–13.
30. APC, 3/365–69; *Il processo,* 43; V.I., July 1935, 50, 54; Cipriani, *Un assurdo,* 323.
31. Fischer, 263–64 (Rossoni); Lessona, *Memorie,* 353–55.
32. Pace, *L'Impero,* 37; Cipriani, *Un assurdo,* 324.
33. R.Med., Nov. 1933, 830; NA, 16.9.1935, 184; I.I., 8.7.1934, 52–54; *Africa: espansionismo,* 149; *"Gerarchia,"* Mar. 1935, 292–96; *"Corriere,"* 22.7.1935, 1; Federzoni, *Italia,* 131, Della Torre, 279–83.
34. V.I., Ap. 1935, 561.
35. *"Gerarchia,"* Ap. 1931, 277–78.
36. REC, Jan. 1937, 16; I.I., 8.9.1935, 455; Alimenti, 98; Gayda, *Che cosa,* 195.
37. De Felice, *Mussolini il fascista,* 2/359; Rochat, *Militari,* 161; Tamaro, *Venti anni,* 3/136.
38. Pirelli, *Considerations,* 7, 16; NA, 16.1.1936, 128 (Federzoni).
39. V.I., Oct. 1931, 386; July 1935, 3–4 (Farinacci).
40. NA, 1.8.1935, 338; I.I., 28.7.1935, 168; *"Gerarchia,"* Aug. 1935, 673, and Feb. 1936, 99.
41. *Italia fra tedeschi,* 67 (De Felice); *Dino Grandi racconta,* 17.
42. Lagardelle, 276–77, 280–86; *"Middle East Journal,"* 1961, XV/71–74 (Watt).
43. Reynaud, 1/176; De Felice, *Mussolini il duce,* 526–33.
44. Romains, 203–204; Laurens, 24–30; Boncour, 3/14–16; Vansittart, 515; Ciano, *1937–1938,* 313; Guariglia, *Ricordi,* 220–21.
45. Thompson, 96–99; Rotunda, 218–22; Gladwyn, 47–48; Strang, 65–66; Harvey, 137; *"The Spectator,"* 18.6.1943, 568 (Perth); Macartney, 309.
46. RSPI, Ap.–June 1958, 188 (Berio); July 1972, 411–14 (Marzari); Petrie, 180; JCH, July 1974, 112–13, 119 (Goldman).
47. Serventi, viii, 34–38.
48. LEI, Oct. 1935, 741; Nicolosi, 14; Bertoldi, *Mussolini,* 271–72; *Il processo,* 19 (Suvich); De Felice, *Mussolini il duce,* 646; Bandini, 297.
49. Bottai, *Vent'anni,* 87; Ojetti, 464; Canevari, *La conquista,* 60–61; *Dizionario,* 3/50 (Valori).
50. Bianchi, *Rivelazioni,* 64, 184; Rochat, *Militari,* 111.
51. Susmel, *Corrispondenza,* 150–51.
52. Caracciolo, 30–31; Fuller, 53; Bianchi, *Rivelazioni,* 153–54; Rochat, *Militari,* 106–108, 161–62, 270.
53. Jones, 191.
54. Lessona, *Memorie,* 171–72.
55. Guariglia, *Ricordi,* 245–46.
56. Federzoni, *Italia,* 140–41.
57. Eden, 227, 421–22.
58. Sarkissian, 151–52 (Toscano).
59. NA, 16.4.1936, 419, and 1.7.1936, 32–33 (Villari); Civ.F., Nov. 1935, 1062; Bianchi, *Rivelazioni,* 680.

60. Funke, 16–17; Salvemini, *Prelude*, 237; Bernotti, 18; Aloisi, *Journal*, 294.
61. Baer, 255 (quoting Chambrun); Guariglia, *Ricordi*, 272; Rotunda, 271, 288 (quoting Drummond); Aloisi, *La mia attività*, 4.
62. *"Gerarchia,"* Aug. 1935, 724, and Sept. 1935, 787.
63. Gambetti, *Cronache*, 88, 151; IF, 28.8.1935, 32.
64. *"Gerarchia,"* Feb. 1936, 98–99 (Guariglia); Lessona, *Verso*, 34–35, 73–74; *Fascism and the Working Classes*, 52; *L'Impero* (A.O.L.), 13; APSR, Dec. 1940, 1168–72 (Wilcox).
65. *"Storia e politica,"* 1966, 5/94 (Cora); Rochat, *Militari*, 377; *"Il Giorno,"* 11.11.1968, 4 (Boca); Salvemini, *Prelude*, 310–11.
66. Rochat, *Militari*, 400–406.
67. I.I., 8.9.1935, 454.
68. Aloisi, *Journal*, 346; St.A. 129/035493 (Balbo); *"Il Rubicone,"* July 1935, 6; Ciano, *1937–1938*, 71.
69. Marder, 77–81; Hart, 1/330.
70. Rossi, F., *Mussolini*, 24–26; Aloisi, *Journal*, 348–49; Rochat, *Militari*, 225–27.
71. Bandini, 331.
72. Guspini, 241; Guariglia, *Ricordi*, 248, 269; Amé, 203–206; Aloisi, *Journal*, 66, 99, 224; Irving, 123.
73. Ciano, *1937–1938*, 61, 75, 309; Ciano, *Diario*, 1/31; Quaroni, 204; Blet, 1/413.
74. Kelly, 227; Jones, 160; Villari, *Storia*, 141.
75. Marder, 86; Chatfield, 2/89; Gladwyn, 60–61; DDI, 9/4/622; Toscano, *Pagine*, 2/82.
76. Leto, *Ovra*, 136–37; St.A. 122/034033; Fischer, 261.
77. Scorza, 35; Gorla, 41; Conti, *Servizio*, 545–46; Lessona, *Memorie*, 178; DGFP, C/4/691; Corbino, 235; *"Corriere,"* 13.10.1967, 5 (De Stefani); Romains, 216.
78. *"Gerarchia,"* Sept. 1935, 787, and Nov. 1935, 946; PS, July 1935, 179–80 (Bottai), Oct. 1935, 303–304, and Nov. 1935, 311 (Bottai); NA, 1.11.1935, 34; OO, XXVII, 203.
79. Theodoli, 176.
80. Begnac, 517.
81. *Inghilterra*, 87–101 (Mack Smith).
82. Lessona, *Memorie*, 276.
83. *"L'azione coloniale,"* 17.10.1935, 1.
84. *Le ragioni*, 7 (Marconi), 11 (Volpe), 25 (De Stefani), 37 (Ojetti), 46 (Coppola); NA, 1.2.1936, 244; Federzoni, *A.O.*, 241; Sergi, 2; *"Il Frontespizio,"* Jan. 1936, 1–6.
85. Maurano, *Ricordi;* Guspini, 135; Biondi, 280.
86. Aloisi, *Journal*, 315.
87. DGFP, C/4/1075.
88. St.A. 123/034279–80 (Farinacci); FO (PRO), 371/19134 (J.4853/1/1); Lessona, *Memorie*, 195; Bottai, *Quaderno*, 56.
89. Lessona, *Memorie*, 182.
90. Rosengarten, 30; DF, 2/1/49.
91. Steer, 231; *Hansard*, 20.5.1936, 1171; AAI, May 1938, 323–25.
92. Rotunda, 272 (quoting Drummond); Romains, 216; Lessona, *Memorie*, 240; Bottai, *Vent'anni*, 132–33, 233, 302.
93. *Il processo*, 57, 103, 258–60; Conti, *Servizio*, 70–75, 148–49, 202–206, 248–51; Bandini, 353–54, 395–96, 527–28, 532–42.
94. DGFP, C/4/927; Amery, 3/184; *Il Gran Consiglio*, 595; Tamaro, *Venti anni*, 3/166; Aloisi, *Journal* 331; NA, Dec. 1973, 488; Bianchi, *Rivelazioni*, 144; Hardie, 197–99.
95. *"Il Giorno,"* 12 and 14.11.1968 (Boca).
96. Dall'Ora, 217–18; *"Gerarchia,"* Jan. 1936, 44; *Il processo*, 30; Izzo, 4–5, 439–41.
97. Villari, *L'Italia*, 154; Lessona, *Un ministro*, 122; Aloisi, *Journal*, 367–68; Bandini, 529–30; Vailati, 240.
98. Matthews. *Eyewitness*, 15, 256–57; Del Boca, 74–75.
99. *"Daily Mail,"* 6.5.1936, 15; Mancini, 21; NA, 1.11.1935, 91 (Bollati).
100. Fuller, 39; Macfie, xi–xii; Brown, 201, 218; Nelson, 218, 222; Schonfield, 53.
101. *"Espresso,"* 26.9.1965, 6–7 (Gambino); Boca, 165, 272–73; Steer, 7–9; *"Le Figaro,"* 26.3.1959, 5.
102. *"The Patriot,"* 7.5.1936, 392; *"Daily Mail,"* 28.4.1936; DDF, 2/1/96–97.

103. "*La Verità*," Ap. 1936, 58; Keene, 191–92 (Salvemini).
104. Vailati, 238–39; St.A. 132/036830.
105. Rochat, *Militari*, 170, 181–87; Graziani, *Ho difeso*, 78–82.
106. "*Gerarchia*," May 1936, 351.
107. Graziani, *Ho difeso*, 115; Tamaro, *Venti anni*, 3/302; Farina, 94; Boca, 58–59.
108. Mecheri, 135; Bonacossa, 103.
109. Leto, *Ovra*, 149; Donosti, 41; Federzoni, *Italia*, 144–45; Caracciolo, 32.
110. *Camera*, 7.5.1936, 2654; V.I., May 1936, 497.
111. St.A. 114/031494 and 122/034030.
112. RPI, July 1935, 5; June 1936, 12–13; *Chi è*, 1940, 653; Santoro, 1/14, 25; Mussolini, R., *La mia vita*, 125.
113. Mussolini, V., *Voli*, 48, 78–79, 141, 150.
114. Aloisi, *Journal*, 367; De Felice, *Mussolini il duce*, 710.
115. "*Lo Stato*," May 1936, 292; *Camera*, 20.3.1936, 2383; "*Daily Mail*," 6.5.1936, 15.
116. Lessona, *Memorie*, 185–86; Bottai, *Vent'anni*, 105; Vailati, 240; Luciano, 8, 14.
117. Marinese, 117; Signoretti, 95–99; FO (PRO), 371/22436 (Perth, 13.1.1938).
118. Graziani, *Ho difeso*, 96; St.A. 132/036936.
119. OO, XXIX, 193, 272; *Nuova Civiltà*, 114.
120. Badoglio, *L'Italia*, 15; Pareti, *I due imperi*, 240.
121. Farago, 16 (Fuller).
122. Maugeri, *Mussolini*, 42; Federzoni, *Italia*, 278.
123. Canevari, *La guerra*, 1/368; De Biase, *L'Aquila*, 400; Salvemini, *Prelude*, 420; Biondi, 288.
124. *Camera*, 18.5.1938, 5014–16 (Di Revel), and 20.3.1936, 2368–69 (Baistrocchi); BD, 3/3/501; Canevari, *La guerra*, 1/374; *Compendio statistico* 1938, 195.
125. Bottai, *Vent'anni*, 125.
126. RPI, Ap. 1936, 45.
127. De Felice, *Mussolini il duce*, 642.
128. Bernotti, 15–16.
129. Harris, 144; Diggins, 290–92.
130. Pricolo, *Ignavia*; Senise, 92; Farina, 83–84; Roatta, 13.
131. "*The Economist*," 6.3.1937, 510–11; Aloisi, *La mia attività*, 4–5, 14; RSPI, Ap. 1958, 211–13 (Berio).
132. OO, XXVIII, 32; SIPS (meeting at Venice), 1938, 2/326.
133. *Camera*, 20.3.1936, 2383, 2385.
134. OO, XXX, 98; Boca, 111; Canevari, *Graziani*, 18; Barker, *The Civilizing Mission*, 158.
135. CF, 1.11.1936, 2.
136. MLI, July 1971, 4–5 (Isnenghi, quoting *Corriere*, 13.5.1936).
137. Tamaro, *Venti anni*, 3/134, 232–33; Spigo, 44–45.
138. IAI, 3/20–22, 105–106 (allegati 14, 80).
139. AAI, 1939, 3/163.
140. "*Il Giorno*," 20–21.11.1968 (Boca); Graziani, *Ho difeso*, 106–107, 129; *Documents*, 1/36–47.
141. Poggiali, *Diario*, 106; "*Il Giorno*," 19.11.1968, 3.
142. Poggiali, *Diario*, 75–78, 90–91, 110, 114.
143. Lessona, *Memorie*, 305–306; Algardi, 142–43.
144. "*Le Figaro*," 25.3.1959, 5.
145. Graziani, *Ho difeso*, 124.
146. Lessona, *Memorie*, 296–97.
147. GAA, 18.6.1936, 2.
148. St.A. 103/027742–43; GAA, 21.7.1936, 1; Poggiali, *Gli albori*, 116–7; MLI, July 1971, 7 (Isnenghi).
149. OO, XXVIII, 93.
150. IAI, 2/381; 5/298 (allegato 1046); Vittorelli, 113.
151. "*Storia e Politica*," 1966, 5/96 (Cora); Rocca, 202.
152. Rochat, *Il colonialismo*, 200; IAI, 2/269; Bianchi, *Rivelazioni*, 210.

153. *Il Gran Consiglio*, 621.
154. Boca, 201–203; Pankhurst, 542–47; Poggiali, *Diario*, 179–83; Bandini, 444–45; Federzoni, *Italia*, 145; Mosley, *Haile Selassie*, 245; Greenfield, 240–41; Barker, *The Civilizing Mission*, 304; Rochat, *Militari*, 201–203; Lessona, *Un ministro*, 14.
155. Poggiali, *Albori*, 5, 105, 485.
156. *Documents*, 1/19–20, 40–47; Rochat, *L'attentato*, 37.
157. *Documents*, 1/26–29; Susmel, *Corrispondenza*, 170; Ciano, *1937–1938*, 19; "Espresso," 26.9.1965, 7 (Gambino); Dower, 242.
158. Pini, U., *Sotto*, 60–63; Poggiali, *Diario*, 246–47; IAI, 5/446–52 (allegati 1249–57).
159. Ciano, *1937–1938*, 17, 19, 22, 94.
160. FO (PRO), 371/22436 (Perth, 13.1.1938, 112); "The Times," 2.2.1938, 8; Poggiali, *Diario*, 86.
161. Waugh, 230.
162. St.A. 15/006516–18; 117/031823.
163. St.A. 290/088936–43; Rochat, *Il colonialismo*, 204.
164. St.A. 290/088914–15.
165. St.A. 122/033901–905; Cavallero, *Il dramma*, 56.
166. DDF, 2/7/281–82; Guarneri, *Battaglie*, 1/437.
167. Ciano, *1937–1938*, 122; Graziani, *Ho difeso*, 162–64; Lessona, *Memorie*, 311–16.
168. Boca, 216–18; Rochat, *Il colonialismo*, 184.

CHAPTER 6: TOWARDS THE AXIS

1. BD, 1a/3/153; FO (PRO), R. 6020/23/22 (5.7.1938, Perth); *Peace and War*, 279 (Long); Di Nolfo, 35–36; *Dino Grandi racconta*, 12.
2. Grazzi, 13.
3. Caviglia, 142; DDB, 5/40 (Spaak).
4. Di Nolfo, 218–19; "Foreign Affairs," Jan. 1928, 201–202; Petersen, 465.
5. DDI, 7/6/282; Aloisi, *Journal*, 340.
6. Ojetti, 325; Guariglia, *Ricordi*, 204.
7. Conti, *Servizio*, 20–21; Tamaro, *Venti anni*, 3/87–88; Starhemberg, 189; D'Amoya, *Declino*, 104–105.
8. DDI, 7/3/57.
9. Aloisi, *Journal*, 238; De Felice, *Mussolini il duce*, 797.
10. Bastianini, 33; Guarneri, *Battaglie*, 2/70, 109; MO, 391 (Pirelli); RI, Nov. 1936, 775; "Romana," Aug.–Sept. 1937, 259; Giglio, *Politica*, 26–27; Fornaciari, 113.
11. MO, 43; PM, Jan.–Feb. 1937, 4.
12. MO, 129.
13. Saracino, 94, 103–104.
14. *Dal regno all'impero*, 34.
15. CF, 1.11.1936, 2; Orestano, *Saggi*, 268; GF, 15.10.1936, 5.
16. "Libro e moschetto," 9.9.1937, 1; CF, 1.11.1936, 5; LS, Sept. 1937, 259; Saracino, 103–104, 109–10.
17. "Daily Mail," 5.5.1936, 15; "Daily Telegraph," 28.5.1936.
18. OO, XXVII, 244.
19. OO, XXVIII, 60.
20. Dinale, 153–54; Bottai, *Vent'anni*, 105; Guariglia, *Ricordi*, 97; DGFP, C/5/1002; Lessona, *Memorie*, 276.
21. Bastianini, 50–51.
22. Lessona, *Memorie*, 333.
23. *Camera*, 18.5.1936, 2722, 2724 (Alfieri).
24. "Daily Telegraph," 28.5.1936; DDF, 2/2/264.
25. Bottai, *Vent'anni*, 113.

26. Aloisi, *Journal*, 382.
27. *"Il Rubicone,"* July 1935, 4–5; Susmel, *Corrispondenza*, 159.
28. CF, 15.2.1937, 127 (Berto Ricci); *"Il Frontespizio,"* 1937, 803 (Papini).
29. *Enciclopedia, appendice*, 1938, 577–78; *"Information,"* 24.2.1933, 388; UF, Dec. 1934, 126–27.
30. CF, 1.7.1934, 245–46; Ledeen, 164–66.
31. Ciano, *1937–1938*, 47, 49.
32. MO, 192 (Volpe).
33. MO, 183–84, 190–92, 267; CF, 15.1.1924, 37; Guariglia, *Ricordi*, 332–34.
34. De Felice, *Mussolini il duce*, 713.
35. Ciano, *1937–1938*, 94; *Ciano's Diary 1937–1938*, 62; St.A. 27/013049.
36. Mussolini, V., *Vita*, 82.
37. CF, 15.5.1933, 195; *"Il Lavoro Fascista,"* 4.4.1933, 1; IML, Aug. 1933, 18; OO, XVIII, 224.
38. OO, XXVI, 10, 24, 45, 302; BF, May 1934, 367, and July 1934, 533; *"Augustea,"* 15.7.1933, 386; *"Il Lavoro Fascista,"* 18.4.1933, 1.
39. Ciano, *1937–1938*, 12, 15; JCH, Jan. 1974, 81–84 (Joseph); St.A. 26/012513, 012518, 012523.
40. Ciano, *1937–1938*, 63; V.I., Jan. 1935, 94 (Daudet).
41. St.A. 15/006441–42; 145/042627–31.
42. DF, Oct.–Nov. 1941, 86.
43. Pascazio, *La rivoluzione d'Irlanda*, 171.
44. St.A. 54/026803, 026812, 026823–25.
45. St.A. 15/006864–66.
46. St.A. 15/006867; 54/026826.
47. *Hansard*, 6.6.1946, 2140.
48. *"The Times,"* 7.6.1946, 6; Cross, 90–91; Benewick, 200, 215; Skidelsky, 463–64.
49. St.A. 15/006516–18; 20/009586; 43/022610; 54/006874.
50. RF, 2.11.1934, 1; V.I., July 1934, 116.
51. NA, 16.4.1936, 419; 1.7.1936, 32–33; and 16.11.1936, 211; *Il fascismo inglese*, 104, 111–12.
52. St.A. 267/077152–53.
53. OO, XXXV, 232; DDI, 7/1/503.
54. DDI, 7/4/324, and 7/7/531; DDF, 1/1/209; CAM, Sept.–Dec. 1936, 236–37, and Sept.–Dec. 1937, 217–19; API, 1936, 785.
55. FO (PRO), 371/22436 (Perth, 13.1.1938), and 371/22444/491 (Consul at Tunis, 29.11.1938).
56. OO, XVI, 432, and XXVI, 268; DDI, 7/4/260; *"Imperium,"* June 1935, 457–60; *"Geopolitica,"* Aug.–Sept. 1941, 384; St.A. 26/012507–23; Rebora, 118.
57. OO, XXXV, 230; Cassels, 86; DDI, 7/7/75; St.A. 26/012567–68, 012617; R.Med., June 1926, 210–18, and Aug. 1926, 284–85.
58. BD, 2/6/257; *"Gerarchia,"* May 1932, 402–403.
59. Ricci, 13, 55; EN, July 1934, 495; BF, May 1932, 269–70; *"Lo Stato,"* Oct. 1934, 691; *"Augustea,"* 15.11.1934, 645; *"Commentari,"* 1.10.1934, 6–7.
60. Ciano, *1937–1938*, 234; PI, 21.5.1940, 3; CF, June 1940, 407 (Ercole); *"Geopolitica,"* Aug.–Sept. 1941, 378–79; *Camera commissioni*, 17.4.1943, 1351–53.
61. Aloisi, *Journal*, 269.
62. *Il processo*, 81 (Baistrocchi); Reynaud, 1/176; Gamelin, 2/167–68.
63. St.A. 20/009447–49.
64. Nuremberg, 9/103; DGFP, D/8/610; Funke, 4.
65. DDI, 9/2/338–39; Donosti, 74–75.
66. Guarneri, *Battaglie*, 2/72; DGFP, C/4/745.
67. *"Le Figaro,"* 26.3.1959, 5; Fest, 495; Funke, 40–45, 60; Kordt, 109, 116.
68. GDFP, D/1/376; Robertson, 66, 95; Starhemberg, 219.
69. De Felice, *Mussolini il duce*, 729, 732; Giglio, *Politica*, 119.
70. Aloisi, *Journal*, 364; DDF, 2/1/700; Bonnefous, 6/403.
71. Tamaro, *Venti anni*, 3/191; Aloisi, *Journal*, 365.

72. *Reichskanzlei*, 31.1.1936 (Strunk).
73. OO, XXXIV, 438.
74. DGFP, C/4/1110, and C/5/576.
75. Boncour, 2/338.
76. DGFP, C/5/1000–1001; Ciano, *1937–1938*, 55.
77. CF, 15.9.1930, 346, and 1.3.1933, 97; Pini, *Filo*, 133, 158; Ricci, 116–17.
78. *"Gerarchia,"* Sept. 1935, 794–95.
79. *"Augustea,"* 30.6.1933, 373–74; BF, June 1934, 457.
80. Begnac, 351.
81. OO, XXIX, 195.
82. Aloisi, *Journal*, 386.
83. OO, XXVIII, 106–107, and XXIX, 51, 257.
84. Bastianini, 49.
85. Bechi-Luserna, 114.
86. Gianturco, 60; Danzi, 44, 46.
87. Cucco, *Amplexus*, 112–39; Cucco, *L'amplesso*, xi–xxiii; Danzi, 20.
88. Calderoli, 53.
89. OO, XXXI, 126; Ciano, *Diario*, 2/225.
90. Pettinato, *Questi inglesi*, 163, 169, 365, 377, 379; Pascazio, *La crisi*, 175, 186; *"Corriere,"* 29.3.1941, 3 (Piovene), and 8.2.1942, 3 (Monelli); Pepys, 9 (Radius).
91. *"Gerarchia,"* Dec. 1935, 1029.
92. LIR, Ap.–May 1940, 95–96; *Il libro della IV classe*, 1938, 44.
93. *"Prospettive,"* 1939, 4/41; Gray, *La chiesa anglicana*, 3, 8; *Inghilterra*, 90–94 (Mack Smith).
94. V.I., June 1936, 549, 552 (Canevari); LAI, June 1938, 66; CF, 1.9.1939, 339.
95. DGFP, 5/1000.
96. OO, XVIII, 198, and XXIX, 29; DGFP, D/1/3; Civ.F., June 1937, 410 (Villari).
97. Federzoni, *Italia*, 132–33; Castellani, 12–13; *"Corriere,"* 9.11.1938, 3.
98. Ricci, 25; Saracino, 8.
99. Bottai, *Vent'anni*, 105–106; DGFP, C/5/1000, C/4/961; Scarfoglio, *L'Inghilterra*, 268; Zanussi, *Guerra*, 1/71–74; Bastianini, 49; Ciano, *1937–1938*, 69–71.
100. Aloisi, *Journal*, 363, 369, 372; Maravigna, 4–5; *"L'azione coloniale,"* 27.3.1936, 1; DGFP, C/5/1000–1002.
101. Puntoni, 64.
102. Begnac, 571; Tamaro, *Venti anni*, 3/196; Giolli, 48; Signoretti, 88; *"Prospettive,"* 1939, 4/31.
103. Donosti, 47; Guariglia, *Ricordi*, 328–29; Vergani, 54–55.
104. Ciano, *L'Europa*, 78; Templewood, 155; RSPI, July–Sept. 1950, 391–92 (Toscano); St.A., 54/026756–79.
105. OO, XXVIII, 69; DGFP, C/2/1000, 1137; Ciano, *L'Europa*, 75, 93–96.
106. *"Lo Stato,"* Feb. 1936, 106; CF., 1.4.1937, 165; Federzoni, *Parole*, 34; AF, Aug. 1937, 2–4.
107. RPI, Sept. 1936, 5; DDF, 2/3/350–51.
108. RPI, July 1937, 5, 9.
109. Magistrati, *L'Italia*, 44–45; Rintelen, 21–24; Tamaro, *Venti anni*, 3/344.
110. Rintelen, 9–10; De Felice, *Storia*, 537–38; Funke, 152–53; Hossbach, 35.
111. *"The Economist,"* 15.5.1937, 393; *"The Times,"* 11.5.1937, 14; 14.5.1937, 12, and 18.6.1937, 16; FO, 371/22346 (Perth, 13.1.1938), 8, 22–26; Ebenstein, 67; RSPI, July–Sept. 1950, 394.
112. Anfuso, 52; Magistrati, *L'Italia*, 71; Kirkpatrick, *Mussolini*, 334.
113. Schmidt, 365; Dollmann, *Roma*, 119.
114. *"Life,"* 26.2.1945 (Grandi); *"Libro e moschetto,"* 30.9.1937, 1; Cucchetti, 216–17; *Italia e Germania* 61–62 (Amicucci); Araldi, 273.
115. Ciano, *L'Europa*, 220.
116. Orestano, *Saggi*, 277; Giolli, 18; *"Lo Stato,"* Nov.–Dec. 1937, 632.
117. Ciano, *1937–1938*, 46, 66.
118. *"Gerarchia,"* July 1935, 605, and Aug. 1935, 677; *"Lo Stato,"* Jan. 1936, 51.

119. Ciano, *1937–1938*, 76, 88–89; Guarneri, *Battaglie*, 2/157; LEI, Dec. 1941, 595.
120. NYT, 28.8.1938, 4/2/3.

CHAPTER 7: CIVIL WAR IN SPAIN

1. Payne, *Politics*, 295, 503.
2. Guariglia, *Ricordi*, 189–90; Robinson, 174–75.
3. JMH, June 1952, 181–83 (Askew); Guariglia, *Primi passi*, xx, 375–78.
4. St.A. 145/042121.
5. Donosti, 53.
6. Cantalupo, *Fu la Spagna*, 63; Tamaro, *Venti anni*, 3/200.
7. Thomas, 233–34; Jackson, 248–49.
8. St.A. 132/036925; Canevari, *La guerra*, 1/419; Aroma, *Vent'anni*, 242.
9. Cantalupo, *Fu la Spagna*, 65; Guarneri, *Battaglie*, 2/132–33.
10. St.A. 230/060500; Caviglia, 319; DGFP, D/11/213–14.
11. *Hansard*, 2.5.1938, 619.
12. Bottai, *Vent'anni*, 113.
13. NP, Jan.–Dec. 1937, 114–5 (Quilici).
14. JCR, Jan. 1974, 55 (Coverdale).
15. Guspini, 146–47; Caracciolo, 36; Guariglia, *Ricordi*, 325.
16. Cantalupo, *Fu la Spagna*, 77, 102, 112.
17. Susmel, *Corrispondenza*, 234; St.A. 53/026380–83; Cantalupo, *Fu la Spagna*, 152; Tamaro, *Venti anni*, 3/245.
18. St.A. 165/048793.
19. JCH, Jan. 1974, 57–72 (Coverdale); St.A. 165/048689, 048692; Canevari, *La guerra*, 1/470.
20. St.A. 165/048739–45.
21. St.A. 165/048750, 048762–63.
22. Susmel, *Corrispondenza*, 162; GDFP, D/3/258–59; Faldella, *Venti mesi*, 503; Bottai, *Vent'anni*, 109; Incisa, 54; OO, XXVIII, 201.
23. FO (PRO), R.2869/1/22; Monghini, 116.
24. Hunt, 56.
25. Harvey, 34.
26. *Foreign Relations*, 1/268; Packard, 36–37; Bowers, 330; Hamilton, 44–45; Buckley, 300.
27. DGFP, D/3/376, 410, 521.
28. Cantalupo, *Fu la Spagna*, 191, 207; St.A. 288/088412.
29. Rintelen, 30; Weizsäcker, *Memoirs*, 113; Magistrati, *L'Italia*, 31–32; Fest, 500; DGFP, D/1/37, and D/3/172–73, 210, 222, 634–35.
30. Tamaro, *Venti anni*, 3/263; DGFP, D/3/443; Susmel, *Corrispondenza*, 238.
31. Ciano, *1937–1938*, 36, 41, 76, 122; FO (PRO), 371/22436 (Perth, 13.1.1938), 6.
32. Guarneri, *Battaglie*, 2/276–79; DGFP, D/3/699; D'Amoya, *La politica*, 185.
33. Cantalupo, *Fu la Spagna*, 231–32; Dinale, 326; Ciano, *1937–1938*, 73, 101; DGFP, D/3/468, 533; Mussolini, E., *Mio fratello*, 153.
34. *Il processo*, 26; Conti, *Servizio*, 215–18, 230, 252, 270–71, 276.
35. Villari, *Italian*, 174.
36. *Il processo*, 27, 77; Conti, *Servizio*, 32, 262; Delzell, 160.
37. Carboni, *Memorie*, 144–45; Ciano, *1937–1938*, 19; Begnac, 591–92, 613; Salvemini, *Scritti*, 2/632.
38. Zangrandi, *Il comunismo*, 110–18.
39. Ciano, *1937–1938*, 6, 51; Ciano, *Diario*, 1/44–45; *Il processo*, 115.
40. St.A. 109/030006A; Ciano, *1937–1938*, 7, 79, 103.
41. Ciano, *1937–1938*, 137, 152.
42. BD, 3/3/329; DGFP, D/3/622–24, 627, 705–706; Vittorelli, 54; *Survey*, 1938, 1/288.

43. GAA, 30.7.1936, 1.
44. DGFP, D/6/241–42; Aroma, *Mussolini*, 188–89; Aroma, *Vent'anni*, 277; "*Prospettive*," 6/8.
45. Cantalupo, *Fu la Spagna*, 279, 317.
46. Merkes, 173; Robertson, 95.
47. Payne, *Politics*, 461–62; "*Gerarchia*," June 1939, 374.
48. DGFP, D/9/541.
49. DGFP, D/3/933; OO, XXXI, 70–71.
50. Spigo, 45.
51. Zachariae, 81; DDI, 9/2/488, and 9/3/15, 433; Canevari, *La guerra*, 1/484; Latronico, 162–63.
52. DGFP, D/2/¡972 and D/3/865; Guariglia, *Ricordi*, 34.
53. Signoretti, 163; Donosti, 52–53; Cantalupo, *Fu la Spagna*, 179.
54. GDFP, D/3/352.
55. GDFP, D/3/501, 566, 570.
56. GDFP, D/3/830–31; Magistrati, *Il prologo*, 151.

CHAPTER 8: THE COLONIES, 1936–1939

1. *Enciclopedia, appendice*, 1938, 66–67; *L'Impero (A.O.I.)*, 159–60 (Volpi); Preti, *Impero*, 63–64 (Appelius); Belluzzo, 243–44.
2. CF, 1.12.1939, 41; *Sintesi*, 22.
3. St.A. 122/033902–903; FO (PRO), 371/22436, 119 (Perth, 13.1.1938); ARA, 1939, 1/91–92; *Camera*, 18.3.1938, 4819 (Teruzzi); "*Romana*," Mar. 1939, 181.
4. Susmel, *Corrispondenza*, 160; AAI, 1939, 3/17.
5. Belluzzo, 241; Pennisi, 44; LEI, Feb. 1937, 1928; Aloisi, *Journal*, 382.
6. CFI, 1937, 48–51, 1341.
7. Guarneri, *Battaglie*, 1/437; 2/141, 196; Sarti, 125.
8. Dower, 224–29.
9. St.A. 53/026388–89; 120/032889; 122/033902; De Biase, *L'impero*, 94.
10. "*Gerarchia*," May 1936, 342.
11. Guariglia, *Ricordi*, 315–16; Bottai, *Vent'anni*, 107.
12. "*Augustea*," 30.4.1937, 191–92.
13. FO (PRO), R.3093/64/22 (10.4.1937, Drummond); "*The Times*," 4.1.1938, 11.
14. DDF, 2/7/282–83.
15. *Camera*, 18.3.1938, 4817–18; St.A. 122/033901–902 (Farinacci).
16. *Dal regno all'impero*, 647 (Bastianini).
17. RSA, Aug. 1942, 462–63, 475.
18. *L'Impero (A.O.I.)*, 148.
19. AAI, 1939, 3/16 (Teruzzi).
20. IAI, 5/278 (allegato 1021).
21. Mondaini, 2/567–68.
22. "*Cronache illustrate*," 25.9.1936, 340.
23. RSA, May 1941, 478–79 (Lessona).
24. Civ.F., Jan. 1936, 39–40 (Montanelli), and Sept. 1938, 788–89; Dinale, 226; DF, Jan. 1939, 97; *L'Impero (A.O.I.)*, ix, 276; Lessona, *Memorie*, 267; Marsanich, 283.
25. RISS, May 1940, 443; AIA, 1939, 3/294; De Felice, *Mussolini il duce*, 784–85; DGFP, D/6/241.
26. St.A., files 124, 125, 168, 267, 290.
27. Villari, *Italian*, 161.
28. Ciano, *1937–1938*, 194.
29. St.A. 53/026388.
30. Leto, *Ovra*, 150–51; Caviglia, 276; Donosti, 42; Vittorelli, 105–106; Iuvenalis, 38.

31. Canevari, *La guerra*, 1/378.
32. St.A. 290/088938, 088941.
33. Guarneri, *Battaglie*, 2/340; Lewis, 111; Dower, 231–35.
34. LS, Mar. 1939, 73–74; LDR, 5.9.1942, 4; De Felice, *Storia*, 238.
35. "*Antieuropa*," Mar. 1933, 137 (Zavattari); Aloisi, *Journal*, 185.
36. Cipriani, *Un assurdo*, 3–6; ACV, 1938, 1/595–98; Cipriani, *Fascismo razzista*, 9, 116–17, 155, 166–67.
37. "*Corriere*," 4.8.1935 (quoted by Melograni, 549); I.I., 25.8.1935, 389.
38. DF, Jan. 1939, 97; RSA, Feb. 1939, 114–16; *Dizionario di politica*, 4/28.
39. Civ.F., Jan. 1936, 40; Vittorelli, 54; "*Lo Stato*," July 1936, 424.
40. Lessona, *Memorie*, 298–99.
41. AAI, 1939, 3/70.
42. DGFP, D/1/2.
43. St.A. 122/033903; AAI, 1938, 4/1391–92; Fossa, 142–43.
44. DF, Jan. 1939, 100; Poggiali, *Albori*, 524.
45. ACV, 1939, 1/47–49 (Orestano), 90 (Biasutti), 717–21; "*Comando*," 1941, 3/207.
46. ACV, 2/1455, 1561.
47. ACV, 1/757–61, 766–71.
48. *Partito e impero*, 10–11.
49. "*Geopolitica*," Dec. 1942, 541–43.
50. AAI, 1939, 3/82.
51. RSA, Feb. 1939, 117–18, 121; IDR, Mar. 1940, 134, and Mar. 1942, 109–10.
52. *Raccolta delle leggi*, 1939, 3/1680–81.
53. AAI, 1939, 3/76–77; "*Giovanissima*," Ap. 1939, 27, 36–37.
54. Pace, *La Libia*, ii.
55. Eden, 227.
56. Moore, 88; AAI, 1941, 1/240–41.
57. Evans-Pritchard, 75–76, 208–11, 225; OM, June 1939, 338–39; Graziani, *Libia redenta*, 301.
58. St.A. 222/057068.
59. Alfieri, 59.
60. Lessona, "*L'Africa*," 155.
61. AAI, Mar. 1943, 1/106; LDR, 20.3.1941, 12; REA, Nov. 1939, 1185–87 (Teruzzi).
62. ACV, 1/735.
63. St.A. 129/035609; *L'Impero (A.O.I.)*, 267–68.
64. CF, 1.11.1938, 1, 3; Pini, *Filo*, 172.
65. DF, Nov. 1938, 13; EI, May 1939, 234; REC, May–June 1940, 389–90; Preti, *Impero*, 96–98; CF, 1.11.1940, 12–13 (Ambrosini).
66. NA, 16.7.1935, 250–51 (Pace).
67. *Senato*, 13.5.1932, 5004.
68. OM, Feb. 1939, 119; "*Gerarchia*," June 1936, 410.
69. Evans-Pritchard, 203–204; Aloisi, *Journal*, 269; ACV, 1938, 1/738, 742, 746; Ciano, *Diario*, 1/15.
70. "*Gerarchia*," Dec. 1935, 1016; Poggiali, *Albori*, 488–90; V.I., May 1940, 587–88; AAI, June 1943, 315–16; FO (PRO), 371/22436 (13.1.1938), 121.
71. *Documents*, 30; AAI, 1939, 3/156; Zaghi, 536, 544.
72. Marco, 36–41.
73. APC, 6/194–95, 209; "*Augustea*," 30.6.1933, 355–56.
74. Carocci, 255; RC, May–June 1927, 299; ACV, 1938, 1/724–26 (De Vecchi).
75. V.I., Jan. 1939, 124.
76. RC, June 1931, 458–59; Jan. 1933, 32–33, 41.
77. Gori, 102–103; Salis, 338; Roletto, 27; Ciano, *1937–1938*, 72.
78. St.A. 166/049071; Ciano, *1937–1938*, 36; Ciano, *Diario*, 1/115–16; Bocca, 219; ACV, 1938, 1/716.
79. LDR, 5.6.1943, 12–13.
80. St.A. 251/068539–42, 068551–52.
81. AAI, 1939, 3/7.

82. Gorla, 305; Lessona, *Memorie*, 269.
83. CF, 1.8.1937, 327; 15.2.1939, 123; 1.12.1939, 41; 1.3.1940,153; *Camera, commissioni*, 5.5.1942, 917.
84. Ebenstein, 216–17.
85. ICE, 76–79; PS, Aug. 1940, 278–79; *"The Economist,"* 7.1.1939, 45.
86. RPE, Feb. 1942, 84; Guarneri, *Battaglie*, 2/199, 289–90; Pistolese, 57; Lessona, *Memorie*, 131.
87. Guarneri, *Battaglie*, 2/199–200; CF, Oct. 1942, 767; St.A. 121/033822; *"Studi storici,"* 1971, 30 (Mori).
88. FO (PRO), 371/22436 (13.1.1938), 133; Guarneri, *Battaglie*, 2/404.
89. Volpe, *Saluto*, 186; Guariglia, *Ricordi*, 315–16.
90. Guarneri, *Battaglie*, 2/198.
91. *La Méditerranée*, 53–56 (De Leone); AAI, Sept. 1941, 3/861–63 (Villa); *Quaderni*, 4/109; Raciti, 82.
92. SIPS, Bologna 1938, 3/580, 587.
93. AAI, 1941, 3/856–57; *La Méditerranée*, 55–56; Zaghi, 545–47.
94. NA, July 1955, 355–56, 362 (Tumedei); St.A. 120/032708 (Benni); Monti, 128–31.
95. RPI, May 1940, 170; PPS, 21.7.1939, 355, and 10.5.1940, 218.
96. Tarchi, 1941, 130; Lojacono, 234; Alimenti, 97, 265; CSC, 188.
97. AAI, 1939, 3/xviii, 12.
98. REA, July 1939, 929–30; *"Lo Stato,"* May 1936, 293; Civ.F., Nov.–Dec. 1941, 17–18 (Bottai); *"Gerarchia,"* May 1938, 304; Volpe, *Storici*, 472; Volpe, *Saluto*, 145.
99. *Camera*, 17.3.1938, 4805.
100. UF, Nov. 1937, 7; EF, May 1933, 409, 415; RSA, May 1941, 478.
101. AAI, 1939, 3/79–80, and 1942, 4/917; Gayda, *Italia e Francia*, 172; Cipriani, *Fascismo razzista*, 153–55; ACV, 1938, 1/596–98, 717–21; PS, May–June 1940, 204.
102. CF, 15.2.1931, 76–77; *L'Impero (A.O.I.)*, 275–76; ACV, 1938, 1/715–76 (De Vecchi); Civ.F., Nov. 1940, 861–63.

CHAPTER 9: 1938: ANSCHLUSS AND MUNICH

1. OO, XXIX, 2.
2. OO, XXVIII, 184, 186; Ciano, *1937–1938*, 188.
3. DF, Oct. 1940, 47–49 (Toscano); Volpe, *Storia*, 243–44.
4. CF, 15.9.1937, 369–70, and 15.4.1938, 187–88; *"Omnibus,"* 2.4.1938, 1; Ciano, *1937–1938*, 191; Perini, 146; SIPS, 1938, 2/326 (Cabiati).
5. Senise, 35.
6. *"Gerarchia,"* Aug. 1938, 526; LDR, Aug. 1938, 69; Rosso, 102, 130; Santelli, 5; Melchiori, 108; NDS, Jan. 1938, 15.
7. Federzoni, *Italia*, 263; Federzoni, *A.O.*, xi; Federzoni, *Parole*, 10.
8. *"Gerarchia,"* Ap. 1935, 316–17.
9. Funke, 171–72; Tamaro, *Venti anni*, 3/91.
10. Starhemberg, 219, 222; Fuchs, 177, 180; Reynaud, 1/178.
11. Tuninetti, 17, 167–68.
12. Ciano, *L'Europa*, 141, 224; Ciano, *1937–1938*, 88, 110; RI, July 1936, 489.
13. *Il Gran Consiglio*, 640; DGFP, D/1/612–13.
14. OO, XXIX, 69–70.
15. *"Omnibus,"* 19.3.1938, 1.
16. *Italia e Germania*, 28–29 (Signoretti); VA, 11.4.1938, 7; RF, 15.5.1938, 1; V.I., Ap. 1938, 421, 431 (Canevari); *Panorami*, 6/1/227 (Missiroli); Porfiri, 7–8; API, 1938, 26.
17. Ciano, *1937–1938*, 115, 132, 164; Ciano, *L'Europa*, 247–48; Mussolini, R., *La mia vita*, 141.

18. BD, 3/3/496; Caviglia, 187; Bandinelli, 78; Zangrandi, *Il lungo viaggio*, 136–37; Ciano, *1937–1938*, 291; Pintor, xix; Tannenbaum, 283.
19. Grifone, 150; Apih, 327; Rusinow, 268; "*The Economist*," 22.7.1939, 165; Gangemi, 77, 90; St.A. 121/033766.
20. Taylor, *Beaverbrook*, 375.
21. Ciano, *L'Europa*, 251 (cf. *Ciano's Diplomatic Papers*, 165).
22. Amery, 3/231; Templewood, 278–79; Colvin, 190; Harvey, 87–89.
23. Page, 77; Driberg, 40.
24. Ciano, *1937–1938*, 150–51.
25. Ciano, *L'Europa*, 245–46.
26. "*The Times*," 26.2.1938, 7.
27. St.A. 20/009476.
28. Canepa, 2/134; "*Augustea*," 15.12.1937, 487.
29. Bottai, *Vent'anni*, 81; Rauschning, 180–81.
30. Ojetti, 516; Magistrati, *L'Italia*, 86–87; Vaccari, 371; Ciano, *1937–1938*, 70.
31. LS, Oct. 1937, 290; CF, 15.4.1938, 181; Volpe, *Storia*, 224; Pellizzi, 177.
32. Speer, *Inside*, 72; Strasser, 219–21.
33. DGFP, C/4/1015; DDF, 2/5/357.
34. DDF, 2/3/603; *Nazi Conspiracy*, Supp. B, 1492 (Neurath).
35. *Testament*, 103; Rauschning, 57, 130; Wiskemann, 94; Fest, 608.
36. DGFP, D/1/1106; Toscano, *The Origins*, 11; Henderson, 183.
37. Rintelen, 46; Donosti, 104.
38. Pini, *Filo*, 150.
39. Navarra, 132; Guspini, 154; Graziani, *Ho difeso*, 167; Ciano, *1937–1938*, 167; "*Augustea*," 15.3.1938, 11.
40. FO (PRO), R.7167/43/22 (20.8.1938, Burrows); BD, 3/2/356; BD, 3/3/335; Dollmann, *Roma*, 124.
41. Westphal, 158–59; Rintelen, 55–56; Toscano, *Origins*, 79.
42. CF, 15.7.1938, 274; Magistrati, *L'Italia*, 212.
43. *Due popoli*, 46 (Bastianini); Bottai, *Vent'anni*, 116.
44. "*Camicia Rossa*," June–Oct. 1938, 112; V.I., Aug. 1938, 172–73.
45. Ciano, *1937–1938*, 112.
46. Ciano, *1937–1938*, 104–105; Ciano, *L'Europa*, 222; DGFP, D/1/1152.
47. Ciano, *1937–1938*, 227,236.
48. Ciano, *1937–1938*, 240, 245–46.
49. BD, 3/3/334, and 3/4/305; Ciano, *1937–1938*, 250; Ciano, *Diario*, 1/21.
50. *In Africa settentrionale*, 47–49.
51. DGFP, D/2/357, 533; Nuremberg, 2/12–13; Ciano, *1937–1938*, 132, 177, 180.
52. Celovsky, 461–64; Donosti, 121–25; Hildebrand, 72; Schmidt, 415; Aroma, *Vent'anni*, 272–73.
53. Anfuso, 100–101; Senise, 46.
54. Gravelli, *Mussolini*, 208; Dollmann, *Roma*, 117; Dinale, 161.
55. OO, XXIX, 192.
56. API, June 1942, 147; Guariglia, *Ricordi*, 344–46.
57. OO, XXIX, 192–94; BD, 3/3/346–48; FO (PRO), R.9/9/22 (27.12.1938, Perth); Bottai, *Vent'anni*, 121; "*Augustea*," 15.3.1938, 11.
58. OO, XXIX, 192–93.
59. Ciano, *L'Europa*, 373–78; Ciano, *1937–1938*, 279–81; DGFP, D/4/515–16.
60. *Camera*, 30.11.1938, 5228.
61. CF, 1.8.1938, 289; 1.11.1938, 13; 15.11.1938, 22–23; 15.1.1939, 82.
62. Bottai, *Vent'anni*, 72.
63. PS, Nov.–Dec. 1938, 2; *Camera, commissioni*, 6.6.1941, 871–72; GDFP, D/4/523.
64. Ciano, *1937–1938*, 102.
65. Guarneri, *Battaglie*, 2/382–83; Simoni, 101; Signoretti, 176–77, 183; Navarra, 94–95; CF, 1.8.1938, 290; "*Corriere*," 7.10.1938, 2.
66. Guariglia, *Ricordi*, 381–82; Ojetti, 503.
67. CF, 1.8.1938, 304; Ardemagni, 42.

68. Ciano, *1937–1938*, 53, 182.
69. St.A. 120/032704; Ciano, *1937–1938*, 289, 294; Spigo, 91–92.
70. Cantalupo, *Racconti*, 330–31; Guarneri, *Battaglie*, 2/380; Guariglia, *Ricordi*, 353–54; PS, May–June 1940, 182.
71. Ciano, *1937–1938*, 282, 286–88.
72. BD, 3/3/466; "*The Economist*," 17.12.1938, 582; Packard, 43; Poncet, *Au palais*, 21–22; Tamaro, *Venti anni*, 3/333–34; Cianfarra, 139–40; VA, 1.12.1938, 1, and 15.12.1938, 1.
73. St.A. 1/000041–43; Acerbo, 452.
74. Ciano, *1937–1938*, 315; St.A. 1/000044.
75. Guspini, 157; Ciano, *Diario*, 1/20; Guariglia, *Ricordi*, 369; Milza, 220.
76. Dollmann, *The Interpreter*, 136.
77. API, 1938, 28.

CHAPTER 10: GROWING TENSION

1. Churchill, 348; NA, 16.1.1961, 161.
2. BD, 3/3/498.
3. Leto, *Ovra*, 168.
4. St.A. 54/026793–94, 026901, 026962–65.
5. Feiling, 329.
6. St.A. 54/026767.
7. DGFP, D/11/708; Ciano, *Diario*, 1/14; Sermoneta, 140.
8. RI, 3.6.1939, 436; "*The Times*," 27.5.1939, 12.
9. St.A. 54/026756; *Il popolo*, 110–17; Sforza, 274; Sermoneta, 128.
10. Ciano, *Diario*, 1/12.
11. BD, 3/3/459–60; RPI, Feb. 1939, 5; Aroma, *Vent'anni*, 276.
12. Navarra, 130; Pini-Susmel, 4/17; Barzini, *From Caesar*, 140.
13. Aster, 49; BD, 3/3/532; Harvey, 239–42.
14. Navarra, 48–49; Anfuso, 82.
15. Guariglia, *Ricordi*, 371.
16. CF, 15.2.1939, 123.
17. CF, 15.2.1939, 123; Faldella, *L'Italia*, 131; RI, 11.2.1929, 93.
18. Ciano, *Diario*, 1/42.
19. Pettinato, *Scritto*, 772–73; Maurano, *Francia*, 266; Maurano, *Ricordi*, 234; OO, XXIX, 295–96.
20. St.A. 1/000039–41; Bottai, *Vent'anni*, 123.
21. Gorla, 194; Phillips, 114.
22. Ciano, *1937–1938*, 23, 111, 132, 171, 185; Bottai, *Vent'anni*, 113.
23. Anfuso, 35, 43; Guariglia, *Ricordi*, 395–96; Giolli, 118–19.
24. Phillips, 92.
25. Cantalupo, *Fu la Spagna*, 52–53; Scoppa, 37; Donosti, 86–87; Tamaro, *Venti anni*, 3/280; Vergani, 208.
26. Gorla, 199; Dollmann, *The Interpreter*, 201; Rotunda, 34–35 (quoting Ingram); Kirkpatrick, *Inner Circle*, 140–42.
27. Cerrutti, 230–31; Leto, *Ovra*, 239; Dollmann, *The Interpreter*, 154; Alfieri, 155.
28. BD, 3/6/658–59.
29. Vergani, 19–20, 54; Signoretti, 156; Leto, *Ovra*, 175.
30. Vergani, 208.
31. Bastianini, 232, 237–38.
32. Vergani, 42, 48; Castellani, 28.
33. Ciano, *1937–1938*, 97, 130, 206; Lessona, *Memorie*, 332.
34. Aroma, *Mussolini*, 152; Maurano, *Ricordi*, 260; Pini-Susmel, 4/132; St.A. 104/028396.
35. Leto, *Ovra*, 198; Spampanato, *Contromemoriale*, 1/226; Rossi, *Personaggi*, 242.

36. Alfieri, 259–60; Bastianini, 244.
37. Aroma, *Mussolini*, 171; Navarra, 144–45.
38. Poncet, *Ricordi*, 247; *Testament*, 103.
39. DGFP, D/1/33; *Testament*, 107–108.
40. Fest, 504; Weizsäcker, *Memoirs*, 147.
41. Dietrich, 248.
42. Ciano, *Diario*, 1/214; Bottai, *Vent'anni*, 113; Badoglio, 30; Dolfin, 116; OO, XXXII, 174.
43. Zachariae, 97; Lessona, *Memorie*, 367; Mussolini, V., *Vita*, 21.
44. Starhemberg, 170; Mussolini, V., *Vita*, 167; "*Life*," 26.2.1945 (Grandi); *Les lettres*, 11 (François-Poncet).
45. Navarra, 154.
46. Salvemini, *Scritti*, 3/386–94; Bertoldi, *Mussolini*, 151–52; Schuschnigg, 220; Papen, 279; Zachariae, 49–50; Dolfin, 159; Pozzi, 122–23; Fuchs, 38.
47. Panzini, 272; Poncet, *Ricordi*, 246; Guariglia, *Ricordi*, 19; Naudeau, 71; CF, 15.11.1934, 40; "*Primato*," 15.10.1940, 11; *Vocabolario*, passim.
48. "*Gerarchia*," Ap. 1939, 255; Anfuso, 411; Zachariae, 41; OO, XXXII, 161.
49. *Mussolini e il fascismo*, 33 (Bodrero); OO, XXIII, 26, and XXVIII, 137.
50. Gravelli, *Mussolini*, 168–69; Barzini, *From Caesar*, 140; Cowles, 255; Bertoldi, *Mussolini*, 152.
51. Aroma, *Mussolini*, 221; CF, 1.3.1943, 115; Begnac, 463; Vergani, 81; D'Amoya, *Declino*, 104–105.
52. Scoppa, 33; Grazzi, 8–10; Donosti, 16–17.
53. Guariglia, *Ricordi*, 204, 381–82; Alfieri, 231; DDI, 9/2/164; Toscano, *Una mancata intesa*, 12; Aloisi, *Journal*, 340.
54. Petrie, 180; Donosti, 113; Bianchi, *Perchè*, 681.
55. Ojetti, 564.
56. Alfieri, 343.
57. Begnac, 596.
58. Carboni, 7; Cowles, 259–60.
59. OO, XXIX, 193; DGFP, D/8/611.
60. Ciano, *Diario*, 1/55–58; Ciano, *L'Europa*, 420; Donosti, 153.
61. Ciano, *Diario*, 1/60; DGFP, D/6/175.
62. Ciano, *Diario*, 1/60, 63; Bottai, *Vent'anni*, 125–26.
63. OO, XXIX, 250–53.
64. OO, XXXII, 178.
65. CF, 1.4.1939, 162; 15.4.1939, 182; 1.5.1939, 197.
66. RI, 29.4.1939, 338.
67. ACN, 1939, 390; PS, May 1939, 189; Ercole, *Storia*, 170–71, 174.
68. DGFP, D/6/40–41, 57–58, 1109; Ciano, *Diario*, 156.
69. GDFP, D/6/1113.
70. Stehlin, 378.
71. GDFP, D/4/521, 530–31.
72. DGFP, D/4/584–87; D/6/240–41, 1108.
73. Vailati, 240; Rintelen, 60; DGFP, D/6/1110–11.

CHAPTER 11: THE INVASION OF ALBANIA

1. Bottai, *Vent'anni*, 107; Ciano, *Diario*, 1/37.
2. APSR, Ap. 1941, 312 (Sereni); GDFP, D/4/578–79.
3. "*La lettura*," May 1939, 399–402 (Montanelli); RISS, May 1940, 420–21.
4. Ciano, *1937–1938*, 190–91.
5. Ciano, *1937–1938*, 140, 165.

6. Ciano, *1937–1938*, 170, 175; and *L'Europa*, 305–15.
7. Donosti, 157; Quaroni, 140; Ciano, *L'Europa*, 307–308; Guarneri, *Battaglie*, 2/347.
8. Ciano, *1937–1938*, 192–93.
9. GDFP, D/1/1134, and D/6/16.
10. Ciano, *1937–1938*, 264, 267, 278, 304; St.A. 132/036521, 036866.
11. Ciano, *1937–1938*, 302–306; Ciano, *L'Europa*, 411.
12. *Lisbon papers*, Jacomoni memo, 9.2.1939, 31–32; Guspini, 160–61.
13. *Lisbon papers*, Jacomoni, 21.3.1939, 40.
14. Ciano, *Diario*, 1/67.
15. BD, 3/5/120–21, 128.
16. *Lisbon papers*, 24.3.1939; Ciano, *Diario*, 1/55–57.
17. Pricolo, *La regia*, 39; Baudino, 32; Ciano, *Diario*, 1/69; Sillani, *Le forze*, 339; *Esercito anno XVII*, 377.
18. Valle, 147–52; Baudino, 54.
19. Anfuso, 115; Donosti, 162–63.
20. Begnac, 617; Bottai, *Vent'anni*, 89, 126.
21. Ciano, *Diario*, 1/90; Donosti, 159.
22. Silva, *Il Mediterraneo*, 505; Silva, *Io difendo*, 135.
23. CF, 1.5.1939, 208–209; RM, May 1939, 185; EI, July 1939, 313; Ceci, 297; Pascazio, *Scopritevi*, 70; *Esercito anno XVII*, 384; *Almanacco fascista*, 1940, 52; AF, May 1939, 3.
24. St.A. 54/026903–908.
25. "Gerarchia," May 1939, 307; DF, June 1939, 280; EI, May 1939, 206–207; Marsanich, 296; CF, 15.4.1939, 181.
26. Ciano, *Diario*, 1/77.
27. Trizzino, *Verità*, 28.
28. DGFP, D/11/802; Badoglio, 20; FO (PRO), R.3397/1335/90 (Ryan, 27.4.1939).
29. Orestano, *Verso*, 390; AAI, Jan. 1941, 1/60 (Ambrosini); APSR, Ap. 1941, 314–16.
30. "Gerarchia," July 1939, 455–58.
31. CF, 1.11.1940, 12–14 (Ambrosini); Lucatello, 77–82.
32. Grazzi, 18; Guariglia, *Ricordi*, 388–89.
33. Ciano, *Diario*, 1/78–79.
34. "*The Economist*," 15.4.1939, 121; Harvey, 275–78.
35. *Hansard*, 13.4.1939, 30.
36. DGFP, D/6/239.
37. Ciano, *Diario*, 1/114.
38. St.A. 121/033830–32; Canevari, *Graziani*, 161.
39. RISS, May 1940, 422–23; Jacomoni, 293; Anfuso, 115–16; CF, 15.10.1939, 385.
40. PPS, 10.5.1940, 218–19; CDI, Ap. 1940, 124.
41. Grazzi, 184; "*Espresso*," 24.11.1956, 13 (Cancogni); Leto, *Ovra*, 178.
42. Leto, *Ovra*, 197; Donosti, 173; Miles, 32–33.
43. Donosti, 171; St.A. 30/014193–94; Begnac, 605.
44. *Il processo*, 56, 60–62, 221–25.

CHAPTER 12: THE PACT OF STEEL

1. "*Augustea*," 3.5.1938, 5–6 (Balella); DGFP, C/1/109; Donosti, 87–88.
2. Guarneri, *Battaglie*, 2/125–28, 225; "*Gerarchia*," Oct. 1932, 933; GDFP, D/4/514; "*The Banker*," Oct. 1937, 13 (Einzig); FO (PRO), R.9/9/22 (Perth, 27.12.1938).
3. LEI, 1937, 291 (Boldrini); "*Lo Stato*," Jan. 1938, 42; GDFP, D/4/574–75; Guarneri, *Battaglie*, 2/307.
4. CF, 1.2.1929, 100; PS, 15.3.1941, 121; *Camera, commissioni*, 8.4.1941, 810.
5. Wiskemann, 55; *Quaderni*, 4/79–80.
6. Guarneri, *Battaglie*, 2/324–25; DGFP, D/4/557.

7. DGFP, D/4/577, 585–86, and D/6/210–11, 470–71; St.A. 120/032899.
8. Faldella, *L'Italia*, 88.
9. DGFP, D/6/40–41.
10. DGFP, D/6/613–14; Aroma, *Vent'anni*, 282.
11. Tamaro, *Venti anni*, 3/372; *La marina*, 21/12.
12. DGFP, D/6/248, 250, 252, 260–61.
13. Rintelen, 61; DGFP, D/6/261–62.
14. Giolli, 141; DGFP, D/6/445–46; BD, 3/5/426–28.
15. Ciano, *Diario*, 1/93; RI, 13.5.1939, 375.
16. SIPS; 1938, 1/621.
17. DGFP, D/6/450–51; Toscano, *The Origins*, 305; Dollmann, *The Interpreter*, 155; Magistrati, *L'Italia*, 341; Ciano, *L'Europa*, 427.
18. Giolli, 143–45; Vergani, 76.
19. Toscano, *The Origins*, 328; Ciano, *Diario*, 1/99; DGFP, D/6/479; Magistrati, *L'Italia*, 344.
20. Luciano, 12–13; OO, XXIX, 273.
21. *"The Times,"* 15.5.1939, 13, and 17.5.1939, 13.
22. Toscano, *The Origins*, 406.
23. Bastianini, 253.
24. CF, 1.6.1939, 229.
25. Gorla, 61.
26. Bianchi, *Perchè*, 789 (De Bono); Guariglia, *Ricordi*, 67; Magistrati, *L'Italia*, 354–55.
27. Badoglio, 30.
28. Gorla, 63.
29. Villari, *Italian*, 227.
30. Scorza, 68; Bottai, *Vent'anni*, 309; Signoretti, 187; Donosti, 192.
31. DDI, 8/12/49–51.
32. Badoglio, 22; Donosti, 191.
33. Simoni, 22; Nuremberg, 10/248.
34. DDI, 8/12/112, 378, 399–400.
35. DGFP, D/6/576, 580; *Testament*, 115.
36. DGFP, D/6/884.
37. DGFP, D/6/444–45; Rintelen, 62.
38. DGFP, D/6/1118.
39. DGFP, D/6/1124–25.
40. DGFP, D/6/909, 1119.
41. Weichold, *War*, 1; DGFP, D/6/984.

CHAPTER 13: THE ARMED FORCES AND PREPAREDNESS FOR WAR

1. Favagrossa, 11.
2. MLI, July 1949, 53–54 (Pieri).
3. Roatta, 47; Canevari, *La guerra*, 2/42–43.
4. *"Augustea,"* 28.2.1935, 98; V.I., Ap. 1935, 536; RDC, Ap. 1935, 18.
5. OO, XXVIII, 32, 59.
6. *"Gerarchia,"* Mar. 1937, 190; Ceci, 218; *"Italiani di Tunisia,"* June 1939, 2; EI, July 1939, 311.
7. Sillani, *Le forze*, xv; RA, Aug. 1939, 398.
8. *Das Heer*, 22; *"Augustea,"* 15.9.1932, 545–46; Susmel, *Corrispondenza*, 166 (Oct. 1937); CF, 1.4.1937, 165; Federzoni, *Parole*, 10 (12.7.1937); Orano, *La difesa*, 9–11.
9. Carboni, 64–65; Caracciolo, 114; Spigo, 51.
10. *Das Heer*, 15; St.A. 168/049424 (24.2.1931, Giuriati).
11. Spigo, 52; Tamaro, *Venti anni*, 3/272, 370; FO (PRO), R.3835/86/22 (4.5.1939, Burrows); Roatta, 37.

12. Reisoli, 44–45; Armellini, *La crisi*, 115–16.
13. Federzoni, *Italia*, 190; St.A. 53/026396 (13.9.1939, Farinacci); Benigno, 319; Rivoire, 96; Zanussi, 1/41.
14. Santoro, 1/25; Pricolo, *Ignavia*, 84; Armellini, *La crisi*, 74, 81.
15. *Senato*, 29.3.1935, 936–38; Canevari, *La guerra*, 1/381; DDF, 1/4/283.
16. OO, XXIX, 74–82; RI, June 1939, 253/113–14 (Soddu), 123–28 (Pariani); July 1939, 254/211–13 (Cavagnari); RM, Jan. 1939, 3–6; V.I., Ap. 1938, 506–508.
17. *Camera*, 20.3.1936, 2383–85; *Senato*, 29.3.1935, 936–38; Valori, *La ricostruzione*, 83–84; Salvemini, *Prelude*, 252; Pugnani, 13, 17.
18. St.A. 122/033883 (Zoppi), 033893 (Caviglia); OO, XXIX, 77; V.I., 15.7.1937, 21; CF, 15.5.1938, 221–22.
19. Senise, 115; Guspini, 150.
20. *In Africa settentrionale*, 181–84; Graziani, *Ho difeso*, 178–82.
21. *Esercito anno XVII*, 312–19; "*Prospettive*," 1939, 6/8.
22. St.A. 163/047668–80, 047708–10; Fuller, 68; Graziani, *Ho difeso*, 178.
23. Caracciolo, 64.
24. Roatta, 79–80; Favagrossa, 231; Guarneri, *Battaglie*, 2/390–91.
25. St.A. 1/000210.
26. Graziani, *Ho difeso*, 178.
27. Spigo, 54; Roatta, 71–72.
28. Bottai, *Vent'anni*, 127; Favagrossa, 13; Faldella, *L'Italia*, 96–101; St.A. 121/033808; Guspini, 162–63.
29. *Speer Papers*, FD 1940–44, 5–8.
30. Spigo, 112; St.A. 114/031605–606.
31. *In Africa settentrionale*, 182–83; Roatta, 216–17; DDI, 9/4/622.
32. *Senato*, 11.1.1934, 7048; St.A. 120/032832.
33. St.A. 1/000087.
34. Amé, 17; *Il processo*, 29; Washington, T.821/127/IT, 1147 (Ap. 1943).
35. Deakin, 214.
36. Algardi, 33–34; *Il processo*, 60; Carboni, 17.
37. Armellini, *Diario*, 275; Carboni, 80–84; *Il processo*, 91.
38. Amé, 4.
39. Bragadin, *Che ha fatto*, 179; Ciano, *Diario*, 1/306.
40. Douhet, *La guerra*, 299–300; Douhet, *Il dominio*, 10, 24, 63–64, 207–11; Pricolo, *La regia*, 31; OO, XXIX, 83.
41. V.I., Mar. 1930, 324; Nov. 1931, 541–43; Orano, *La difesa*, 12; Pagano, 41; EN, Nov. 1936, 739; RA, Aug. 1939, 217, and Oct. 1939, 156.
42. *Senato*, 11.1.1934, 7034; *Camera*, 24.3.1936, 2431–33, and 16.3.1938, 4719; OO, XIX, 277–78; Valle, 122–23, 128; RPI, Ap. 1933, 14; I.I., 29.10.1933, 644; Schuschnigg, 235; "*Omnibus*," 29.1.1938, 1; Pricolo, *La regia*, 94–95.
43. RPI, Aug. 1933, 8; Sillani, *Le forze*, 275.
44. Heinkel, 121; FO (PRO), 371/16800/362 (7.11.1933, Hetherington).
45. St.A. 133/037401, 037404–405.
46. St.A. 221/056657–78; 141/040077–97.
47. *Senato*, 19.5.1931, 3702–705; CF, 1.2.1931, 58.
48. St.A. 129/035631–37; 109/030017A; Santoro, 1/17–18; Pricolo, *La regia*, 73, 86, 93–98, 102, 125; Bianchi, *Rivelazioni*, 14 (De Bono).
49. Ojetti, 400; Canevari, *La guerra*, 1/220–21; Tamaro, *Venti anni*, 2/456; Aroma, *Vent'anni*, 213.
50. Luciano, 7; Ciano, *Diario*, 1/15.
51. Dinale, 321.
52. DGFP, D/8/901.
53. Pricolo, *La regia*, 49.
54. Valle, 155; Aloisi, *Journal*, 346, 369; Ciano, *1937–1938*, 71.
55. RPI, July 1937, 16–17; "*Augustea*," 31.1.1935, 35; St.A. 54/026919–20 (Grandi).
56. Belot, 42–43; RM, Sept. 1947, 88–89; "*Comando*," 1942, 1/39; Pricolo, *La regia*, 115–22.

57. *Enciclopedia, appendice*, 1938, 752; *"Gerarchia,"* Oct. 1939, 668; Sillani, *Le forze*, 249–50; *Camera*, 16.3.1938, 4718–19 (Valle); *"Augustea,"* 31.1.1939, 3; BF, Oct. 1939, 809–10; SIPS, *Atti* (Sept. 1937, Venice), 2/329.

58. *Venti anni*, 3/36; LAI, June 1938, 66; *Il cittadino*, 72; Perini, 101–102; Infante, 71; RA, Feb. 1940, 186–88 (Pricolo); CDI, June 1940, 170–71.

59. Canevari, *La guerra*, 1/582–83.

60. Ciano, *Diario*, 1/90.

61. Santoro, 1/35; Pricolo, *La regia*, 95–96.

62. Ciano, *Diario*, 1/92; Pricolo, *La regia*, 125; FO (PRO), R.10066/424/22 (17.12.1938 Perth); *"Harper's Magazine,"* Ap. 1938, 516.

63. Senise, 115; Maurano, *Ricordi*, 238; Spampanato, *Contromemoriale*, 1/157; Mussolini, R., *La mia vita*, 133.

64. R. Gentile, *Storia*, 137, 281; Halder, *Kriegstagebuch*, 2/138; Santoro, 1/61; GDFP, D/12/137.

65. FO (PRO), R.4721/173/22 (11.4.1940, Lorraine, 9).

66. *In Africa settentrionale*, 187.

67. *La marina*, 21/75–76; St.A. 1/000128–29; Iachino, 51–53.

68. Pricolo, *La regia*, 257, 286; Trizzino, *Navi*, 197; Ciano, *Diario*, 1/292.

69. Scorza, 40.

70. *Camera*, 15.3.1938, 4695–97; *"Brassey's,"* 1938, 84 (Sansonetti); R.It., July 1939, 191–92; Maugeri, *From the Ashes*, 19; RM, Sept. 1947, 90 (Bernotti).

71. Maugeri, *Mussolini*, 41.

72. NA, 16.8.1935, 522–23; V.I., June 1936, 549; Ciano, *1937–1938*, 109; Perini, 101; *Gli scacchieri*, 2/43–44; PN, 31.3.1940, 186–87.

73. Weichold, *War*, 9; Ruge, 122–23; Iachino, 54–56; *Rommel Papers*, 139; Cocchia, 123; Arena, 1/21; Ghetti, 1/18.

74. RF, 20.10.1934, 1 (Canevari); NA, 16.5.1938, 138–39; Sillani, *Le forze*, 190 (Sansonetti), 200–201 (Giamberardino), 213 (Cavagnari); LM, Nov. 1938, 321.

75. R.It., Nov. 1933, 769–70; *Italia e Germania*, 54–55; *"Echi,"* 25.6.1937, 574; LAI, June 1938, 5 (Valle); EI, July 1939, 313; Ceci, 222; Perini, 107–108; *"Brassey's,"* 1938, 84; RA, Sept. 1939, 426, and Feb. 1940, 189.

76. *La marina*, 21/322–23; Bragadin, *Che ha fatto*, 15; Iachino, 69–70; Weichold, *War*, 8; Belot, 270; Santoro, 1/566; Puntoni, 74.

77. FO (PRO), R.9/9/22 (27.12.1938, Perth); *"Harper's Magazine,"* Ap. 1938, 514–15.

78. Weichold, *La marina*, 24; Weichold, *War*, 4; DDI, 9/4/192; Ruge, 104–105.

79. *La marina*, 21/65; Bernotti, 10, 17; Maugeri, *Mussolini*, 16.

80. Bottai, *Vent'anni*, 110; Scorza, 31–34; RPI, Sept. 1938, 31; Mussolini, B., *Il tempo*, 7.

81. Belot, 63; Weichold, *War*, 3; Iachino, 66–67; Bragadin, *Che ha fatto*, 26–27.

82. PN, 30.11.1939, 762; *Gli scacchieri*, 2/42–43; Caracciolo, 54.

83. Marder, 101.

84. Gabriele, 296–97; *La marina*, 21/319–21.

85. Ceva, 195 (Pio Perrone).

86. St.A. 114/031608–609 (14.10.1939, Farinacci); Favagrossa, 46; Spigo, 130; Caracciolo, 72; Santoro, 1/23; Tamaro, *Venti anni*, 3/364; Miles, 11.

87. Guarneri, *Battaglie*, 1/395, 435; 2/46, 338; De Stefani, 520; Acerbo, 559; Begnac, 544–45 (Scialoja).

88. Conti, *Dal taccuino*, 549; Schuschnigg, 238; Ciano, *Diario*, 1/216.

89. Scorza, 40; St.A. 159/046313; Pricolo, *La regia*, 159; *Camera*, 21.3.1935, 1110.

90. DDI, 9/2/624; AF, Ap. 1939,3.

91. V.I., March 1930, 322–39 (Gazzera, Baistrocchi); Balbo, *La politica*, 10–11; *Senato*, 7.4.1930, 2219; *Camera*, 27.4.1932, 6595–97 (Balbo); Canevari, *La guerra*, 1/197–98 (3.5.1933).

92. Acerbo, 408; Tiffen, 125,248–49; Miles, 28–29.

93. Federzoni, *Italia*, 167–68.

94. Rintelen, 61–62; FO (PRO), R.3835/86/22 (4.5.1939, Burrows); R.4721/173/22 (Ap. 1940, Charles).

95. Bottai, *Vent'anni*, 315.

96. Ciano, *Diario*, 1/171; St.A. 53/026447 (Pariani); Pricolo, *Ignavia*, 66.
97. Rintelen, 87; Valle, 147; Armellini, *Diario*, 8; St.A. 121/033841.
98. Bertoldi, *Badoglio*, 103–107; Cilibrizi, 81–82; Carboni, 66; Vailati, 245–46.
99. St.A. 1/000074; 132/036870, 036919, 036934.
100. Ciano, *Diario*, 1/42, 90, 92.
101. *"Corriere,"* 19.1.1939, 3; *"Il Nuovo Giornale,"* 1; *Italia e Germania*, 55–56; Sillani, *Le forze*, vii, 114; NM, July–Aug. 1939, 539, 561, 566; RI, 27.5.1939, 397; CF, 15.5.1939, 213; 1.6.1939, 229; 1.9.1939, 336 (Canevari); *Almanacco fascista*, 1940, 35; Perini, 108, 393.
102. Ciano, *Diario*, 1/51.
103. St.A. 1/000074–75; *L'esercito italiano*, 137; Favagrossa, 25–27; Canevari, *La guerra*, 1/211, 548–49.
104. St.A. 120/032925; Conti, *Il taccuino*, 625; Ciano, *1937–1938*, 106, 108.
105. St.A. 120/032929 (10.2.1939).
106. Spigo, 94.
107. Spigo, 88; St.A. 121/033781.
108. *"Educazione politica,"* Dec. 1926, 568.
109. *"Gerarchia,"* Oct. 1932, 917.
110. CF, 15.4.1930, 150, and 1.7.1934, 250; Marconi, 29.
111. I.I., 29.10.1933, 643 (Severi).
112. OO, XXIII, 285–86; V.I., June 1936, 612; RS, 15.12.1933, 427; 15.5.1935, 463; Marconi, 21; *Dizionario*, 4/212; *Dal regno all'impero*, 541–54 (Marconi); UF, July–Aug. 1935, 576–79, and Nov. 1937, 41.
113. *"Augustea,"* 30.5.1937, 234; NA, 16.5.1938, 150; *"Romana,"* July 1939, 394; SIPS: *Un secolo di progresso scientifico*, 1939, 2/36, 40; *"Lo Stato,"* Sept.–Oct. 1942, 259.
114. OO, XXXI, 104–105.
115. OO, XXVI, 291; Marconi, 29; *"Augustea,"* 31.10.1942, 611; *Italia d'oggi*, 244–46; Cione, 188.
116. V.I. Nov. 1933, 523 (De Stefani).
117. Toscano, *The Origins*, 79.
118. *Senato*, 1.5.1935, 1027 (Cini); CF, 15.10.1938, 377.
119. *"Romana,"* Nov. 1939, 702–704; UF, Feb. 1942, 118–19; Barzini, *La guerra*, 4–5.
120. LPEA, Nov. 1935, 19–21; OO, XXIX, 334–35; ACN, 367; RS, Ap. 1940, 280.
121. *Camera, commissioni*, 12.5.1942, 1023–24; Bianchi, *Perchè*, 728; *"Gerarchia,"* Dec. 1942, 501–502.
122. Tamaro, *Venti anni*, 3/272; Aroma, *Vent'anni*, 248.
123. Arena, 1/47; *La marina*, 21/168–69; *Enciclopedia, appendice*, 1948, 2/636.
124. Iachino, 67–68; Pricolo, *La regia*, 101.
125. OO, XXXII, 176.

CHAPTER 14: NEUTRALITY OR NON-BELLIGERENCE?

1. OO, XXVI, 248, and XXIX, 117; Ciano, *Diario*, 2/146; Sermoneta, 94–95.
2. Federzoni, *Italia*, 260; Settimelli, *Edda*, 73–75; Carboni, 153; Waterfield, 259.
3. Riboldi, 42.
4. Dinale, 128; Iraci, 103.
5. Bottai, *Vent'anni*, 113; Ciano, *1937–1938*, 50, 264.
6. Ciano, *Diario*, 1/219–21; Navarra, 86.
7. *"Prospettive,"* 1937, 1/2; CF, 15.9.1937, 369; SIPS, July–Aug. 1937, 236; *"Romana,"* July–Aug. 1938, 327; Giglio, *Politica*, 30.
8. *"Il libro italiano,"* May 1939, 273–74 (Alfieri); *Camera, commissioni*, 14.4.1943, 1251 (Polverelli): *"Prospettive,"* 1937, 1/56; DF, Mar.–May 1939, 243.
9. BD, 3/6/288–89.

10. Ciano, *Diario*, 1/92, 99, 106, 145, 209; DDI, 8/13/50; GDFP, D/6/451; DF, June 1939, 282; Faldella, *L'Italia*, 251; Giolli, 129.
11. Ciano, *Diario*, 1/101.
12. DDI, 8/12/379, 389, 399–400, 555–59.
13. Ciano, *Diario*, 1/52; Badoglio, 30.
14. DDI, 8/12/497–98; Wiskemann, 153; *Nazi Conspiracy*, 4/463.
15. BD, 3/6/658–59.
16. Washington, T.120/101 (7.8.1939, Weizsäcker, *Memoirs*, 206.
17. Nuremberg, 2/153.
18. Nuremberg, 2/79; Ciano, *L'Europa*, 454–55.
19. Schmidt, 439; Rintelen, 70.
20. Ciano, *L'Europa*, 457; Halder, *Kriegstagebuch*, 1/15.
21. Ciano, *Diario*, 1/141.
22. DGFP, D/7/53, 432.
23. DDI, 8/13/22–23; BD, 3/7/60; Siebert, 262.
24. Ciano, *Diario*, 1/142.
25. Ciano, *Diario*, 1/144.
26. Ciano, *Diario*, 1/146; Bastianini, 62–63.
27. NA, Dec. 1973, 495 (Vitetti); BD, 3/7/139, 147–48.
28. DGFP, D/6/259–60; Toscano, *L'Italia*, 83.
29. Bottai, *Vent'anni*, 81–82, 138; CF, 15.10.1939, 382, and 1.1.1940, 66.
30. Begnac, 659; Bottai, *Vent'anni*, 140; Ciano, *Diario*, 1/172; GDFP, D/8/64–65.
31. Rintelen, 72; NA, Dec. 1973, 496.
32. *Hitler e Mussolini*, 10–11.
33. Faldella, *L'Italia*, 111; Favagrossa, 106–107; Canevari, *La guerra*, 1/622; Ciano, *Diario*, 1/148–52.
34. CF, 1.9.1939,336; *Almanacco fascista*, 1940,43; Canevari, *La guerra*, 1/570.
35. St.A. 53/026397.
36. Ciano, *Diario*, 1/40; Ciano, *1937–1938*, 246; DGFP, D/6/1114; *"Comando,"* 1940, 6/507.
37. St.A 114/031609–612, 031618.
38. NA, Dec. 1973, 495; Fest, 597.
39. Ojetti 525–26.
40. Donosti, 214; NA, Dec. 1973, 496 (Vitetti); *"Life,"* 26.2.1945 (Grandi).
41. DDI, 8/13/144; Favagrossa, 105–107; *Hitler e Mussolini*, 12–13.
42. Schmidt, 452–53; Halder, *Kriegstagebuch*, 1/34; Gisevius, 366–67.
43. Keitel, 88–89; Gilbert, 32; Siebert, 288–89; Nuremberg, 9/300 and 10/183.
44. Matteini, 68.
45. Donosti, 204–205; Guarneri, *Battaglie*, 2/471; Bianchi, *Perchè*, 709; Blet, 1/297.
46. VA, 1.9.1939, 1 (Pallotta); *"Augustea,"* 31.6.1939, 1–2.
47. *"Nord e Sud,"* Jan. 1964, 122–25 (Aquarone); DGFP, D/8/23–24; Leto, *Ovra*, 205; Blet, 1/261.
48. Ojetti, 513, 527, 530, 534.
49. Bianchi, *Perchè*, 789.
50. Bianchi, *Perchè*, 103–104; Federzoni, *Italia*, 290; *"Life,"* 26.2.1945.
51. RI, 9.9.1939, 661–62.
52. Washington, T.120/101 (14.9.1939); Tamaro, *Venti anni*, 3/420.
53. *"Gerarchia,"* Sept. 1939, 608, 635; CF, 15.9.1939, 347.
54. Ciano, *Diario*, 1/167–68.
55. NA, Dec. 1973,498.
56. Ciano, *Diario*, 1/159; St.A. 1/000256–57; *"Gerarchia,"* Nov. 1939, 715–16.
57. Ciano, *Diario*, 1/176; Giolli, 182–83; Guarneri, *Battaglie*, 2/430.
58. Blet,1/417; Dollmann, *Interpreter*, 136–37.
59. LIR, Sept. 1939, 396.
60. Salvatorelli, 880.
61. Bottai, *Vent'anni*, 136, 144; Ciano, *Diario*, 1/165, 176, 187–89; Amicucci, 82.
62. Matteini, 74, 77; Ciano, *Diario*, 1/178.
63. PN, 30.9.1939, 667; *"Prospettive,"* 15.10.1939, 3.

64. Papini, *Italia mia*, 30, 141–47, 177–78.
65. Favagrossa, 110, 115, 236; Spigo, 48; Roatta, 66–68.
66. Rossi, F., *Mussolini*, 153; St.A. 1/000074–81 and 121/033786.
67. Valle, 157; Santoro, 1/39; Canevari, *La guerra*, 1/622; DDI, 9/3/172–73.
68. Guarneri, *Battaglie*, 2/442–43; Canevari, *La guerra*, 2/70–71; Badoglio, 33.
69. Roatta, 225; Tamaro, *Venti anni*, 3/431; RPI, Oct. 1939, 5; *"Civiltà,"* 21.4.1940, 5.
70. Gorla, 77; Caviglia, 219; Roatta, 89–90; Acerbo, 432–24; Cavallero, *Comando*, 307.
71. St.A. 121/033841.
72. Dollmann, *Roma*, 120, 123.
73. Aroma, *Mussolini*, 388; Simoni, 87; Guspini, 162–63.
74. Ciano, *Diario*, 1/144, 201–203.
75. Bottai, *Vent'anni*, 153–54.
76. Acerbo, 422.
77. DDI, 9/5/26; Bottai, *Vent'anni*, 151.
78. DDI, 9/2/501.
79. DGFP, D/8/511; Ciano, *Diario*, 1/202–204, 209; DDB, 5/447–48; Weizsäcker, *Memoirs*, 222.
80. Carboni, 62.
81. FO (German), C. 938/15/18 (Goerdeler); Weichold, *War*, 1; Roatta, 89–90.
82. DGFP, D/8/442; *Fuehrer Conferences*, 9 (26.1.1940).

CHAPTER 15: MUSSOLINI CHOOSES WAR

1. Ciano, *Diario*, 1/219–20, 251; Dinale, 164.
2. *"Gerarchia,"* Nov. 1939, 715, and Jan. 1940, 17, 21.
3. OO, XXIX, 330, and XXXI, 144; Gorla, 242; Begnac, 295.
4. Ciano, *Diario*. 1/209–11.
5. Ciano, *Diario*, 1/217.
6. DGFP, D/8/907–908; *"Lo Stato,"* Nov.–Dec. 1939, 562; Barzini, *La guerra*, 19.
7. CF, 1.1.1940, 65, and 15.3.1939, 147; Cucchetti, xiii (Valsecchi).
8. OO, XXXV, 139; St.A. 121/033775.
9. Ciano, *Diario*, 1/212.
10. Ciano, *Diario*, 1/214.
11. *Hitler e Mussolini*, 36–38; *Italia fra tedeschi*, 119 (André).
12. Badoglio, 34.
13. St.A. 121/033769–70; Silvestri, *I responsabili*, 175–77; Ciano, *Diario*, 1/248.
14. St.A. 121/033782–86.
15. Bottai, *Vent'anni*, 158.
16. St.A. 121/033775.
17. St.A. 121/033787.
18. St.A. 121/033769.
19. St.A. 121/033841.
20. St.A. 121/033745, 033776, 033840.
21. St.A. 121/033761.
22. St.A. 121/033758, 033762; Guarneri, *Autarchia*, 23.
23. St.A. 121/033754, 033771, 033775; *"Romana,"* Mar. 1939, 144–45; *"Le Vie,"* Ap. 1939, 457–58.
24. St.A. 121/033842; Ciano, *Diario*, 1/225.
25. Ciano, *Diario*, 1/233; Guariglia, *Ricordi*, 452.
26. *In Africa settentrionale*, 182; Ciano, *Diario*, 1/213.
27. St.A. 128/035329–30.
28. Messe, *La mia armata*, 20; Favagrossa, 25.
29. Matteini, 84.

30. *L'esercito italiano*, 137; Messe, *La mia armata*, 13; Faldella, *L'Italia*, 266–67; Canevari, *La guerra*, 1/211, and 2/37, 74.
31. *"Epoca,"* 8.2.1975, 83 (De Felice); Mosca, 339; Blet, 1/469.
32. Ciano, *Diario*, 1/233–34.
33. Dinale, 164; Alfieri, 40; OO, XXIX, 436; Guarneri, *Battaglie*, 2/499.
34. Ciano, *Diario*, 1/236.
35. Ciano, *L'Europa*, 525–29; DGFP, D/8/894–95.
36. Guspini, 167–68; *Italia fra tedeschi*, 119–20 (André).
37. Ciano, *L'Europa*, 526, 531, 534, 539–40; Ciano, *Diario*, 1/236–37; *Weizsäcker-Papiere*, 193.
38. GDFP, D/9/5–14; Ciano, *Diario*, 1/239–40.
39. Warlimont, 79; Schmidt, 479.
40. St.A. 1/000325.
41. St.A. 1/000328; DDI, 9/3/579.
42. Santoro, 1/76.
43. Vailati, 340–44.
44. Vailati, 340–41; *In Africa settentrionale*, 161–62.
45. FO (German), 1/41/G (1.4.1940, Mackensen to Ribbentrop); Ciano, *Diario*, 1/249.
46. GDFP, D/9/13; DDI, 9/3/103.
47. Westphal, 123–24; Halder, *Hitler*, 33; Warlimont, 70; Jacobsen, 128–29; Rintelen, 81–82.
48. Graziani, *Ho difeso*, 204; *In Africa settentrionale*, 168–71.
49. Messe, *La mia armata*, 23; Graziani, *Ho difeso*, 201; Canevari, *La guerra*, 2/15; Tamaro, *Venti anni*, 3/415; De Biase, *L'aquila*, 417.
50. Iachino, 23; Ciano, *Diario*, 1/207 (D'Andrea); Federzoni, *Italia*, 207–208; Halder, *Kriegstagebuch*, 1/278.
51. Lessona, *Memorie*, 426; Bianchi, *Perchè*, 177–78, 674; Mariano, 243; FO (PRO), 371/24949/R.1507 (20.1.1940, Loraine); Ciano, *Diario*, 1/224.
52. Waterfield, 257; Welles, 116; Bottai, *Vent'anni*, 163.
53. FO (PRO) R.5033/58/22 (20.4.1940, Loraine); R.5202/58/22 (19.4.1940, Burrows); Caviglia, 246; Carboni, 65; Bianchi, *Perchè*, 739.
54. Signoretti, 196–97; Hoettl, 261; Ciano, *Diario*, 1/268.
55. *Bollettino*, July 1940, 63–64; PI, 28.4.1940, 1; Arpinati, 142.
56. *Camera, commissioni*, 2.4.1940, 181–82; Simoni, 124; Ciano, *Diario*, 1/241.
57. PI, 27.4.1940, 1; Ciano, *Diario*, 1/233.
58. CF, 1.4.1940, 179; PN, 15.3.1940, 131; *"Economia,"* Ap. 1940, 264 (Serpieri); RPI, Ap. 1940, 5.
59. OO, XXXII, 194.
60. Gorla, 80; OO, XXIX, 378.
61. Dinale, 161.
62. PI, 19.4.1940, 1; Ciano, *Diario*, 1/251.
63. OO, XXIX, 375–76; Bertoldi, *Mussolini*, 53; Ciano, *Diario*, 1/254.
64. DDI, 9/4/192; GDFP, D/9/235; Halder, *Kriegstagebuch*, 1/270, 277.
65. Grazzi, 100.
66. Marder, 161; CF, 15.5.1940, 235 (Canevari).
67. Capoferri, *Venti anni*, 219.
68. Pricolo, *La regia*, 194; Ciano, *Diario*, 1/264.
69. DDI, 9/4/397.
70. Guspini, 170; Ciano, *Diario*, 1/264.
71. PI, 17.4.1940, 1; OO, XXIX, 394–95.
72. Poncet, *Au palais*, 173; Ciano, *Diario*, 1/270.
73. Ciano, *Diario*, 1/266.
74. *"Primato,"* 1.6.1940, 1 (Bottai); PI, 23.5.1940, 1; CF, 15.5.1940, 227; Ciano, *Diario*, 1/274.
75. Anfuso, 406; DGFP, D/9/472; Tamaro, *Venti anni*, 3/398.
76. Mussolini, V., *Vita*, 106.
77. Leto, *Ovra*, 212.

78. LEI, May 1940, 382.
79. DF, Oct. 1940–Jan. 1941, 236.
80. Canevari, *Graziani*, 174, and *La guerra*, 2/21; Tamaro, *Venti anni*, 3/400–404; Rintelen, 82; Cowles, 354; Pini, *Filo*, 204, 210; Ciano, *Diario*, 1/270.
81. Begnac, 651 (Aug. 1939).
82. Rintelen, 146.
83. Giolli, 108; Ciano, *Diario*, 1/308.
84. FO (PRO), 434/7/7006 (11.4.1940, Charles).
85. *"Il libro italiano,"* May 1939, 271 (Alfieri); Civ.F., Jan.–Feb. 1941, 37 (Cantimori).
86. CF, 1.3.1940, 153.
87. *"Gerarchia,"* June 1942, 237.
88. Giolli, 213.
89. Borsa, *Gli inglesi*, 73.
90. Matthews, *I frutti*, 300.
91. PI, 14.5.1940, 1.
92. *"Costruire,"* May 1940, 4; *"Libro e moschetto,"* 6.4.1940 (Lajolo: reproduced in *Eia*, 409–10).
93. Garland, 27–29.
94. Bottai, *Vent'anni*, 174; Federzoni, *Italia*, 166; IM, 28.10.1935, 9–10; BF, June 1940, 476–78 (Pavolini); *Weizsäcker-Papiere*, 212.
95. Armellini, *La crisi*, 98.
96. Scorza, 85, 156; Federzoni, *Italia*, 273.
97. *In Africa settentrionale*, 186–87.
98. PI, 12.6.1940, 1.
99. Ciano, *Diario*, 1/271.
100. Badoglio, 37–38; Puntoni, 315.
101. Aroma, *Mussolini*, 400.
102. Puntoni, 13, 88; Giolli, 214; PI, 7.4.1940, 1.
103. Maugeri, *From the Ashes*, 14; Bertoldi, *Badoglio*, 29, 142; Armellini, *Diario*, 22–23; Pieri, 746 (Rochat); Vailati, 71–72.
104. Carboni, 91; Mussolini, B., *Il tempo*, 45; *"Il Ponte,"* 1952, 1103 (Salvemini); Pricolo, *La regia*, 224.
105. *Peace and war*, 537; Langer, 1/461, 465; Ciano, *Diario*, 1/270.
106. Badoglio, 36; Ciano, *Diario*, 1/270.
107. Rossi, F., *Mussolini*; Matteini, 92.
108. Maugeri, *Mussolini*, 25; Pricolo, *La regia*, 212.
109. Keitel, 111–12; Halder, *Kriegstagebuch*, 1/308; Dollmann, *Roma*, 125; Nuremberg, 15/351.
110. Testament, 102.
111. CDG, 29.6.1940, 895; Rintelen, 88; Poncet, *Au palais*, 178; Canevari, *La guerra*, 2/74.
112. Lessona, *Memorie*, 399.
113. Badoglio, 36–37; Guarneri, *Battaglie*, 2/498; Guspini, 173; Bianchi, *Perchè*, 188.
114. Maugeri, *Mussolini*, 28, 42.
115. *Camera, commissioni*, 6.5.1942, 953 (Riccardi).
116. Armellini, *Diario*, 18; Favagrossa, 16–18; Faldella, *L'Italia*, 108; Messe, *La mia armata*, 29.
117. Cabianca, 179; *Fianco a fianco*, 165–66.
118. *Hitler e Mussolini*, 42, 48; DGFP, D/9/541.
119. *L'esercito italiano*, 149; Roatta, 44–45.
120. Rossi, F., *Mussolini*, 14–15.
121. DDI, 9/4/622; Maravigna, 407; *In Africa settentrionale*, 93.
122. *La marina*, 21/311.
123. Ciano, *Diario*, 1/277.
124. CDI, June 1940, 163 (Silva).
125. Iachino, 163; Roatta, 195; Doenitz, 156; Ruge, 195.
126. Killen, 112; Poolman, 42–51, 71.
127. Belot, 52.

128. Gabriele, 43.
129. *Gli scacchieri*, 1/11–12, 18, and 2/36–44.
130. *Hitler e Mussolini*, 48; Ciano, *Diario*, 1/271; Faldella, *L'Italia*, 742 (Pricolo).
131. Washington, T.821/127/IT A.1141 (25.5.1940, Geloso; 6.6.1940, Visconti-Prasca).
132. Santoro, 1/77–78, 94.

CHAPTER 16: AN UNCERTAIN START

1. Ciano, *Diario*, 1/272.
2. Rintelen, 85; Bottai, *Vent'anni*, 175; Gorla, 83; Zangrandi, *Il lungo viaggio*, 185; Dollmann, *The Interpreter*, 106, 187; Monelli, 14; Badoglio, 45.
3. FO (PRO), R.4721/173/22 (11.4.1940, Lorraine).
4. *"Politica,"* June 1940, 133/20–22 (Coppola).
5. Cione, *Storia*, 473 (Flora).
6. CF, 15.6.1943, 212.
7. CF, 1.11.1941, 1; DF, Sept. 1941, 118 (Curcio).
8. *"Economia,"* Ap. 1940, 263–64; DF, Feb.–Mar. 1942, 256–57, 261 (Mezzasoma).
9. AAI, Dec. 1940, 4/24–25 (Orano); *"Civiltà Cattolica,"* Oct. 1936, 468–69.
10. *"Primato,"* 1.10.1942, 351; LEI, Mar. 1940, 216; *"Comando,"* 1940, 2/181; Fenizio, 10; Spampanato, *Contromemoriale*, 1/164.
11. DF, Oct. 1940, 47–49 (Toscano); Borntraeger, x (Pini); Volpe, *Storia*, 243–44.
12. PI, 31.7.1942, 1; Tur, 40; Scorza, 71.
13. OO, XXX, 50, and XXXII, 175; PI, 10.5.1943, 1; Italicus, 3; *"Lo Stato,"* May 1941, 199; *Tamaro, Venti anni*, 3/372; Orano, *Mussolini*, 40; Capoferri *L'ora*, 223.
14. Barzini, *La guerra*, 102, 105; Ciano, *Diario*, 1/263; *"Echi,"* 20.9.1940, 530 (Villari).
15. Villari, *Italian*, 245, 257; Bocca, *Storia*, 75 (Umberto); Pettianto, *Tutto*, 49; Lessona, *Un ministro*, 145–46; Gentizon, *Souvenirs*, 97–98; Mussolini, E., *Mio fratello*, 225.
16. Caracciolo, 60.
17. Pricolo, *La regia*, 210–11; Santoro, 1/94.
18. Rintelen, 89; *La battaglia*, 128.
19. *Hitler e Mussolini*, 50.
20. MLI, July 1973, 80 (Marchelli).
21. Boelcke, 392; Bojano, 158, 165.
22. Luciano, 14; Ciano, *Diario*, 1/279–80.
23. *La battaglia*, 137.
24. CDI, 14.6.1940, 169, 179; PI, 4.6.1940, 1; Ciano, *Diario*, 1/279; Rossi, F., *Mussolini*, 174–75.
25. Rossi, F., *Mussolini*, 174.
26. Messe, *La mia armata*, 28; Canevari, *La guerra*, 2/68.
27. Anfuso, 161–62; Bottai, *Vent'anni*, 298; Iachino, *Marina*, 166.
28. Ciano, *L'Europa*, 603; Deakin, 61.
29. PS, July 1940, 225 (Trevisani); CDG, 29.6.1940, 895; RI, 6.7.1940, 913.
30. DDI, 9/5/45.
31. St.A. 1/000868–69; Ciano, *Diario*, 1/280.
32. Matteini, 106.
33. PI, 18.6.1940, 1; 19.6. 1940,3.
34. BF, Sept. 1942, 562; Zanussi, 1/23.
35. Santoro, 1/108–109.
36. *La battaglia*, 118.
37. Halder, *Kriegstagebuch*, 1/370.
38. Signoretti, 204.
39. *L'apporto*, 1/207–209; Pascazio, *Scopritevi*, 70; DF, Sept. 1940, 850 (Corselli); Massani, 20–22; Mayneri, 38; V.I., Sept. 1940, 318 (Canevari).

40. Bastianini, 257.
41. Azeau, 307, 334.
42. Ciano, *Diario*, 1/289; Di Bella, 31.
43. Bottai, *Vent'anni*, 181; Ciano, *Diario*, 1/281.
44. DGFP, D/10/150; Ciano, *L'Europa*, 596; De Matteis, 166; Caprarelli, 122; ASNS, 1940, 2/22.
45. PI, 19.7.1940, 1; DGFP, D/11/332–33, 418; DDI, 9/5/757; CDI, July 1940, 183.
46. *"Lo Stato,"* Aug.–Sept. 1940, 356–57; CDI, July 1940, 199.
47. PI, 20.6.1940, 3; DF, June 1940, 776.
48. Matteini, 112; Monghini, 264.
49. Ciano, *L'Europa*, 563, 571–72; Ciano, *Diario*, 1/294.
50. Zachariae, 86–87.
51. *"Corriere,"* 14.7.1940, 1; RI, 20.7.1940, 1043; Cucco, *Le ragioni*, 30–31; LAI, 30.6.1940, 17; CDI, 14.6.1940, 167.
52. Sillani, *Le forze*, 265 (Pinna); CDG, 22.6.1940, 880, and 10.8.1940, 160; *La marina*, 4/97; Canevari, *La guerra*, 1/593; Villa, *Nemica*, 129.
53. PN, 31.8.1940, 467; CF, 15.11.1940, 18; VM, July 1940, 598.
54. DGFP, D/10/151, 252; Simoni, 141–42.
55. Boelcke, 72; Meissner, 546–47.
56. PS, Aug. 1940, 291–92; *Almanacco fascista*, 1940, 279; *"Geopolitica,"* Dec. 1940, 534; EF, Dec. 1941, 25 (Missiroli); *"Comando,"* 1941, 6/417–18.
57. Ciano, *L'Europa*, 564; Usai, 148.
58. DDI, 9/5/105; DF, Aug. 1940, 836; OM, July 1941, 337.
59. *"Primato,"* 1.7.1940, 17; Baravelli, 46–47; BF, July 1940, 562–63 (Bodrero); *"Geopolitica,"* Dec. 1940, 558.
60. Mainardi, 181–82; *"Politica,"* July 1940, 85; *Convegno*, 1/236–39.
61. DF, June 1940, 763; *"Geopolitica,"* June–July 1940, 292; CF, 15.5.1941, 218–19.
62. Appelius, *La vittoria*, 20; PS, Oct. 1940, 322; *"Comando,"* 1941, 3/240.
63. Quartara, 467–68; PS, Sept. 1942, 218; *Vademecum Africano*, 1943, 2/75–76; *Orientamenti*, 37; VM, Oct. 1940, 902; *Senato, commissioni*, 30.5.1942, 1576 (Aloisi).
64. OO, XXIX, 404; Ciano, *Diario*, 1/117, 227; Phillips, 157; CF. 1.9.1940, 339; Orestano, *Verso*, 384.
65. AAI, Dec. 1940, 40 (Astuti).
66. *"Geopolitica,"* 31.3.1942, 119; Pennisi, 45–46; Monterisi, 192–93.
67. DF, Jan. 1942, 226, 230–31; *"Comando,"* 1941, 3/206–207, 223.
68. EF, Dec. 1940, 12; REC, Ap. 1941, 246, 258; Baistrocchi, 27–29; *Convegno*, 1/478; *"Echi,"* 5.8.1942, 364.
69. DDI, 9/5/40–41, 106; Lubera, 50; Volpe, *Saluto*, 147.
70. DGFP, D/12/951; DDI, 9/5/105, 721; Ciano, *1937–1938*, 132; Puntoni, 21; Gorla, 282, 303, 325.
71. OO, XXXII, 194; DF, June 1939, 280; CF, 15.6.1941, 249.
72. Matteini, 115; Mainardi, 181; *"Comando,"* 1941, 5/389.
73. PS, May–June 1941, 182; EF, May 1941, 44–45; DGFP, D/10/153–54.
74. Halder, *Kriegstagebuch*, 2/21, 33.
75. DGFP, D/10/153; DDI, 9/5/149; Ciano, *L'Europa*, 570; Simoni, 144–45.
76. Washington, T.821/126/IT A.1139 (11–12.7.1940); Roatta, 117; Schramm, 64.
77. Armellini, *Diario*, 49; Rossi, F., *Mussolini*, 72; Canevari, *La guerra*, 2/226.
78. Armellini, *Diario*, 81, 102–103; Roatta, 143–44.
79. Alfieri, 4.
80. Rintelen, 103–104; Bottai, *Vent'anni*, 182.
81. Westphal, 211; Tur, 39; Zanussi, 1/133; Carboni, 36.
82. Armellini, *Diario*, 81–82.
83. Senise, 113.
84. St.A. 231/061184.
85. St.A 231/061182, 061189, 061191.
86. PI, 17.5.1940, 2; DF, June 1940, 775, and Oct. 1940–Jan. 1941, 234–36.
87. Flora, 7.

88. Pini, *Mussolini* (1940), 267.
89. Maurano, *Ricordi*, 212–13; Monelli, 36; Cavallero, *Il dramma*, 102–103.
90. DDI, 9/5/239–40; Greiner, 1/118–19.
91. CF, 15.7.1940,299 (Paresce); Orano, *Mussolini*, 40; *"Corriere,"* 26.6.1940,3; *"Politica,"* June 1940, 133/52 (Coppola); Luongo, *L'Inghilterra*, 66.
92. CF, 1.12.1940, 41; 15.12.1941, 53; *"Corriere,"* 8.2.1941, 1.
93. Canevari, *La guerra*, 2/358.
94. PI, 27.10.1940, 1; *Annuario RA*, 24.11.1940, 145 (Crocco); CDG, 2.11.1940, 580–81; *"Corriere,"* 13.11.1940, 1, 6; Barzini, *La guerra*, 217.
95. *"Corriere,"* 20.10.1940, 2; 15.11.1940, 6; Mandillo, 55–56.
96. Kesselring, *Soldat*, 103, 154; Kesselring, *Gedanken*, 29; Valle, 171–72; Guariglia, *Ricordi*, 482; Soffici, 111; Simoni, 182.
97. Armellini, *Diario*, 91; Ciano, *Diario*, 1/304; DGFP, D/11/254–55.
98. Cambria, 73, 76; OO, XXXI, 34.
99. RI, 19.10.1940, 1491; LAI, 31.12.1940, 3; RA, Dec. 1940, 497 (Mecozzi); *"Corriere,"* 1.9.1940, 1; PS, Oct. 1940, 321.
100. Appelius, *Vincere*, 40; *Venti anni*, 3/26, 36.
101. Halder, *Kriegstagebuch*, 2/138; GDFP, D/12/137; OO, XXX, 33.
102. CDG, 27.7.1940, 95 (Lioy); *"Rassegna di cultura,"* Nov. 1940, 275.
103. St.A. 1/001047 (20.6.1940); DDI, 9/4/191; Trizzino, *Navi*, 197; Pricolo, *La regia*, 286.
104. Rossi, F., *Mussolini*, 98–99; Faldella, *L'Italia*, 246.
105. Guariglia, *Ricordi*, 478; Bastianini, 258; Ciano, *Diario*, 1/317.
106. DDI, 9/5/699–705; *Senato, commissioni*, 25.5.1942, 1486 (U. Ricci).
107. *"Comando,"* 1941, 6/481; LM, Nov. 1940, 319; *"Echi,"* 5.7,1942, 315.
108. PI,1.11.1940, 1; CDG, 9.11.1940, 602, and 16.11.1940, 634; Tamaro, *Venti anni*, 3/426.
109. *La prima offensiva*, 45–46; Ciano, *Diario*, 1/298, 306–307.
110. Dolfin, 215; Roatta, 363; Scala, 10/340; *Ambrosini papers* (It. 3029), July 1943.
111. Warlimont, 124; Greiner, 1/73; Halder, *Kriegstagebuch*, 2/149; Westphal, 155; Rintelen, 101–102; Spampanato, *Contromemoriale*, 1/164–65; Canevari, *La guerra*, 2/106–108; Messe, *La mia armata*, 40, 66.

CHAPTER 17: THE LOGICAL CONCLUSION OF FASCISM

1. Araldi, 308, 316.
2. *"Primato,"* 1.3.1940, 1; CF, 1.6.1940, 243, and 15.6.1940, 259; PI, 24.10.1940, 1; Pirelli, *Economia*, 2/8; *"Lo Stato,"* May 1941, 190, and Aug.–Sept. 1941, 343; LEI, Dec. 1941, 596; *Nuova civiltà*, 223–27; Gambetti, *Controveleno*, 156; Fanelli, 43, 105–107.
3. Volpe, *Storia*, 224–25; PI, 27.4.1940, 1 (Buffarini); *"Lo Stato,"* Sept.–Oct. 1942, 260 (Costamagna); LM, Oct. 1940, 282; Araldi, xv.
4. CF, 15.4.1941, 179; 15.6.1940, 251; 1.8.1941, 292; 15.11.1941, 32.
5. *"Lo Stato,"* Sept.–Oct. 1942, 258; DF, Sept. 1941, 108 (Curcio); *Camera, commissioni*, 14.4.1943, 1243 (D'Aroma).
6. PI, 27.4.1940, 1, and 26.5.1940, 1.
7. *"Comando,"* 1942, 6/275 (Orestano); *"Echi,"* 20.8.1940, 453–55.
8. CF, 15.6.1940, 257; DF, Oct. 1940, 105.
9. *"Corriere,"* 22.9.1940, 3 (Luzio); *"Lo Stato,"* Ap. 1941, 129; EFG, June 1942, 1–2.
10. LIR, June–July 1940, 180; CDI, 14.6.1940, 160; PS, July 1940, 231 (Panunzio); Appelius, *La guerra*, 13–14.
11. CF, 1.11.1941, 3–4 (Panunzio); Berlutti, 43, 63.
12. EI, 20.1.1941, 31; CF, 15.12.1941, 53; EFG, Jan. 1942, 15; Valori, *Parole*, 46; PN, 1.11.1942, 170–71 (Spampanato).
13. Sottochiesa, 12, 34. Luongo, *La guerra*, 39.

14. BF, Sept. 1940, 663, and Nov. 1940, 879; CF, 1.11.1940, 5; Civ.F., Nov.–Dec. 1941, 14–17 (Bottai).
15. Soffici, 51; *"Camicia rossa,"* Sept. 1940, 11; EF, May 1941, 12 (Riccardi).
16. Armellini, *Diario,* 47.
17. EF, Dec. 1940, 12/3; *Orientamenti,* 165; Mainardi, 144; De Matteis, 160–62.
18. SPI, June 1942, 169–70; *Venti anni,* 3/8–9, 26; *"Echi,"* 5.7.1942, 322–23.
19. Appelius, *La vittoria,* 7; Matteini, 280.
20. PI, 12.9.1940, 1; RPE, Sept. 1940, 625–26.
21. EI, 20.1.1941, 29–30; EFG, Mar. 1942, 21–22; Mazzei, *Commenti,* 16–19.
22. DDI, 9/5/315.
23. DF, Oct. 1940, 141 (Bodrero); OO, XXX, 57; LDR, 5.1.1942, 31.
24. DDI, 9/5/309; *Senato, commissione di finanza,* 23.9.1942, 1731.
25. EF, Dec. 1940, 11/7–9; May 1941, 4–5 (Riccardi); *"Giovane Europa,"* 1942, 12/38.
26. *Il Gran Consiglio,* 620; Ciano, *L'Europa,* 531.
27. Saraceno, 257; *L'economia italiana dal 1861,* 454–56 (Baffi).
28. Rossi, F., *Mussolini,* 8–9; Anfuso, 151; Messe, *La mia armata,* 25; Roatta, 26–27.
29. Matteini, 128.
30. Senise, 104.
31. PS, Aug. 1940, 279–80.
32. CF, 15.5.1941, 217.
33. CF, 15.2.1941, 128, and 1.4.1941, 165; *"Echi,"* 5.2.1942, 86–89; V.I. Aug. 1942, 217; LM, July 1941, 2–4; Giani, 188; *La disoccupazione,* 2/2/149–50; REC, Ap. 1941, 245–46.
34. Rintelen, 163; Kesselring, *Soldat,* 142–43; *Il popolo,* 23.
35. *Camera, commissioni,* 6.5.1942, 951–53; 12.5.1942, 1026; 13.5.1942, 1061–62.
36. *Camera, commissioni,* 12.5.1942, 1021.
37. CF, 15.1.1940, 105.
38. PS, May–June 1941, 189; CDG, 27.7.1940, 101; PI, 22.1.1941, 1–2 (Appelius); V.I., Aug. 1940, 194; EF, May 1941, 13, and Oct. 1941, 3–4 (Riccardi); *"Vità,"* 21.9.1941, 1.
39. Roatta, 64.
40. *Camera, commissioni,* 8.5.1941, 798.
41. Gorla, 242; DGFP, D/13/755.
42. *Camera, commissioni,* 8.5.1942, 1002–1003 (Buffarini), and 13.5.1942, 1090; Gorla, 303; Guspini, 193–94.
43. CF, 15.1.1941, 85; 1.3.1941, 129; 15.5.1941, 217; 1.7.1941, 265; 15.7.1941, 281; 15.10.1941, 367, 369; 1.11.1941, 16; 15.6.1942, 219; 1.8.1942, 252; and 1.11.1942, 7; Vergani, 152; Caviglia, 366.
44. Gorla, 91–92, 115; *Camera, commissioni,* 10.1.1941, 629, and 18.7.1941, 893–94.
45. *Camera, commissioni,* 12.5.1942, 1044–46; *Senato, commissioni,* 27.9.1942, 402.
46. Gorla, 353.
47. Gorla, 315–16.
48. Senise, 80–81; Arpinati, 60; St.A. 221/056682–83, 056689, 056701–702, 056706, 056714–19, 056725.
49. Senise, 40–42.
50. Leto, *Ovra,* 178; Leto, *Polizia,* 163.
51. Pini-Susmel, 4/159; *"Gerarchia,"* June 1942, 259; St.A. 103/027843 (Suardo); Soffici, 24–25, 147, 151; Ciano, *Diario,* 2/38.
52. St.A. 234/062183–84, 062189; FO (German), 4924/E.257596 (29.5.1942, Mackensen); Spampanato, *Contromemoriale,* 1/176; Bianchi, *Perchè,* 713.
53. Leto, *Polizia,* 42; Luciano, 6–7; Ciano, *Diario,* 2/167–68; Pini-Susmel, 4/182.
54. Wagnière, 204; Minney, 118; Poncet, *Au palais,* 20; Rintelen, 148.
55. Dolfin, 116; OO, XXXII, 174; Scorza, 70.
56. *Hitler e Mussolini,* 38, 152; Messe, *La guerra,* 16, 20; CSIR, 36.
57. Gorla, 216–17; Ciano, *Diario,* 2/56; Alfieri, 199.
58. V.I., July 1941, 18; EI, 10.7.1941, 171.
59. Keitel, 159–60.
60. Roatta, 186; Faldella, *L'Italia,* 467.
61. Pricolo, *La regia,* 213.

62. Valle, 172.
63. Messe, *La guerra*, 25.
64. Anfuso, 239.
65. DGFP, D/13/654, 660; Messe, *La guerra*, 50.
66. CF, 15.11.1941, 27–28 (Canevari); *"Civiltà,"* 21.1.1942, 12; *"Gerarchia,"* Oct. 1942, 386; AF, Feb. 1942, 5–6.
67. CF, 1.11.1936, 4, and 15.10.1938, 382; RSA, Sept. 1941, 795–96.
68. Messe, *La mia armata*, 69; DGFP, D/13/222, 695.
69. *"Comando,"* 1942, 6/280.
70. Anfuso, 561.
71. Ciano, *Diario*, 2/56, 101; Bianchi, *Perchè*, 792; Gorla, 268.
72. PI, 2.6.1940, 3, and 6.5.1941, 1; VM, Jan. 1940, 29.
73. OO, XXX, 100; Ciano, *Diario*, 2/56; Grazzi, 219; Ciano, *L'Europa*, 590; CF, 15.12.1941, 57.
74. Bottai, *Vent'anni*, 189–90; Bragadin, *Il dramma*, 180; Ciano, *Diario*, 2/79.
75. Senise, 99; Galbiati, 127.
76. Gorla, 275; OO, XXX, 155; Ciano, 2/104.
77. Barzini, *La guerra*, 23, 39–40; Gayda, *Gli Stati Uniti*, 377, 592; CF, 15.12.1941, 57.
78. *"Politica,"* Ap. 1943, 167 (Coppola).
79. Interlandi, 4–5, 19, 35–37; LDR, 5.2.1942, 6.
80. St.A. 268/077750, 077760.
81. Gorla, 362; RHDG, July 1972, 48 (Vujosevic); *Senato, commissioni*, 18.3. 1942, 1382–83.
82. SPI, June 1942, 171–75 (Bastianini); Civ.F. Nov.–Dec. 1941, 22–23 (Bottai); Federzoni, *L'ora*, 153.
83. Cavallero, *Comando*, 298; OO, XXXI, 97.
84. Ciano, *Diario*, 2/110; Apih, 423–26; LDR, 5.3.1941, 8.
85. Maurano, *Ricordi*, 287, 293; Blet, 8/622–23; Rusinow, 280; Zbornik, 5/9/519; 6/3/425, 597; *Human and Material sacrifices*, 5, 8, 52.
86. Caviglia, 326; Ciano, *Diario*, 2/58, 140; Puntoni, 77; Mussolini, V., *Vita*, 104.
87. *"Lo Stato,"* May 1942, 142; *"Gerarchia,"* May 1942, 219.
88. Puntoni, 99; Ciano, *Diario*, 2/156.
89. Canevari, *Graziani*, 149; Benedetti, 96; Navarra, 105.
90. Ciano, *Diario*, 1/339 and 2/66; Soffici, 140.
91. Gorla, 348; OO, XXXI, 72–73, 76.
92. Matteini, 293; Appelius, *La vittoria*, 21.
93. St.A. 116/031768–69; 117/031883, 031993; 249/067570.
94. *"Primato,"* 15.7.1942, 263; *Camera, commissioni*, 17.5.1943, 1350; Civ.F., Aug. 1942, 604–605; OO, XXXII, 197; Zachariae, 178.
95. Appelius, *Parole*, 210, 212, 250, 269; Rysky, 458–59.
96. PI, 19.7.1942, 3 (Soffici); CF, 15.11.1942, 16 (Bottai); 15.12.1942, 40 (Bottai); 1.3.1943, 112 (Paresce); 15.3.1943, 123; and 15.6.1943, 197; *"Gerarchia,"* May 1943, 150 (Bottai).
97. St.A. 26/012620–42.
98. *"Il Giornale d'Italia,"* 17.2.1943, 1 (Gayda); Pozzi, 165; OO, XXXII, 198; St.A., 151/044537 (Giannini).
99. Caracciolo, 102; Luciano, 14–15.
100. Leto, *Polizia*, 76.
101. Bertoldi, *Mussolini*, 142 (De Stefani).
102. Gorla, 305; Bottai, *Vent'anni*, 250, 263; Soffici, 101–102, 179.
103. Federzoni, *Italia*, 273; Bottai, *Vent'anni*, 315.
104. Dinale, 172; PI, 23.2.1941, 1.
105. Scorza, 181–82; Bottai, *Vent'anni*, 229; Castellano, 34.
106. Rivoire, 108–109; *Camera, commissioni*, 14.4.1943, 1244 (D'Aroma); Gambetti, *Controveleno*, 147.
107. Acerbo, 485, 523; Bastianini, 114–15; Plehwe, 17.
108. Blet, 7/188–89 (Cardinal Montini); Puntoni, 73; Castellano, 32.
109. Bellotti, 63 (Sept. 1943); *"Tempo,"* 12.1.1960 (De Vecchi); Dinale, 197–98.
110. OO, XXXIV, 296, 437; Dolfin, 187; Pareti, *Passato*, 428.

111. Vergani, 144, 151, 228.
112. OO, XXXII, 175–76, 200; Caviglia, 333; Bottai, *Vent'anni*, 237, 314.
113. OO, XXXII, 188; Vergani, 151.
114. Bottai, *Vent'anni*, 260.
115. Zachariae, 70–71; Anfuso, 407; Aroma, *Mussolini*, 274.
116. OO, XXXI, 119, 128.
117. St.A. 292/089626; Dolfin, 152, 218; OO, XXXII, 164; Tamaro, *Due anni*, 1/77; Gorla, 393–94; Bottai, *Vent'anni*, 234, 250; Dinale, 181, 184.
118. Zachariae, 67–68; Maugeri, *Mussolini*, 42.
119. Blet, 7/335.
120. Fanelli, 38; CF, 15.2.1943, 95; Deakin, 219, 283.
121. PN, 15.4.1942, 37 (Spampanato).
122. St.A. 159/046270 (11.5.1943).
123. *"Costruire,"* Ap. 1943, 36; Deakin, 220.
124. Gambetti, *Controveleno*, 139–41.
125. Rintelen, 196.
126. Benjamin, 240.

LIST OF WORKS CITED AND
NOTE ON FURTHER READING

The English-speaking reader has easily available what is still the most fascinating and useful source for the declining years of Mussolini, the posthumously published diaries of Count Ciano. Although in some few places these diaries have evidently been tampered with before publication and though the English version is sometimes far from reliable, they give an authentic and often hour-by-hour account of what happened in Rome between 1937 and 1943. Another excellent book on the early development of Mussolini's aggressive temperament is that which Gaudens Megaro wrote while an exile in America. For the middle period, when Mussolini was at his most self-important and narcissistic, there is the account of his revealing interviews with Emil Ludwig: the pose is obvious, the opinions often quite patently false and histrionic, but this book shows as no other does the myth in the process of fabrication.

More than a dozen books have appeared in English which give a short version of Mussolini's life, of which the best is by Laura Fermi, who is the wife of the great scientist and another Italian exile writing in America. Somewhat drier is another by Sir Ivone Kirkpatrick, who witnessed something of Italian affairs at the time as a member of the British foreign service. Two official biographies, by Giorgio Pini and Margherita Sarfatti, were translated from Italian into English, but are full of rhetorical falsity and serve only as indications of what Mussolini wanted the world to believe about himself. One of several "autobiographies" purporting to be by Mussolini himself came out first in English and, interestingly enough, was never allowed to appear in Italian in case it gave Italians the wrong impression: it was in fact the product of collaborative authorship between Mussolini's brother and a former United States ambassador to Rome, Washburn Child.

Specifically on foreign policy, there are some excellent books in English. Two general but very substantial and thoroughly researched volumes are by Alan Cassels for the earlier period and Bill Deakin for the last years of defeat. On the Corfu incident of 1923 an authoritative study has been written by J. Barros; another on the origins of the Ethiopian war by G. W. Baer; and of considerable interest is another by J. P.

Diggins on the reactions in America towards Italian fascism. In 1949 Elizabeth Wiskemann published a pioneer investigation of the German alliance and Mussolini's relations with Hitler, and on the Pact of Steel there has subsequently been translated Mario Toscano's thorough monograph. More recently has appeared a study of "universal fascism" by M. A. Ledeen.

Of general surveys of foreign policy in the period, one by Luigi Villari is interesting because of the facts and arguments with which he tries to justify Mussolini. More satisfactory is that written by Maxwell Macartney and Paul Cremona, and more recently we have another outline history by C. J. Lowe and F. Marzari. But the best of all is still Salvemini's book on the origins of the Second World War.

In addition might be mentioned a well-balanced chapter on foreign policy in Christopher Seton-Watson's book on modern Italy, and a few pages by Adrian Lyttleton that are particularly interesting on the relations between fascism and nationalism. The best treatise in English on propaganda in fascist Italy is by Edward Tannenbaum. Some of the relevant documents on foreign policy can be found in an anthology edited by Charles Delzell, and others on the years 1942 and 1943 in another volume of Mussolini's memoirs edited by Raymond Klibansky.

AAI: *"Gli annali dell'Africa italiana"* (ed. A. Piccioli), Rome 1938–

Acerbo, G., *Fra due plotoni di esecuzione: avvenimenti e problemi dell'epoca fascista*, Rocca S. Casciano 1968

ACN: *Atti del convegno nazionale di studi autarchici*, Milan 1939–40

ACV: *Atti del Convegno Volta* (Reale Accademia d'Italia)

AF: *"Annali del Fascismo"* (ed. F. Paoloni), Naples 1931–

"Affari Esteri," Rome

"Africa," London

Africa: espansionismo fascista e revisionismo, ed. A. Gravelli, Rome 1933

Albertini, L., *Epistolario 1911–1926*, ed. O. Barié (4 vols.), Milan 1968

Alfassio Grimaldi, U., and Bozzetti, G., *Farinacci il più fascista*, Milan 1972

Alfieri, D., *Due dittatori di fronte*, Milan 1948

Algardi, Z., *Processi ai fascisti*, Florence 1958

Alimenti, C., *La questione petrolifera italiana*, Turin 1937

Almanacco fascista del "Popolo d'Italia"

Aloisi, Baron, *Journal: 25 Juillet 1932–14 Juin 1936*, Paris 1957

Aloisi, P., *La mia attività a servizio della pace*, Rome 1946

Ambrosini Papers, Cabinet Offices, London

Amé, C., *Guerra segreta in Italia 1940–1943*, Rome 1954

Amery, L. S., *My Political Life* (3 vols.), London 1955

Amicucci, E., *I 600 giorni di Mussolini: dal Gran Sasso a Dongo*, Rome 1948

Amministrazione fiduciaria all'Italia in Africa: atti del secondo convegno di studi coloniali, Florence 1948

Anfuso, F., *Roma Berlino Salò: 1936–1945*, Cernusco 1950

Annuario RA: Annuario della Reale Accademia

"Antieuropa" (ed. A. Gravelli), Rome 1929–

APC: *Atti del primo congresso di studi coloniali*, Florence 1931

API: *"Annuario di Politica Internazionale"* (Istituto per gli Studi di Politica Internazionale), Milan 1935–

Apih, E., *Italia fascismo e antifascismo nella Venezia Giulia: 1918–1943*, Bari 1966

Appelius, M., *La guerra dell'asse e il mondo di domani*, Rome 1941

——, *La vittoria liberatrice*, Rome 1943

——, *Parole dure e chiare*, Milan 1942

——, *Vincere*, Rome (c. 1942)

APSR: *'American Political Science Review'*, New York

ARA: *Atti della Reale Accademia*, Rome

Araldi, V., *Mussolini parla*, Rome 1943

Ardemagni, M., *La Francia sarà fascista?*, Milan 1937

Arena, N., *Bandiera di combattimento: storia della marina militare italiana, 1925–1945*, Rome 1974

Armellini, Q., *Diario di guerra: nove mesi al comando supremo*, Cernusco 1946

——, *La crisi dell'esercito*, Rome 1945

Aroma, N. d', *Mussolini segreto*, Rocca S. Casciano 1958

——, *Vent'anni insieme: Vittorio Emanuele e Mussolini*, Rocca S. Casciano 1957

Arpinati, G. C., *Arpinati mio padre*, Rome 1968

ASC: *"Archivio Storico di Corsica"* (ed. G. Volpe), Livorno 1925–

ASNS: *"Archivio Storico di Nizza e Savoia"* (ed. F. Bonazzi), Turin 1940–

Aster, S., *The Making of the Second World War*, London 1963

"Augustea" (ed. F. Ciarlantini), Rome 1925–

Avenati, C. A., *Perchè difendiamo l'indipendenza dell'Austria*, Turin 1934

Azeau, H., *La guerre franco-italienne: juin 1940*, Paris 1967

Badoglio, P., *L'Italia nella seconda guerra mondiale: memorie e documenti*, Milan 1946

Baer, G. W., *The Coming of the Italian-Ethiopian War*, Cambridge Mass. 1967; Oxford 1967

Baistrocchi, A., *La certezza della vittoria*, Livorno 1941

Balbo, I., *La politica aeronautica dell'Italia fascista*, Rome 1927

Bandinelli, R. B., *Dal diario di un borghese e altri scritti*, Milan 1948

Bandini, F., *Gli Italiani in Africa: storia delle guerre coloniali, 1882–1934*, Milan 1971

Baravelli, G. C., *La profanazione anglo-giudaica dei luoghi santi*, Rome (c. 1941)

Barker, A. J., *The Civilizing Mission: A History of the Italo-Ethiopian War of 1935–1936*, New York 1968; London 1968

Barker, E., *Macedonia: Its Place in Balkan Power Politics*, London 1950; New York 1950

Barros, J., *The Corfu Incident of 1923*, Princeton 1965

Barzini, L., *From Caesar to the Mafia: Sketches of Italian Life*, London 1971; Freeport 1971

——, *La guerra all'Inghilterra: commenti e spiegazioni*, Milan 1941

Bastianini, G., *Uomini, cose, fatti: memorie di un ambasciatore*, Milan 1959

Baudino, C., *Una guerra assurda: la campagna di Grecia*, Milan 1965

BD: *Documents on British Foreign Policy 1919–1939*, ed. E. L. Woodward, Rohan Butler, etc.

Bechi-Luserna, A., *Noi e loro: cronache di un soldato vagabondo*, Milan 1941

Begnac, Y. de, *Palazzo Venezia: storia di un regime*, Rome 1950

Bellotti, F., *La repubblica di Mussolini, 26 Luglio 1943–25 Aprile 1945*, Milan 1947

Belluzzo, G., *L'autarchia Italiana vista da un ingegnere*, Milan 1940

Belot, R. de, *The Struggle for the Mediterranean 1939–1945*, Princeton 1951; Oxford 1952

Benedetti, U., *Beneditto Croce e il fascismo*, Rome 1967

Benewick, R. J., *The Fascist Movement in Britain*, London 1972

Benigno, Jo di, *Occasioni mancate: Roma in un diario segreto 1943–1944*, Rome 1945

Benito Mussolini: Memoirs 1942–1943, with Documents Relating to the Period, ed. R. Klibansky, trs. F. Lobb, London 1949; Philadelphia 1949

Benjamin, R., *Mussolini et son peuple*, Paris 1937

Berlutti, G., *Noi crediamo nel Duce*, Rome 1941

Bernotti, R., *Storia della guerra nel Mediterraneo: 1940–43*, Rome 1960

Berselli, A., *L'opinione pubblica inglese e l'avvento del fascismo: 1919–1925*, Milan 1971

Bertoldi, S., *Badoglio*, Milan 1967

——, *Mussolini tale e quale*, Milan 1965

Bertoni, R., *Russia: trionfo del fascismo*, Milan 1937

BF: *"Bibliografia Fascista"* (ed. E. Bodrero, B. Giuliano, A. Pavolini, C. di Marzio), Rome, 1926–

Bianchi, G., *Perchè e come cadde il fascismo*, Milan 1970

——, *Rivelazioni sul conflitto italo-etiopico*, Milan 1967

Biondi, D., *La fabbrica del Duce*, Florence 1967

Blet, P.; Graham, R. A.; Martini, A.; Schneider, B., *Actes et documents du Saint Siège relatifs à la seconde guerre mondiale* (8 vols.), Rome 1964–74

Blondel, J.-F., *Au fil de la carrière: récit d'un diplomate 1911–1938*, Paris 1960

Boca, A. del, *La guerra d'Abissinia 1935–1941*, Milan 1966

Bocca, G., *Storia d'Italia nella guerra fascista 1940–1943*, Bari 1969

Boelcke, W. A., ed., *Kriegspropaganda 1939–1941: Geheime Ministerkonferenzen im Reichspropagandaministerium*, Stuttgart 1966

Bojano, F., *In the Wake of the Goose-step*, London 1944; New York 1945

'Bollettino delle Assemblee Legislative', Rome

Bonacossa, C., *Quando il mondo ha vent'anni*, Milan 1938

Boncour, P.-P., *Entre deux guerres: souvenirs sur la 111e République*, Paris 1945

Bonnefous, G. and E., *Vers la guerre*, Paris 1965

Borntraeger, C., *Dal trattato di Versaglia al patto Mussolini: 15 anni di politica estera italiana*, Genoa 1942

Borsa, M., *Gli inglesi e noi*, Milan 1945

——, *Memorie di un redivivo*, Rome 1945

Bottai, G., *Mussolini costruttore d'impero*, Mantua 1927

——, *Quaderno Affricano*, Florence 1939

——, *Vent'anni e un giorno*, Cernusco 1949

Bowers, C. G., *My Mission to Spain*, London 1954; New York 1954

Bragadin, M'A., *Che ha fatto la marina? (1940–1945)*, Milan 1949

——, *Il dramma della marina italiana 1940–1945*, Milan 1968

"Brassey's Naval Annual," London

Braunthal, J., *The Tragedy of Austria* (appendix by P. R. Sweet), London 1948

Brown, S. H., *Für das Rote Kreuz in Aethiopien*, Zurich 1939

BSOA: *"Bulletin of the School of Oriental and African Studies,"* London

Buckley, H., *Life and Death of the Spanish Republic*, London 1940

Cabianca, E., *L'Italia in prima linea*, Bologna 1940

Calderoli, G., *I senza tonsille*, Bergamo 1941

CAM: *"Corsica Antica e Moderna"* (ed. F. Guerri), Florence 1932–

Cambria, A., *Maria José*, Milan 1966

Camera, commissioni legislative riunite (Camera dei Fasci e delle Corporazioni), Rome 1943

Camera dei deputati: Atti del parlamento italiano, discussioni

"Camicia Rossa" (ed. E. Garibaldi), Rome 1924–

Canepa, A., *Sistema di dottrina del fascismo* (3 vols.), Rome 1937

Canevari, E., *Graziani mi ha detto*, Rome 1947

———, *La conquista inglese dell'Africa*, Rome 1935

———, *La guerra italiana: retroscena della disfatta* (2 vols.), Rome 1948

Cantalupo, R., *Fatti europei e politica italiana 1922–1924*, Milan 1924

———, *Fu la Spagna: ambasciata presso Franco, Febbraio–Aprile 1937*, Milan 1948

———, *Racconti politici dell'altra pace*, Milan 1940

Capoferri, P., *L'ora del lavoro*, Milan 1941

———, *Venti anni col fascismo e con i sindacati*, Milan 1957

Caprarelli, G., *Opinioni e saggi politici*, Milan 1941

Caracciolo di Feroleto, M., *"E poi?": la tragedia dell'esercito italiano*, Rome 1946

Carboni, G., *Memorie segrete 1935–1948: più che il dovere*, Florence 1955

Carli, M., *Antisnobismo*, Milan 1929

———, *Cervelli di ricambio*, Rome 1928

———, *Colloqui coi vivi*, Rome 1928

———, *Fascismo intransigente (contributo alla fondazione di un regime)*, Florence 1926

Carocci, G., *La politica estera dell'Italia fascista 1925–1928*, Bari 1969

Castellani, A., *Tra microbi e re*, Milan 1961

Castellano, G., *Come firmai l'armistizio di Cassibile*, Milan 1945

Cassels, A., *Mussolini's Early Diplomacy*, Princeton 1970

Cavallero, C., *Il dramma del Maresciallo Cavallero*, Milan 1952

Cavallero, U., *Comando supremo: diario 1940–43 del Capo di Stato Maggiore Generale*, Rocca S. Casciano 1948

Caviglia, E., *Diario (aprile 1925–marzo 1945)*, Rome 1952

CDG: *"Cronache Della Guerra"* (ed. D. S. Piccoli, for Ministero della Cultura Popolare), Rome, 1939–

CDI: *"Conquiste d'Impero"* (ed. C. Petrone), Rome, 1933–

Ceci, P., *Lineamenti di cultura militare a seconda dei programmi ministeriali per l'insegnamento universitario*, Rome 1939

Celovsky, B., *Das Münchener Abkommen, 1938*, Stuttgart 1958

Cerruti, E., *Ambassador's Wife*, London 1952; New York 1953

Ceva, L., *La condotta italiana della guerra: Cavallero e il comando supremo 1941–1942*, Milan 1975

CF: *"Critica Fascista"* (ed. G. Bottai and G. Casini), Rome 1923–

CFI: *Confederazione Fascista degli Industriali, Annuario*, Rome 1937

Chatfield, Lord, *It Might Happen Again*, London 1947

Chi è? Dizionario degli italiani d'oggi, Rome 1940

Chiurco, G. A., *Storia della rivoluzione fascista 1919–1922* (5 vols.), Florence 1929

Churchill, W., *Step by Step, 1936–1939*, London 1939; New York 1939

Cianfarra, C. M., *The War and the Vatican*, London 1945; *The Vatican and the War*, New York 1944

Ciano, G., *Diario 1939–1943* (2 vols.), Milan 1946

———, *1937–1938 Diario*, Bologna 1948

———, *L'Europa verso la catastrofe*, Milan 1947

Ciano's Diary 1937–1938, trs. A. Mayor, Introduction by M. Muggeridge, London 1952;

Ciano's Diary 1939–1943, ed. M. Muggeridge, London 1947; New York 1946

Ciano's Diplomatic Papers, ed. M. Muggeridge, London 1948

Ciarlantini, F., and Cuesta, U., *Antologia coloniale*, Milan 1929

Ciarlantini, F., *Hitler e il fascismo*, Florence 1933

——, *Mussolini imaginario*, Milan 1933

——, *Vicende di libri e di autori*, Milan 1931

Cilibrizzi, S., *Pietro Badoglio rispetto a Mussolini e di fronte alla storia*, Naples n.d.

Cione, E., *Storia della repubblica sociale italiana*, Caserta 1948

Cipriani, L., *Fascismo razzista*, Rome 1940

——, *Un assurdo etnico: l'impero etiopico*, Florence 1935

Civ.F.: *"Civiltà Fascista"* (ed. G. Gentile, P. De Francisci, and C. Pellizzi for the Istituto Nazionale di Cultura Fascista), Rome 1934–

"Civiltà" (ed. E. Cecchi), Milan, 1940–

"Civiltà Cattolica" (ed. F. Rinaldi), Rome, 1850–

Cocchia, A., *Submarines Attacking*, London 1956; *Hunters and Hunted*, Annapolis 1958

Cogni, G., *I valori della stirpe italiana*, Milan 1937

Colvin, I. G., *Vansittart in Office: An Historical Survey of the Origins of the Second World War*, London 1965; *None So Blind: A British Diplomatic View of the Origins of World War II*, New York 1965

"Comando: rassegna di studi politici e militari" (ed. A. E. Folchi), Rome 1940–

"Commentari dell'azione fascista" (ed. U. Nani), Rome, 1934–

Compendio statistico Italiano (16 vols.), Rome 1927–42

Conti, C., *Servizio segreto: cronache e documenti dei delitti di stato*, Rome 1945

Conti, E., *Dal taccuino di un borghese*, Cremona 1946

Convegno economico: Convegno per lo studio dei problemi economici dell'ordine nuovo, 18–23 Maggio 1942 (2 vols.), Pisa 1942

Coppola, F., *La pace coatta*, Milan 1929

Corbino, O. M., *Conferenze e discorsi*, Rome (c.1938)

"Corriere Della Sera," Milan (ed. A. Borelli)

Corso, G., *Lo stato fascista*, Rome 1929

"Costruire" (eds. D. Lischi and O. Mosca), Rome 1924–

Cowles, V. S., *Looking for Trouble*, London 1941; New York 1941

Croce, B., *Terze pagine sparse*, Bari 1955

"Cronache illustrate della azione italiana in AO" (ed. O. Zoppi), Milan 1936

Cross, C., *The Fascists in Britain*, London 1961; New York 1963

CSC: *Congresso di studi coloniali, relazioni e communicazioni*, Florence 1937

CSIR: *Le operazioni del C.S.I.R. e dell'Armir dal guigno 1941 all'ottobre 1942*, Rome 1947

Cucchetti, G., *Italia Germania*, Palermo 1940

Cucco, A., *"Amplexus interruptus": effetti deleteri alla salute*, Milan 1940

——, *L'amplesso e la frode alla luce della scienza medica moderna*, Rome 1961

——, *Le ragioni biologiche della disfatta demoplutocratica*, Rome (c.1942)

——, *Non volevamo perdere*, Rocca S. Casciano 1950

——, *Perchè perderanno*, Rome (c.1942)

"Daily Mail," London

"Daily Telegraph," London

Dall'Ora, F., *Intendenza in A.O.*, Rome 1937

Dal Regno all'Impero, 17 Marzo 1861–9 Maggio 1936, Accademia dei Lincei, Rome 1937

D'Amoja, F., *Declino e prima crisi dell'Europa di Versailles 1931–1933*, Milan 1967

———, *La politica estera dell'impero dalla conquista dell'Etiopia all'Anschluss*, Padua 1967

Danzi, G., *Europa senza europei?*, Rome 1934

Das Heer des faschistischen Italien, Rome 1934

DDB: *Documents diplomatiques belges, 1920–1940*, Brussels

DDF: *Documents diplomatiques français, 1932–1939*, Paris

DDI: *Documenti diplomatici italiani* (ed. R. Moscati, M. Toscano), Rome

Deakin, F. W., *The Brutal Friendship: Mussolini, Hitler and the Fall of Italian Fascism*, London 1962; New York 1962

De Biase, C., *L'aquila d'oro: storia dello Stato Maggiore Italiano 1861–1945*, Milan 1970

———, *L'impero di "Faccetta Nera,"* Milan 1966

De Felice, R., *Mussolini il duce, 1921–1936*, Turin 1975

———, *Mussolini il fascista, 1921–1929* (2 vols.), Turin, 1966–68

———, *Mussolini il rivoluzionario, 1883–1920*, Turin 1965

———, *Storia degli ebrei italiani sotto il fascismo*, Turin 1972

Della Torre, F. M., and Santagata, F., *Panorama economico africano*, Naples 1935

Delzell, C. F., *Mussolini's Enemies: The Anti-Fascist Resistance*, Princeton 1961; Oxford 1961

De Matteis, G., *Verso l'equilibrio della nuova Europa*, Florence 1941

De Stefani, A., *Baraonda bancaria*, Milan 1960

DF: *"Dottrina Fascista"* (ed. N. Giani), Milan, 1937–

DGFP: *Documents on German Foreign Policy, 1918–1945*, London

Dietrich, O., *The Hitler I Knew*, London 1957; *Hitler*, Chicago 1955

Diggins, J. P., *Mussolini and Fascism: The View from America*, Princeton 1972

Dinale, O., *Quarant'anni di colloqui con LUI*, Milan 1953

Dino Grandi racconta, Venice 1945

Di Nolfo, E., *Mussolini e la politica estera italiana 1919–1933*, Padua 1960

Dizionario di politica (ed. Partito nazionale fascista) (4 vols.), Rome 1940

Documents on Italian War Crimes Submitted to the United Nations War Crimes Commission by the Imperial Ethiopian Government, Addis Ababa, 1949

Doenitz, K., *Memoirs: Ten Years and Twenty Days*, London 1959; Cleveland 1959

Dolfin, G., *Con Mussolini nella tragedia: diario del capo della segreteria particolare del Duce 1943–1944*, Cernusco 1949

Dollmann, E., *The Interpreter*, London 1967

———, *Roma nazista*, Milan 1951

Donosti, M. (Mario Luciolli), *Mussolini e l'Europa: la politica estera fascista*, Rome 1945

Douhet, G., *Il dominio dell'aria*, Milan 1932

———, *La guerra integrale*, ed. E. Canevari, Rome 1936

Dower, K. Gandar, *Abyssinian Patchwork: An Anthology*, London 1949

Driberg, T., *Guy Burgess*, London 1956

"Dublin Review," Dublin

Due popoli una guerra, ed. P. Orano, Rome 1938

Ebenstein, W., *Fascist Italy*, New York 1939

"Echi e Commenti" (ed. P. de Francisci), Rome

"Economia" (ed. V. Fresco and P. Corti), Trieste and Rome, 1922–

Economia italiana dal 1861 al 1961: studi nel 1° centenario dell'unità d'Italia, Milan 1961

Eden, A., *Facing the Dictators*, London 1962; Boston 1962

Ed.F.: *"Educazione Fascista"* (Istituto Nazionale Fascista di Cultura), Rome, 1927–34

"Edinburgh Review," Edinburgh

"Educazione Politica" (ed. G. Gentile), Rome 1923–

EF: *"Economia Fascista"* (ed. R. Riccardi), Rome 1940–

EFG: *"Europa Fascista Giovanissima"* (ed. C. Ferri), Rome 1941–

EI: *"Espansione Imperiale"* (ed. S. Scorza), Rome 1937–

Eia, eia, eia, alalà, ed. O. del Buono, Milan 1971

EN: *"Esercito e nazione: rivista per l'ufficiale italiana"* (ed. A. Baldini), Rome 1926–

Enciclopedia Italiana, Rome 1932–48

"English Review," London

EO: *"L'Europa Orientale"* (ed. A. Giannini and E. Lo Gatto), Rome 1921

"Epoca," Milan

Ercole, F., *Pensatori e uomini d'azione*, Milan 1935

———, *Storia del fascismo* (2 vols.), Milan 1939

"Espresso," Rome

Evans-Pritchard, E. E., *The Sanusi of Cyrenaica*, Oxford, 1949; New York 1949

Faldella, E., *L'Italia e la seconda guerra mondiale: revisione di giudizi*, Rocca S. Casciano 1960

———, *Venti mesi di guerra in Spagna, Luglio 1936–Feb. 1938*, Florence 1939

Fanelli, F. A., *Agonia di an regime (Gennaio–Luglio 1943)*, Rome 1971

Farago, L., ed., *Abyssinian Stop Press*, London 1936

Farina, G. G., *Follie delle folle*, Rome 1945

Fascism and the Working Classes, Rome 1936

Favagrossa, C., *Perchè perdemmo la guerra: Mussolini e la produzione bellica*, Milan 1946

Federzoni, L., *A.O.: il "posto al sole,"* Bologna 1938

———, *Italia di ieri per la storia di domani*, Milan 1967

———, *Parole fasciste al Sud-America*, Bologna 1938

Feiling, N., *The Life of Neville Chamberlain*, London 1946; New York 1946

Fenizio, F. di, *L'Economia di guerra come economia di monopoli*, Milan 1942

Fermi, Laura, *Mussolini*, Chicago 1961; London 1961

Fest, J. C., *Hitler*, London 1974; New York 1974

Fianco a fianco fino alla vittoria, Rome 1941

Fischer, L., *Men and Politics: An Autobiography*, London 1941; New York 1941

Flora, F., *Stampa dell'era fascista: le note di servizio*, Rome 1945

FO: Foreign Office, London

FO (German): photostats of German documents, FO Library, London

Foglio d'ordine (intermittent publication by the Fascist Party)

"Foreign Affairs," New York

Foreign Relations of the United States: Diplomatic Papers, Washington

Fornaciari, J., *Nel piano dell'impero: risorse locali Africane*, Bologna 1937

Fortunati, P., *L'importanza delle colonie per la scienza e la politica della popolazione*, Rome 1940

Fossa, D., *Lavoro italiano nell'impero*, Milan 1938

Fuchs, M., *A Pact with Hitler: The Death of Austria*, London 1939; *Showdown in Vienna: The Death of Austria*, New York 1939

Fuehrer Conferences on Naval Affairs 1943, Admiralty, London 1947

Fuller, Maj. Gen. J. F. C., *The First of the League Wars*, London 1936

Funke, M., *Sanktionen und Kanonen: Hitler, Mussolini und der internationale Abessinienkonflikt 1934–36*, Düsseldorf 1970

GAA: *"Giornale di Addis Abeba"* (ed. C. Milanese), Addis Ababa 1936–

Gabriele, M., *Operazione C. 3: Malta*, Rome 1965

Galbiati, E., *Il 25 Luglio e la M.V.S.N.*, Milan 1950

Galland, A., *The First and the Last: The German Fighter Force in World War II*, London 1955; New York 1954

Gambetti, F., *Controveleno*, Parma 1942

———, *Cronache del tempo fascista*, Bologna 1936

Gamelin, M. G., *Servir* (3 vols.), Paris 1946–47

Gangemi, L., *Conseguenze economiche delle mutazioni territoriali nell'Europa centrale*, Naples 1939

Garland, A. N., and Smyth, H. McGaw, *The Mediterranean Theater of Operations: Sicily and the Surrender of Italy*, Washington 1965

Gasparotto, L., *Diario di un deputato: cinquant'anni di vita politica italiana*, Milan 1945

Gayda, V., *Che cosa vuole l'Italia?*, Rome 1940

———, *Gli Stati Uniti nella guerra mondiale*, Rome 1943

———, *Italia e Francia* (6th ed.), Rome 1939

Gehl, J., *Austria, Germany and the Anschluss 1931–1938*, London 1963; New York 1963

Gentile, R., *Storia dell'acronautica dalle origini ai giorni nostri*, Rome 1959

Gentizon, P., *Souvenirs sur Mussolini*, Palermo 1958

"Geopolitica" (ed. R. Roletto), Milan 1938–

"Gerarchia" (ed. B. Mussolini, M. G. Sarfatti, Vito Mussolini, C. Ravasio), Milan 1922–

GF: *"Gioventù Fascista"* (ed. A. Starace), Rome 1931–

Ghetti, W., Storia della marina italiana nella seconda guerra mondiale (4 vols.), Milan 1974

Giani, P., *Autarchia e guerra: lineamenti, realizzazioni e sviluppi dell'autarchia*, Turin 1942

Gianturco, M., *La guerra degli imperi capitalistici contro gli imperi proletari*, Florence 1940

Giglio, C., *La confraternita senussita, dalle sue origini ad oggi*, Padua 1932

———, *Politica estera italiana*, Padua 1936

Gilbert, F., ed., *Hitler Directs His War*, New York 1950; Oxford 1951

Ginnari, B., *Il fascismo in difesa dell'Europa*, Naples 1929

Giolli, P. (U. d'Andrea), *Come fummo condotti alla catastrofe*, Rome 1950

"Giovane Europa: organo del combattentismo universitario europeo" (ed. R. Rupp), Berlin 1942–

"Giovanissima" (ed. C. Ferri), Rome 1931–

Giovannucci, F. S., *Il problema austriaco e l'Italia*, Rome 1934

Gisevius, H. B. *To the Bitter End*, London 1948; New York 1947

Gladwyn: *The Memoirs of Lord Gladwyn*, London 1972

Gli scacchieri Mediterranei (ed. Istituto Superiore di Guerra) (9 parts), Rome 1939–40

Gori, F., *Egeo fascista*, Rome 1938

Gorla, G., *L'Italia nella seconda guerra mondiale: memorie di un milanese, ministro del re nel governo di Mussolini*, Milan 1959

Gravelli, A., *Mussolini aneddotico*, Rome (c. 1950)

———, *Verso l'internazionale fascista*, Rome 1932

Gray, E. M., *Credenti nella patria*, Milan 1938

———, *La chiesa anglicana contro Roma fascista e cristiana*, Milan 1937

———, *L'Italia ha sempre ragione*, Milan 1938

Graziani, R., *Cirenaica pacificata*, Milan 1932

———, *Ho difeso la patria*, Cernusco 1947

———, *Libia redenta: storia di trent'anni di passione italiana in Africa*, Naples 1948

Grazzi, E., *Il principio della fine (l'impresa di Grecia)*, Rome 1945

Greenfield, R., *Ethiopia: A New Political History*, London 1965; New York 1965

297

Gregory, J. W., *Report of the Work of the Commission Sent Out by the Jewish Territorial Organization*, London 1909

Greiner, H.; Schramm, P. E.; and Jacobsen, H-A., eds., *Kriegstagebuch des Oberkommandos der Wehrmacht* (5 vols.), Frankfurt 1961–65

Grifone, P., *Il capitale finanziario in Italia*, Turin 1971

Guariglia, R., *Primi passi in diplomazia e rapporti dall'ambasciata di Madrid, 1932–1934*, ed. R. Moscati, Naples 1972

——, *Ricordi, 1922–1946*, Naples 1950

Guarneri, F., *Autarchia e scambi internazionali*, Rome 1941

——, *Battaglie economiche tra le due grandi guerre* (2 vols.), Milan 1953

Guida generale degli Italiani a Londra, London 1932

Guspini, U., *L'orecchio del regime: le intercettazioni telefoniche al tempo del fascismo*, Milan 1973

Halder, F., *Hitler als Feldherr*, Munich 1949

——, *Kriegstagebuch*, ed. H. A. Jacobsen (3 vols.), Stuttgart 1962–66

Hamilton, T. J., *Appeasement's Child*, London 1943; New York 1943

Hansard: Parliamentary Debates, Official Report, London

Hardie, F., *The Abyssinian Crisis*, London 1974; Hamden 1974

"Harper's Magazine," New York

Harris, B., *The United States and the Italo-Ethiopian Crisis*, Stanford 1964

Harvey, J., ed., *The Diplomatic Diaries of Oliver Harvey 1937–1940*, London 1970; New York 1972

Heinkel, E., *HE 1000*, London 1956; *Stormy Life: Memoirs of a Pioneer of the Air Age*, New York 1956

Henderson, N. M., *Water Under the Bridges*, London 1945

Hess, R. L., *Italian Colonialism in Somalia*, Chicago 1966; London 1966

Hildebrand, K., *The Foreign Policy of the Third Reich*, London 1973

Hitler, A., *Mein Kampf*, London 1939; Harrisburg 1939

Hitler e Mussolini: lettere e documenti, Milan 1946

Hitler's Secret Book (intro. by T. Taylor), New York 1962

Hoepke, K. P., *Die Deutsche Rechte und der Italienische Fascismus*, Düsseldorf 1968

Hoettl, W., *The Secret Front: The Story of Nazi Political Espionage*, London 1953; New York 1954

Hossbach, F., *Zwischen Wehrmacht und Hitler 1934–38*, Göttingen 1965

Human and Material Sacrifices of Yugoslavia in her War Efforts 1941–1945, Belgrade 1946

Hunt, D., *A Don at War*, London 1966

Iachino, A., *Tramonto di una grande marina*, Milan 1966

IAI: *Il 3 anno dell'Impero* (5 vols.), Addis Ababa 1937–38

ICE: *Relazione sull'attività dell'ICE*, Rome 12.7.1939

IDR: *"Il Diritto Razzista"* (ed. S. M. Cutelli), Rome 1939–

I.I.: *"Illustrazione Italiana"* (ed. E. Cavacchioli), Milan 1874–

Il cittadino italiano, ed. Partito Nazionale Fascista, Rome 1936

Il fascismo inglese, ed. A. Gravelli, Rome (c. 1935)

"Il Frontespizio" (ed. P. Bargellini), Florence, 1929–

"Il Giornale d'Italia" (ed. V. Gayda), Rome

"Il Giorno," Milan

Il Gran Consiglio del fascismo nei primi quindici anni dell'era fascista, Bologna 1938

"Il Lavoro Fascista" (ed. A. de Marsanich), Rome

Il libro della IV classe elementare, letture, 1938

"Il Libro Italiano" (ed. G. Casini), Rome 1937–

"Il Nuovo Giornale" (ed. E. Novelli), Florence

"Il Politico," Pavia

"Il Ponte," Florence

Il popolo italiano non ha capitolato (2d ed.), Venice 1944

"Il Primato" (ed. V. Zangara), Rome 1930–

Il processo Roatta, Rome 1945

"Il Rubicone" (ed. G. Massani), Rimini 1931–

IM: *"Impero Fascista"* (ed. E. Settimelli), Rome 1933–

IML: *"Il Mondo Latino"* (ed. F. D. Sapio), Rome 1933–

"Imperium" (ed. S. Maurano), Rome and Como, 1926–

In Africa settentrionale: la preparazione al conflitto. Ottobre 1935–settembre 1940, Rome 1955

Incisa, L., *Spagna nazional-sindacalista,* Bologna 1941

Infante, A., *Problemi del Mediterraneo,* Tripoli 1937

Information: Weekly Guide to Current Politics," London

Inghilterra e Italia nel '900: atti del convegno di Bagni di Lucca, Florence 1973

Interlandi, T., ed., *Pagine di documentazione sugli Stati Uniti,* Rome (c. 1943)

Iraci, A., *Arpinati l'oppositore di Mussolini,* Rome 1970

Irving, D. J. C., *Breach of Security,* London 1968

Italia d'oggi, Rome 1941

Italia e Germania: Maggio XVI, Rome 1938

Italia fra tedeschi e alleati: la politica estera fascista e la seconda guerra mondiale, ed. R. De Felice, Bologna, 1973

"Italiani di Tunisia" (ed. G. B. Cerchiai), Tunis 1934–

Italicus, *La guerra contro l'Inghilterra, guerra di liberazione,* Rome (c. 1940)

Iuvenalis, *Mussolini alla luce infrarossa,* Rome 1944

Izzo, A., *Guerra chimica e difesa antigas,* Milan 1935

Jackson, G., *The Spanish Republic and the Civil War: 1931–1939,* Princeton 1965

Jacobsen, H. A., *Fall Gelb, der Kampf um den deutschen Operationsplan zur Westoffensive, 1940,* Wiesbaden 1957

Jacomoni, F. di San Savino, *La politica dell'Italia in Albania,* Rocca S. Casciano 1965

JCR: *"Journal of Contemporary History,"* London

JMH: *"Journal of Modern History,"* Chicago

Jones, T., *A Diary with Letters 1931–1950,* Oxford 1954; New York 1954

Keene, F., ed., *Neither Liberty nor Bread: The Meaning and Tragedy of Fascism,* London 1940; New York 1940

Keitel: *The Memoirs of Field Marshal Keitel,* London 1945

Kelly, D. V., *The Ruling Few, or The Human Background to Diplomacy,* London 1952

Kesselring, A., *Gedanken zum zweiten Weltkrieg,* Bonn 1955

——, *Soldat bis zum letzten Tag,* Bonn 1953

Killen, J., *A History of Marine Aviation 1911–68,* London 1969

Kirkpatrick, I., *Mussolini: Study of a Demagogue,* London 1964; Englewood Cliffs 1964

——, *The Inner Circle: Memoirs,* London 1959; New York 1959

Klibansky, R., ed., see *Benito Mussolini*

Kordt, E., *Nicht aus den Akten,* Stuttgart 1950

La battaglia delle Alpi occidentali: giugno 1940, ed. U. Marchini, Rome 1947

La colonizzazione dell'Africa del Nord, Padua 1960

La disoccupazione in Italia: commissione parlamentare di inchiesta sulla disoccupazione (16 vols.), Rome 1953

Lagardelle, H., *Mission à Rome: Mussolini*, Paris 1955

La guerre en Méditerranée 1939–1945 (Colloque international, April 1969), Paris 1971

LAI: *"L'Ala d'Italia"* (ed. V. Federigo), Rome 1919–

"La Lettura" (ed. E. Radius), Milan 1901–

La marina italiana nella seconda guerra mondiale, ed. G. Fioravanzo (21 vols.), Rome 1958–72

La Méditerranée de 1919 à 1939 (Colloque organisé par le Centre de la Méditerranée moderne et contemporaine), Paris 1969

Langer, W. L., and Gleason, S. E., *The World Crisis and American Foreign Policy* (2 vols.), New York 1953; London 1953

La nuova Italia d'oltremare: l'opera del fascismo nelle colonie italiane, ed. A. Piccioli (2 vols.), Milan 1933

L'apporto dell'Italia alla guerra dell'asse, ed. V. Varanini and G. Salocchi, Milan 1941

La prima offensiva Britannica in Africa settentrionale (ottobre 1940–febbraio 1941), Stato Maggiore Esercito, Rome n.d.

La rinascita della Tripolitania: memorie e studi sui quattro anni di governo del conte Giuseppe Volpi di Misurata, Milan 1926

Latinus, *L'Italia e i problemi internazionali*, Milan 1935

Latronico, E., *Spagna economica oggi e domani*, Milan 1938

Laurens, F. D., *France and the Italo-Ethiopian Crisis 1935–1936*, Hague 1967

"La Verità" (ed. N. Bombacci), Rome 1936–

"L'Azione Coloniale" (ed. M. Pomilio), Rome 1930–

LDR: *"La Difesa della Razza"* (ed. T. Interlandi and G. Almirante), Rome 1938–

Ledeen, M. A., *Universal Fascism: The Theory and Practice of the Fascist International, 1928–1936*, New York 1972

"Le Figaro," Paris

Legatus, *Vita diplomatica di Salvatore Contarini: Italia fra Inghilterra e Russia*, Rome 1947

LEI: *"L'Economia Italiana"* (ed. L. Lojacono), Rome 1915–

Leone, E. de, *La colonizzazione dell'Africa del nord* (2 vols.), Padova 1960

Le ragioni dell'Italia: dichiarazioni pronunziate nell'adunanza generale della Reale Accademia d'Italia, Rome 1936

L'esercito italiano tra la 1ª e la 2ª guerra mondiale, novembre 1918–giugno 1940, Rome 1954

Les lettres secrètes échangées par Hitler et Mussolini (intro. by François-Poncet), Paris 1946

Lessona, A., *Il fascismo per le colonie*, Rome (c.1933)

———, *Memorie*, Rome 1963

———, *Scritti e discorsi coloniali*, Milan 1935

———, *Un ministro di Mussolini racconta*, Milan 1973

———, *Verso l'impero: memorie per la storia politica del conflitto italo-etiopico*, Florence 1939

Leto, G., *Ovra, fascismo, antifascismo*, Rocca S. Casciano, 1952

———, *Polizia segreta in Italia*, Rome 1961

Le Vie d'Italia, ed. C. Bonardi, Milan 1895–

Lewis, I. M., *The Modern History of Somaliland: From Nation to State*, London 1965; New York 1965

"Libro e Moschetto," Milan

Liddell Hart, B. H., *The Memoirs of Captain Liddell Hart* (2 vols.), London 1965; New York 1966

"Life," New York

L'Impero (A.O.I.), ed. T. Sillani, Rome 1937

LIR: *"L'Idea di Roma"* (ed. E. Coselschi), Rome 1938–

Lisbon Papers: Ciano's Material on Albania, FO Library, London

Lischi, D., *Sotto i segni del littorio*, Pisa 1933

"L'Italia Coloniale" (ed. C. Palombi), Rome 1923–

Litvinov, M., *Notes for a Journal*, London 1955; New York 1955

LM: *"L'Italia Marinara"* (ed. A. Starace and A. Sulliotti), Rome 1900–

Lojacono, L., ed., *L'indipendenza economica italiana*, Milan 1937

Longanesi, L., *Vade-mecum del perfetto fascista*, Florence 1926

Longrigg, S. H., *A Short history of Eritrea*, Oxford 1945; New York 1946

"Lo Stato" (ed. C. Costamagna), Rome 1930–

Lowe, C. J., and Marzari, F., *Italian Foreign Policy, 1870–1940*, London 1975

LPEA: *"Le Professioni e le Arti"* (ed. E. Bodrero), Rome 1931–

LS: *"La Stirpe"* (ed. E. Rossoni and A. Signoretti), Rome 1923–

Lubera, G., *La catena mediana delle Alpi*, Milan 1941

Lucatello, G., *La natura giuridica dell'unione Italo-Albanese*, Padua 1943

Luciano, C., *Rapporto al Duce: nel racconto dell'ex capo-gabinetto alla stampa*, Rome 1948

Ludecke, K. G. W., *I Knew Hitler*, London 1939

Ludwig, E., *Colloqui con Mussolini: riproduzione delle bozze dalla prima edizione con le correzioni autografe del duce*, Milan 1950

——, *Leaders of Europe*, London 1934; *Nine Etched from Life*, New York 1934

——, *Talks with Mussolini*, trs. E. and C. Paul, London 1932

Luongo, G., *La guerra del lavoro contro l'oro*, Rome 1941

——, *L'Inghilterra nemica del mondo*, Rome 1940

Lyttelton, Adrian, *The Seizure of Power: Fascism in Italy 1919–1929*, London 1973; New York 1973

Macartney, M. H. H., and Cremona, P., *Italy's Foreign and Colonial Policy, 1914–1937*, London 1938

Macfie, J. W. S., *An Ethiopian Diary: A Record of the British Ambulance Service in Ethiopia*, Liverpool 1936

Magistrati, M., *Il prologo del dramma: Berlino 1934–1937*, Milan 1971

——, *L'Italia a Berlino (1937–1939)*, Milan 1956

Mainardi, L., *Nazionalità e spazi vitali*, Rome 1941

Malaparte, C., *Technique du coup d'état*, Paris 1931

Mancini, A., *La donna fascista nell'irrobustimento della razza*, Rome 1937

Mandillo, E., *Fronti attraverso l'Europa in guerra*, Rome 1942

Maravigna, P., *Come abbiamo perduto la guerra in Africa*, Rome 1949

Marco, R. de, *The Italianization of African Natives, 1890–1937*, New York 1943

Marconi, G., *Per la ricerca scientifica*, Rome 1935

Marder, A. J., *From the Dardanelles to Oran: Studies of the Royal Navy in War and Peace 1915–1940*, London 1974

Mariano, N., *Forty Years with Berenson*, London 1966; New York 1966

Marinese, L., *Giornalisti per il mondo*, Palermo 1937

Marsanich, A. de, *Civiltà di masse*, Florence 1940

Martini, E., *Civiltà e decadenza demografica: civiltà fascista Mediterranea*, Turin 1934

Massani, G., *La battaglia delle Alpi*, Rome 1941

Massuero, F. N., *Ombre e luci di due continenti: due anni di politica coloniale e Mediterranea 1923–1924*, Milan 1926

Matteini, C., *Ordini alla stampa: la politica interna ed estera del regime fascista nelle "disposizioni" emanate ai giornali dal Ministero della Cultura Popolare*, Rome 1945

Matthews, H., *Eyewitness in Abyssinia*, London 1937

——, *I frutti del fascismo*, Bari 1945

Maugeri, F., *From the Ashes of Disgrace*, New York 1948

——, *Mussolini mi ha detto: confessioni di Mussolini durante il confino a Ponza e alla Maddalena*, Rome 1944

Maurano, S. *Francia la sorellastra*, Milan 1939

——, *Mentalità fascista*, Rome (c.1930)

——, *Ricordi di un giornalista fascista*, Milan 1973

Mayneri, C. C., *Parla un comandante di truppe*, Naples 1947

Mazzei, J., *Commenti alla riorganizzazione economica europea*, Rome 1940

Mecheri, E., *Chi ha tradito? Rivelazioni e documentazioni inedite di un vecchio fascista*, Milan 1947

Mediterranean Fascism, 1919–1945, ed. C. F. Delzell, New York 1970

Megaro, G., *Mussolini in the Making*, London 1938; Boston 1938

Meissner, O., *Staatssekretär unter Ebert, Hindenburg, Hitler*, Hamburg 1950

Melchiori, A., *Roma e Mosca*, Rome 1937

Melograni, P., ed., *"Corriere della sera" (1919–1943)*, Rocca S. Casciano 1965

Merkes, M., *Die deutsche Politik gegenüber dem Spanischen Bürgerkrieg 1936–1939*, Bonn 1961

Messe, G., *La guerra al fronte russo: il corpo di spedizione italiano*, Milan 1947

——, *La mia armata in Tunisia: come finì la guerra in Africa*, Milan 1960

"Middle East Journal," London

Miles, *Come si andò alla disfatta: l'esercito beffato e tradito*, Rome 1945

Milza, P., *L'Italie fasciste devant l'opinion française 1920–1940*, Paris 1967

Minney, R. J., *The Private Papers of Hore-Belisha*, London 1960; New York 1961

Missiroli, M., *Studi sul fascismo*, Bologna 1934

MLI: *"Il Movimento di Liberazione in Italia,"* Milan

MO: *Mediterraneo orientale: 1° convegno nazionale di politica estera*, Milan 1936

Mondaini, G., *La legislazione coloniale italiana nel suo sviluppo storico e nel suo stato attuale, 1881–1940* (2 vols.), Milan 1941

Monelli, P., *Roma 1943* (4th ed.), Rome 1946

Monghini, A. S., *Dal decennale alla catastrofe, 1 gennaio 1933–25 luglio 1943*, Milan 1954

Monterisi, M., *La libertà dei mari e l'Inghilterra*, Milan 1943

Monti, M., *L'Italia e il mercato mondiale del petrolio*, Rome 1930

Moore, M., *Fourth Shore: Italy's Mass Colonization of Libya*, London 1940

Morgan, T. B. *Spurs on the Boot*, London 1942; New York 1941

Mosca, O., *Nessuno volle i miei dollari d'oro*, Naples 1958

Mosley, L. *Haile Selassie, The Conquering Lion*, London 1964; Englewood Cliffs 1965

Mowrer, E. A., *Triumph and Turmoil: A Personal History of Our Time*, London 1968; New York 1968

Mussolini, A., *La lotta per la produzione*, Milan 1937

——, *Le forze dominanti*, Florence 1928

——, *Tripolitania*, Rome n.d.

——, *Verso il nuovo primato*, Milan 1929

Mussolini, B., *Il tempo del bastone e della carota: storia di un anno (ottobre 1942–settembre 1943)*, Milan 1944

——, *La dottrina del fascismo*, Rome 1941

————, *My Autobiography*, trs. R. W. Child, London 1928

————, *Opera Omnia* (see OO)

Mussolini e il fascismo, ed. O. Daffinà, Rome 1929

Mussolini, E., *Mio fratello Benito: memorie*, ed. R. R. Crisolini, Florence 1957

Mussolini, R., *La mia vita con Benito*, Milan 1948

Mussolini, V., *Vita con mio padre*, Milan 1957

————, *Voli sulle ambe*, Florence 1937

NA: *"La Nuova Antologia"* (ed. L. Federzoni and F. Ercole), Rome 1866–

Naudeau, L., *L'Italie fasciste ou l'autre danger*, Paris 1926

Navarra, Q., *Memorie del cameriere di Mussolini*, Milan 1946

Nazi Conspiracy and Aggression (8 vols.), Washington, 1946–48

NDS: *"La nobiltà della stirpe"* (ed. S. M. Cutelli), Rome 1931–

Nelson, K. and Sullivan, A., *John Melly of Ethiopia*, London 1937

Nicolosi, V. M., *Giornale del tempo armato*, Catania 1936

Niekisch, E., *Gewagtes Leben: Begegnungen und Begebnisse*, Cologne 1958

Nitti, F. S., *Rivelazioni: dramatis personae*, Naples 1948

"Nord e Sud," Naples

NM: *"Nazione Militare"* (ed. A. Baldini), Rome 1926–

NP: *"Nuovi Problemi di Politica Storia ed Economia"* (ed. N. Quilici), Ferrara 1930

Nuova civiltà per la nuova Europa, Rome 1942

Nuremberg: *The Trial of Major German War Criminals* (23 vols.), London 1946–51

NYT: *"New York Times"*

"Oggi" (ed. A. Benedetti and M. Pannunzio), Milan 1938–

Ojetti, U., *I taccuini 1914–1943*, Florence 1954

OM: *"Oriente Moderno"* (ed. C. A. Nallino), Rome 1921–

"Omnibus" (ed. L. Longanesi), Milan 1937–41

OO: *Opera omnia di Benito Mussolini*, ed. E. and D. Susmel (36 vols.), Florence 1951–63

Orano, P., ed., *Le direttive del Duce: la difesa nazionale*, Rome 1937

————, *Mussolini al fronte della storia*, Rome 1941

————, *Rodolfo Graziani generale scipionico*, Rome 1936

Orestano, F., *Revisione filosofica*, Rome 1934

————, *Saggi giuridici*, Milan 1941

————, *Verso la nuova Europa*, Milan 1941

Orientamenti dell'economia dell'Europa fascista (Centro Studi Economici e Sociali), Turin 1941

"Ottobre" (ed. A. Gravelli), Rome 1932–

Pace, B., *La Libia nella politica fascista (1922–1935)*, Milan 1935

————, *L'impero e la collaborazione internazionale in Africa*, Rome 1938

Packard, R. and E., *Balcony Empire: Fascist Italy at War*, London 1943; New York 1942

Pagano, S., *Stormi aerei e divisioni corazzate in cooperazione*, Rome 1941

Page, B., Leitch, D.; Knightley, P., *Philby: the Spy who Betrayed a Generation*, London 1968; *The Philby Conspiracy*, New York 1968

Pankhurst, S., *Ethiopia, a Cultural History*, London 1955

Panorami di realizzazioni del fascismo (12 vols.), Rome 1942

Panunzio, S., *Che cos'è il fascismo*, Milan 1924

Panzini, A., *Dizionario moderno delle parole che non si trovano nei dizionari comuni* (10th ed.), Milan 1963

Papen, F. von, *Memoirs*, London 1952; New York 1952

Papini, G., *Italia mia*, Florence 1939

——, *Tutte le opere*, Rome 1963

Pareti, L, *I due imperi di Roma*, Catania 1938

——, *Passato e presente d'Italia*, Venice 1944

Partito e Impero (Istituto Fascista dell'Africa Italiana), Rome 1938

Pascazio, N., *La crisi sociale dell'impero Britannico*, Milan 1941

——, *La rivoluzione d'Irlanda e l'impero Britannico*, Rome 1934

——, *Scopritevi! Passa il soldato italiano*, Milan 1943

Payne, S. G. *Falange: A History of Spanish Fascism*, Stanford 1962; Oxford 1962

——, *Politics and the Military in Modern Spain*, Stanford 1967; Oxford 1967

Peace and War: United States Foreign Policy 1931–1941, Washington 1943

Pellizzi, C., *Una rivoluzione mancata*, Milan 1949

Pennisi, P., *L'espansione fascista in Africa*, Rome 1942

Pepys: *Il diario di Samuel Pepys*, ed. M. Dandolo, Milan 1941

Perini, F. A., *Giano: manuale introduttivo di "Cultura Militare" per i docenti*, Padua 1938

Petersen, J., *Hitler-Mussolini: die Entstehung der Aschse Berlin-Rome 1933–1936*, Tübingen 1973

Petrie, C. A., *Chapters of Life*, London 1950

Pettinato, C., *Questi inglesi*, Milan 1944

——, *Scritto sull'acqua*, Milan 1963

——, *Tutto da rifare*, Milan 1966

Phillips, W., *Ventures in Diplomacy*, London 1955; Boston 1953

"Picture Post," London

Pieri, P., and Rochat, G., *Pietro Badoglio*, Turin 1974

PI: *"Il Popolo d'Italia,"* Milan

Pini, G., *Benito Mussolini* (15th ed.), Bologna 1940

——, *Filo diretto con Palazzo Venezia*, Rocca S. Casciano 1950

——, *La civiltà di Mussolini fra l'oriente e l'occidente*, Rome 1930

——, *The Official Life of Benito Mussolini*, trs. L. Villari, London 1939

Pini-Susmel: Pini, G., and Susmel, D., *Mussolini: l'uomo e l'opera* (4 vols.), Florence 1953–55

Pini, U., *Sotto le ceneri dell'impero*, Milan 1967

Pintor, G., *Il sangue d'Europa (1939–1943)*, Turin 1966

Plehwe, F.-K. von, *The End of an Alliance: Rome's Defection from the Axis in 1943*, London 1971

PM: *"Problemi Mediterranei"* (ed. G. Frisella Vella), Palermo 1924–

PN: *"Politica Nuova"* (ed. B. Spampanato), Naples 1933–

Pirelli, A., *Considerations on the Italo-Ethiopian conflict*, Milan 1936

——, *Economia e guerra* (2 vols.), Milan 1940

Pistolese, G. E., *L'economia dell'impero*, Rome 1937

Poggiali, C., *Albori dell'impero: l'Etiopia come è e come sarà*, Milan 1938

——, *Diario AOI (15 giugno 1936–4 ottobre 1937)*, Milan 1971

"Politica," (ed. F. Coppola), Rome 1919–

Poncet, A. François-, *Au palais Farnèse: souvenirs d'une ambassade à Rome 1938–1940*, Paris 1961

——, *Ricordi di un ambasciatore a Berlino*, Milan 1947

Poolman, K., *Faith, Hope and Charity: Three Planes Against an Air Force*, London 1954

"Popolo di Roma," Rome

Porfiri, F., *L'Anschluss e l'Italia*, Rome 1939

Portsmouth, Earl of, *A Knot of Roots*, London 1965; New York 1965

Pozzi, A., *Come li ho visti io: dal diario di un medico*, Milan 1947

PPS: *"Petroleum Press Service,"* London

Prasca, S. Visconti, *Io ho aggredito la Grecia*, Milan 1946

Preti, L., *Impero fascista africani ed ebrei*, Milan 1968

Pricolo, F., *Ignavia contro eroismo: l'avventura Italo-Greca, ottobre 1940–aprile 1941*, Rome 1946

——, *La regia aeronautica nella seconda guerra mondiale*, Milan 1971

"Primato" (ed. G. Bottai), Rome 1940–

PRO: Public Record Office, London

"Prospettive" (ed. C. Malaparte), Rome 1937–

PS: *"Politica Sociale"* (ed. R. Trevisani), Rome 1929–

Pugnani, A., *La motorizzazione dell'esercito e la conquista dell'Etiopia*, Rome 1936

Puntoni, P., *Parla Vittorio Emanuele III*, Rome 1958

Quaderni sull'autarchia in Italia (4 vols.), Rome 1939

Quaroni, P., *Valigia diplomatica*, Milan 1956

Quartara, G., *La futura pace*, Milan 1942

RA: *"Rivista Aeronautica"* (ed. V. Lioy), Rome 1925–

Raccolta delle circolari e istruzioni ministeriali riservate, ed. A. Toscani (2 vols.), Rome 1934

Raccolta delle leggi e dei decreti del Regno d'Italia, Rome

Raciti, M., *L'opera coloniale dell'Italia fascista in Cirenaica*, Rome 1934

"Rassegna di Cultura" (ed. L. Pollini), Milan 1933–

Rauschning, H., *Hitler Speaks: A Series of Political Conversations with Adolf Hitler on his Real Aims*, London 1939; New York 1940

RC: *"Rivista Coloniale,"* Rome 1919–27. Later *"Rivista delle Colonie"* (ed. A. Bollati for Ministero delle Colonie), Rome 1927–

R.Civ: *"Razza e Civiltà"* (ed. A. Le Pera for Ministero dell'Interno), Rome 1940–

RDC: *"Rassegna dei Combattenti"* (ed. B. Biagi), Rome 1920–

RDO: *"Rassegna d'Oltremare"* (ed. G. Berlutti), Rome 1930–

RDP: *"Rivista di Diritto Pubblico"* (ed. M. D'Amelio), Rome 1908–

REA: *"Rassegna Economica dell'Africa Italiana"* (ed. R. Giannini), Rome 1936–

Rebora, L., *La storia delle nuove rivendicazioni Ticinesi*, Milan 1942

REC: *"Rassegna Economica delle Colonie"* (ed. R. Giannini), Rome 1913–

Reichskanzlei Adjutantur des Führers, Hoover Institute, Stanford

Reisoli, G., *Fuoko su Adolfo, fuoko su Benito*, Naples 1948

"Resto del Carlino," Bologna

"Revue des Deux Mondes," Paris

Reynaud, P., *La France a sauvé l'Europe*, Paris 1947

RF: *"Regime Fascista"* (ed. R. Farinacci), Cremona

RHDG: *"Revue d'Histoire de la Deuxième Guerre Mondiale,"* Paris

RI: *"Relazioni Internazionali"* (ed. V. Varale for ISPI), Milan 1935–

Riboldi, E., *Vicende socialiste: trent'anni di storia italiana nei ricordi di un deputato massimalista*, Milan 1964

Ricci, B., *Avvisi*, Florence 1943

Rintelen, E. von, *Mussolini als Bundesgenosse: Erinnerungen des deutschen Militärattachés in Rom 1936–1943*, Tübingen 1951

RISS: *"Rivista Internazionale di Scienze Sociali"* (ed. A. Fanfani), Milan 1892–

R.It.: *"Rassegna Italiana"* (ed. T. Sillani), Rome 1918–

Rivoire, M., *Vita e morte del fascismo*, Milan 1947

RM: *"Rivista Marittima"* (ed. G. Po), Rome 1868–

R.Med: *"Rassegna del Mediterraneo e della Espansione Italiana"* (ed. T. Sillani), Rome 1925–

Roatta, M., *Otto milioni di baionetti: l'esercito italiano in guerra dal 1940 al 1944*, Milan 1946

Robertson, E. M., *Hitler's Pre-war Policy and Military Plans, 1933–1939*, London 1963

Robinson, R. A. H., *The Origins of Franco's Spain*, Newton Abbott, 1970; Pittsburgh 1971

Rocca, M., *La sconfitta dell'Europa*, Milan 1960

Rocco, A., *Scritti e discorsi politici*, (3 vols.), Milan 1938

Rochat, G., *Il colonialismo italiano: documenti*, Turin 1973

——, *L'attentato a Graziani e la repressione italiana in Etiopia 1933–37* (offprint from *"Italiana Contemporanea,"* Jan. 1975)

——, *L'esercito italiano da Vittorio Veneto a Mussolini (1919–1925)*, Bari 1967

——, *Militari e politici nella preparazione della campagna d'Etiopia: studio e documenti 1932–1936*, Milan 1971

Roletto, G., *Rodi: la funzione imperiale nel Mediterraneo orientale*, Milan 1939

Romains, J., *Seven Mysteries of Europe*, London 1941; New York 1940

"Romana" (ed. U. Biscottini), Rome 1937–

Rommel Papers, ed. B. H. Liddell Hart, London 1953; New York 1953

Rosenberg, A., *Das politische Tagebuch*, Munich 1964

Rosengarten, F., *The Italian Anti-Fascist Press (1919–1945)*, Cleveland 1968

Rossi, A., *The Russo-German Alliance*, London 1950; Boston 1951

Rossi, C., *Mussolini com'era*, Rome 1947

——, *Personaggi di ieri e di oggi*, Milan 1960

——, *Trentatre vicende Mussoliniane*, Milan 1958

Rossi, F., *Mussolini e lo Stato Maggiore: avvenimenti del 1940*, Rome 1951

Rosso, G., *Orma di Mussolini*, Rome 1938

Rotunda, D. T., *The Rome Embassy of Sir Eric Drummond, 16th Earl of Perth 1933–39*, London 1972 (Ph.D. thesis)

RPE: *"Rivista di Politica Economica"* (ed. G. Balella, G. Olivetti, A. Scialoja), Rome 1911–

RPI: *"Rivista Illustrata del 'Popolo d'Italia' "* (ed. M. Morgagni), Milan, 1923–

RS: *"La Ricerca Scientifica e il Progresso Tecnico nell'Economia Nazionale"* (ed. U. Frascherelli), Rome 1930–

RSA: *"Rassegna Sociale dell'Africa Italiana"* (ed. N. Bonfatti), Rome 1938–

RSPI: *"Rivista di Studi Politici Internazionali"* (ed. G. Bosco), Florence 1934–

Ruge, F., *Sea Warfare 1939–1945: A German Viewpoint*, London 1958; *Der Seekrieg*, Annapolis 1957

Rumi, G., *Alle origini della politica estera fascista (1918–1923)*, Bari 1968

Runciman, Sir Walter, *"Sunbeam" in the Mediterranean During the Regime of Mussolini* (London?) 1926

Rusinow, D. I., *Italy's Austrian Heritage 1919–1946*, Oxford 1969

Rysky, C. de, *La guerra moderna: il nuovo imperialismo italiano*, Milan 1942

Saint-Aulaire, A. F., Comte de, *Confession d'un vieux diplomate*, Paris 1954

Salata, F., *Il patto Mussolini: storia di un piano politico e di un negoziato diplomatico*, Milan 1933

Salis, R. Sertoli, *Le isole italiane dell'Egeo dall'occupazione alla sovranità*, Rome 1939

Salter, J. A., *Personality in Politics*, London 1947; New York 1948

Salvadori, M., *L'unità del Mediterraneo*, Rome 1931

Salvatorelli, L., and Mira, G., *Storia del fascismo: l'Italia dal 1919 al 1945*, Rome 1952

Salvemini, G., *Mussolini diplomatico*, Rome 1945

————, *Prelude to World War II*, London 1953; New York 1954

————, *Scritti sul fascismo*, ed. R. Vivarelli, N. Valeri, A. Merola (3 vols.), Milan 1961–74

Santelli, A., *Il primato italiano nelle testimonianze degli stranieri*, Rome 1939

Santoro, G., *L'aeronautica italiana nella seconda guerra mondiale* (2 vols.), Milan 1957

Saraceno, P., *Ricostruzione e pianificazione 1943–1948*, Bari 1969

Saracino, G., *L'Impero italiano e l'Inghilterra*, Milan 1936

Sarfatti, M., *Dux*, Milan 1926

————, *The Life of Benito Mussolini*, trs. F. Whyte, London 1925; New York 1925

Sarkissian, A. Q., ed., *Studies in Diplomatic History and Historiography*, London 1961; New York 1962

Scala, E., *Storia delle fanterie italiane*, Rome 1956

Scarfoglio, C., *L'Inghilterra e il continente*, Rome (c.1938)

Scaroni, S., *Con Vittorio Emanuele III*, Milan 1954

Schmidt, P., *Statist auf diplomatischer Bühne 1923–45*, Bonn 1949

Schonfield, H. J., *Italy and Suez*, London 1940

Schramm-von-Thadden, E., *Griechenland und die Grossmächte im zweiten Weltkrieg*, Wiesbaden 1955

Schuschnigg, K. von, *Ein Requiem in rot-weiss-rot*, Zurich 1946

Scoppa, R. Bova, *Colloqui con due dittatori*, Rome 1949

Scorza, C., *La notte del Gran Consiglio*, Milan 1968

Seeckt: aus seinem Leben 1918–1936, ed. F. von Rabenau, Leipzig 1941

Seldes, G., *Sawdust Caesar: The Untold History of Mussolini and Fascism*, London 1936; New York 1935

Senato: Atti del parlamento italiano, discussioni

Senato, commissione della finanza

Senato, commissioni legislative riunite

Senise, C., *Quando ero capo della polizia 1940–1943*, Rome 1946

Sergi, G., *I Britanni*, Milan 1941

Sermoneta, Duchess of, *Sparkle Distant Worlds*, London 1947

Serventi, G. N., and Balbis, P., *Inglesi 1935*, Rome 1935

Seton-Watson, Christopher, *Italy from Liberalism to Fascism, 1870–1925*, London 1967; New York 1967

Settimelli, E., *Edda contro Benito: indagine sulla personalità del duce attraverso un memoriale autografo di Edda Ciano Mussolini*, Rome 1952

————, *Mussolini visto da Settimelli*, Rome 1929

Sforza, C., *Gli Italiani quali sono*, Milan 1946

Siebert, F., *Italiens Weg in den zweiten Weltkrieg*, Frankfurt 1962

Signoretti, A., *La stampa in camicia nera, 1932–1943*, Rome 1968

Sillani, T., ed., *La Libia in venti anni di occupazione italiana*, Rome 1932

————, ed., *Le forze armate dell'Italia fascista: studi e documenti*, Rome 1939

————, ed., see *L'Impero* (A.O.I.)

Silva, P., *Il Mediterraneo dall'unità di Roma all'impero italiano* (7th ed.), Milan 1942

————, *Io difendo la monarchia*, Rome 1946

Silvestri, C., *I responsabili della catastrofe italiana: guerra, 1940–43*, Milan 1946

Simoni, L. (M. Lanza), *Berlino ambasciata d'Italia 1939–1943*, Rome 1946

Sintesi economica dell'Etiopia: ieri, oggi, domani (Istituto Coloniale Fascista), Rome 1936

SIPS: *Società Italiana per il Progresso delle Scienze*

Skidelsky, R., *Oswald Mosley*, London 1975; New York 1975

Slocombe, G. E., *The Tumult and the Shouting*, London 1936; New York 1936

Soffici, A., and Prezzolini, G., *Diari 1939–1945*, Milan 1962

Sottochiesa, G., *Religiosità di questa guerra: per una coscienza di guerra*, Turin 1941

Spampanato, B., *Contromemoriale* (3 vols.), Rome 1952

————, *L'Italia di noi*, Rome 1935

Speer, A., *Inside the Third Reich*, London 1970; New York 1970

Speer papers: Imperial War Museum, London

SPI: "*Storia e Politica Internazionale*" (ed. ISPI), Milan 1939–

Spigo, U., *Premesse tecniche della disfatta*, Rome 1946

St.A.: St. Antony's College, Oxford (photostats of *Segreteria particolare del Duce*)

Spigo, U., *Premesse tecniche della disfatta*, Rome 1946

St.A.: St. Antony's College, Oxford (photostats of *Segeteria particolare del Duce*)

Starhemberg, E. R., *Between Hitler and Mussolini*, London 1942; New York 1942

Steer, G. L., *Caesar in Abyssinia*, London 1936; Boston 1937

Steffens: *The Autobiography of Lincoln Steffens* (2 vols.), London 1931; New York 1931

Stehlin, P., *Témoignage pour l'histoire*, Paris 1968

Stimson, H. L., and Bundy, McGeorge, *On Active Service in Peace and War*, New York 1948

"*Storia Contemporanea*," Bologna

"*Storia e Politica*," Milan

Strang, W., *Home and Abroad*, London 1956

Strasser, O., *Hitler and I*, London 1940; Boston 1940

"*Studi Storici*," Rome

"*Survey of International Affairs*" (Royal Institute of International Affairs), London

Susmel, D., ed., *Corrispondenza inedita di Mussolini*, Milan 1972

Susmel, D., *Vita sbagliata di Galeazzo Ciano*, Milan 1962

Suster, R., *La Germania repubblicana*, Milan 1923

Szembek, J., *Journal 1933–1939*, Paris 1952

Tamaro, A., *Due anni di storia 1942–45* (3 vols.), Rome 1948–50

————, *Venti anni di storia 1922–1943* (3 vols.), Rome 1953–54

Tannenbaum, E. R., *Fascism in Italy: Society and Culture 1922–1945*, London 1973; *The Fascist Experience: Italian Society and Culture 1922–1945*, New York 1972

Tarchi, A., *Prospettive autarchiche: rassegna economica delle produzioni nazionali e lineamenti dei problemi autarchici*, Florence 1941

Taylor, A. J. P., *Beaverbrook*, London 1972; New York 1972

Templewood, Viscount, *Nine Troubled Years*, London 1954

"*Tempo*," Milan

"*Terzo Mondo*," Milan

Testament politique de Hitler, Paris 1959

"*The Banker*," London

"*The Economist*," London

"*The Geographical Journal*," London

"*The Labour Magazine*," London

"*The National Review*," London

Theodoli, A., *A cavallo di due secoli*, Rome 1950

"*The Patriot*," London

"*The Spectator*," London

"*The Sunday Times*," London

"*The Times*," London

Thomas, H., *The Spanish Civil War*, London 1961; New York 1961

Thompson, G. H., *Front-Line Diplomat*, London 1959

Tiffen, C., *La course aux armements et les finances publiques*, Paris 1937

"*Time and Tide*," London

Toscano, M., *L'Italia e gli accordi tedesco-sovietici dell'agosto 1939*, Florence 1955

——, *Pagine di storia diplomatica contemporanea* (2 vols.), Milan 1963

——, *Storia dei trattati e politica internazionale*, (2 vols.), Turin 1963

——, *Storia diplomatica della questione dell'Alto Adige*, Bari 1967

——, *The Origins of the Pact of Steel*, Baltimore 1967

——, *Una mancata intesa italo-sovietica nel 1940 e 1941*, Florence 1955

Trevaskis, G. K. N., *Eritrea: A Colony in Transition, 1941–1952*, Oxford 1960; New York 1960

Trial of the Major War Criminals before the International Military Tribunal (42 vols.), Nuremberg, 1947–49

"*Tribuna*" (ed. R. Forges-Davanzati), Rome

Tritonj, R., *Politica indigena Africana*, Milan 1941

Trizzino, A., *Navi e poltrone*, Milan 1952

——, *Verità e menzogne sulla spedizione in Albania*, Rome 1940

Tuninetti, D. N., *La mia missione segreta in Austria 1937–1938*, Milan 1946

Tur, V., *Con i marinai d'Italia da Bastia a Tolone, 11 Novembre 1942–23 Maggio 1943*, Rome 1948

UF: "*Universalità Fascista*" (ed. O. Fantini), Rome 1929–

VA: "*Vent'Anni*" (ed. G. Pallotta), Turin, 1932–

Vaccari, W., *Vita e tumulti di F. T. Marinetti*, Milan 1959

Vademecum Africano (Istituto Fascista Africa Italiana), Milan 1943

Vailati, V., *Badoglio risponde: con una appendice del Professor Guido Gigli*, Milan 1958

Valle, G., *Pace e guerra nei cieli*, Rome 1966

Valori, A., *La Ricostruzione militare*, Rome 1930

——, *Parole di fede*, Milan 1942

Vansittart, R. G., *The Mist Procession: The Autobiography of Lord Vansittart*, London 1958

Varanini, V., *La ricostruzione fascista delle forze armate italiane*, Milan 1929

Vecchi, C. M. de, *Bonifica fascista della cultura*, Milan 1937

Vedovato, G., *Organizzazione internazionale e patto a quattro*, Florence 1939

Venti anni, ed. A. Pugliese (3 vols.), Rome 1942

Vergani, O., *Ciano, una lunga confessione*, Milan 1974

V.I.: "*La Vita Italiana*" (ed. G. Preziosi), Rome and Cremona, 1913–

Villa, C., *Nemica Inghilterra*, Milan 1941

Villari, L., *Italian Foreign Policy under Mussolini*, New York 1956

——, *L'Italia come non è: polemica con gli anglosassoni*, Rome 1941

——, *Storia diplomatica del conflitto italo-etiopico*, Bologna 1943

"*Vita*" (ed. S. Visco), Rome, 1940–

"*Vita Nova*" (ed. L. Arpinati and G. Saitta), Bologna 1925–33

Vittorelli, P., *Dal fascismo alla rivoluzione: storia della caduta del fascismo*, Cairo 1945

VM: "*Le Vie del Mondo*" (ed. C. Bonardi), Milan, 1933–

Vocabolario della lingua Italiana, ed. G. Bertoni (Reale Accademia), Milan 1941

Volpe, G., *Guerra dopoguerra fascismo*, Venice 1928

——, *Il risorgimento dell'Italia*, Rome 1934

——, *Saluto a un maestro*, Rome 1951

——, *Storia del movimento fascista* (2d ed.), Milan 1943

——, *Storici e maestri*, Florence 1967

Wagnière, G., *Dix-huit ans à Rome 1918–1936*, Geneva 1944

Warlimont, W., *Im Hauptquartier der deutschen Wehrmacht 1939–1945*, Frankfurt 1962

Washington: microfilm held by the National Archives of the United States

Waterfield, G., *Professional Diplomat, Sir Percy Loraine*, London 1973

Waugh, E., *Waugh in Abyssinia*, London 1936; New York 1937

Weichold, E., *La marina italiana in guerra: opinioni d'un ammiraglio tedesco*, Rome 1955

——, *War in the Mediterranean* (Admiralty Library, London)

Weizsäcker, E., *Memoirs of Ernst von Weizsäcker*, London 1951; Chicago 1951

Weizsäcker-Papiere 1933–1950, ed. L. E. Hill, Frankfurt 1974

Welles, S., *The Time for Decision*, London 1944; New York 1944

West, R., *Black Lamb and Grey Falcon* (2 vols.), London 1941; New York 1941

Westphal, S., *Heer in Fesseln: aus den Papieren des Stabschefs von Rommel, Kesseling und Rundstedt*, Bonn 1950

Wiskemann, E., *The Rome-Berlin axis: A History of the Relations between Hitler and Mussolini*, London 1949; New York 1949

Zachariae, G., *Mussolini si confessa: rivelazioni del medico tedesco inviato da Hitler al Duce*, Cernusco 1948

Zaghi, C., *L'Africa nella coscienza europea e l'imperialismo italiano*, Naples 1973

Zangrandi, R., *Il comunismo nel conflitto Spagnolo*, Florence 1939

——, *Il lungo viaggio attraverso il fascismo: contributo alla storia di una generazione*, Milan 1963

Zanussi, G., *Guerra e catastrofe d'Italia, giugno 1940–giugno 1943*, Rome 1945

Zbornik documenta i podataka o Narodno-oslobodilačkom ratu jugoslovenskih naroda (13 vols.), Belgrade 1949–68

Zingarelli, I., *Questo è il giornalismo*, Rome 1946

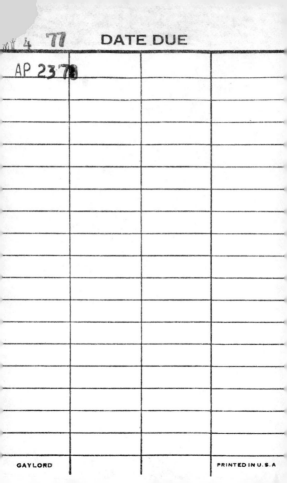